THE *LETTERS* OF SYMMACHUS: BOOK 1

Society of Biblical Literature

Writings from the Greco-Roman World

Number 30

THE *LETTERS* OF SYMMACHUS: BOOK 1

THE *LETTERS* OF SYMMACHUS: BOOK 1

Translation by Michele Renee Salzman and Michael Roberts

General Introduction and Commentary by Michele Renee Salzman

Society of Biblical Literature
Atlanta

THE *LETTERS* OF SYMMACHUS: BOOK 1

Library of Congress Cataloging-in-Publication Data

[Epistulae. English]
The letters of Symmachus. Book 1 / translation by Michele Renee Salzman and Michael Roberts ; general introduction and commentary by Michele Renee Salzman.
p. cm. — (Society of Biblical Literature. Writings from the Greco-Roman World ; no. 30)
Includes bibliographical references and index.
ISBN 978-1-58983-597-9 (paper binding : acid-free paper)— ISBN 978-1-58983-598-6 (electronic format)
1. Symmachus, Quintus Aurelius, d. 405—Correspondence. 2. Authors, Latin—Correspondence—History and criticism. 3. Letter writing, Latin—History—To 1500. 4. Rome—History—Theodosians, 379–455—Sources. I. Salzman, Michele Renee.
PA6704.S7A4 2011
937'.08092—dc22 2011031821

Printed on acid-free paper.

Contents

Acknowledgments

Researching a commentary, writing an introduction, and creating a translation of the first book of Symmachus's *Letters* has been a project that has allowed me to make the friendship of some extraordinarily generous and learned scholars. Michael Roberts has demonstrated repeatedly his graciousness and keen insight into the intricacies of Late Latin. It has truly been a joy to work with him on the translations of these letters. His careful questioning of the text and of the commentary has improved this manuscript significantly. I am grateful for his patience and friendship as Symmachus passed back and forth between coasts and computers. We have tried to render these letters into modern English, while maintaining the style of the original text. This has been a challenging undertaking, given Symmachus's propensity for archaism, formality, and literariness, but a task not without its rewards.

We are pleased to be able to publish a Latin text along with our translation. The Latin text was prepared on the basis of Seeck's edition of Symmachus's *Letters*, incorporating improvements from J. P. Callu's later edition. Controversial points are discussed in the commentary.

The present manuscript owes much to those who have read it and offered their advice at various stages in its production. Above all, we appreciate the helpful suggestions of David Konstan, co-editor of the Writings from the Greco-Roman World series, and the series editorial board, as well as those of Robert Kaster, who read the manuscript for Brill. In addition, we thank Neil McLynn and William Klingshirn, who read earlier drafts of the manuscript and made many helpful suggestions. The commentary has benefited from the generosity of several scholars who shared their work and read the manuscript at various stages. I wish to thank especially Alan Cameron, who very kindly shared drafts of *The Last Pagans of Rome* before it was published. Similarly, Kimberly Bowes, Robert Chenault, Carlos Machado, Cristiana Sogno, and Rita Lizzi Testa have shared conversations and writings that have helped improve this manuscript.

Composing a social and historical commentary for these letters has required me to consult several research institutions and to rely on their excellent librarians and staff. In particular, I wish to thank the Interlibrary Loan staff at the University of Riverside, California, for their never-ending willingness to search for recondite volumes. Similarly, my residency at the American Academy in Rome in spring 2008 and the wonderful librarians and resources at the American Academy in Rome Library have been of great aid. My graduate assistants, Lucia Gusti and Ingrid deHaas, have been of special help in the final stages of this manuscript.

This work would not have been possible without the loving support of my husband, Steven Brint, and of my children, Juliana and Ben. They have truly taught me what Symmachus knew about the value of family.

I have come to appreciate the *Letters* of Symmachus, both for their Latin, and for their contents. They are unique documents from a world that I find endlessly fascinating. Of course, in re-creating this world, there is room for differences of opinion about the best translation or the correct reconstruction of the circumstances of each letter. So, in the end, this book reflects my vision of this world, for better or for worse.

Michele Renee Salzman
24 August 2010

It is a great pleasure to have the opportunity to revisit the *Letters of Symmachus, Book 1*, to make some changes and corrections to the text and commentary. Advances in scholarship come about through the collective efforts of a community of scholars, past and present. This 2015 printing has benefited from scholars who have generously shared their thoughts and works with me. I owe special thanks to Michael Roberts for his unfailing willingness to discuss the Latinity of Symmachus's *Letters* and to Gavin Kelly, whose research and conversations have convinced me to return to these letters. The 2015 printing, however, allows for limited alterations to the text. Nonetheless, I am pleased to be able to offer this improved version to interested readers. I thank the SBL Press and Bob Buller for making these changes possible through the marvels of twenty-first-century publishing.

29 November 2015

Abbreviations

CIL	*Corpus inscriptionum latinarum*. Berlin: Reimer, 1862–.
CSEL	Corpus scriptorum ecclesiasticorum latinorum
C. Th.	*Codex Theodosianus*. For the Latin, see Theodor Mommsen, Paul M. Meyer, and Jacques Sirmond, *Theodosiani libri XVI: Cum Constitutionibus Sirmondianis et Leges novellae ad Theodosianum pertinentes*. Berlin: Weidmann, 1954 ed. of 1905 ed. For the English, see the translation, with commentary, glossary, and bibliography, by Clyde Pharr, *The Theodosian Code and Novels and the Sirmondian Constitutions*. Princeton: Princeton University Press, 1952.
FHG	*Fragmenta historicorum graecorum*. Edited by Karl Müller. 5 vols. Paris: Didot, 1841–1870.
ILS	*Inscriptiones latinae selectae*. Edited by Hermann Dessau. 5 vols. Berlin: Weidmann, 1892–1916. Repr., Chicago: Ares, 1979.
LCL	Loeb Classical Library
OCD	*The Oxford Classical Dictionary*. Edited by Simon Hornblower and Antony Spawforth. 3rd ed. Oxford: Oxford University Press, 1996.
OLD	*Oxford Latin Dictionary*. Edited by P. G. W. Glare. Oxford: Clarendon, 1982.
PCBE	*Prosopographie chrétienne du Bas-Empire*. Vol. 1: *Prosopographie de l'Afrique chrétienne (303–533)*. Edited by André Mandouze and Anne-Marie La Bonnardière. Paris: Éditions du Centre national de la recherche scientifique,1982. Vol. 2: *Prosopographie de l'Italie chrétienne (313–604)*. Edited by Charles Pietri and Luce Pietri. Rome: École Française de Rome, 2000.
PECS	*Princeton Encyclopedia of Classical Sites*. Edited by Richard Stillwell, William MacDonald, L. McAlister, and Marian Holland. Princeton: Princeton University Press, 1976.

PL	Patrologia latina [= Patrologiae cursus completus: Series latina]. Edited by J.-P. Migne. 217 vols. Paris: Migne, 1844–1864.
PLRE	*The Prosopography of the Later Roman Empire.* Vol. 1 (260–395 c.e.) edited by A. H. M. Jones, J. R. Martindale and J. Morris. Cambridge: Cambridge University Press, 1971. Vol. 2 (395–527 c.e.) edited by J. R. Martindale. Cambridge: Cambridge University Press, 1980.
ThLL	*Thesaurus linguae latinae.* Leipzig: Teubner, 1900–.

Introduction

Quintus Aurelius Symmachus signo Eusebius is best known to historians as a staunch traditionalist, "the leading proponent of the pagan religious cause against the Christian emperors" and author of the eloquent *State Paper* 3 (*Relatio* 3), which in 384 C.E. petitioned the boy emperor Valentinian II to return the Altar of Victory to the Roman Senate House.[1] In Symmachus's lifetime, however, he was famous rather for his eloquence. Even Christians who were hostile to his religious views, such as the Spanish poet Prudentius, admired the orator for his "speech flowing with a marvelous fountain of words." Prudentius called Symmachus "the glory of Roman eloquence, surpassing even Tullius [Cicero] himself!"[2] Symmachus used his considerable rhetorical talents to advance senatorial political goals as well as his own interests; he was a prominent senatorial leader throughout the fourth century, one of the key reasons, along with his rhetorical skills, that he was chosen to advance that body's request for the return of the Altar of Victory. Symmachus's family, wealth, and connections, along with his great political and rhetorical skills, made him one of the most influential men in the fourth-century western empire.

Unfortunately, Symmachus's reputation as an orator can only be partly substantiated by his extant works. Although he delivered and circulated many of his *Orations* in his lifetime, only eight survive, and all are missing sections.[3] We learn more of Symmachus as a writer from his extant works in other genres. Some forty-nine of Symmachus's *State Papers* survive from his term of office as urban prefect, the office he held from 384 through early 385. But it is his *Let-*

1. *OCD*, *s.v.* Symmachus, (2) Quintus Aurelius provides the standard view of the man. For a recent political biography of the man, see Sogno 2006.

2. Prudentius, *Contra Symmachum* (*Against Symmachus*) 1.632–634 (Thomson): "O linguam miro verborum fonte fluentem, / Romani decus eloquii, cui cedat et ipse / Tullius!"

3. The edition by Otto Seeck (1883) remains the standard modern edition of Symmachus's *Orations*, *State Papers*, and his *Letters*, although some of these have also been edited in more recent publications in French, German, Italian, and Spanish; see xv nn. 10–12 below.

ters—of which there are some 902 extant in ten books[4]—that allow us not only to admire his rhetorical expertise but also to gain a clearer, more nuanced view of the man and of the complex political and social world in which he lived.

The 107 letters of Symmachus's book 1 included in this present volume were sent to some of the most influential men living in the western Roman Empire in the 370s and early 380s; none of the letters in this first book can be dated after 384.[5] The letters in book 1 are organized by correspondent, probably by order of their importance to Symmachus; these letters demonstrate an elaborate but coherent set of themes as well as a consistent style.[6] As I shall argue below (liii–lxvi), it was probably Symmachus himself who collected the correspondence and circulated it in book form after 384 and no later than the early 390s. His was one of several books of letters that were in circulation at the end of the fourth century and one of the first, I will suggest, to present a book of letters as a sort of autobiography.[7] Symmachus probably intended to publish more books of letters, but he died circa 402, before concluding this project; his son, Q. Fabius Memmius Symmachus, was left to conclude the work. According to my reconstruction, Memmius probably then published books 2–7 of the letters; books 8–10 of Symmachus's letters were a later addition, although this view of Symmachus's ten books of letters is not uniformly accepted (see section 3).

Regardless of how one reconstructs the publication history of Symmachus's ten books of letters, the letters in book 1 are in many ways unique; only in this case, I would argue, can we be fairly confident that the book that survives reflects the authorial intent and arrangement of Symmachus himself. This contributed to my decision to translate this first book and to publish it, with a commentary, as a separate volume, thereby in my view corresponding to Symmachus's original intentions.

But there are several other good reasons why I chose to publish this book of letters. There is, first of all, no English translation of Symmachus's letters yet available for historians, religionists, classicists, and literary scholars. Only random letters of Symmachus appear in English in collections on the reli-

4. As I will discuss (liii–lxvi), the ten books of Symmachus's *Letters* did not include the *State Papers,* although some scholars have argued that they did.

5. Callu 1972, 18 states that no letter is later than 385; I see no letter in book 1 later than 384. See table, lxiv; see also my discussion, lviii–lxvi.

6. Bruggisser 1993, 25–31; Callu 1972, 18.

7. For general discussions of letter collections, see Peter 1965, 142–43; Mullett 1997, 31–37; Cugisi 1983; and Morello and Morrison 2007, v–xii. For the dating of Symmachus's collection in relation to other, mostly Christian, books of letters, see lvii nn. 212–13, 215 below.

gious, social, or political history of the period.[8] Two of his eight orations are available in English in a Ph.D. dissertation.[9] Readers of French, Italian, and Spanish are better served; all of Symmachus's letters are available in French and Spanish, and books 2–6 and 9 can be found with extensive commentaries in Italian.[10] His *Orations* have been translated into French, German, and Spanish, and the *First Oration* also has appeared in Italian.[11] Unfortunately, the only work by Symmachus currently available in full in English is his *State Papers*, which appeared in 1973.[12]

The lack of English translations of Symmachus's letters is odd, for there are good modern editions of these letters in Latin. As early as 1883 Otto Seeck provided a sound critical edition with commentary not only of the *Letters* but also of the *Orations* and *State Papers*.[13] Jean Pierre Callu augmented Seeck's work on the manuscripts and improved the Latin text of the *Letters* when he published his French translation and commentary.[14]

There are several reasons for the lack of English translations of Symmachus's letters, but chief among them is the belief among historians and classicists that Symmachus's personal letters do not have enough specific information to make them worthwhile historical documents. Edward Gibbon was most vociferous in his criticism: "Few facts, and few sentiments, can be extracted from his verbose correspondence"; A. H. M. Jones lamented that Symmachus "tells us less than might have been expected of the events of the day."[15] Even Callu, the scholar who translated all of Symmachus's *Letters* into French, observed that, of the small number of Latinists who have actually

8. See, e.g., Croke and Harries 1982, 108–11, which includes six of Symmachus's letters from book 1.

9. Hall 1977.

10. Callu (1972, 1982, 1995, 2002) has published a French translation of the *Letters* in four volumes. Gallego (2000, 2003a) has published a Spanish translation with an abbreviated commentary. The Italian translations and commentaries are, in order of their publication, book 9 by Roda 1981a, book 6 by Marcone 1983, book 4 by Marcone 1987, book 5 by Rivolta Tiberga 1992, book 3 by Pellizzari 1998, and book 2 by Cecconi 2002a.

11. There is a French translation of the *Orations* by Callu 2009b, a German translation by Pabst 1989, a Spanish translation by Gallego 2003b, and an Italian translation of *Oration* 1 for the emperor Valentinian I by Del Chicca 1984.

12. Barrow 1973. This may explain why these works are better known to British and American scholars and historians than the letters.

13. Seeck 1883, i–ccxl, includes a discussion of the textual transmission of the *Orations*, *State Papers*, and *Letters*, as well as providing a chronology of Symmachus's life and a prosopography of the correspondents.

14. Callu 1972, 1982, 1995, 2002.

15. Gibbon 1901, 3:193 n. 21; Jones 1986, 1:155.

bothered to read Symmachus's letters, many were left wondering whether it was worth their while.[16]

Yet, if Symmachus's letters frustrate historians by their lack of specific names and dates and have alienated classicists by their elaborate rhetorical style, they can nevertheless be rewarding for those who have learned how to read them as windows into the social, political, and cultural landscape of the late fourth century.[17] Indeed, even the critical Jones recognized that Symmachus's letters "reveal much about the life of a Roman noble."[18] Historians and classicists have come, only recently, to appreciate these letters—and the epistolary genre as a whole—for what they can reveal about late Roman social and cultural history. Support for this positive view of Symmachus and his letters in particular increased with the publication of papers after a 1984 Colloquium held in Geneva on the 1600th anniversary of the Altar of Victory controversy.[19] This volume is presented here in the hope that, after learning to read these letters within the coded language of late Roman epistolography, students and scholars will come to appreciate the literary, political, and religious importance of Symmachus.

This introduction is divided into three sections: (1) The Life and Works of Symmachus; (2) The World of Symmachus's *Letters*: Themes in Book 1; (3) The Publication and Survival of Symmachus's *Letters*.

1. The Life and Works of Symmachus

Literary achievement had been, for centuries, a source of pride in Roman aristocratic circles; rhetorical expertise especially signaled high status, which, it was presumed, went hand in hand with public office and honor.[20] Symmachus's desire to become known as an orator and statesman was very much in keeping with traditional Roman notions of what constituted success in aristocratic circles. To augment his honor and that of his family, Symmachus circulated and published his *Orations* and his first book of *Letters,* no doubt with the intention of publishing more books of letters subsequently; some scholars think that he also published his *State Papers*, but this seems less likely.[21]

---

16. Callu 1972, 7.

17. Especially important has been the work of Matthews, notably 1974 and 1975, and Bruggisser 1993.

18. Jones 1986, 1:155.

19. See the series of important papers in Paschoud 1986.

20. See Symmachus, *Letter* 1.20.1; Salzman 2002, 44–49.

21. Symmachus notes that he circulated his *Orations* to friends in several letters, such as *Letter* 1.44, 1.52, 4.29, 5.9. Seeck (1883, vi–vii) lists the speeches and notes that no less

Symmachus's successful attainment of high office and honors was not based solely on his rhetorical and literary skills. On the contrary, Symmachus was born into one of the most powerful families in Italy, and although Rome was no longer the sole capital of the empire, its elite remained among the most influential and wealthy in the fourth century.[22] Moreover, Rome's aristocracy had ties that extended well beyond the city, especially to the western provincial elites of Africa, Spain, and Gaul, but also to the imperial courts resident in Gaul and northern Italy as well as to the military and civic administrative elites both in the West and in the East. Not surprisingly, given their position and resources, Roman and Italian elites were also eager to strengthen their connections with emperors, generals, and imperial administrators.[23] Symmachus and his family assiduously maintained their ties to powerful men at the imperial court and in the state bureaucracy, men such as Ausonius, the grammarian and tutor of Gratian, who turned palatine minister, and the general Stilicho, who could further Symmachus's and his family's quest for honor and influence.[24] Through such connections, Symmachus extended his networks of patronage and won favors for friends, clients, and family. This was one of the key ways in which nonmilitary elites secured their power, making the Symmachi "one of the most important families in Rome from the fourth to the sixth centuries."[25]

Symmachus's Family

Given the honors, wealth, and connections of Symmachus and his father, it would be somewhat surprising if Symmachus's family was new to Rome's elite. Then, as now, achieving prominence and high office required influential connections and economic resources, which, in most cases, was acquired over generations. However, Seeck, the first modern editor of Symmachus's works, argued that Symmachus's family was a newcomer to the Roman aristocracy; he considered the consul of 330, Aurelius Valerius Tullianus Symmachus,

than seven were edited by Symmachus himself. For the arguments that Symmachus and later his son, Memmius, published his *Letters*, see liii–lxvi below; for the scholarly disagreements about the publication of the *State Papers*, see lxii–lxiii below.

22. See Salzman 2002, 19–68.

23. See especially Matthews 1975, 24–33, 319–20, and *passim*; Salzman 2002, 19–68; Sogno 2006, 8–17, 85–88, 48, and *passim*.

24. For more on Ausonius and his career as *quaestor sacri palatii*, see the introduction to *Letters* 13–43, pp. 35–40; for more on the life and career of the general Flavius Stilicho, see *PLRE* 1:835–58.

25. Cameron 1999a, 477.

the first member of this family to attain high status.[26] Seeck posited a link between this man and M. Aurelius Nerius Symmachus on the basis of two shared names, and since Nerius was attested as *vir perfectissimus,* the equivalent of an equestrian, in 312 or 337, Seeck argued that the consul of 330 was most likely not of senatorial birth either.[27] Seeck's views on Symmachus's family have been widely influential; François Paschoud suggested that Aurelius Valerius Tullianus Symmachus may have been a barbarian.[28]

More recently, Alan Cameron has argued convincingly against the idea that the Symmachi were newcomers to Rome's elite. He observes that the proper reading of Nerius's name is Symmachius, not Symmachus, making any ties between the two men virtually impossible. In addition, Cameron proposes that a reference by Elias, a sixth-century Alexandrian Neoplatonist, in his commentary on the *Isagoge* (*Introduction*) of Porphyry to a Symmachus who fathered one Chrysaorius, "a leading man in the senate of Rome," should be taken at face value and used as evidence that by 270 the Symmachi had been "a prominent Roman family for three generations."[29] If Cameron's evidence is accepted, as I think it should be, the Symmachi were influential members of the Roman senatorial elite from as early as the last quarter of the third century, a situation that seems far more in keeping with the wealth, honors, and standing of this family in the late fourth century.

Aside from Aurelius Valerius Tullianus Symmachus, the consul of 330,[30] several other prominent members of Symmachus's family can be identified; in all likelihood, the *consularis* of Numidia, M. Aurelius Valerius Valentinus, was the uncle of the orator and letter writer, Q. Aurelius Symmachus.[31] Symmachus's father, L. Aurelius Avianius Symmachus, was one of the most successful and active members of the family. Like his son, the elder Symmachus was

---

26. Aurelius Valerius Tullianus Symmachus 6, cos. ord. 330, *PLRE* 1:871; identified by Seeck 1883, xxxix–xli, in his preface to the works of Symmachus; and followed by Paschoud 1965, 228.

27. On M. Aurelius Nerius Symmachus 5, *PLRE* 1:870–71, with the critical inscription giving his name, *CIL* 6:1747.

28. Seeck 1883, xxxix–xli; Paschoud 1967, 73; also suggested by Arnheim 1972, 19 and 164.

29. Cameron (1999a, 477–78) notes that Elias describes Chrysaorius as "a leading man in the senate of Rome, for he was descended (ἀπόγονος) from that Symmachus of whom it was written, 'Symmachus, son of Symmachus, man of many allies, ally of Rome.'"

30. Cameron (1999a, 481–84, 488–92) argues against there being two different men, one called Valerius Tullianus, the other Aurelius Valerius Symmachus. The papyri make it clear that the man was both a Valerius and an Aurelius; for M. Aurelius Valerius Valentinus, see Bagnall, Cameron, Schwarz, and Worp 1987, 182.

31. Valentinus 12, *PLRE* 1:936; see Cameron 1999a, 484; and Salzman 1990, 201.

praised for his rhetorical and political talents; his leadership is demonstrated by his role as *princeps senatus*, "First Man of the Senate," an honor that allowed him to give his opinion first in senatorial deliberations and that was manifested by his leadership of numerous embassies to the imperial court.[32] On the way home from one such endeavor to the court of the emperor Constantius II in 361, Avianius stopped at Naissus, where he was treated with honor by the new aspirant to the imperial throne, Julian, even though he was passed over for the position of urban prefect that year.[33] Probably during that trip, too, Avianius made the acquaintance of the rhetor Libanius, to whom he later wrote about educating his son.[34] But within three years, Avianius attained the highly prized office of the urban prefectureship of the city of Rome (364–365), and his career culminated with his designation as consul for 377; unfortunately, he died before holding this last office.[35] At the time of his death, Avianius's prestige was such that he received, on 9 April 377, imperial consent to honor him with two gold statues, one in the monumental center of Rome and the other in Constantinople.[36]

Avianius had married well; his wife was most likely the daughter of Fabius Titianus, himself a man who held multiple offices, including the consulship in 337 and urban prefectureship twice, once between 339 and 341 and again between 350 and 353.[37] Titianus's prestige was well advertised; in Rome, nine statue bases have been found on the Via Sacra and another two on the Caelian Hill that commemorate his efforts as urban prefect.[38] Titianus's daughter, whose name we still do not know, bore Avianius several children; all their known sons attained high public office. One son, Avianius Valentinus, *consul-*

---

32. For his role as *princeps senatus* as bestowing the honor of *primus in senatu sententiam rogari solitus* (*CIL* 6:1698 = *ILS* 1257), see also Lizzi Testa 2004, 342.

33. Ammianus Marcellinus, *Res Gestae* 21.12.24.

34. Libanius, *Letter* 1004 (Foerster 11:132–34), has been associated with this visit, and this date is persuasively defended by Lizzi Testa 2004, 444–46.

35. L. Aurelius Avianius Symmachus signo Phosphorius 3, *PLRE* 1:863–65. For more on this man and his career, see the introduction to *Letter* 1.1, pp. 1–6.

36. For these statues, see the inscription, note 32 above, and Weisweiler 2010.

37. Fabius Titianus 6, *PLRE* 1:918–19.

38. Niquet 2000, 200–221. The association of statues with personal honor and as a sign of virtue was already common in the time of the republic. This phenomenon is well-attested for fourth-century Rome, where, with the emperor largely absent, the Senate and magistrates, like the urban prefect, competed for such honors within the status-oriented elite society. For statues in fourth century Rome, see Machado 2006, ch. 4, who remarks that it seems most "sensible" to assume that statues erected by the urban prefect would have been paid for by public monies, though very few inscriptions (three out of ca. 365) make this explicit.

aris of Campania between 364 and 375, has been identified as Symmachus's brother because of the unusual name Avianius, which repeats that of his father, L. Aurelius Avianius Symmachus; the name Valentinus lived on in the family of the Symmachi, one of whose Christian members can be identified as the recipient of the deluxe and richly ornamented *Codex-Calendar of 354*.[39] Another of Avianius's sons, Avianius Vindicianus, again identified because of the unusual name, was *consularis* of Campania in the second half of the fourth century but died sometime before 380.[40] The third son, recipient of several letters in book 1, was Celsinus Titianus; he was vicar of Africa in 380, the year in which he died.[41] Another relative, Aurelius Anicius Symmachus, is attested in the early fifth century, probably a son of one of Symmachus's brothers or sisters.[42] Through this relative's marriage, the Symmachi would have been linked with one of the most powerful Christian families of Rome, the Anicii. It is into this well-connected, ambitious family that Q. Aurelius Symmachus nicknamed Eusebius was born, probably as the eldest son, probably in the year 340.[43]

The Early Years: Youth and Education

We can assume that, as the son of a wealthy, highly honored Roman senator, Symmachus's youth was spent comfortably, but we know little else in much detail. He must have received the best education possible, and his father's reputation for eloquence indicates that this was a family that valued such skills. They certainly could engage the very best teachers possible. Avianius was in touch with the celebrated rhetorician Libanius about the possibility of sending his son to him as his pupil.[44] That did not happen, for Symmachus was apparently too young, but we do know that Symmachus had been taught by a Gallic teacher of rhetoric, an elderly man familiar to Ausonius; through him, Sym-

---

39. Valentinus 7, *PLRE* 1:938; see Cameron 1999a, 484. The *Codex-Calendar of 354* was dedicated to a Valentinus, identified as a member of the Symmachi; Salzman 1990, 201–2.

40. Avianius Vincidicanus 4, *PLRE* 1:968. Symmachus, *Letter* 3.6.2, notes that, with the death of Celsinus Titianus, Symmachus had lost his third brother.

41. Celsinus Titianus 5, *PLRE* 1:917.

42. Aurelius Anicius Symmachus was urban prefect between 418 and 420; for this man, see Symmachus 6, *PLRE* 2:1043–44.

43. Seeck (1883, xliv) observed that in *Letter* 1.15, written in 375, Symmachus speaks of himself as enjoying "a young man's glory" ("inter iuvenile decus"), and in *Letter* 4.18.2, written in 396, he was not yet an old man ("annis in senectam vergentibus"). Since Symmachus's first magistracy was in 365, Seeck reasoned that he could not have been born much before or after 340, and no later than 345. According to Seeck (1883, xxxix), it was the custom of the family to give the cognomen "Symmachus" to the oldest son.

44. Libanius, *Letter* 1004 (Foerster); see also n. 34 above. Cf. Seeck 1883, xliv n. 105.

machus claimed familiarity with the precepts of the celebrated Gallic schools of rhetoric.[45] This elderly teacher has been identified with the illustrious rhetorician Tiberius Victor Minervius, who came from Bordeaux and taught at Rome in the year 352.[46]

Most likely Symmachus followed the standard curriculum, with its heavy emphasis on classical authors. In his writing he tends to cite the standard Roman authors studied in school, notably Cicero, Terence, Plautus, Horace, and, of course, Vergil. Wilhelm Kroll argued, on the basis of an extensive study of Symmachus's use of earlier authors, that Symmachus's learning was rather narrow in terms of Greek and Latin authors,[47] but Gerd Haverling's study of the language and style of Symmachus's works led her to somewhat different conclusions. Haverling argues that in his choice of words Symmachus demonstrated a "profound familiarity with early Latin literature" and suggests that he read more widely in Latin than his direct citations would indicate.[48] But Haverling's claims about Symmachus's knowledge of archaic Latin literature rely heavily on his use of verbal formulae (e.g., *cautio est alicui, fors fuat, proquam*) and syntax rather than on familiarity with the texts per se. As such, these are perhaps not the best indicators of Symmachus's deep knowledge of early or later Latin literature.[49] Thus, at the level of syntax and usage, Symmachus's writings show familiarity with a range of Latin authors, including early imperial Latin writers; although there are few uncontested direct citations from Pliny the Younger's *Letters* and *Panegyric*, verbal echoes and lexical usage similarly indicate a high level of rhetorical training and education in Latin.[50] Symmachus's familiarity with Greek, however, was far less

---

45. See pp. 39–41 below for this letter, which, in my view, began the correspondence with Ausonius. Symmachus refers to his teacher as "senex olim Garumnae alumnus."

46. The proposed identification with Tiberius Victor Minervius is found in Seeck 1883, xliv n. 106; McGeachy 1942, 7; Matthews 1975, 86, but the *PLRE* reference to Minervius 4 (1:603–4) notes the large number of Gallic rhetoricians and rightfully questions this identification. On this man, see Jerome, *Chronica* (*Chronicle*), s.a.352; Ausonius, *Commemoratio professorum Burdigalensium* (*Poems Commemorating the Professors of Bordeaux*) 1, Green 1991, 41–42.

47. Kroll 1891, 1–99.

48. Haverling 1988, 135. Kroll (1891, 1–99) included citations or allusions to some sixteen Latin authors. His views have influenced others, notably Ruggini 1984, 477–521.

49. For criticism of Haverling's view of Symmachus's knowledge of early Latin, see Cameron 2011, 366–83, 408. Cameron's position is similar to that of Kroll 1891, 26–29.

50. For imperial literary echoes, note, for example, a phrase found in *Letter* 1.26, "in specula honorum locato," which has been rightly seen as a Plinian metaphor by Callu 1972, 221 n. 1, who cites as parallels Pliny, *Letters* 2.12.3; 3.18.3; *Panegyric* 86.4. Symmachus does not quote Pliny directly, as Sidonius does. Cameron (1965, 289–98) has argued that Sido-

impressive.[51] Unlike Pliny and earlier epistolographers, Symmachus quotes only single words in Greek, never whole phrases, and he uses these far less frequently than his predecessors in the genre; leaving aside the few shared Greek words found in contemporary Latin writers (e.g., *apophoreta*, *diptychum*), Alan Cameron counts some six words transmitted in Greek in the manuscripts.[52] Symmachus's remark about the need to "devote himself anew to the study of Greek" (*Letter* 4.20) at the time that his son was beginning to learn the language seems an honest assessment of his rather limited contact with Greek literature in the original.

Symmachus's emphasis on the Latin literary tradition fits well with what we can gather about where Symmachus lived. His letters indicate that Rome was his primary domicile but that he made frequent trips to various of his estates throughout Italy, with occasional forays to Gaul and North Africa. He does not refer to traveling in the eastern empire, although he may well have done so.[53] Like many late Roman estate owners, he traveled mostly to the areas where he and his family owned property; Symmachus lists among his holdings some thirteen estates in central Italy as well as properties in Samnium, Apulia, Sicily, Mauretania, and perhaps Lucania.[54] In addition to these, his family had no less than three urban villas, one located across the Tiber and one very large, opulent house on the Caelian Hill in Rome; a brick stamp and gold glass cup with the family name of the Symmachi on them has allowed identification of this house.[55]

We wish we knew more about Symmachus's youth. He probably devoted some of his time to the typical pursuits of Rome's elite—hunting, dining, and visiting friends and family—alternating his time between town and country properties but staying mostly within the western empire, where he and his friends owned comfortable villas and townhouses.

---

nius only added direct quotations when he edited his letters for publication; since Symmachus did not have the opportunity to do that, his letters contain no direct quotes from Pliny. However, there is no evidence to support this hypothesis. Moreover, since Symmachus himself probably prepared the letters of book 1 (see liv–lviii below), this argument does not explain the absence of direct quotations from Pliny in this book.

51. Haverling (1988, 135) concurs with Kroll (1891, 1–99) that the Greek element in Symmachus's vocabulary is not particularly prominent.

52. Cameron 2011, 385.

53. Seeck (1883, lx–lxiv) recounts Symmachus's travels between 395 and 402; see also Salzman 2004, 81–94.

54. Symmachus, *Letters* 6.11, 6.12, 6.66, 7.66, 9.32, 9.52. See also Vera 1986, 231–76.

55. Symmachus, *Letter* 1.44 (across the Tiber); *Letter* 3.12 (on the Caelian Hill); *Letter* 3.14 notes a third villa in Rome. See Stirling 2005, 224 and nn. 16 and 18.

360–370: First Honors and Travel to the Imperial Court in Gaul.

Symmachus's home on the Caelian Hill in Rome has provided a key inscription for tracing his career; on a base for an honorific statue, set up by Symmachus's son, Memmius, we find the father's career listed in chronological order:

> To Quintus Aurelius Symmachus, nicknamed Eusebius, *vir clarissimus, quaestor, praetor, pontifex maior*, corrector of Lucania and the Brutii, count of the third order, proconsul of Africa, prefect of the city, *consul ordinarius*, a most eloquent orator—Quintus Fabius Memmius Symmachus, *vir clarissimus*, to the best of fathers.[56]

At some date before 365, Symmachus had embarked on a senatorial, civic career, holding the requisite magistracies of quaestor and praetor.[57] By the late fourth century, these were largely honorific positions whose primary responsibilities entailed arranging for and contributing toward the financing of the public games and entertainments at Rome. The position of quaestor also bestowed upon its holder the right to sit in the Senate of Rome for life, and hence it was a key position for those aspiring to enter public careers.[58] These lower offices were valued because they gave rising aristocrats and their families the opportunity to advertise themselves against the appropriate, traditional backdrop, Rome.

One of Symmachus's early honors was his appointment as *pontifex maior*, a priesthood that he held no later than 365 (judging by the date of the next office on the inscription, that of *corrector*, which he held in 365). It is the only priesthood attested for Symmachus, but his letters suggest that he took the associated duties seriously. So, for example, he tells Praetextatus, the eminent pagan senator and Symmachus's close friend, of his plan to summon the college to expiate an unfavorable omen (*Letter* 1.49), and he chides Praetextatus for not returning to Rome to fulfill his (Praetextatus's) priestly duties (*Letters* 1.47, 1.51). Symmachus proudly notes that his priestly college condemned to death

---

56. *CIL* 6:1699 = *ILS* 2946: "Eusebii—Q. Aur(elio) Symmacho v(iro) c(larissimo), quaest(ori), praet(ori), pontifici maiori, correctori Lucaniae et Brittiorum, comiti ordinis tertii, procons(uli) Africae, praef(ecto) urb(i), co(n)s(uli) ordinario, oratori disertissimo, Q. Fab(ius) Memm(ius) Symmachus v(ir) c(larissimus) patri optimo."

57. If Symmachus was born ca. 340, he could have held the early offices of quaestor, praetor, and pagan priest by ca. 360, by age twenty. There do not seem to have been strict age limits on these offices, hence there is no reason to follow Heather (1998, 191) and to assume that Symmachus held these before the age of twenty.

58. For more on these offices, see Jones 1986, 523–45; Salzman 2002, 49–53; and Heather 1998, 184–210.

Primigenia, the Vestal from Alba, for her failure to keep her vow of chastity, although we do not know if this sentence was executed.[59] His earnest desire to meet his priestly responsibilities contrasts with the attitudes of many of his contemporaries, or so Symmachus would have us believe from a letter to Praetextatus: "I do not intend a colleague to take my place when there is such negligence among the priests. Once this sort of delegation of religious affairs was straightforward; now to desert the altars is, for Romans, a kind of careerism."[60] Co-option into a priestly college was one sign of status and acceptance into elite circles in Rome, explaining Symmachus's pride in his priesthood and his duties. Yet Symmachus's remark (*Letter* 1.51) here also suggests that Christianity was making inroads into the traditional status that pagan priests once held.

It was in 365, the same year that his father held the prestigious office of urban prefect, that Symmachus was made governor (*corrector*) of Lucania-Bruttium, at around age twenty-five. This was a position that held higher prestige but also included certain administrative responsibilities in financial and judicial matters.[61] Symmachus fulfilled his duties, but it was probably his friendships and family connections, combined with his political and rhetorical skills, that resulted in his receiving the signal honor of being designated as senatorial envoy to the imperial court in Trier to convey to Valentinian I the traditional speech of praise on the fifth year anniversary of his rule. This speech, delivered in 368, is preserved as Symmachus's first *Oration*.[62] At this time, he also brought to the emperor the Senate's gift (*aurum oblaticium*), a voluntary tax collected by the Senate from all senators.[63]

Symmachus seems to have used his time at the imperial court to his advantage, apparently winning the approval even of Valentinian I, for we find

59. Primigenia is discussed in Symmachus, *Letters* 9.147 and 148; both letters are dated before 382.

60. Symmachus, *Letter* 1.51: "Neque enim fert animus in tanta sacerdotum neglegentia sufficere collegam. Fuerit haec olim simplex divinae rei delegatio: nunc aris deese Romanos genus ambiendi."

61. For an excellent discussion of the role of the governors, including *correctores*, see Cecconi 1994.

62. For the 368 date for Symmachus's first *Oration*, see Chastagnol 1987, 255–68. Older editions follow the 369 date for this *Oration*, proposed by Seeck 1883, 318–23; so also Del Chicca 1984, 7–23. Sogno (2006, 6) suggests that it was the influence of Praetextatus, then urban prefect, that smoothed the way for this honor. Though there is no evidence for this, and Praetextatus was probably a generation older than Symmachus, the elites of Rome were closely connected. As urban prefect, Praetextatus presided over the senate and was regarded as the leader and spokesman of the senatorial order; see Chastagnol 1960, 66, 68, 182, 459. See Kahlos 2002, 17, for Praetextatus's date of birth between 310 and 324.

63. Jones 1986, 1:430–31.

the rising senator accompanying the emperor on one of his campaigns against the Alamanni, probably in the spring/summer of 368.[64] This first-hand view of battle enlivens Symmachus's next speech, a panegyric delivered at court on Valentinian's assumption of his third consulship on 1 January 370, preserved as his second *Oration*.[65] Either in conjunction with this *Oration*, or soon after in the same year, Symmachus also delivered a panegyric on the young prince Gratian, his third *Oration*.[66] The distinction of delivering these *Orations* attests to Symmachus's access to the court and his positive reception; it was probably during his time at court that he received the honorific title of *comes tertii ordinis*, or "count of the third order," a new status that may be associated with his patronage of guilds in Rome.[67]

Symmachus's time at court also enabled him to extend his network of friends to include rising and influential provincials at court. It is probably to this period that we can date the beginnings of his friendship with the Spanish general Flavius Theodosius, father of the future emperor Theodosius.[68] From this period, too, comes evidence of Symmachus's relationship with his Gallic friend and mentor, the rhetorician, poet, and politician Ausonius, whose correspondence figures prominently in Symmachus's first book of *Letters*. The two men shared a deep interest in literature.[69] Their time together at court reinforced a bond that had been initiated by Ausonius; as Sergio Roda has shown, on the basis of *Letter* 9.88, Ausonius apparently read something writ-

64. Symmachus, *Oration* 2.2 and 18, implies that he was present in person on Valentinian's campaign. The date of this campaign is disputed; Chastagnol (1987, 256) would date Symmachus's presence to Valentinian's campaign in the spring/summer of 368, while Lorenz (1997, 118–22) prefers Valentinian's campaign of summer 369. Given the redating of the Symmachus's first *Oration*, the likelihood is greater that Symmachus went on the campaign of 368, but we cannot be certain.

65. Seeck 1883, 323–30; see Hall 1977, xiv–xlv.

66. Seeck (1883, 330–32) dated this third *Oration* to the same time as his first *Oration* to Valentinian I, which Seeck dated to 25 February 369. However, Shanzer (1997, 286–88) has argued convincingly that references to fortifications on the Rhine indicate a later date. If so, the *Oration* should be dated to the period after his trip to the frontier but while Symmachus was still at court.

67. Jones (1986, 1:528) proposes that by the 370s the title of count of the third order was an honor conferred in general on "persons of humble degree, decurions … and the patrons of the guilds of bakers and butchers at Rome." It is in this last category that Symmachus's title is appropriate. Indeed, other elites were proud to be patrons of such guilds; see, e.g., Proculus honored as patron of the guild of bakers in Rome (*CIL* 6:1692 = *ILS* 1242). Hence, I do not agree with Heather (2006, 43) that this was a "dismally dismissive" honor.

68. Matthews 1971, 122–28. See Flavius Theodosius 3, in *PLRE* 1:902–4, and n. 76 below.

69. Symmachus, *Letter* 1.14.

ten by Symmachus, perhaps a now lost *Oration*, and sought to connect with the young man, who, for his part, was eager and almost fawning in his praise of the elder rhetorician.[70] Symmachus's second *Oration* suggests the influence that Ausonius exerted; it includes images and ideas that appear also in Ausonius's poem, the *Moselle*, when describing Valentinian's campaign against the Alamanni.[71] After Symmachus's departure from Trier, Ausonius's presence at court and his subsequent appointment as praetorian prefect of Gaul, Italy, and Africa in 378–379 proved extremely helpful to Symmachus's interests.

Symmachus used his letters to build and maintain friendships with other important provincials within the military and imperial bureaucracy. Two such relationships, which may well have begun when Symmachus was still at court in Trier, are featured prominently in the last part of book 1. Fl. Claudius Antonius, who received *Letters* 1.89–93, was appointed as quaestor of the sacred palace and rose to praetorian prefect of Gaul 376–377, then of Italy 377–378 and consul in 382.[72] Like Ausonius, Antonius is praised for his rhetorical abilities by Symmachus. As quaestor for the sacred palace, Antonius also wrote speeches for the emperor (Symmachus, *Letter* 1.89.1). Of similar prominence is the provincial Syagrius who received *Letters* 94–107; most likely he can be identified with the man who became *magister officiorum* in 379, praetorian prefect of Italy in 380–382, and consul in 381.[73] Symmachus's friendships with such upwardly mobile provincials would later prove invaluable to himself and his family, as well as to his numerous friends and clients.

370–380: The Ascendancy of Gratian

Symmachus returned to Rome, probably in the spring of 370.[74] He did not have to wait long for his next honor; by early March 373, approximately at the

70. Roda (1981b, 273–80) identifies this anonymous *Letter* 9.88 as written to Ausonius on the basis of internal evidence; 9.88.2 indicates that Ausonius has read some of Symmachus's writing. For more on this letter, see my discussion, 35–41.

71. Symmachus, *Oration* 2.18, claims that the fortresses built by Valentinian excel those of the famed craftsmen Archimedes, Epius, and Daedalus; Ausonius's *Mosella* (*Moselle*), lines 298–317 (Evelyn-White 1988), makes the same declaration, that the edifices along the Moselle equal or surpass those of the great builders, Archimedes, Daedalus, and twelve others.

72. Fl. Claudius Antonius = Antonius 5 in *PLRE* 1:77.

73. Flavius Syagrius is likely to be identified with Syagrius 3, *PLRE* 1:862–863. There is another Syagrius, named Flavius Afranius Syagrius, = Syagrius 2 in *PLRE* 1:862, with whom this letter's recipient is possibly identified; see my discussion of Symmachus, *Letter* 1.94.

74. We cannot be certain exactly when Symmachus left Trier, but *Letter* 9.112 has been

age of thirty-three, he was in Africa, once again holding public office, this time the proconsulship of that province.[75] This was a position with administrative, judicial, and financial responsibilities. In a letter of 375/376, Symmachus congratulated the general Flavius Theodosius, whom he had probably met earlier in Trier, for ending the African revolt led by the Moor Firmus (372/3–374/5); Symmachus had supported this campaign in his official capacity as proconsul.[76] One measure of Symmachus's success as proconsul is indicated by the desire of the local elites to erect a statue in his honor, a fact that Symmachus proudly advertised; only the envy of unnamed people—commentators have suggested local rivalries or the jealousy of Chilo and Paulus Constantius, Symmachus's successors as proconsuls—deterred his African supporters from carrying through with their plan to erect an honorific statue.[77] Nevertheless, Symmachus's time as proconsul had been well spent, for he used his time in office there, from winter/spring 373 to spring or summer 374,[78] to reinforce and expand his ties to friends and clients; one of these friends, a bishop, appears in book 1 as the recipient of a letter of recommendation from Symmachus, in large measure on the basis of actions taken during Firmus's revolt (*Letter* 1.64).

---

identified as written from Rome, to Probus and dated to the year before Probus's consulship, hence to late 370, as Seeck (1883, xxv n. 49) suggested. This is the Probus addressed in *Letters* 1.56–61. Also, *Letter* 1.14, which mentions Ausonius's *Moselle,* was written after Symmachus left court; this letter can be dated to soon after 370 and was sent from Rome. Hence Symmachus was back in Rome by the end of 370 at the latest.

75. *C. Th.* 12.1.73, dated November 373, is the first extant law sent to Symmachus as proconsul; the last extant legislation to his predecessor is dated to February 373 (*C. Th.* 16.6.1). That means he probably arrived after April 373, with the opening of the sailing season. The first dated law to his successor is from July 374 (*C.Th.* 8.5.33); see Lizzi Testa 2004, 378 n. 186.

76. Symmachus, *Letter* 10.1.2–3, to the elder Theodosius, dated to 375/376. Symmachus inserts a proverb that refers to mutual praising: literally, "Mules scratching each other's backs." It is a proverb that Symmachus liked, for he used it also in a letter to Ausonius (*Letter* 1.31.1). For their earlier meeting, see Matthews 1971, 122–28. For more on the general, see Flavius Theodosius 3, in *PLRE* 1:902–4; he was the father of the future emperor, Theodosius, and was *magister equitum* in the West between 369 and 375. The revolt of Firmus is described by, among others, Ammianus Marcellinus, *Res Gestae* 28.6.25, 29.5; Aurelius Victor, *Epitome de Caesaribus* 45.7; and Orosius, *Historiarum adversus paganos libri septem* 7.33.5.

77. Symmachus, *Letter* 9.115: "nihil moror statuas et publica falsa titulorum." *Letter* 8.5 advertises his success as proconsul in Africa. Callu (2002, 127 n. 1 to *Letter* 9.115) suggests that the envy of his successors prevented the statue's erection; see Constantius 11, *PLRE* 1:227; Chilo, *PLRE* 1:201.

78. See xxvii n. 75 above and xxviii n. 79 below.

Symmachus left the province of Africa in the late spring or summer of 374 to return to Rome to start his own family.[79] He married well. His wife Rusticiana was the daughter of Memmius Vitrasius Orfitus, a man from a noble family with close ties to the court of Constantius II, judging from Orfitus's rapid rise through a series of appointments; indeed, Orfitus held the urban prefectureship of Rome twice (353–355, 357–359), a signal honor.[80] Probably Orfitus was no longer alive at the time of his daughter's wedding, which removed any embarrassment his son-in-law might have felt about Orfitus's alleged lack of refinement. The Greek historian Ammianus Marcellinus decried Symmachus's father-in-law as a man whose learning in the liberal arts was "less than befits a noble."[81] Nonetheless, Orfitus's influence, his record in public office, and his ties at court were enough to make the marriage desirable to the Symmachi.

Symmachus and Rusticiana had two children who survived into adulthood, a daughter whose name and date of birth are not securely attested (see below), and a son, Quintus Fabius Memmius Symmachus, born probably in 382 or at the latest 384.[82] Both children married into the same noble, politically engaged, and influential family, the Nicomachi, a family with whom the

79. Seeck (1883, xlvii–xlviii, lxxiii) thinks Symmachus stayed on in Africa as a private citizen for several months into 375 after he left office; he returned to Rome to wed in the summer of 375. Lizzi Testa (2004, 375–79) argues for a longer time frame; i.e., he left Africa in the spring or summer of 374 and married soon after in Rome. Her view allows more time to accommodate events such as his marriage and the burning of his father's house, before the opening letter of book 1, securely dated to 375. A 374 marriage date would also fit better with Marcone's (1983, 24) dating for the wedding of Symmachus's daughter in 388 (see xxix n. 85 below). Palanque (1931, 346–56) argued, however, that the marriage of Symmachus took place in 370, a little before Orfitus died, to make the marriage coincide with the emancipation of Rusticiana. Although this seems likely, there is no evidence to prove the date of the wedding or anything to necessitate her marriage before the death of her father, as observed by Lizzi Testa (2004, 379).

80. Memmius Vitrasius Orfitus signo Honorius 3, *PLRE* 1:651–53, lists his appointments at court: "comes ordinis secundi, comes ordinis primi, item comes intra consistorium ordinis primi, comes ordinis primi iterum intra consistorium." Cameron (1996, 295–30) suggests that Orfitus was married to an imperial woman, Constantia, thus explaining his rapid success at the imperial court. *CIL* 6:1741 = *ILS* 1243 claims that Orfitus was born from a noble family ("genere nobili"), as do *CIL* 6:1739, 1740, and 1742, and Symmachus, *State Paper* 34.12.

81. Ammianus Marcellinus, *Res Gestae* 14.6.1 (Rolfe 1935–1939).

82. For Memmius's birth, see Symmachus, *Letters* 2.47, 2.48, 8.69. Cecconi (2002a, 314–15) argues convincingly for his birth date of 382, against the 384 dating offered by Seeck; but *PLRE* 2:1047, Symmachus 10, dates his birth to 383/384.

Symmachi had already made marriage ties.[83] Symmachus's daughter married Nicomachus Flavianus the Younger;[84] if the date for her marriage of 388 is correct and she was (as was the norm for the elite) between the ages of twelve and fourteen at her wedding, then she must have been born between late 374 and 376.[85] She was Flavianus's second wife, and she and her husband were in constant contact with Symmachus; they are the recipients of an entire book of letters (book 6, dating from 394–401). Much later, Symmachus's son also married into the Nicomachi, to a granddaughter of Virius Nicomachus Flavianus the Elder.[86] Hence, the ties between these two families were secured for at least two generations; I suspect shared financial interests, as well as social and political ties, made these matches desirable.

We know far more about Memmius than his sister, for his father was intimately involved in his son's life, health, education, and private as well as public affairs. Symmachus expended much time, money and influence on his son's behalf; perhaps best documented are his efforts to organize Memmius's praetorian games, held in 401. Symmachus called in favors from friends scattered over the empire and spared no effort in preparing the entertainments for the day. The more exotic the animal, the better; horses from Spain and entertainers from far and wide were sought for games that cost at least 2,000 pounds of gold, a sum that suggests how wealthy the family was.[87]

Yet despite Symmachus's fortune and connections, the mid-370s presented trials to him and his family. His father, L. Aurelius Avianius Symmachus, had

83. Ammianus Marcellinus, *Res Gestae* 23.1.4, states that Flavianus the Elder's father, Volusius Venustus, was of noble birth, "clare natus." Marcone (1983, 24) believes that Symmachus was probably already related to Flavianus the Elder through marriage, since he accepts Seeck's suggestion that Symmachus's father, Avianius Symmachus, had married the sister of Volusius Venustus, father of Flavianus the Elder. But not all agree with this identification of Avianius's wife; the *PLRE* (1:1146), Stemma of the Symmachi, based on the work of Chastagnol (1962, 159–60), proposes that Avianius Symmachus had wed the daughter of Fabius Titianus, the brother of Flavianus the Elder's mother, and that it was a sister of Symmachus the elder who wed Volusius Venustus; I follow that line of argument. However, regardless of who married Avianius, the point remains true that the Symmachi and Nicomachi were already related by marriage ties. This preexisting link may explain why Symmachus chose to wed his children to the Nicomachi, whom Cameron (1999a, 503) characterizes as a "relatively minor family (by Roman standards)."

84. For more on this man, see Nicomachus Flavianus 14, *PLRE* 1:345–47.

85. Marcone 1983, 50–51; contra Seeck 1883, lii, who dates the marriage to 392–394.

86. For more on Flavianus the Elder, see Virius Nicomachus Flavianus 15, *PLRE* 1:347–49. Memmius's wife's identity is not certain, although *PLRE* 2:1047 suggests that she be identified with Galla 1. In any case, Flavianus is called Memmius's "prosocer" (grandfather-in-law) in an inscription, *CIL* 6:1782 = *ILS* 2947; see also Symmachus, *Letter* 4.14.

87. Olympiodorus, *Fragment* 44 M = 41.2B; Cameron 1999a, 492–505.

been forced to flee Rome before an angry mob; his father's alleged remark during a wine shortage that he would rather use his wine to quench lime-kilns than sell it at a reduced rate had incensed the crowd, who proceeded to burn down his house in Trastevere.[88] Avianius went into self-enforced exile in 375, the point of departure for *Letters* 1–5 to his father that open book 1. Avianius was recalled to Rome at the end of 375 by the Senate and subsequently honored.[89] His son delivered a speech of gratitude for his father's recall on 9 January 376; the speech, although fragmentary, is preserved as Symmachus's fifth *Oration*.[90]

After Avianius's recall and in the midst of hope for better times with the ascension to the throne of Ausonius's pupil Gratian (375–383), a new note of optimism and enthusiasm emerges in Symmachus's correspondence (*Letter* 1.13 to Ausonius). Symmachus's friendship with Ausonius now proved especially helpful. In these early years, the bulk of Symmachus's letters to Ausonius preserved in book 1 (*Letters* 1.13–43) are letters of recommendation and requests for favors. The beginning of Gratian's reign also brought new honors to Symmachus and his family; Symmachus's father, Avianius Symmachus, was singled out for the consulship for 377, although he died before holding it; Symmachus's relative and future in-law, Nicomachus Flavianus the Elder, was made vicar of Africa this same year.[91] Symmachus himself was given a special distinction when, in lieu of the urban prefect of Rome, he was granted the honor of reading aloud the message from Gratian concerning victories over the Alamanni in the spring or summer of 376 (*Letter* 10.2). A similar distinction was accorded to him in the fall of 379, when again he was asked to convey to the Roman Senate the words of the emperor Theodosius concerning victories over the Goths (*Letters* 1.95, 3.18).

Although Symmachus held no other public office until 384, he was active in public life; he wrote letters in support of friends and clients, delivered orations, and served on senatorial embassies. His *Orations* 6–8 were probably delivered in this period, although they are fragmentary and cannot be dated precisely.[92] Sogno has proposed, with justification, that the success of his speeches probably led Symmachus to publish a selection of his orations in the

---

88. Ammianus Marcellinus, *Res Gestae* 27.3.4; and see pp. 1–3.

89. The first notice of the elder Symmachus's return to Rome is a speech of thanks given by his son in the Senate on 9 January 376 (*Or.* 5); see also Symmachus, *Letters* 1.44, 2.38; Seeck 1883, xliii.

90. Symmachus, *Or.* 5; see also Symmachus, *Letters* 1.44 and 2.38.

91. See Virius Nicomachus Flavianus 15, *PLRE* 1:347; and *C. Th.* 1.16.6.2.

92. *Orations* 6–8 were all delivered to the Senate in connection with the advancements of individual senators; see Sogno 2006, 25–30; Seeck 1883, v–xv; and Callu 2009b, vii–xvi.

early years of Gratian's rule, with the idea of advancing his reputation.[93] His letters indicate that Symmachus was also busy in these years with his own affairs; we hear of his travels to his various estates to attend to necessary business, the standard sorts of managerial work of the Roman elite.[94]

Symmachus's prominence in public life in the early years of Gratian's rule explains why, for example, he was invited to consular inaugurations, a much desired sign of status. Indeed, Symmachus was so secure in society that he felt free enough to decline some invitations. So, for example, he sent regrets for not attending the consular inauguration of Ausonius scheduled for 1 January 379, probably in Trier; Symmachus begged off because of poor health and claimed that he was not up to the trials of travel (*Letter* 1.20.3). He also excused himself from the consular inauguration of Syagrius in January 381 on the grounds that he was still in mourning for the death of his brother, Celsinus Titianus, vicar of Africa, who had died in 380 (*Letter* 1.101). Some scholars have read Symmachus's apologies and claims of ill health quite literally. Just as likely, they are gracious excuses; Jerome, too, felt free to dwell on his maladies as a reason for avoiding responsibilities.[95] Symmachus was feeling in perfectly good health by 382, when he went to Gratian's court as an envoy of the Senate in what has become his most memorable historical role.

382–385: Symmachus as an Advocate of Traditional Religion? His Months as Urban Prefect

In 382 Symmachus traveled to Milan as head of a senatorial delegation to ask Gratian, among other things, to restore the Altar of Victory to the Roman Senate House. The altar had stood next to a statue of Victory ever since the time of Augustus, who had set up both in 29 B.C.E. in his newly built Senate House to commemorate his victories over Antony and Cleopatra.[96] Neither the altar nor the statue survives, but it seems likely that the statue was the standard one, a representation of Victory as a woman poised on bare feet with outstretched wings as if about to land, wearing long, flowing garments, depicted much as she appears, for example, as the Victory of Samothrace in the Louvre Museum. The altar, whatever shape it took, was of political and religious significance, for it was here that senators traditionally vowed their

93. Sogno 2006, 30; in this she follows the views of Callu 1972, 17; and 2009b, viii–ix.

94. See *Letter* 1.49 for Rome in 378; 1.15 for Rome in 379; 3.50 for Praeneste; and Seeck 1883, liii n. 191.

95. Lançon 1988, 355–66.

96. See *Fasti Maffeiani* in A. Degrassi 1963, 79, for August 28; H. A. Pohlsander 1969, 591.

loyalty to the emperor on his accession; it was here that oaths were taken and incense was offered to the gods before any major undertakings.[97] As a symbol of such activities, the altar was offensive to some Christians. In 357, during his visit to Rome, the emperor Constantius II, acting in response to such sensibilities, removed the altar but probably not the statue of Victory from the Roman Senate House; the altar was soon returned to its place in the Senate, probably by the pagan emperor Julian, and there it remained under his Christian successors Jovian and Valentinian I.[98]

In 382 Gratian took a more aggressive stance against the traditional state cults. He not only removed the Altar of Victory, but he also confiscated the estates and their income from the Vestal Virgins and from the other state cults; these monies had funded cult rituals and supported the upkeep of the temples.[99] As Symmachus argued, Gratian's predecessor Constantius II had allowed the financial status quo to continue and had recognized the privileges of the Vestals as he also filled the public priesthoods.[100] The Senate responded by sending an embassy, headed by Symmachus, to the imperial court to request the return of these funds. When the bishop of Rome, Damasus, objected to the embassy on the grounds that it was not representative of the sentiments of the Senate as a whole, Gratian refused to hear the delegation.[101] Symmachus was forced to return to Rome, embarrassed, no doubt, by his inability to gain admission even for a hearing at the imperial court. Gratian's new policy represented a change in the financing of the public cults of Rome that ultimately threatened their viability as state cults. Thus, while Gratian did not remove himself as head of the state cults, it is perhaps indicative of changing Christian sensibilities that from the 380s on we find the title *pontifex inclitus* displacing the old imperial title *pontifex maximus*.[102]

97. For incense and libations, see Herodian, *Roman History* 5.5.7; for oaths, see Ambrose, *Letter* 72 (Maur. 17).9–10; and Symmachus, *State Paper* 3.5.

98. Symmachus, *State Paper* 3.4 and 3.6; Ambrose, *Letter* 73 (Maur. 18).11–17.

99. Symmachus, *State Paper* 3.11–15. Lizzi Testa (2007, 251–62) argues that Gratian removed these privileges and estates only from the Vestal Virgins. She focuses largely on the rhetoric of Symmachus's *State Paper* 3. However, this privileges the remarks of Symmachus over those of Ambrose who, in *Letter* 73 (Maur. 18).16 notes that estates in general were confiscated. For a full discussion of the extent of Gratian's policies, see Cameron 2011, 33–51.

100. Symmachus *State Paper* 3.7.

101. Symmachus, *State Paper* 3.1; Ambrose, *Letter* 72 (Maur.17).10.

102. Zosimus, *New History* 4.36. See Cameron 1968, 96–99; 2007, 341–84, especially 371–73, for a correction of Zosimus's statement that Gratian was the first emperor to reject the priestly robes of the office of *pontifex maximus*.

As the focus of senatorial attempts to retain state support for traditional public cult, the Altar of Victory remained an issue in Roman elite circles through the end of the century. When political circumstances changed, Symmachus used his position as urban prefect to once more advance a senatorial request for its return. The emperor Gratian had been killed in August 383 in Lyons as he unsuccessfully tried to put down a coup by the usurping general Magnus Maximus.[103] Maximus then set up an independent court in Trier, which, however, was not recognized by Gratian's younger brother, Valentinian II, who, aged twelve or thirteen, established his court in Milan. Valentinian II's position was not a secure one, however, and the religious in-fighting at the court between his Arian mother, Justina, and the orthodox bishop of Milan, Ambrose, further weakened the boy-emperor's standing. In light of these events, some scholars have argued that the emperor's advisers urged Valentinian II to seek the support of the senatorial elites in Rome. Hence, Valentinian II appointed Symmachus prefect of the city of Rome by spring 384, an office that was one of the most influential and powerful to which a senator could aspire.[104] Symmachus accepted this honor for several reasons, one of which was the support of his friend, the eminent pagan senator Vettius Agorius Praetextatus, who had been appointed praetorian prefect of Italy, Illyricum, and Africa earlier in this same year. (Praetextatus is the recipient of *Letters* 44–55 published by Symmachus in book 1.)[105]

In his official capacity as urban prefect, Symmachus also represented the emperor at festivals and ceremonies pertaining to the state and its cults, especially since the emperor was no longer resident in Rome.[106] In this capacity, and with senatorial support, Symmachus sent a speech in the form of a state paper, his third *State Paper*, in the summer of 384 to the emperor Valentinian II.[107] In it he argued eloquently for the return of the Altar of Victory to the Senate House; key to his position was the importance of the altar for the well-being of the Roman state: only after its return, he argued, and with the restoration of public monies (i.e., the estates and inheritances granted to the

---

103. Liebeschuetz 2005, 14–15; and see xxxvi n. 120.

104. For the date of his taking office in May or June, see Vera 1981, liv–lvi, although Coşkun (2003), 3–10, makes a strong case for April 384.

105. *C. Th.* 6.5.2, dated to 21 May 384, indicates that Praetextatus was already in office by then. For more on his career, see pp. 91–96.

106. For the religious duties of the urban prefect, see Barrow 1973, 4–5; Chastagnol 1960, ch. 5.

107. The bibliography on the Altar of Victory controversy is vast. For a good introduction to the problem with a translation of the documents pertaining to it in English, see Croke and Harries 1982, 30–51; see also Salzman 1990, 221, 233–34; McLynn 1994, 406; Evenepoel 1998, 283–306; and Liebeschuetz 2004, 61–94. See also xxxii n. 99.

state cults) could Rome's survival and success be guaranteed. In a world that had been recently shaken by the barbarian victories at Adrianople in 378, and after a famine in Italy in the winter of 383, such arguments were deemed particularly persuasive, or so Symmachus hoped. Ambrose, then bishop of Milan, was made aware of the *Relatio* and, as he claims, demanded to see it, threatening Valentinian II with excommunication if he refused to send it to him.[108] Once more the request for the altar's restoration was denied by the imperial court. But, as Neil McLynn has observed, that did not stop Ambrose from preparing a letter in response to the failed *State Paper* in which he ridiculed Symmachus's arguments point by point,[109] and it was Ambrose who then circulated and published both of his letters to Valentinian, together with Symmachus's *State Paper*, in order to publicize his "victory" over the senator and orator. The incident was later immortalized—and Symmachus's reputation as an eloquent pagan advocate advanced—by the poet Prudentius in a long poem, the *Contra Symmachum* (*Against Symmachus*), completed in the spring of 402 or early 403.[110]

Symmachus's willingness to act as senatorial envoy concerning the Altar of Victory controversy and his authorship of the third *State Paper* won him the reputation of a traditionalist and politically active leader of a "pagan party." Yet the degree to which Symmachus and his friends were motivated by "religion," as opposed to "senatorial tradition," has been contested. Herbert Bloch and, more recently, Charles Hedrick, have emphasized his religious motivations, while others, such as Alan Cameron and François Paschoud, emphasize Symmachus's concern for senatorial tradition and the economic viability of the state cults.[111] In my view, this dichotomy is a false one; traditional religion was part of Symmachus's identity and part of the Roman state. Defense of senatorial religious tradition was central to maintaining his and his family's and friends' position; the altar, emblematic of the status quo, was important precisely because it represented the symbiosis of traditional religion and politics. Symmachus proved himself eager to defend senatorial tradition, since he

---

108. Ambrose, *Letter* 72 (Maur.17).13.

109. Ambrose, *Letter* 73 (Maur. 18); McLynn 1994, 167–68. The third *State Paper* survives both in Ambrose's edition of Symmachus's and his own writings on the controversy, as well as in the independent manuscript tradition of Symmachus's *State Papers*; see Vera 1981, lxxix; Seeck 1883, xvii–xviii.

110. For dating Prudentius's poem to 402/3, see especially Barnes 1976, 373–86; Shanzer 1989, 442–62. This was also probably the year in which Symmachus died, perhaps prompting the poem. Ambrose's letters included a copy of the third *State Paper* (Klein 1970, 335–71; Liebeschuetz 2005, 27–37; and n. 109 above).

111. Bloch 1963, 193–218; Hedrick 2000; Paschoud 1965, 215–35; 1997, 275–80; Cameron 1999b, 109–22; 2011, 41–48, 75–89.

believed in the central role of the Senate and its religious as well as political role in the state. This stance is a far cry, however, from viewing Symmachus as a pagan provocateur. Rather, in his defense of tradition and his willingness to engage in a dialogue with the imperial court, he adopts a markedly moderate stance. Although he put his reputation behind his request, the fact that he chose to do so in a formal state paper suits the values and character of a man who was firmly wedded to the status quo.

Symmachus left the office of the urban prefect before the customary twelve-month period. His successor, Pinianus, a Christian, was in office by 24 February 385.[112] A combination of factors—growing frustration at his inability to win concessions from Valentinian II, the burdens of governing a city without being able to select the lower officials upon whom he had to rely, and then the death of his friend Praetextatus in October or November 384—led Symmachus to request an early departure.[113] Symmachus's failure to win concessions in the Altar of Victory controversy was not, therefore, the only or even necessarily the principal reason for his decision.

Yet if Symmachus's term as urban prefect was brief, it nonetheless has left us with a unique record of the kinds of demands and pressures on the holder of this position in the fourth century in the form of his *State Papers*. Although it is unlikely that Symmachus published these official reports in his lifetime (see section 3 below), their survival has enriched our understanding of the details of late Roman government immensely.

From Urban Prefect to Consul: 385–391

Although no longer urban prefect, Symmachus's influence on politics remained strong. It was at some point after he left this office that he received the honor of *princeps senatus*, "first man of the Senate," indicating that he, like his father, was first in precedence in the Senate; this title may also have granted him some prerogatives usually granted to other magistrates (e.g., calling the Senate to meet).[114] Another sign of his status was the invitation he

---

112. *Collectio Avellana* (*Avellana Collection*), *Letter* 4, Guenther 1895.

113. For the request to be relieved from office, sometime after the death of Praetextatus, see *State Papers* 10–12 and 24. For the death of Praetextatus, see p. 92. For complaints about the burdens of the office, see Symmachus, *Letter* 3.28; for complaints about inferior officials whom he did not appoint, see Symmachus, *State Paper* 17.

114. Socrates, *Historia ecclesiastica* (*Church History*) 5.14.6, notes Symmachus's role as *princeps senatus* in a discussion of the usurpation of Maximus, implying that he had attained this honor around the same time, ca. 388. For his father as *princeps senatus*, see xix n. 32 above. By the late fourth century, the prerogatives of this office beyond precedence

received to attend the consular inauguration in Milan for Valentinian's third consulship in 387.[115] One year later, however, Valentinian's position looked precarious. In late summer 387, Magnus Maximus had successfully invaded Italy. To avoid direct conflict, the emperor Valentinian II fled to Greece, to the eastern emperor Theodosius. Maximus took control of the state in Milan. In January 388, Symmachus, acting as senatorial representative, traveled to Milan to deliver a panegyric on the usurper, Maximus.[116] Given Maximus's success and his control of Italy, some have argued that Symmachus and the Senate had little choice but to support the usurper.[117] Others, however, have contended that dissatisfaction with the pro-Christian religious policies of his predecessors led Symmachus and other pagan senators to support Maximus and to oppose the Christian faction led by Ambrose and Petronius Probus that supported Valentinian II in exile.[118] This second view cannot be substantiated, nor can we know with any certainty if Symmachus was pressured to deliver his panegyric to Maximus.[119] Admittedly, Symmachus had failed to influence the previous regime on issues such as the Altar of Victory and funding for the state cult, and there is little to suggest that Maximus would have changed course. We do know that in delivering his panegyric Symmachus acted as senatorial representative, and he certainly tried to influence Maximus's policy on religious as well as on other issues to be favorable to the Senate.[120]

Unfortunately for Symmachus, Maximus's control of Italy was short-lived; the eastern emperor Theodosius came to the support of Valentinian II, and a swift overland march, instead of the expected naval attack, surprised Maximus and led to his defeat at Aquileia in August 388.[121] His demise put Symmachus

---

in speaking are not entirely certain. However, it is a sign of the influence of the Senate that individual senators and not the emperor (who was no longer resident in Rome) held this honored role. This transition occurred over the course of the third century; see *Scriptores Historiae Augustae, Vita Trium Gordianorum* (*Life of the Three Gordians*) 9.7; and Lizzi Testa 2004, 342 n. 61.

115. For Symmachus's attending the consular inauguration, see his *Letters* 3.52 and 63.

116. Socrates, *Church History* 5.14.6; cf. Symmachus, *Letters* 2.31; Matthews 1975, 223.

117. For scholars who diminish Symmachus's involvement in the usurpation by emphasizing his role as representative of the Senate, see, e.g., Seeck 1883, lvii; Rivolta Tiberga 1992, 27.

118. Pellizzari 1998, 47–48; hesitations raised by Cecconi 2002a, 51.

119. Sogno 2006, 68, proposes this hypothesis.

120. On Magnus Maximus, see Matthews 1975, 173–82; McLynn 1994, 218–19, 293–94; and Magnus Maximus 39, *PLRE* 1:588.

121. Date of execution in *Fasti Idatiani*, Mommsen 1892–1898, 1:245, 388,2; cf. Zosimus, *New History* 4.46–47.

in a dangerous position. According to the church historian Socrates, Symmachus was forced to seek asylum in a church, and only the intervention of Leontius, the Novatian bishop of Rome, saved him from punishment for treason.[122] In fact, in the autumn of 388 we find Symmachus suffering the presence of soldiers on his Ostian estates, a sign of his loss of influence and suggestive of possible punitive actions against him by Theodosius.[123] Although the military occupation of his property ended with Theodosius's visit to Rome in June–September 389, it was only after Symmachus delivered a speech of apology before Theodosius (which does not survive) that he was able to earn a full pardon.[124]

Pardon, however, did not mean the end of his marginalization from politics. For that, Symmachus had to call upon his friends. Symmachus now benefited from the influence of his in-law Nicomachus Flavianus the Elder (Symmachus's daughter had married Flavianus the Younger in 387/388) and from the network of imperial and military officials, such as the Frankish general Richomeres and the imperial official Flavius Rufinus, who helped Symmachus mend ties to the court of Theodosius.[125] Working through these friends and family, Symmachus was back in the court's good graces by late 389 and was even invited to attend the consular inauguration for Valentinian II and Neoterius in 390; he declined, claiming the invitation had arrived late, but only after many letters of regret sent to all involved.[126]

Perhaps the most obvious sign of Symmachus's rehabilitation was the fact that he was designated consul for 391.[127] This signal honor was reserved for

---

122. Socrates, *Church History* 5.14.6; some scholars have doubted this incident. Libanius, *Letter* 1004.8 (Foerster), notes that Symmachus had just survived a crisis, which may refer to this moment.

123. Cecconi 2002a, 50–51 and 323–24, on *Letter* 2.52.

124. Symmachus, *Letter* 2.13: "cum civiles et bellicas laudes domini nostri Theodosii stili honore percurrerem" ("When I was recounting, honoring him with my pen, the civic and military praises of our lord Theodosius"); *Letters* 2.28, 2.30, 2.31: "in panegyrici defensione" ("in defense of the panegyric"); *Letters* 2.32 and 8.69. See also Cecconi 2002a, 52–53. Other fragmentary evidence supports this view; see Seeck 1883, 340, with a fragment by Arusianus Messius (Keil 1880, 489): "solere principes bona verba largiri" ("Emperors are accustomed to grant favorable speeches"). See also Socrates, *Church History* 5.14.

125. For Richomeres, *magister militum* in the east in 383, and again, 388–393, see *PLRE* 1:765–66; for Flavius Rufinus, master of offices between 388 and 392 (under the emperor Theodosius) and later praetorian prefect of the Orient from 392 to 395, see Rufinus 18, *PLRE* 1:778–81.

126. Symmachus, *Letters* 3.85, 5.34. Sogno (2006, 76) thinks the late-arriving invitation was an intentional snub; this cannot be known.

127. Symmachus, *Letter* 2.62.

men whom the emperor favored; it was rarely granted to senators and hence all the more significant that Symmachus received it.[128] The intervention of his friends at court paved the way for this honor, but perhaps most influential was his in-law Nicomachus Flavianus the Elder; Flavianus had been at court for some time and had recently become the praetorian prefect of Italy.[129] Symmachus planned to celebrate his consulship, probably in Rome.[130] He had reached the highest office in the land and had matched the honors his father had attained, a traditional desire of the Roman aristocracy.

After assuming the consulship, Symmachus's reintegration into Roman politics and into the good graces of the Theodosian court appears secure. For this reason, and perhaps also because of his recent experiences, Symmachus seems not to have taken a leadership role in continuing protests about the Altar of Victory. This remained an issue even after Theodosius had returned to the east and left the west nominally under the control of Valentinian II, now aged twenty-one, who established his court at Vienne, though in reality the Frankish general Arbogastes, who had been given the duty of protecting Valentinian II, was in control.[131] In 391 another senatorial delegation requesting the return of the Altar of Victory went to see Valentinian II, following an earlier delegation, most probably in 389.[132] Both delegations were denied access to the emperor, but Symmachus is not mentioned on either embassy in any reliable source.[133]

---

128. Bagnall, Cameron, Schwarz, and Worp 1987, 4–6.

129. Symmachus, *Letter* 3.90, on Flavianus's appointment; this chronology follows that of Matthews 1975, 25; see also Sogno 2006, 77–78.

130. Seeck 1883, lviii, supposes that Symmachus traveled to Milan for these games, but as Matthews (1975, 16 n. 5) observes on the basis of *Letters* 4.60.1–2 and 4.58.2, it is more likely that the games were celebrated in Rome. For the meeting between Theodosius and Symmachus, see Quodvultdeus, *De promissionibus et praedictionibus Dei* (*On the Promises and Predictions of God*), 3.38(41) (Braun 1964). This meeting probably never happened (see xxxviii n. 132 below). If it did, it probably occurred in 389; see Sogno 2006, 75 n. 114; Pellizzari 1998, 190–91.

131. Zosimus, *New History* 4.53.1; Paulinus, *Vita Ambrosii* (*Life of Ambrose*) 26–30; Matthews 1975, 238.

132. For the delegation in 389, see Ambrose, *Epistula extra collectionem* (*Letter outside the Collection*) 10.4 (Maur. 57.4). For the delegation in 391, see Ambrose, *Letter outside the Collection* 10.5 (Maur. 57.5); *De obitu Valentiniani* (*On the Death of Valentinian*) 52. Scholars, including Croke and Harries (1982, 50 n. 33) and Matthews (1975, 238), connect the 389 delegation with the erroneous story from Quodvulteus, *On the Promises and Predictions of God* 3.38(41), about the emperor Theodosius, so infuriated by the delegation that he had Symmachus taken off in a carriage and set down one hundred miles from Milan.

133. See xxxviii nn. 130–32.

The Last Decade: Flavianus, the Battle of Frigidus, and Family Affairs

The last decade of Symmachus's life, 392–402, was most tumultuous for the orator and his family, especially for his in-laws, the Nicomachi. Only through his assiduous exercise of influence was Symmachus able to protect and advance his family and friends during the violence that overtook the western empire. The sudden death of Valentinian II in May 392—the emperor was found hanging from a noose, either a suicide or a murder—left Arbogastes in a difficult position; he had held the office of *magister militum* and had refused to be dismissed by the emperor Valentinian II.[134] Arbogastes looked guilty; although he at first tried to reconcile with Theodosius, by August 392 war seemed inevitable.[135] Eugenius, a Christian imperial bureaucrat and former teacher of rhetoric, was advanced as western emperor.[136] But even as Eugenius and Arbogastes sent envoys to Theodosius in the east to try to win recognition, they cultivated ties with potential supporters in the west, including the senatorial aristocracy and Christian clerics. One of the senators who lent their names to the cause of the usurpers after Eugenius entered Italy in 393 was Nicomachus Flavianus the Elder; he was rewarded with the office of praetorian prefect of Italy and in the next year, 394, was granted the further honor of holding the ordinary consulship. In this same year his son, now Symmachus's son-in-law, Flavianus the Younger, was appointed urban prefect.[137]

Flavianus the Elder's decision to establish ties with the imperial usurper and cut off his relationship with Theodosius's court has puzzled historians. If he was hopeful that Theodosius would recognize the usurpers, he was woefully misguided; Theodosius's legitimacy was based on his position as defender of the house of Valentinian. On the contrary, in January 393 Theodosius advanced his own son Honorius to the rank of Augustus.[138] Some historians have argued that Flavianus the Elder was motivated by concern for the state

134. Zosimus, *New History* 4.53.

135. Rufinus, *Historia ecclesiastica* (*Church History*), 11.31 (Amidon), on the death of Valentinian II; for the delay, see Matthews 1975, 239.

136. Symmachus, *Letters* 3.60 and 3.61, were conveyed by Eugenius to Ricomeres, who was the uncle of Arbogastes (Zosimus, *New History* 4.53.2). See Pellizzari 1998, 198–200 on the close ties between Eugenius and Arbogastes. For Arbogastes, see *PLRE* 1:95–97; for Eugenius, see Fl. Eugenius 6, *PLRE* 1:293.

137. This account follows the dates of these offices proposed by *PLRE*: Flavianus 15 (1:347–48) and Flavianus 14 (1:345–47); see also O'Donnell 1978, 129–43.

138. Matthews 1975, 239 and n. 7.

cult and for the survival of traditional religion. Certainly both sides called on divine support in the events between 392 and 394. According to the bishop Ambrose's *Letter* to Eugenius, Eugenius tried but failed to win over Christians but also pagans by granting gifts to outstanding, practicing pagan individuals, though he denied requests from pagan senators for public concessions to the state cult; Ambrose's *Letter* is the likely source for the statement by his biographer, Paulinus of Milan, that Eugenius allowed the Altar of Victory to be returned to the Roman Senate House and restored income to the state cults, as Cameron has argued.[139] Although many modern historians have been persuaded by Paulinus's *Life of Ambrose*, a close reading of these texts indicates that even Ambrose refrains from saying this, making it unlikely that Eugenius granted such concessions to pagan senators.[140] Nonetheless, Eugenius's openness to western pagan senators about such matters appears a conscious policy that contrasts sharply with that of his opponent, Theodosius, whose February 391 legislation sent to Albinus, prefect in Rome, announced stiff fines for pagans who performed animal sacrifice, visited temples, or revered the images of their gods; in November of the following year, in dealing with matters in Constantinople, Theodosius went even further and outlawed all kinds of sacrifice, specifying even the offering of incense within a domestic context to the Lares and Genius of the household.[141]

It seems unlikely, however, that Flavianus's opposition to Theodosius was part of a widespread reaction to such imperial religious policies. One primary piece of evidence for the idea of a pagan reaction—an inscription recording the restoration of a temple of Hercules at Ostia—offers little to support such an interpretation; the restored building was not a temple but probably a bath

139. Ambrose, *Ep. extra coll.* (*Letter outside the Collection*) 10.6 (Maur. 57); Liebeschuetz 2005, 258: "But when your clemency [Eugenius] took over the helm of government, it was later discovered that these gifts were made to men outstanding in public life, but practicing pagans. And it could perhaps be said, august emperor, that you have made a donation not to temples, but to men who have deserved well of you." Paulinus of Milan, *Life of Ambrose* 26, says that Eugenius granted the return of the Altar of Victory and funding for the cults. See Cameron 2011, 74–89.

140. Ambrose, *Ep. extra coll.* (*Letter outside the Collection*) 10.6 (Maur. 57; Liebeschuetz 2005, 258), only intimates the notion of restored funding, as Cameron (2011, 74–89) has rightly argued. The bibliography on these events that read this conflict as a "pagan-Christian conflict" brought on by a "pagan reaction" is large; see Salzman 2010, 191–224; Hedrick 2000, 47–58; and Cameron 2011, 74–89.

141. *C. Th.* 16.10.10, February 391, was sent to the urban prefect of Rome, Albinus. However, the more restrictive edict, *C. Th.* 16.10.12, November 392, was sent to Rufinus, praetorian prefect of the East, and hence would not have been applicable to Rome and Italy.

complex decorated with the labors of Hercules.[142] An anecdote that claims to show Flavianus's hostility to Christians—his threat to use Ambrose's basilica in Milan to stable his horses—appears the product of the propaganda that followed the decisive battle at the River Frigidus on 5 September 394 between Theodosius and the usurpers Eugenius and Arbogastes; later Christians, much influenced by Ambrose's views, saw this imperial victory as a triumph of their God.[143] Flavianus's desire to support the usurpers must be explained primarily by ambition and dynastic politics; he and his son, as well as his friends, stood to gain much from the court of Eugenius and Arbogastes.[144]

The defeat of the usurpers presented a real danger to the fortunes of Symmachus's family; although Symmachus had not been involved in this civil war, his daughter was married into the family of the Flaviani. In the aftermath of the battle, Flavianus the Elder chose suicide over dishonor.[145] His name was effaced from public monuments, and the life of his son, Symmachus's son-in-law Flavianus the Younger, was in danger; Augustine claims that the sons of the rebels were either killed in battle or sought asylum in church and were forced to convert.[146] Some scholars have gone so far as to argue that Flavianus the Younger was one of these men who, once pardoned, converted to Christianity, although the evidence for this is far from certain.[147] Later sources allege that Theodosius visited Rome after his victory to encourage the conversion of this group to Christianity, and while this trip appears unlikely, and probably a conflation with an earlier visit, it does suggest an emperor eager to be clement and to mend relations with this powerful group.[148]

---

142. See especially O'Donnell 1979, 43–77, citing the critical inscription, republished by Bloch 1963, 193–218. On the monument as no longer probably a temple of Hercules, see Boin 2010, 253–66.

143. Rufinus, *Historia ecclesiastica* 2.33 (Amidon); Ambrose, *Letters* 57 and 61; *Enarrationes in XII Psalmos davidicos* (*Interpretations of the Twelve Psalms of David*) *In Psalmum* 36.25 (PL 14:1025–26); Socrates, *Church History* 5.25; Theodoret, *Historia ecclesiastica* (*Church History*) 5.24. See also Salzman 2010, 191–224.

144. See Salzman 2010, 191–224.

145. Rufinus, *Historia ecclesiastica* 2.33 (Amidon).

146. Augustine, *De civitate Dei* (*The City of God*) 5.26

147. There is no firm evidence for the conversion of the younger Flavianus, since the passage in Augustine, *De civitate Dei* 5.26, does not name him, nor is he known to have sought refuge in a church; for doubts about this identification, see O'Donnell 1978, 129–43; Salzman 2002, 246; 2010, 191–224. Nonetheless, many historians, such as Hedrick (2000, 70), assume that this passage refers to the conversion of the younger Flavianus, based largely on his subsequent succcessful career.

148. Ancient sources recount a visit of Theodosius to Rome to convert the aristocracy, though some modern scholars have questioned its historicity; for discussion, see Salzman 2002, 1; Zosimus, *New History* 4.59 (Ridley 1982, n. 153).

But if we cannot be certain about the religious affiliation of Flavianus the Younger, we can be confident that his return to political life was owed in large measure to Symmachus's influence and network of powerful friends. In a letter to Stilicho, Theodosius's general, Symmachus expressed gratitude for the special dispensation granted his son-in-law Flavianus the Younger, exempting him from having to return to the state his father's salary as praetorian prefect.[149] Later, Symmachus urged his son-in-law to join a senatorial delegation to the emperor in 397 in the hopes of improving his standing at court.[150] Soon after we find a sign of his success: Flavianus the Younger was invited to the consular inauguration of Theodorus in late 398.[151] Flavianus the Younger's full reintegration into politics is evidenced by his attaining the office of urban prefect in 399–400, an honor for which Symmachus expresses gratitude in another letter to Stilicho.[152]

We find Symmachus in this last period of his life deeply involved in politics, in family matters, and in maintaining the friendships so critical for the exercise of influence in the late Roman world. As his intervention on behalf of Flavianus the Younger suggests, Symmachus's influence extended well beyond Rome to men in the military as well as in the imperial administration. The mechanism for maintaining these friendships was the writing of letters. Indeed, almost two-thirds of the letters contained in the collection belong to the period after Theodosius's victory at Frigidus, that is, 395 and later.[153]

The center of Symmachus's political activities remained in Rome; his influence was especially strong in the western empire. So, for example, as leader of the Senate, he was the man to whom that body turned in times of crisis, as, for example, in 397–398, when the Mauretanian rebel Gildo withheld the grain shipments from Rome. After Stilicho referred the problem to the Senate, it must have fallen to Symmachus, as Senate leader, to take up the matter and convince the Senate to declare Gildo a public enemy, which they did.[154] This action proved to be dangerous to Symmachus personally, as the populace blamed him for the ensuing food shortage. Like his father, Symma-

149. Symmachus, *Letters* 4.19, 4.51, 5.47 indicate that the salary was not paid back but that the threat had been real.

150. Symmachus, *Letters* 6.52, 6.56, 6.63.

151. For Symmachus's gratitude, see *Letter* 4.6, dated to 398 by Callu 1982, 89; for Flavianus's invitation to the consular inauguration of Theodorus, see *Letters* 4.6, 4.39, 6.6, 6.10.

152. Symmachus, *Letter* 4.4; for Flavianus the Younger's offices, see *PLRE*, Flavianus 14, 1:346.

153. Seeck 1883, lx.

154. Symmachus, *Letter* 4.5; Marcone 1987, 42–44; Claudian, *De consulatu Stilichonis* (*On the Consulship of Stilicho*) 1.306–350; for the Senate's decree, see *CIL* 9:4051 = *ILS* 795, *AE* 1926, 124.

chus was forced into exile by an angry mob that later recognized the error of their ways and asked him back, bestowing on him honors on his return.[155]

In the years after Gildo's uprising, Symmachus focused his attentions and efforts on his son's praetorian games. This, too, was politically motivated. Quaestors and praetors were expected to give games upon attaining office; indeed, by the late fourth century, this was their primary obligation, and the Roman elite were engaged in a pattern of competitive expenditure on such activities as a means of advertising the family name. His son Q. Fabius Memmius Symmachus had already given impressive quaestorian games in 393, but Symmachus seems to have felt compelled to outdo these, judging from the amount of effort and expense that he describes for his son's praetorian games.[156] Symmachus wrote to friends in all corners of the empire for favors. He asked his correspondents in Spain to obtain the best horses available for the chariot races.[157] He wrote to friends in Dalmatia for bears to be sent across the Adriatic to Rome.[158] His correspondent, the general Stilicho, also contributed by sending a gift of leopards for the hunt.[159] But Symmachus wanted more from Stilicho; he petitioned for the prerogative usually only granted to consuls, to hold the games in the Flavian Amphitheater.[160]

It is a sign of how important these games were that, although they were initially scheduled for 400, Symmachus delayed them until 401 for a variety of reasons. It is likely that Stilicho requested that Symmachus attend Stilicho's inauguration ceremonies for his consulship in 400 in Milan. The difficulties of making the trip at the same time as preparing for the games of his son in Rome, as well as a desire not to compete with Stilicho's celebrations, would

---

155. For Symmachus's exile in 398, see Symmachus, *Letters* 6.66, 8.64, 8.65, 9.81. The ability of the mob in Rome to riot and force the exile of leaders must be seen as a political tool, one of the few left to the people in the late Roman city. Often such riots were occasioned by food shortages, as in the case of Gildo.

156. Symmachus, *Letters* 4.58 and 4.59.2: "I must outdo the fame of my earlier displays, which, after the consular munificence of our house and the quaestorian exhibition of my son, portend nothing mediocre from us." See also Olympiodorus frag. 44M = 41.2B. For the ruinous nature of aristocratic expenditure, see Symmachus, *State Paper* 8.1–2; Marcone 1983, 107.

157. Symmachus, *Letters* 4.58, 4.59, 4.63, 5.56, 5.82, 5.83, 7.97, 9.12, 9.18, 9.19, 9.21, 9.23.

158. Symmachus, *Letters* 7.121, 9.132, 9.135, 9.137, 9.142.

159. Symmachus, *Letters* 4.12, 7.59.

160. Symmachus, *Letters* 6.33 (cf. Symmachus *State Paper* 8) and 4.11, requesting all the prerogatives of consular games for the games of Memmius. The Flavian Amphitheater is known in modern times as the Colosseum.

have led to the delay.[161] It was critical that Symmachus maintain his friendship with the powerful Stilicho; hence, he traveled to Stilicho's inauguration. It was in this same period that Symmachus sent a wedding gift (*sportulae*) to Stilicho, seeking his blessing for the forthcoming marriage of Symmachus's son Memmius to Galla, a member of the family of the Nicomachi, plausibly identified as the daughter of Flavianus the Younger's brother; the marriage took place in the course of 401.[162]

Symmachus's last known official act was his journey as senatorial envoy to the imperial court at Milan in 402. The reason for this delegation is unknown. Symmachus, now about sixty-two, became ill during this trip, and we have no further letters from him after 402.[163] Hence, Symmachus is presumed to have died in 402. When Prudentius, writing in late 402 or early 403 in Spain, praised Symmachus's eloquence as beyond that of anyone living now, his remark is generally understood as either an indication that Prudentius had not yet heard the news of Symmachus's death or was praising a recently deceased man.[164]

2. The World of Symmachus's *Letters*: Themes and Concerns in Book 1

The first book of Symmachus's letters is particularly important. These letters present an idealized image of this Roman aristocrat as he wished to be perceived by contemporaries and posterity. The first letter of book 1 serves well as both a summation and an introduction to this projected ideal. Symmachus focuses on age-old notions of honor among Rome's elite—his prestigious family, his accomplished father, his wife's distinguished family, his literary and political accomplishments, his education, wit, material wealth, and cultural attainments—which allow him to affirm his social status. His inclusion of epigrams, peppered with literary allusions to myths, like that of Hercules, and to figures from the Roman past, like Hortensius and Aeneas (*Letter* 1.1.5), underscores the traditional cultural values with which he wishes to associate

161. See McGeachy 1942, 104–5; Symmachus, *Letters* 4.63, 4.12, 7.1; Matthews 1975, 267.

162. Symmachus, *Letter* 4.14, notes the *sportulae*; so also 6.32. See also Marcone 1987, 53–54.

163. Symmachus, *Letters* 4.13, 5.94–96. The claim that this delegation was sent to once more request the return of the Altar of Victory after the defeat of Eugenius and Arbogast appears highly doubtful; see Cameron 1970, 240–41.

164. Prudentius, *Against Symmachus* 2. *Preface* 56: "quo nunc nemo disertior" ("than whom no one is now more eloquent"). For the arguments about the dating of this poem, see xxxiv n. 110.

himself. Good-humored yet polished, this first letter, and the subsequent letters to his father (1.3–12), portray Symmachus, the successful Roman senator and son, at work and at play. He alludes to the venerable Cato and represents himself as embodying the age-old balancing of *otium* and *negotium* that informs the social life of the Roman elite: "it is no less pleasing to offer an account of our leisure time than of our work time."[165] Book 1 shows us Symmachus pursuing the customary working activities of the Roman aristocrat as he delivers orations on state matters, as he manages his estates, as he deliberates on business pertaining to the state and its cults, and, most frequently, as he writes letters of recommendation for friends and clients.

Symmachus's activities as letter writer highlight the primary way that influence and power functioned in late Roman civic society; as a "friend"—as the Romans tactfully phrased this exercise of patronage—Symmachus developed ties to a wide network of men in all areas of late antique society: teachers, philosophers, bureaucrats, generals, Christian priests, and senators all relied on and sought Symmachus's support, as his letters of recommendation reveal. In advancing these requests and writing letters of recommendation for his "friends," Symmachus accrued honor, favors, and influence, since the successful friend was hereafter in Symmachus's debt. In essence, Symmachus acted as a power broker who could, for example, ask the powerful aristocrat Probus to grant the request of his friend Romanus (*Letter* 1.60). At times Symmachus asks for favors for himself or for his own family, such as the special privilege of having his son's praetorian games in the Flavian Amphitheater in Rome (*Letter* 4.8). Symmachus's letters reveal how personal influence was the *sine qua non* for success at all levels in late Roman society. Advancement was based on connections much more than on merit. The ability to advance the interests of clients augmented one's own reputation, and certainly Symmachus's name and career advanced in large part through his letter writing, especially his letters of recommendation. We can only wish that the letters of recommendation that others had written for Symmachus had survived; unfortunately, they do not.

Symmachus was a master at manipulating the conventions of epistolary etiquette. One measure of his reputation as a successful letter writer is the fact that his letters were copied and recopied, and they became models of style and etiquette. Indeed, Symmachus was keenly aware of the rules of epistolary conduct. So, for example, when Praetextatus wrote a single letter jointly to Symmachus and his father, Symmachus pointedly complains that this failure to write to them individually was a breach of epistolary propriety and

165. Symmachus, *Letter* 1.1.2, and see 9 n. 9.

something of an insult (*Letter* 1.50); similarly, the style of the letter should suit the correspondent's status and education.[166] The length of each letter was also calibrated to suit the importance of the person and the issue at hand. A short letter of greeting (*salutatio*) was acceptable under certain circumstances and better than not writing, for it functioned as a calling card that served to sustain the friendship (see *Letter* 1.57, to Probus). Symmachus's art lies in his ability to individualize the greeting or recommendation, reworking the formula to match the correspondent. Longer letters (see *Letter* 1.45, to Praetextatus) and requests for frequent communications (see *Letter* 1.34, to Ausonius) were signs of more intimate ties.

The language used to describe the recipient of the recommendation in Symmachus's correspondence is also revealing of the values important to Symmachus. He describes this relationship as if part of a metaphorical family. Often the person recommended is called *frater*, "brother," or, if younger, *filius*, "son." The latter term underscores the fidelity owed to Symmachus, who is in the more powerful position and hence is the metaphorical parent (see *Letter* 6.25). It is very much in keeping with the ethos of these ties that the demands of friendship were felt to be especially sacrosanct if performed for the sons of friends (*Letter* 9.34).[167]

The true Roman aristocrat knew how to play as well as work. Symmachus takes what can only be considered a traditional view of the appropriate use of leisure time when, following the venerable Cato the Elder (*Letter* 1.1.2), he demands it be devoted to "good" purposes. For an aristocrat, such activities included literary composition; in addition to writing letters and orations and reading and arranging for the copying of texts, Symmachus also wrote poetry (*Letter* 1.1). Sidonius Apollinaris ranked him high as a poet, quoting an epigram by him not found in any of his extant letters (Sidonius Apollinaris, *Epistle* 8.10.1). Symmachus saw such shared literary interests as a means to cement friendship ties. So, to indicate his relationship with the poet Ausonius, Symmachus includes a letter describing how he has had a manuscript of Pliny's *Natural History* copied for him.[168] Indeed, Symmachus's attention to classical literature was based on a deep regard for the past and for Roman traditions.

166. See Symmachus's complaint, *Letter* 3.32, that Ambrose sent a single letter of recommendation for two men; for Symmachus's use of epistolary etiquette to advance his prestige, see Salzman 2006a, 360–63. For the notion that the epistolary writer should calibrate his style to his correspondent, see the chapter "on letters" in Julius Victor's *Ars rhetorica* (*Rhetorical Art*) (Giomini and Celentano 1980), 105,36–106,6.

167. Vera 1983, 135–36. For more discussion on letters of recommendation, see especially Roda 1986, 177–207. On *frater*, see 51 n. 4.

168. Symmachus, *Letter* 1.24, also laments the carelessness of the scribe working on

The terms *vetustas*, "the olden days," and *antiquitas*, "antiquity," are used in a positive sense throughout Symmachus's writing.[169] Similarly, Symmachus's references to the *veteres*, "the ancients," as Symmachus likes to call republican or early imperial writers, are positive.[170] Such an attitude explains, too, the archaizing tendencies observed in Symmachus's vocabulary and syntax in his *Letters*, especially prevalent in book 1, which, as I propose, Symmachus himself polished for publication (see below).[171]

Symmachus's veneration for classical texts has been construed by some historians as a meaningful ideological statement in favor of traditional religion and opposed to Christianity, especially after Julian's failed efforts to remove Christian professors of rhetoric and literature from the schools.[172] However, having a high regard for classical texts did not, in Symmachus's world, convey such a polarized view of society.[173] Rather, Symmachus's allusions to classical literature, though certainly indicative of veneration for these texts, were intended to express a shared cultural and world view, a unanimity of purpose (see *unanimitas, Letter* 1.61) that united all well-educated men, be they Christian, such as the writer Ausonius, or pagan, such as Praetextatus or Symmachus himself.[174] Love of the classics should ignore religious affiliation.

Proof of Symmachus's desire to ignore religious difference in favor of a shared aristocratic culture is articulated, too, by Symmachus's apparent willingness to use formulaic language that speaks of the "gods" smiling even on Christians such as Ausonius and Probus; both men are addressed with the plural "gods" without regard for their religious affiliation (*Letters* 1.14.5, 1.57). Alternatively, the use of the singular in the phrase "with god willing" in a letter to his pagan father Avianius (1.3.5), which Seeck corrected to "with the gods willing," may have been intentional; Symmachus's openness to noncontrover-

---

Pliny's *Natural History*; see Symmachus, *Letter* 9.13, for the correction of Livy's works as a cause for delaying a gift.

169. For more on this attitude in the letters, see Bruggisser 1993, 414–17, concerning especially the letters between Symmachus and Avianius. See also the frequent references to *vetustas* and *antiquitas* in Lomanto 1983.

170. Symmachus, *Letter* 1.53.1, for this term in his letter to Praetextatus.

171. Haverling 1988, 135–37, 254–57.

172. See, e.g., Roda 1981a, 120–22, on the ideological implications of editing texts; argued again by Hedrick 2000, 183–214.

173. See especially Cameron 1977, 1–31, and his forceful amplification in 2011, 421–23, 451–60.

174. For Symmachus's use of classical texts in this way, see, for example, his *Letters* 1.20 and 1.21 to Ausonius and 1.53 to Praetextatus; see also xlviii n. 177 below. Most scholars consider Symmachus's *State Paper* 3 a good expression of his own religiosity; see xxxii n. 99 and xxxiii n. 107 above for bibliography on this *State Paper*.

sial, generic language for the divine emerges in other contexts.[175] Indeed, the alternation of the plural and singular of god or gods in addressing pagans and Christians in this and later books is interpreted by Alan Cameron as a sign of Symmachus's attentiveness to the religiosity of his correspondent in a carefully worked out world that divided people into pagans and Christians.[176] This view does not fit easily this first book of letters, set mostly in the 370s, which seeks to ignore such religious differences and assumes a shared set of social and cultural values; moreover, Cameron's view requires special pleading on a case-by-case basis even for the later books.[177] Certainly in book 1 religion does not stand in the way of patronage; as Symmachus himself notes (*Letter* 1.64), he is more than willing to recommend even a bishop for a favor.

Shared literary pursuits were a key component of Symmachus's view of elite society, but there were other aspects of aristocratic culture that Symmachus was eager to depict. So, for example, the aristocratic pursuit of hunting is appreciated by Symmachus for its health-giving benefits for Probus's sons.[178] However, he himself does not partake and preferred to picture Praetextatus reading rather than hunting, indicating the higher value of cultural pursuits.[179] Symmachus is also keen to show himself socializing with his peers and family members. So, Symmachus's letters depict him in the company of friends and family (e.g., *Letters* 1.1, 1.14, 1.62) and as a desired guest at consular ceremonies (1.101) as well as among the elite villas on the Bay of Naples at Baiae (1.3). He exercises the role of protector of the weak by coming to the aid of senatorial women in need of protection (1.70, 1.74).

---

175. See, for example, Symmachus, *State Paper* 3.5: "everywhere is full of god" ("omnia quidem deo plena sunt"). For Seeck's corrections, see 20 nn. 8 and 10 below.

176. Cameron 2011, 377–82.

177. Cameron (2011, 378–90) assumes that five correspondents whose religious affiliations are unknown are pagan because of polytheistic language in Symmachus's letters. Similarly, Cameron reasons that correspondents are Christian if Symmachus addressed them with monotheistic religious language. However, this way of reasoning assumes the very point Cameron is arguing, that Symmachus had a systematic and religiously divided approach to his correspondents. Nor does this logic work well for the letters in book 1, where we find Symmachus using polytheistic language to address Christians such as Probus, *Letter* 1.57. It may be that Symmachus became more sensitive to polytheistic terminology in the years after Theodosius's 391 legislation against paganism, but there is little to support such a systematic approach for the pre-384 period reflected in book 1 of his letters. Rather, Symmachus seems to be appealing to more generic principles of "the divine" as a means to obscure religious differences. See *Letter* 1.3.4 about Beneventum, *Letter* 1.3.5, and 20 n. 10.

178. Symmachus, *Letter* 5.67; for more on hunting and its value as an epistolary *topos*, see Bruggisser 1993, 397–407.

179. Symmachus, *Letters* 1.47.2 and 1.53 for Praetextatus; 4.18 for the reuse of this *topos* for Protadius.

Certainly Symmachus's epistolary self-portrait presents an idealized view of himself and his family. He circulated these letters in part to promulgate this image and thereby to advance not only his reputation and career but also his views on how late Roman society should be oriented. The popularity of these letters, alluded to by Symmachus himself, suggests how successful he was in this endeavor.[180]

Symmachus's support for traditional senatorial culture extended to the public cults and priesthoods.[181] Symmachus's adherence to pagan cult is part of his self-presentation in this first book of letters. His religiosity manifested itself primarily in his scrupulousness in the performance of religious duties. This "scrupulousness" or "conscientiousness" in one's duties toward the gods translates the Latin term *religio*. It is a major theme in book 1, occurring as a noun (*religio*) or adjective (*religiosus*) no less than seventeen times in the first book of letters.[182] How deeply Symmachus felt about the deities or rituals attendant upon his religious affiliation is not a topic that he would address outright necessarily; traditionalist classical Roman writers rarely speak of religion in personal or overtly introspective terms.[183] At most, we hear descriptions of rituals or outward manifestations of cult practice (see, e.g., *Letter* 1.49). Symmachus thus adheres to religious and literary norms in his private correspondence that are in keeping with his traditionalist stance.

Among traditional Romans, *religio* is conceptualized in a positive light as a binding moral principle demonstrated not just to gods but also to men.[184] Symmachus's conscientiousness in performing his duties is key to his portrait. Already in *Letter* 1.1.1, his first letter to his father, Symmachus speaks of writing from a sense of obligation (*noster* [*sermo*] *ex debito* [*proficiscitur*]), and throughout this first book of letters Symmachus reiterates his scrupulous concern to fulfill the responsibilities of friendship, and he expects the same in return from friends (see, e.g., *Letter* 1.47, to Praetextatus). The morality implicit in this concept comes close to modern notions of duty and responsibility, ideas that Symmachus expressed with other Latin words as well, such

180. Symmachus, *Letter* 2.48.

181. Bruggisser 1993, on *Letter* 1.1, and especially pp. 78–87, makes this point clearly, but see also my commentary on this letter.

182. See Lomanto 1983, 808–809, s.v. *religio; religiosus*.

183. North 2007, 318–63.

184. The man who demonstrates this quality, according to Festus, "values not only the sanctity of the gods but is also dutiful toward men" ("non mod[ic]o deorum sanctitatem magni aestimans sed etiam officiosus erga homines," Festus, *De verborum significatione* (*On the Meaning of Words*) 348.22; Lindsay 1913). For the term *religio* for friendship, see Wistrand 1950, 87–89 = 1972, 229–31, and examples from Lomanto 1983, s.v. *religio*.

as *officia* (duties) and *munera* (responsibilities). Indeed, Symmachus proudly claims to show such scrupulousness toward all friends and makes no note of their religious affiliation (see *Letter* 1.16.1, to the Christian Ausonius). Hence, the scrupulous attention to the responsibilities of friendship was a code of conduct that extended not only across religious lines but also across generational and institutional ones. It was the glue that held late Roman society together, as Symmachus's letters so well reveal.

Symmachus's conscientious attention to his friendships in book 1 is of wider interest because, in part, his correspondents were all men of high status in late Roman society. Indeed, book 1 provides us with portraits of some of the most accomplished men in the 360s and 370s in the late Roman western world: consuls, praetorian prefects, learned rhetoricians, and family predominate. Although each of these correspondents will be given detailed descriptions in the introduction to the letters addressed to them, it is worth pausing here to consider briefly this group as a whole and how Symmachus represented them.

(1) *Letters* 1.1 and 3–12 were written to Symmachus's father, the eminent L. Aurelius Avianius Symmachus. *Letter* 1.2 is Avianius's response. Their correspondence is unique in preserving for posterity both sides of a traditional, aristocratic father-son relationship. Symmachus highlights both his and his father's literary activities and accomplishments. So *Letter* 1.1 presents Symmachus's poetry, and 1.2 includes the biographical epigrams that Avianius wrote when in exile. The epigrams are consciously modeled on Varro's lost work, the *Hebdomades* (see Section 3 below). Their correspondence is a window into the concerns of the Roman elite, for they discuss personal interests, including literary, familial, and to some degree political, but also material concerns such as their estates and income.[185]

(2) *Letters* 1.13–31 and 33–43 were written to the Christian poet and influential courtier Decimius Magnus Ausonius. *Letter* 32 is Ausonius's response to Symmachus's letter. Only Ausonius and Symmachus's father are distinguished by speaking in their own words in this epistolary collection. This formal link underscores the notion that Ausonius was, metaphorically, Symmachus's literary "father" or mentor; Symmachus calls Ausonius his *parens* or relative in *Letter* 1.33, in response to Ausonius's calling him his son, *filius* (*Letter* 1.32.4). Symmachus's tie to Ausonius was also extremely useful; most of the letters to Ausonius are recommendations written to Ausonius when the latter was at court and holding high office. After Ausonius's consulship in 379 and his return to private life, Symmachus's correspondence with

185. Salzman 2006a, 357–75.

Ausonius seems to grow silent, an eloquent testimonial to the practical benefit Symmachus derived from the friendship, regardless of any personal satisfactions their relationship offered.[186]

(3) *Letters* 1.44–55 were written to the pagan senator Praetextatus. They provide a human and somewhat surprising image of this man that contrasts markedly with our other sources. Praetextatus emerges as a man far less engaged in religious matters than Symmachus deemed appropriate, and hence far less pious than the image portrayed by the inscription from Praetextatus's funerary monument (*CIL* 6:1779= *ILS* 1259) or by Macrobius' fifth-century work the *Saturnalia,* where Praetextatus is the expert on Roman festivals as well as Vergil's knowledge of pontifical lore.[187] Symmachus's letters underscore Praetextatus's learning as well as his wit. Somewhat older than Symmachus, Praetextatus offered the younger man advice on civic/state cult matters as well as personal ones in a friendship that is depicted as close and affable.

(4) *Letters* 1.56–61 were written to the powerful Christian senator Sex. Claudius Petronius Probus, father of Olybrius and Probinus, the consuls of 395 with whom Symmachus would also later correspond.[188] Symmachus's relationship with Probus emerges as somewhat distant and reserved but useful; the letters to him are mostly recommendations for clients. Probus's extraordinary record of office-holding reflects his status in senatorial and imperial networks; the historian Ammianus Marcellinus describes him as a fish out of water when not so engaged (27.11.3). It is more than a little ironic that one of these letters depicts Symmachus as encouraging Probus to meet the demands of office (*Letter* 1.58). Further, despite the likely possibility that the families of Symmachus and Probus came into some conflict when Symmachus was urban prefect in 384, none of that later hostility appears in these earlier letters.[189]

---

186. For more on their bond, see Bruggisser 1993, 28 and 153; for more on their correspondence, see my introduction to *Letters* 1.13–43.

187. Macrobius, *Saturnalia* 1.7–10; 1.12–23 (Praetextatus on the Saturnalia and the Roman calendar); 3.4–14 (Praetextatus on Vergil's knowledge of pontificial lore). Macrobius calls Praetextatus, "sacrorum omnium unice conscius" ("uniquely familiar with all sacred matters"; 1.7.17). For more on his image in the Saturnalia, see Kahlos 2002, 180–200; Liebeschuetz 1999, 185–205.

188. Probus's sons, Olybrius and Probinus, were the recipients of *Letters* 5.67–71.

189. Matthews (1986, 174) suggests some hostility between Symmachus and Probus on the basis of Symmachus, *Letter* 3.88; Rufinus chides Symmachus for not writing of the death of an eminent Roman, identified as Probus in a letter dated to 389/390 by Pellizzari (1998, 60) or before 396 by Callu (1982, 78). If this identification is accepted, the reason for this hostility is not explained in this letter. One likely cause of friction was Symmachus's actions against Probus's father-in-law Olybrius over a complicated case involving land rights when he was urban prefect; see *State Paper* 28 and Chastagnol 1960, 105–6. The

(5) *Letters* 1.62–74 were written to Symmachus's brother, Celsinus Titianus, who died in 380.[190] The majority of these letters are given over to business concerns, taking the form either of letters of recommendation or letters pertaining to family properties. Expressions of brotherly affection are reserved and, to a modern eye, rather limited. Nonetheless, we know from subsequent letters how hard Symmachus took his brother's death at what appears to have been a relatively early age.

(6) *Letters* 1.75–88 were written to Ausonius's son Hesperius.[191] Hesperius's advancement to the praetorian prefectureship of Italy and Africa made him a key contact in the imperial administration; not surprisingly, many of Symmachus's letters to Hesperius are recommendations or requests for favors for his friends and clients.

(7) *Letters* 1.89–93 were written to Fl. Claudius Antonius. Symmachus's correspondent was an important imperial official; he attained the position of praetorian prefect of Gaul, 376–377, then of Italy, 377–378, and consul in 382 and may have had ties to the imperial family. [192] He was, indeed, an accomplished and valuable friend.

(8) *Letters* 1.94–107 were written to the upwardly mobile Flavius Syagrius, another important imperial official who held either the praetorian prefectureship of Italy in 380–382 or urban prefectureship in this period, before becoming consul in 381. In my view, he was the same Syagrius who was friendly with Ausonius, making him a fitting figure with whom to conclude this book.[193]

Through Symmachus's eyes, we receive personalized yet carefully selected images of these and numerous other key figures. These are not full biographies but carefully crafted snapshots. Indeed, the omission of personal details is maddening at times. For example, no reasons are given for the elder Symmachus's forced retirement from Rome (*Letters* 1.3, 1.44, 2.38); we must discover them in other sources.[194] Nor does Symmachus explain some of his own actions and motivations during this period; we do not hear about

---

publication of book 1 should, in my view, postdate his year in office and hence this conflict; see liv–lxii.

190. See Titianus 5, *PLRE* 1:917–18, and my introduction to Symmachus's *Letters* 1.62–74, pp. 129–30.

191. For more on this man, see Decimius Hilarianus Hesperius 2, *PLRE* 1:427–28 and my introduction to *Letters* 1.75–88, pp. 145–46.

192. For this man, see Fl. Claudius Antonius, Antonius 5 in *PLRE* 1:77 and my discussion of Symmachus's *Letters* 1.89–93, pp. 161–62.

193. For this man, see Syagrius 3, *PLRE* 1:862–63, with changes to his career noted in my introduction to *Letters* 1.94–107, pp. 169–70.

194. Ammianus Marcellinus, *Res Gestae* 27.3.4; Symmachus, *Or.* 5.

what he did to aid his father's return from exile or even how he felt about his father's forced absence from Rome.[195] We do not know, either, how Symmachus felt about his wife or even his own priesthood.

But despite their limitations, the letters of Symmachus can provide revealing insights into the private life and attitudes that the historian searches for in vain in more elevated historical writing. Symmachus's clear note of exasperation with Praetextatus's delayed return to Rome (*Letter* 1.51), for instance, is a telling detail that conveys a good sense of these men as individuals. Moreover, Symmachus's letters reveal just what aspects of personal affairs his late Roman readers were keen to hear most about: friendships, patronage links, family ties, and literary interests predominate in the first book, with public life and office referred to for the most part only in passing. Ammianus's critique of the devotion of the late Roman elite to gossipy biography and satire rather than serious pursuits (28.4.14) is borne out to some degree by the attention here to private connections and personal interests.

Symmachus's decision to publish his letters (see liii–lxvi below) fits with the late fourth-century resurgence of interest in private lives, not only of pagans such as Libanius but of Christian leaders such as Augustine and Ambrose. This interest, along with the more easy accessibility of the codex as a book form, fueled the marked increase in gathering and publishing epistolary collections in the late fourth and early fifth centuries.[196]

3. The Publication and Survival of Symmachus's *Letters*

Although written as private correspondence to specific individuals, each of Symmachus's letters would be read aloud to its recipient in the presence of members of his household; this was standard practice. Confidential bits of information or controversial views on public affairs would be conveyed by the letter carrier in private conversation.[197] Symmachus kept copies of the letters he wrote; he claims that he did so for fear that his letters would be lost or

195. His correspondence in later books omits his more problematic political errors. So, for example, Symmachus composed and delivered a panegyric to the usurper Maximus, but he notes only the fact that he delivered a speech of apology to Theodosius and obtained pardon (*Letters* 2.13, 2.28, 2.30, 2.31, 2.32, 8.69). On this, see also Socrates, *Church History* 5.14.6; Libanius, *Letter* 1004.8 (Foerster).

196. Peter 1965, 142–43; Mullett 1997, 31–37; and Cugusi 1983.

197. Symmachus mentions information being delivered orally by letter carriers often; see, e.g., *Letters* 1.11, 1.46, 1.87.2, 1.90.1; 2.11, 2.21, 3.30, 4.44, 6.13, 8.31, 9.37. *Letter* 6.18 notes that Symmachus gave oral information about a grain shortage to his letter carrier, so the recipient of the letter will "learn more by listening than by reading" ("Plura igitur auribus quam lectione noscetis").

delayed by an unreliable letter carrier.[198] Such concerns, real or not, suggest that Symmachus's letters had high prestige. However, we should also remember that this was fairly standard practice; the Greek orator Libanius and the Christian ascetic Jerome as well as the bishop Ambrose kept copies of their own letters as well, lest a letter go astray.

The Publication of Book 1

It is likely that at some time after 384, when he stepped down from the urban prefectureship, but by the early 390s, Symmachus organized and published book 1 of his letters.[199] This is not the case for books 2–10 of his letters; these were published after Symmachus's death, circa 402, although books 2–7, in my view, were probably prepared and organized by Symmachus before his death. However, the nature of the publication of these later books presents controversial problems that I will discuss shortly. First I want to present the evidence to support my view that Symmachus personally prepared and published the first book of letters in his lifetime.

Chronological evidence. All the letters in book 1 date to the earliest period in Symmachus's life, but none are earlier than the priesthood that he acquired between 360 and 365. However, none that are securely dated are earlier than 370, and none that are securely dated are later than 381 or 384, depending on the dating of letters to Praetextatus and *Letter* 1.86.[200] Moreover, all the recipients were men active in the 370s and 380s but who were, by 394 at the latest, either known to have died, as is true for Symmachus's father, Praetextatus, Probus, and his brother, Titianus, or no longer active in public life, as was the

198. See, e.g., Symmachus, *Letters* 2.12, 2.48, 2.54, 3.28, 5.85; Cecconi 2002a, 177–79; Roda 1981a, 224–25; and McGeachy 1942, 122–23.

199. This is also the view proposed by Callu 1972, 17–18; Roda 1981a, 69 n. 34 and 79; and Bruggisser 1993, 25–31. Sogno (2006, 61) takes *Letter* 4.34, written in 395 to the Gallic aristocrat Protadius, to indicate that others were urging Symmachus to publish his correspondence as well, but this seems a rather literal reading of a playful jest among two well-educated men. It seems likely that he published book 1 before the 392 usurpation of Eugenius and the defeat of Frigidus, which raised serious political problems for his in-laws.

200. For the dating of *Letter* 1.86 to Hesperius, see 157 n. 1 below. Callu (1972, 18) notes that no letter postdates ca. 385, although some cannot be securely dated. There are no more than a handful of letters that can possibly date after 380: these include *Letters* 1.45, 1.47, 1.48, 1.49, 1.51, 1.53–55, 1.57–59, 1.94, 1.97–100, 1.102, 1.103, and 1.105–107. Roda (1981a, 69) dates the earliest letters to 367 (without reasons), but this is far from certain either. The most we can say is that the earliest letters date from the period after Symmachus's priesthood, which we know was held between 360 and 365, and probably after 365, when he held the office of corrector.

case of Ausonius, Antonius, Syagrius, and Hesperius.[201] Hence the letters fall within a clearly defined time frame, from 360/365 through 381/384. All the other books contain letters going down to the period shortly before Symmachus's death, circa 402. If Symmachus published book 1 soon after he stepped down from the urban prefectureship in 385, sometime in the late 380s or by the early 390s, the letters would not have roused any embarrassing issues for Symmachus or for his correspondents, be they deceased or retired.[202]

Organization and contents. The most compelling evidence that book 1 was published together as a single book is provided by its organization and contents. The letters in book 1 are grouped by correspondent, arguably in order of the person's importance to Symmachus, beginning with letters to Symmachus's father. As the book progresses, we move forward in Symmachus's life and also, for the most part, in time. Moreover, as Callu and Bruggisser have shown, book 1 has an elaborate but coherent set of themes as well as a consistent style.[203]

This high degree of organization, consistency, and thematic development has not been detected in the later books of Symmachus's letters. Books 2–7 are organized by correspondent, like book 1, but the letters in these books are not distributed in so clear a chronological order or by unified themes that develop, integrate, and advance one another.[204] Cristiana Sogno has argued for the beginnings of a pattern of organization for these books, based on periods in Symmachus's political career, but there is much overlap if this is the case in books 2–7. [205] But books 8–9 are far less coherent than even this, for the letters in these last books are not grouped by recipient or by chronology. Book 9 is filled only with letters of recommendation, a practice at odds with all the other books. Moreover, these two books contain several anonymous letters, as well as some letters to correspondents already included in earlier

---

201. Callu 1972, 18. Cameron (2011, 369) suggests that all but Ausonius and Hesperius were dead by 390. We cannot know this for certain; see the introduction to the letters to each of these men for specific details, but none held a high public office after 384.

202. The concern not to embarrass living men may also explain why Symmachus, *Letter* 1.2, includes epigrams praising only men who were no longer living. For 392, see liv n. 199 above.

203. Bruggisser 1993, 25–31; Callu 1972, 17– 18; see also Roda 1981a, 69–79.

204. Roda 1981a, 69.

205. Sogno (2006, 61) contends that this is the case, with book 3 (ca. 370–390), book 4 (ca. 398–402), book 5 (ca. 376–396), and book 7 (379–402), with books 2 and 6 as exceptions, entirely devoted to one recipient, with the former to Nicomachus Flavianus Sr. and the latter to the Nicomachi filii, Symmachus's daughter and her husband, Nicomachus Flavianus the Younger. The amount of overlap suggests an unfinished organizational structure, if at all.

books. So, for example, *Letter* 9.88 lacks a heading, but internal evidence has led scholars to identify it as a very early letter written by Symmachus to the poet Ausonius; all other correspondence to Ausonius was published as *Letters* 1.13–43.[206] Book 10 is too fragmentary to allow for comparison, since only two letters are extant. So in terms of organization and content, book 1 stands apart from the corpus as a whole.

The manuscript evidence. The manuscript evidence lends some support to my argument for a separate publication of book 1. Callu, its most recent editor, noted an unusually high number of variant readings for the book that he attributed to the willingness of recipients to take liberty with this widely promulgated text. This observation, coupled with the nature of the content and the careful organization of book 1, led Callu to posit that Symmachus published this first book of letters separately; he dated the publication of this first book to the period after 384, right after Symmachus stepped down from the office of urban prefect, when he also, in Callu's view, published his *Relationes*, or *State Papers*.[207]

Literary precedents for publishing books of letters. There are strong literary precedents for publishing a book of letters to present oneself to the world. Pliny polished and then published nine books of private letters in regular intervals from 104/5 C.E. on, as he noted in the dedicatory letter to his collection.[208] The tenth book of "public letters" to the emperor Trajan was part of the design of Pliny's published collection.[209] His corpus was probably known to Symmachus, for Pliny's letters were circulating in the fourth century and were read by such figures as Jerome, Ambrose, and Ausonius.[210] A high number of epistolary collections from the fourth- and fifth-century Latin west have survived, and many of these provide evidence that the letters included in them were polished and prepared before being circulated as a book. It is this act that signifies "publishing" in the ancient world, not the modern notion of simultaneously releasing on the market multiple copies of a single work.[211]

206. See my discussion of this letter, 37–41.

207. For the variant versions, see Callu 1972, 18 and n. 1. In this, Callu follows the argument of Seeck (1883, xvi–xxii) for the publication of the *State Papers* at this early date. See also Roda 1981a, 79; Callu 2009b, viii–ix.

208. Pliny, *Letter* 1.1.1 (Radice 1969): "Frequenter hortatus es ut epistulas, si quas paulo curatius scripsissem, colligerem publicaremque" ("You have often encouraged me to collect and publish any letters which I have written with more care than usual"). See Trapp 2003, 14; Sherwin-White 1966, 54–56.

209. For Pliny's ten-book publication and its influence in the fourth century on Ambrose in particular, see Zelzer 1989, 203–8; Liebeschuetz 2005, 31–32; and lvii n. 214.

210. Cameron 1965, 289–98; see also note 209 above for Pliny and Ambrose.

211. Conybeare (2000, 14–16) discusses the ancient notion of "publication" entailing

Jerome, for one, writing in Bethlehem in 393, appends to his work *On Illustrious Men* (135) a list of his published works that includes: "one book of *Letters to Different Persons*" and "one book of *Letters to Marcella*," along with seven free-standing epistolary compositions. The exact dates of these two books of letters are disputed, with the most likely dates falling between Jerome's arrival in Rome in 382 and his writing *On Illustrious Men* in 393.[212] Ambrose also published his letters, probably a bit later, between 395 and 397, in response to the requests of his correspondents.[213] Ambrose, who was in epistolary contact with Symmachus (Symmachus, *Letters* 3.30–37), may well have been inspired by the example of his contemporaries, including Symmachus, who in my view had already circulated his own first book of letters. In structuring his correspondence for publication, likely after 395, Ambrose also conceived of it as a whole but divided into books, arguably in imitation of Pliny's *Letters*.[214] At the end of the fifth century, Sidonius Apollinaris tells us that he carefully revised his letters before publishing them in a single volume, and in this he claimed that he was following the examples of Quintus Symmachus and Pliny.[215]

"merely sending it to another party, under a covering letter bestowing the right—or even the obligation—to publicize its contents." However, I am using the term "publishing" here to indicate not merely this act of promulgation but also the conscious editing that is evidenced by epistolographers such as Pliny, Sidonius Apollinaris (*Letter* 1.1.1), and Augustine (*Letter* 265.1); these letter writers reveal a self-consciousness in promulgating and shaping their finished works, with careful placement and polishing of the individual letters in the book, a degree of thematic organization that is familiar to readers of ancient poetry books.

212. The date of Jerome's *De viris illustribus* (*On Illustrious Men*), written in 393, provides the *terminus post quem*. Vessey (1993, 135–45) makes a convincing case that Jerome sent a collection of his exegetical letters to his patroness Marcella when he was in Rome, 382–385. Cain (2006, 500–525; 2009, 68–98) argues that Jerome's book of *Letters to Diverse People* should also be dated to the period while he was in Rome, 382–385, before he left Rome, i.e., post-385 but before 392/3 C.E.

213. Liebeschuetz (2005, 27–32) argues for this dating based on the evidence of Ambrose, *Letter* 32 (48).

214. For scholars opposed to this view, see Liebeschuetz 2004, 26, 31–32; Savon 1995, 3–17; and Zelzer 1989, 203–8. For the opposing view, see Nauroy 2009, 228–31.

215. Sidonius Apollinaris, *Letter* 1.1: "Diu praecipis, domine maior … ut, si quae mihi litterae paulo politiores varia occasione fluxerint, prout eas causa persona tempus elicuit, omnes retractatis exemplaribus enucleatisque uno volumine includam, Quinti Symmachi rotunditatem, Gai Plinii disciplinam, maturitatemque vestigiis praesumptuosis insecuturus" ("My honoured Lord, you have this long while been pressing me … to collect all the letters making any little claim to taste that have flowed from my pen on different occasions as this or that affair, person, or situation called forth, and to revise and correct the originals and combine all in a single book. In so doing, I should be following, though with

The publication of books of letters from late antiquity attests to a widespread interest in the lives of famous men. Although individual motivations for publishing letter collections varied, concern for self-presentation and a desire to shape and promulgate one's image was shared by all epistolographers. The Greek rhetorician Libanius, for one, probably prepared and published a six-book collection of his letters, not only for self- presentation, but to advertise his teaching and his rhetorical skills, soon after 361.[216] His letters, like those of his Christian contemporaries, were intended to be models. Similarly, Jerome's letters were probably circulated in order to "introduce himself to the Latin-speaking West as the next Origen and thereby to help jump start his fledgling career as a biblical scholar"; his second book of letters also served to announce himself as "the quintessential ascetic."[217] Ambrose, similarly, published his letters in order to present himself as a political and theological figure of great influence toward the end of his life.[218]

A like concern with his public persona and a desire for self-promotion led Symmachus to circulate his own letters as a book, likely after 384 or by the early 390s, and before 392. In doing this, Symmachus was also articulating and spreading the traditional senatorial values and ideals that he and the circle of elites to which he belonged wanted to maintain in a changing world. Hence, I would argue, they also served a propagandistic purpose. Finally, Symmachus no doubt also intended that his letters be viewed as models of epistolary form and etiquette that other letter writers could imitate.

The Publication of the Corpus as a Whole

I have argued that Symmachus himself published this first book of letters. He may well have been preparing the later books for publication, as did many of his contemporaries. Unfortunately, he died before finishing this work, which is why his son Memmius had to publish the remaining books of letters. There is, however, no scholarly consensus on Memmius's edition. Much depends on how much credence one gives to the evidence of the subscriptions to the

---

presumptuous steps, the path traced by Quintus Symmachus with his rounded style and by Gaius Plinius with his highly developed artistry"; Anderson 1936.) Sidonius is imitiating the publication of a single book, not the style of Symmachus, as some scholars have mistakenly argued.

216. Trapp 2003, 17, following the suggestion of Norman 1992, 1:41. Bradbury (2004, 21–22) concedes that Norman may be correct here but suggests that the corpus as a whole was the result of the efforts of a literary executor.

217. Cain 2006, 506; 2009, 33–42.

218. Liebeschuetz 2004, 95–107. For Ambrose, see also lvii n. 214 above.

manuscripts. Two subscriptions, inserted between books 2 and 3 and between books 4 and 5, are preserved in the only Carolingian manuscript of the letters (*Par. Lat.* 8623) and follow the same formula as they record what seems authentic information: "Book 2 of the letters of Quintus Aurelius Symmachus *vir clarissimus* ordinary consul ends, published after his death by his son, Q. Fabius Memmius Symmachus vir clarissimus. Book 3 begins well."[219] Disagreement centers on the evidence provided by a third subscription that preceded book 10 of the letters in a now-lost manuscript that was reprinted in Juretus's 1580 edition; this subscription differs in form from the previous two by specifying the contents of the tenth book as "private letters to the emperors, expressions of opinion in the Senate, and minor works."[220] All that survives of book 10 is a letter to the elder Theodosius (375) and another to the emperor Gratian (376). Since the elder Theodosius was not an emperor, this does not fit the subscript well. Moreover, as Roda observes, the subscription to book 10 not only differs from the two other *explicit*s found in earlier books, but its formulation is strikingly similar to other headings found in this printed edition.[221] So, Roda argues, the subscription to book 10 is not trustworthy and should not be used as evidence that Memmius prepared book 10, or books 8–9, for that matter. And Cameron notes, the same lost manuscript cited by Juretus described book 9 as containing recommendations, a detail that applies to most of the other books as well and hence raises suspicions as to the authenticity of these headings.[222]

Roda's notion of a seven-book publication by Memmius of Symmachus's letters has not, however, been accepted by all scholars. Some, such as Callu, take the position that there was an early first publication of book 1 by Symmachus himself, followed by a second publication by his son Memmius of books 1–10 that was modeled on Pliny's ten books of letters; Pliny's corpus had appeared as nine books of private letters in his lifetime, followed by one book of letters, perhaps published posthumously, written to the emperor

---

219. Roda (1981a, 69) notes that the *explicit*s are located between books 2 and 3 and between books 4 and 5. As printed by Seeck (1883, xxiii n. 42), the *explicit* between books 2 and 3 reads: "Q. Aureli Symmachi v.c. consulis ordinarii epistolarum liber II explicit editus post eius obitum a Q. Fabio Memmio Symmachos v.c. filio, incipit liber III feliciter." The formula is the same for the explicit between books 4 and 5; see Matthews 1974, 66–68.

220. Seeck (1883, 276): "Liber Decimus continens epistulas familiares ad imperatores, sententias senatorias et opuscula: editus post eius mortem a Q. Flavio [*sic*] Memmio Symmacho V. C."

221. Roda (1981a, 71–73 and n. 38) observes that this inscription is also very similar to that found in a series of *florilegia* noted by Callu 1976, 197–217; 1972, 19.

222. Cameron 2011, 367.

Trajan when Pliny was imperial special legate in Bithynia with Pontus in 110.[223] Callu also believes that Symmachus published his first book of letters at the same time as he published his *State Papers*, right after stepping down from the urban prefectureship in 384. In this, he agrees with the first modern editor of the Symmachan corpus, Otto Seeck;[224] however, Callu does not accept Seeck's idea that Memmius republished these *State Papers* in order to imitate Pliny's ten-book model. Rather, because Callu accepts as authentic the subscription to Symmachus's book 10, he considers that there was but one publication by Memmius, concluding with book 10, but that book 10, now fragmentary, had contained a diverse selection of letters, senatorial opinions, and other lesser works, such as his orations. So, Callu concludes, the *State Papers* were never part of a ten-book Symmachan corpus that imitated Pliny's example.

A third view of Symmachus's corpus has been advanced by John Matthews. He proposes one single edition of Symmachus's letters, prepared by Memmius but following the model of Pliny and hence including his *State Papers* as book 10 of the letters after his father died.[225] Matthews, like Callu and Seeck, accepts the authenticity of the subscription to book 10 but not the language of the subscription and instead would substitute the *State Papers* as book 10 of Symmachus's published works.

In my view, the publication schema advanced by Roda is best able to account for the evidence provided by the letters themselves. Roda's doubts about the authenticity of the subscription to book 10 are compelling, and there are substantial arguments in favor of seeing books 8–10 as a later addition. As already noted, these last three books are very different in organization and content from the first seven. The letters in books 2–7, as in book 1, are grouped by recipient; this is not the case for the last three books. Books 8 and 9 are randomly arranged, and book 9 contains only letters of recommendation.[226] Moreover, as Callu notes, it appears significant that fourteen of the manuscripts of Symmachus's letters do not contain the last three books of letters.[227] Sogno has argued that "the existence of a tradition of *florilegia* compiled from the first seven books provides indirect support for this theory," that is, of an ancient edition of books 1–7 by Memmius.[228] This publication should not, however, be taken to mean that Memmius arranged these first seven books. As Callu and Cameron have argued, Symmachus himself may

223. Callu 1972, 18–19; on Pliny's correspondence, see Trapp 2003, 14–15.
224. Callu 1972, 18–19; Seeck 1883, xxii–xxxix; and Callu 2009b, x–xi.
225. Matthews 1974, 66–68.
226. Roda 1981a, 71–74.
227. Callu 1972, 18 n. 3.
228. Sogno 2006, 61.

well have selected and prepared the first seven books of letters, intending to publish them, but died before that happened; the fact that Sidonius Apollinaris originally prepared an edition of seven books of letters, inspired by the examples of Symmachus and Pliny, lends further indirect support for an ancient edition of seven books published by Memmius.[229]

This scenario leaves open the question of who added books 8–10 to Memmius's seven-book edition. Because Seeck accepted the subscription to book 10 as authentic, he proposed that Memmius simply lost interest in this project and threw the last three books of letters together in a haphazard fashion.[230] This is not compelling. But since a number of manuscripts with ten books of letters survive, it seems likely that these last three books were added at an early point in the manuscript tradition; Roda proposed that the last three books were compiled from the family archives in the late fifth century or early sixth century, in response to Symmachus's growing reputation as an epistolographer.[231]

To sum up, the evidence suggests the likelihood that Symmachus himself published book 1 after leaving the office of urban prefect in 384 but no later than the early 390s, before 392. After the initial success of his first book of letters, he then began preparing books 2–7 for publication, organizing and arranging these by recipient. He did not live to complete the task, and that is why, after his father's death (ca. 402), his son Quintus Fabius Memmius Symmachus had to publish the letters. Hence Memmius's edition of the letters—probably of books 1–7—explains why his name, Quintus Fabius Memmius Symmachus, appears in subscriptions in reliable manuscripts between books 2 and 3 and between books 4 and 5 as having published (*editus*) the *Letters*. This publication appeared, in all likelihood, after 402 and before August 408; the execution of Stilicho in August 408 provides a *terminus ante quem*, since his fall would have probably prompted the removal of Symmachus's letters to Stilicho from book 4.[232] Books 8–10, however, were a late fifth- or early sixth-century addition, on the heels of a renewed interest in Symmachus and his correspondence; among the most likely possibilities is the late fifth-century

229. Callu 1972, 18; Cameron 2011, 366–73; for Sidonius's imitation of Symmachus and Pliny in publishing his first edition of seven books of letters, see lvii n. 215 above; for his decision to add two more books of letters, see Sidonius Apollinaris, *Letter* 8.1.

230. Seeck 1883, 70, 124, 276.

231. Roda 1981a, 69–79; see also Cameron 2011, 253–98.

232. Cameron 2011, 368; Seeck 1883, xxii–xxiii. Seeck argued that the letters to the usurper Priscus, which are still in the collection, would have been removed after Priscus's proclamation as emperor in 409, hence providing a *terminus ante quem* for books 1–7.

consul and father-in-law of Boethius, Quintus Aurelius Memmius Symmachus.[233]

Were Pliny's Letters a Model for Symmachus?

This seven-book reconstruction of the letters of Symmachus provides little evidence for the idea, advanced by several scholars, that Symmachus or Memmius intended to imitate the ten-book organization of the *Letters* of Pliny the Younger; as noted above, Pliny's *Letters* were arranged into nine books of private letters to friends, followed by one book of letters to the emperor Trajan, written when Pliny held office. Yet this Plinian organizational model has convinced many scholars to accept the view of the first modern editor of Symmachus's letters, Seeck, who proposed that Memmius added his father's already published *State Papers* to what we now have as book 10.[234] Seeck's reconstruction led scholars to seek further Plinian influences on Symmachus's letters, in part because of this presumed imitation of Pliny's organization.[235]

Seeck's reconstruction and identification of the *State Papers* with book 10 of Symmachus's letters are not likely for several reasons. First, if one accepts the evidence of the subscription to book 10, then the letters to the emperor in that book should have been private ones (*familiares*), not official state papers. Second, although the third and eleventh *State Papers* are extant in some manuscripts of the letters, as Seeck observed in support of his position, this is not the norm; most of the manuscripts of the letters do not include these *State Papers*, and there are two very different manuscript traditions for the *Letters* and the *State Papers*.[236] More recently, Domenico Vera has argued that the *State Papers* were not published by Symmachus or his son; rather, Vera contends that the errors in the headings of the *State Papers* that indicate the imperial addressees show that these documents were Symmachus's private copies that he never intended for publication and hence never corrected. Vera proposes that the *State Papers* were taken from the family archives and published only after a renewal of interest in Symmachus as an epistolographer.[237] Sogno has lent further support to Vera's technical arguments by observing that, since

233. Roda 1981a, 69–79, especially 76–77 for the suggestion that this was the work of Quintus Aurelius Memmius Symmachus.

234. Seeck 1883, xvii and xxii–xxvi.

235. Matthews 1974, 58–99, esp. 66–68; Cameron 1965, 289–98; see Callu's discussion in 1972, 20–22.

236. On the addition of *State Papers* 3 and 11 to the *florilegia* of Symmachus's letters, see Callu 1972, 21.

237. Vera 1981, lxxxix–xcv; 1977, 1003–36.

"his term as urban prefect had been difficult and ended bitterly," he would not have wanted to publish his state papers and hence call attention to his difficult year in office.[238] It is of interest, though not decisive, that the *State Papers* have a different manuscript tradition, and the suspect subscription to the later books provides no good reason to suggest that book 10 ever contained the *State Papers*, for it mentions only "personal letters to the emperors, expressions of opinion in the senate, and minor works." Far more relevant, in my view, is the fact that the *State Papers*, like books 8–10 of the *Letters*, lack any pattern of organization that they presumably would have had if they had been intended for publication.

But there still remains the possibility that book 10, now fragmentary, was modeled on Pliny's book 10. Sogno has called attention to the fact that Pliny's book begins with several personal letters to Trajan, before launching into letters dealing with more official business.[239] The two letters that open Symmachus's tenth book may arguably be construed in the same light, as more personal missives. However, the first letter (*Letter* 10.1) is not written to the emperor but rather to Theodosius (375), father of the emperor of the same name. Symmachus's second letter (10.2), written to the emperor Gratian (376), presents a closer parallel. But it is important to note that, even if book 10 did imitate Pliny's correspondence by including letters to the imperial family, we are still not sure who was responsible for this imitation. The organizational similarities might be the work of Symmachus's son Memmius, or of a later editor, if, as seems most likely, books 8–10 were added from the family archives in the late fifth or early sixth century. Indeed, since we know that Pliny's letters were being circulated and read in the late fifth and early sixth centuries, this last scenario appears more than likely.[240]

But if Pliny's *Letters* did not provide Symmachus with the inspiration for a ten-book epistolary collection, they could, nonetheless, have inspired him in other regards. Scholars have found echoes of Pliny's epistolary vocabulary in Symmachus's letters, though direct quotes are absent.[241] In addition, Pliny set an important generic precedent when he published his letters in books that were carefully edited to present himself to "the world." [242]

238. Sogno 2006, 34.

239. Sogno 2006, 60.

240. Cameron 1965, 289–98.

241. For example, Bruggisser (1993, 95 n. 32) observes the rare repetition of the verb *exarare* for composition. Used by Pliny only once, of his poems, it is also the word that Avianius uses of his poetic compositions; see Pliny, *Letter* 7.4.5.

242. Trapp 2003, 14; Pliny, *Letter* 1.1.1; see xxi n. 50 above.

A Seven-Book Model

If my reconstruction is correct, the question remains as to why Symmachus intended and Memmius published seven books of letters. That this was the intention is supported by the neat parallelism, observed by Sogno, between books 1 and 7: the opening letters of Symmachus to his father in book 1 (1.1–12) are echoed in book 7 with those to his son Memmius (7.1–14).[243] The parallels indicate care, but to what end? Why seven books?

Symmachus's letters may provide the answer. As the second item in book 1, Symmachus published a letter sent by his father Avianius in response to his first letter, *Letter* 1.1. His father's letter is in a prominent position and contains material that is of thematic import for the book as a whole. As Pierre Bruggisser observes, this second letter establishes Avianius as a "new Varro," for it includes epigrams that he had composed in imitation of those in Varro's *Hebdomades*, or the *Imagines*, as it is also called. This famous work, arguably the first illustrated Latin book, contained seven hundred portraits of celebrated Greeks and Romans, mostly drawn from sculpture, and was accompanied by epigrams and discussions of the evidence for the portraits.[244] On the basis of this publication, Pliny the Elder praised Varro as the "father of the epigram" and honored him for conferring immortality on his subjects.[245] Varro's literary output and learning made him a legendary literary force; as the "father of erudition," he was a figure for all Romans—pagans and Christians—to contend with.[246]

Unfortunately, the *Hebdomades* do not survive, and we have only fragmentary information about its organization and structure. Aulus Gellius reports that when Varro was in his twelfth *hebdomad* (i.e., over seventy-seven years old) he had composed some "seventy *hebdomades* of books," that is, seventy groups of seven, or 490 books, but many of these were lost when he was proscribed and forced to flee in the civil war.[247] The title *Hebdomades* certainly alludes to groups of seven and indicates, along with Gellius's testimony, that the number seven had special importance in this work. To give one

243. Sogno 2006, 62.

244. Bruggisser (1993, 9) calls Avianius a "nouveau Varron."

245. Pliny, *Natural History* 35.11.

246. Varro's import in the fourth century is well-attested; see Augustine, *De civitate Dei* 6.2; and especially Jerome, *De viris illustribus*, preface and 54, where Jerome notes that he has written a letter against Varro to Paula (*Letter* 33), only parts of which survive. He contrasts a catalog of Varro's works with those of Origen to prove the latter's superiority; see Schanz and Hosius 1909, 431–34. See also Bruggisser 1993, 97 n. 44.

247. Gellius, *Noctes Atticae* (*The Attic Nights*) 3.10.17.

example, we learn from Aulus Gellius that Varro praised the number seven as it appears in human development: "The teeth appear in the first seven months, seven at a time in each jaw, and fall out in seven years, and the back teeth are added, as a rule, in twice seven years."[248] Indeed, the importance of seven, which derives in part from Pythagorean ideas, has been found throughout Varro's writings.[249] Based on manuscript evidence and testimony by Jerome, scholars reconstruct that after the civil wars there was a shortened edition of Varro's *Hebdomades*, now lost, that was circulated as a work in fifteen books; most posit that there were two groups of seven books (*hebdomades*), perhaps one group for Romans and a second for Greeks, plus an introductory book.[250] Although Ausonius refers to book 10 of Varro's work (*Mosella* 307), epitomes were in circulation with fewer books; it may be that Avianius and Symmachus consulted a seven-book epitome. But even if we cannot be certain of the number of books of the *Hebdomades* that Symmachus saw, the importance of the number seven as an organizing principle in the work and in Varro's thinking is obvious.

As Avianius asserts (*Letter* 1.2), Varro's *Hebdomades* inspired him to compose his own epigrams, what Bruggisser has cleverly called his "*New Hebdomades*." Avianius's epigrams praise five former prefects of Rome under Constantine. Avianius's motivation, like that of Varro's, was to commemorate famous men as he also inculcated the lessons of their lives in his son and readers. The letter casts Avianius as a new Varro, the "Parent of Roman learning."[251] But the similarities do not end there. Like Varro, Avianius had been forced into exile; like Varro, Avianius had lost his property; and like Varro, Avianius would also, eventually, regain both his property and his reputation.[252] Finally, in what may be a subtle compliment to himself, like Varro, Avianius received letters from important people, including his own son.[253] Given the similarities and the very real veneration in which Varro was held by fourth-century elites, it seems likely that the reputation and significance of the number seven in Varro's *Hebdomades* inspired Symmachus to prepare and his son Memmius

248. Gellius, *Noctes Atticae* 3.10; Osgood (2006, 210 n. 34) observes that this particular idea is also found in Solon, frag. 17.1–4 (West 1971–1972).

249. Conte 1994, 214.

250. Schanz and Hosius cite the manuscripts for the existence of Varro's *Imagines* in fifteen books (1909, 423–24) and note its contents (431–34). See also Conte 1994, 214.

251. See Bruggisser 1993, 94–101, esp. n. 44, for the tradition that praises Varro's erudition.

252. For a good discussion of Varro's tribulations, see Osgood 2006, 209–10, 293–94.

253. Cicero, *Epistulae ad Familiares* (*Letters to Friends*) 9.1–9.8, although these are dated to Varro's first exile from Rome and in anticipation of Caesar's return ca. 47/46 B.C.E.; see Leach 1999, 139–79.

to publish seven books of letters. In this Symmachus could count on wide recognition of the symbolic value of seven and of Varro's work. But it is worth noting that this association may also have been very personal. A house in Rome on the Caelian Hill, identified as belonging to the Symmachi, had an apsidal room with seven niches for statues that was renovated at some point in the fourth century, to allow for more luxurious marble display.[254]

Survival

The circumstances of publication of Symmachus's letters have important implications for understanding both how and why his letters survived across the centuries. During his lifetime Symmachus wrote his letters for pragmatic ends: to maintain and augment his circle of friends though greetings; to extend his patronage through the writing of letters of recommendation; and to request favors. Yet the literary reputation of the letter writer, along with the status of the recipients, made his letters so valued that he feared that they would be delayed or kept by unreliable letter carriers. Certainly the people with whom Symmachus corresponded were among the leading figures of his day, and his private correspondence to them was of general interest.[255] Book 1 in particular can be read not only as a life of Symmachus but as a series of personalized depictions of some of the key figures of his age, now safely dead or retired. In addition, even in his lifetime, and certainly in the centuries after his death, the letters were preserved for their literary qualities and as models for epistolographers to imitate. Macrobius, writing in the 430s, attests to Symmachus's fame as a Latin stylist, although the quality he praises in Symmachus, his "luxuriousness" (*luxuriatur*), is arguably more easily observed in his *Orations* than his *Letters*.[256] Sidonius Apollinaris in the late fifth century asserts that Symmachus's style was what he admired in Symmachus's letters; in the dedicatory letter written to his own published book of letters, Sidonius notes that he is following the path traced by Symmachus, whose famed "rounded style" and whose self-publication of letters had inspired him to do the same.[257]

Certainly, the publication of Symmachus's letters after he died added to the reputation of his family; hence Memmius's willingness to edit the letters

254. Stirling 2005, 166–67 and n. 17. See *Letter* 1.12.

255. For the interest in reading and preserving Symmachus's letters, see Peter 1965, 142–43. For letter carriers, see note 198. For the reception of letters, see Mullett 1997, 31–37, with remarks pertaining to fourth- and fifth-century practice; and Cugisi 1983; see also Sogno 2006, 34 n. 17.

256. Macrobius, *Saturnalia* 5.1.7. Cameron 1965, 295 and n. 4.

257. Sidonius Apollinaris, *Letter* 1.1.1, on lvii–lviii n. 215 above.

is easily understandable as a means of augmenting Symmachus's reputation as an orator and thereby the prominence of his family. Symmachus's *Letters* continued to be read in elite circles through the end of the sixth century.[258] The growing reputation of Symmachus as a Latin stylist underlies the notion of posthumous publications of his letters (books 8–10) in the fifth and sixth centuries.[259]

As Callu and Polara have observed, after the sixth century, explicit reference to Symmachus's letters does not emerge again until the eleventh century with Hildebert of Lavardin (born 1056) and Yves de Chartres (died 1116).[260] The twelfth century saw a revival of interest in his letters, fueled by the resurgence of interest in the art of literary letter writing, *ars dictaminis*, and the widespread production of epistolary handbooks. One particularly telling sign of Symmachus's popularity in this century is the number of *florilegia*, or collections of selected letters, that circulated. By Callu's estimate, some 357 of the 902 letters, or 39.5 percent, survive in *florilegia* that date from the twelfth to the fourteenth centuries.[261]

But Symmachus's letters also survived as entire books and were recopied as such, even if we do not have direct references to the letters of Symmachus between the sixth and eleventh centuries. Books of his letters continued to be copied; the best extant manuscript of Symmachus's letters (*Parisinus* 8623) is dated to the ninth century and the "best of the worst" (*Vaticanus* 1576) to the eleventh century.[262]

It is easy to understand why Symmachus's letters would be valued, especially in the twelfth century: Symmachus's stylish, elegant correspondence, with its lack of specific detail, easily served as an exemplar for would-be epistolographers. For example, Symmachus's book 9, which is made up almost entirely of letters of recommendations, is a virtual textbook of how to write such a letter. For Alain de Lille (writing ca. 1181–1184), Symmachus was as gifted a writer as the very best Latinists: Cicero, Quintilian, or Sidonius.[263]

---

258. See Callu 1972, 35–39, and the survey by Polara 1972, 250–63. For the late fifth–early sixth century, we can see his influence in the works of Ennodius, *Opera* (Vogel 1885, 332); in Cassiodorus, the *Tripartite History* (*Historia tripartita*) 9.3 (Jacob and Hanslik 1954), which is the source for the twelfth-century manuscript notes discussed now by Chronopoulos 2010, 232–91. Symmachus's *Letters* are cited in the early sixth century by his relative Q. Aurelius Memmius Symmachus iunior 9 in *PLRE* 2:1044–45; see Callu 2005, 184. Another early sixth-century citation is in Caesarius of Arles, *Sermon 1* (Délage 1971, 95).

259. See lxi n. 231 and lxii n. 233 above.

260. See n. 258 above.

261. Callu 1972, 39–40.

262. Callu 1972, 29–35.

263. Alain de Lille, *Anticlaudianus* 3.235–238: "Symmachus in verbis parcus sed

Further, the confusion of identity of this Symmachus with the father-in-law of Boethius found in twelfth-century authors and continuing through the fourteenth century added extra prestige to his name and letters.[264]

The first printed edition of Symmachus's letters appeared in Venice in 1503; with the sixteenth century, there was a revival of interest in the man and his letters.[265] His fortunes then waned, arousing only modest degrees of enthusiasm until the present day. This volume is aimed at opening up his world and his letters to a new generation of twenty-first-century students and scholars who are willing to learn the rules of epistolary etiquette in late antiquity and hence can come to appreciate Symmachus and his letters as I, grudgingly, have.

mente profundus, / Prodigus in sensu, verbis angustus, abundans / Mente" ("Symmachus is sparing in his words but boundless in his thought, generous in his emotions, restricted with his words, overflowing with his thoughts").

264. See now Sogno 2005, 412–13, citing the twelfth-century Aegidius Benevantanus and Vincentius Bellovacensis as authors who confused these two Symmachi. This confusion continued into the fourteenth century in the writings of Vincent de Beauvais; see Polara 1972, 256–57.

265. The *editio princeps* was by Bartholomaeus Cynischus; see Callu 1972, 29–35.

Proposed Dating of Letters in Book 1

* None of the letters in book 1 can be dated earlier than Symmachus's priesthood, 360/365. None can be securely dated after 381/384. See pages liv–lv.

Letter	Correspondent	M. R. Salzman	J. P. Callu 1972
1	Symmachus to his father, Avianius	375	375
2	Symmachus's father, Avianius, to Symmachus	375	375
3	Symmachus to his father, Avianius	375	375
4	Symmachus to his father, Avianius	375	375
5	Symmachus to his father, Avianius	375	375
6	Symmachus to his father, Avianius	before 375/376	370
7	Symmachus to his father, Avianius	375	375
8	Symmachus to his father, Avianius	370/371–375	375
9	Symmachus to his father, Avianius	375	375
10	Symmachus to his father, Avianius	375	375
11	Symmachus to his father, Avianius	375	375
12	Symmachus to his father, Avianius	before 377	before 377
9.88	anepigraphic, but Symmachus probably to Ausonius	probably 366–367	before 369
13	Symmachus to Ausonius	376	376
14	Symmachus to Ausonius	after 370/371	after 370
15	Symmachus to Ausonius	before 379	before 379

16	Symmachus to Ausonius	376–380	after 376
17	Symmachus to Ausonius	probably 377–379	378–379
18	Symmachus to Ausonius	377–379	376–379
19	Symmachus to Ausonius	378	378
20	Symmachus to Ausonius	378	378
21	Symmachus to Ausonius	378–379	379
22	Symmachus to Ausonius	378	378
23	Symmachus to Ausonius	before 377	before 377
24	Symmachus to Ausonius	370–379	after 370
25	Symmachus to Ausonius	soon after January 379	379
26	Symmachus to Ausonius	377–379	376–379
27	Symmachus to Ausonius	probably 378	379–380
28	Symmachus to Ausonius	375–379	376–379
29	Symmachus to Ausonius	370–379	before 380
30	Symmachus to Ausonius	370–379	before 380
31	Symmachus to Ausonius	370–379	379–380
32	Symmachus to Ausonius	370–379	379–380
33	Symmachus to Ausonius	375–379	before 380
34	Symmachus to Ausonius	375–379	before 380
35	Symmachus to Ausonius	375–379	after 370
36	Symmachus to Ausonius	375–379	around 379
37	Symmachus to Ausonius	375–379	around 373–376
38	Symmachus to Ausonius	375–379	around 373–376
39	Symmachus to Ausonius	375–379	379
40	Symmachus to Ausonius	376–377	376–377
41	Symmachus to Ausonius	after 370	after 370
42	Symmachus to Ausonius	377–379	379
43	Symmachus to Ausonius	370–379	370–379
44	Symmachus to Praetextatus	376	376
45	Symmachus to Praetextatus	before fall 384	before 385
46	Symmachus to Praetextatus	360/365–380	before 381
47	Symmachus to Praetextatus	360/365–before fall 384	around 383
48	Symmachus to Praetextatus	before fall 384	before 385

49	Symmachus to Praetextatus	360/365–before fall 384	around 378
50	Symmachus to Praetextatus	before 377	before 377
51	Symmachus to Praetextatus	360/365–before fall 384	383
52	Symmachus to Praetextatus	376	376
53	Symmachus to Praetextatus	before fall 384	before 384
54	Symmachus to Praetextatus	380–381	380
55	Symmachus to Praetextatus	probably 384	384
56	Symmachus to Probus	after 364	after 370
57	Symmachus to Probus	364–375/384	around 383
58	Symmachus to Probus	364–384	around 383
59	Symmachus to Probus	364–373 or 374–376	370–375/383–384
60	Symmachus to Probus	after 364	before 375
61	Symmachus to Probus	364–366; 368–375; 383–384	before 375
62	Symmachus to his brother, Celsinus Titianus	before 380	before 377
63	Symmachus to his brother, Celsinus Titianus	before 374–378	374
64	Symmachus to his brother, Celsinus Titianus	380	380
65	Symmachus to his brother, Celsinus Titianus	380	380
66	Symmachus to his brother, Celsinus Titianus	380	380
67	Symmachus to his brother, Celsinus Titianus	before 381	380
68	Symmachus to his brother, Celsinus Titianus	380	380
69	Symmachus to his brother, Celsinus Titianus	380	380
70	Symmachus to his brother, Celsinus Titianus	380	380
71	Symmachus to his brother, Celsinus Titianus	380	380
72	Symmachus to his brother, Celsinus Titianus	380	380

73	Symmachus to his brother, Celsinus Titianus	probably 380	380
74	Symmachus to his brother, Celsinus Titianus	380	before 381
75	Symmachus to Hesperius	376–before 381	before 381
76	Symmachus to Hesperius	376–before 381	before 381
77	Symmachus to Hesperius	376–before 381	before 381
78	Symmachus to Hesperius	376	376
79	Symmachus to Hesperius	378–before 381	378–380
80	Symmachus to Hesperius	376–before 381	before 381
81	Symmachus to Hesperius	376–before 381	before 381
82	Symmachus to Hesperius	376–before 381	before 381
83	Symmachus to Hesperius	after late 380	380
84	Symmachus to Hesperius	376–before 381	before 381
85	Symmachus to Hesperius	after 376	around 378
86	Symmachus to Hesperius	378–before 381	378–380
87	Symmachus to Hesperius	376–before 381	before 381
88	Symmachus to Hesperius	376–before 381	before 381
89	Symmachus to Antonius	370–373 or late spring–fall 374	370–373
90	Symmachus to Antonius	after 370	after 370
91	Symmachus to Antonius	after 370	after 370
92	Symmachus to Antonius	before 378	before 378
93	Symmachus to Antonius	after 370	after 370
94	Symmachus to Syagrius	after 379 and before 382	before 382
95	Symmachus to Syagrius	379 or soon after	379
96	Symmachus to Syagrius	376	376
97	Symmachus to Syagrius	before 382	before 382
98	Symmachus to Syagrius	before 382	before 382
99	Symmachus to Syagrius	before 382	before 382
100	Symmachus to Syagrius	380	380–382
101	Symmachus to Syagrius	380	380
102	Symmachus to Syagrius	380–382	380–382
103	Symmachus to Syagrius	381	381
104	Symmachus to Syagrius	379	379
105	Symmachus to Syagrius	after 376	376
106	Symmachus to Syagrius	before 382	before 382
107	Symmachus to Syagrius	before 382	before 382

Book 1, *Letters* 1–12: Symmachus to His Father

Q. Aurelius Symmachus opens his first book of letters with a series of elegant, highly stylized letters written as if in the middle of an ongoing correspondence with his father, L. Aurelius Avianius Symmachus. In the first letter, the younger Symmachus expresses not only his sense of obligation, traditional *pietas*, toward his father but his desire for paternal approval as he relates his most recent activities. To impress his father and other readers with the eminence of his family, Symmachus tells of his setting in order a series of painted portraits at his estate at Bauli on the Campanian coast, property that belonged to his wife's family.[1] These portraits inspired Symmachus to turn to writing verses, which, with professed diffidence, he shared with his father; Symmachus sought his father's advice on emending his poems, as well as encouragement for his literary endeavors. Symmachus wanted to call attention to his literary attainments as a means of establishing his reputation in this traditional area of a Roman senator's identity.[2] Symmachus's opening letter includes none of the pragmatic concerns of estate management for which he will, in his following letters, also seek paternal approval.

Symmachus's desire for his father's respect is all the more understandable given the elder Symmachus's distinguished public career. His father had held the office of prefect of the grain supply under Constans between 340 and 350, had served on numerous imperial embassies, and had held the prestigious office of urban prefect of Rome in 364–365. The elder Symmachus had been designated for the honor of consul in 377 but died before entering office.[3] After his demise, the Senate voted to erect a gilded statue in his honor in Rome in the Forum of Trajan, and a similar one was put up in

1. See *Letter* 1.1.2 and 9–10 nn. 11–12. It is interesting that Symmachus's son Quintus Aurelius Memmius Symmachus would later act similarly in creating an ancestral gallery in his house on the Caelian Hill by erecting statues for his father and the grandfather of his wife; *CIL* 6:1699; 6:1782 = *ILS* 2947. See also Hillner 2003, 139. For evidence in Rome of efforts by Romans to create ancestral galleries in their homes, see Niquet 2000, 26–31.

2. See also Lizzi Testa 2002, 187–99.

3. Symmachus, *Oration* 4.1 (*Pro patre*); and Seeck 1883, xliii–xliv.

Constantinople.[4] His stature is indicated also by the fact that the emperor praised Avianius's accomplishments in a letter (no longer extant) that was once carved and attached to these statues.[5]

However, the opening letter to the book, written with great literary flair and set in 375,[6] the year before his father's death and just after the younger Symmachus had returned from his year as proconsul in Africa, makes no mention of his father's public honors. Rather, the younger Symmachus emphasizes his father's literary skills as well as his own wife's family's honors. This may have been a politic thing to do given the date of composition of their correspondence; as the book opens, the elder Symmachus was still in voluntary exile from Rome. He had been forced to flee the city, sometime between late summer/fall 374 and winter/spring of 375, because of a rumor to the effect that he would rather use his wine to extinguish lime kilns than sell it at a reduced rate.[7] In response, an enraged mob burned down a house of the elder Symmachus's in the Transtibertine district in Rome.[8] The intent of this remark has been much discussed; Rougé suggests that throwing wine into lime kilns was a procedure utilized in the production of a material (*maltha*) that Romans employed in construction to repave floors and walls.[9] Hence, the elder Symmachus's remarks may not have been as arrogant as they were taken to be. In

---

4. For more on the elder Symmachus's career, see also Symmachus 4, *PLRE* 1:863–65.

5. Weisweiler forthcoming.

6. Seeck (1883, lxxiv) dated the correspondence between Symmachus and his father to autumn 375. However, ten of the letters (*Letters* 1.1–4, 1.5, 1.7–11) indicate seasonal changes that Lizzi Testa (2004, 375–79) rightly observes demonstrate a longer period of time for the exchange of letters, i.e., between the end of June to the middle of October 375. The *terminus post quem* for the father-son correspondence is the reference in *Letter* 1.3.4 to an earthquake that destroyed Beneventum; this was identified by Seeck as the one mentioned by Zosimus, *New History* 4.18, in Pannonia before the demise of Valentinian I, i.e., before November 375. Ammianus Marcellinus, *Res Gestae* 30.5.16, lists portents before his death as well. In any case, it is unlikely that the Pannonia quake is the same as that in Beneventum. Although we cannot use this earthquake to date *Letter* 1.3, we can suggest a date based on its affinities to *Letters* 1.1–2, and 1.4.

7. Seeck (1883, lxxiv) fixed the elder Symmachus's flight from Rome to the autumn of 375 and dated the letters between the two to this same period because of an allusion to this in *Letter* 1.2.2. I would date the mob reaction earlier, probably occurring between the time Symmachus left his proconsulship in Africa in the late spring or summer of 374 and no later than the spring/fall of 375, when the exchange of *Letters* 1.1–12 is set. In this, I agree with the chronology proposed by Lizzi Testa 2004, 375–79.

8. Ammianus Marcellinus, *Res Gestae* 27.3.4.

9. Rougé 1961, 59–77, cites the evidence of Pliny, *Naturalis historia* (*Natural History*) 36.181; Palladius, *De re rustica* (*On Agriculture*) 1.17.2 (Martin 1976, 22). For more on this incident, see also Roda 1981a, 257.

fact, mob violence directed at the homes of powerful men was a political act recorded for fourth-century Rome on several occasions.[10] Indeed, such violence against the homes of wealthy aristocrats is another indicator of the close identification of property with elite status.

In time, the tide of public opinion did turn; the elder Symmachus was recalled to Rome by the Senate and subsequently honored, no later than January 376.[11] But his return had not yet happened as *Letter* 1.1 opens the book. Consequently, as the elder Symmachus's reply indicates (*Letter* 1.2.2), the father had plenty of time on his hands to pursue literary projects, since he was still in retirement. Indeed, ten of the twelve letters between father and son can be dated to these months of voluntary exile; based on references to weather and to harvesting, *Letters* 1.1–4, 1.5, and 1.7–11 probably fall in the period between the end of June and the middle of October 375, although the letters themselves do not adhere to a strict chronological sequence.[12] *Letters* 1.6 and 1.12 lack indications of chronology and could have been written during his exile or at any time before the death of the elder Symmachus in 376.

While *Letters* 1.1–12 indicate that the older Symmachus was out of favor and out of public office, the younger Symmachus was in the midst of a rising career. As noted in the introduction, Symmachus had been governor of Lucania-Bruttium in 365, probably at the age of twenty-five; he had been proconsul of Africa beginning in winter/spring 373 until spring/summer 374, probably at age thirty-three. In this year he returned to Rome to wed Rusticiana, daughter of the noble and well-connected Memmius Vitrasius Orfitus, whose villa is the setting for *Letter* 1.1.[13] At a date later than this set of letters to his father, Symmachus would attain the pinnacle of a senatorial career, namely, the office of urban prefect of Rome in 384, probably at age forty-four, and he would later hold the consulship in 391, probably now age fifty-one.[14] These great honors lie ahead, as this book of letters opens.

---

10. See especially Ammianus Marcellinus, *Res Gestae* 27.3.4 and 8; for the phenomenon more broadly, see now Machado 2006.

11. The first notice of the elder Symmachus's return to Rome is *Oration* 5, a speech of thanks given by his son in the Senate on 9 January 376; see also Symmachus, *Letters* 1.44 and 2.38. For the chronology, see Seeck 1883, xlii and lxxiv.

12. Lizzi Testa 2004, 375–79.

13. Seeck (1883, xlvii–xlviii, lxxiii) thinks Symmachus remained in Africa as a private citizen for several months after he left office and returned to Rome to wed in the summer of 375, but I am convinced that the references to seasons and the narrowness of the time frame favors a wedding date in 374, as proposed by Lizzi Testa 2004, 375–79. For more on this, see xxviii n. 79.

14. These dates are predicated on his birth in 340, which is not certain; see xxiii n. 57.

This career, interrupted by long periods out of office, was typical for the late Roman senatorial aristocracy, yet it would be wrong to suppose that these periods between holding office were spent in idleness. As these twelve letters to his father demonstrate, members of the late Roman senatorial aristocracy had to attend to their private affairs. True, most of Symmachus's estates were managed by a hierarchy of estate managers and lessees who sent their rents and revenues to Rome every year.[15] However, this did not mean that it was not advantageous and at times critical for Symmachus or a member of his family to visit their properties and oversee the activities on their estates. Both father and son regularly traveled between their properties in central Italy and Campania through the summer months. In book 1 we can trace their visits to ancient Formiae, Cumae, Puteoli, Baiae, Bauli, Naples, and Capua.[16] Despite Symmachus's professed dislike of travel especially to estates overseas or further afield in Italy (i.e., Apulia and Sicily), his trips to oversee his properties in central Italy offered opportunities for socializing and leisurely activities.[17]

The twelve opening letters of book 1 emphasize Symmachus's literary talents along with his active involvement in his family's patrimony. *Letters* 1.1, 1.6, 1.10, and 1.12 highlight Symmachus's attention to villas and property as a means not only of broadcasting his status but of "describing himself."[18] With his letters and poetry, Symmachus extended these self-descriptions into written form, as did other senatorial elites from Ausonius to Sidonius Apollinaris. The revival of villa *ekphrases*, out of vogue since the time of Pliny, permitted learned late Roman elites new opportunities for self-representation in the construction of their friendship and patronage networks.[19]

That so many of his letters are devoted to estate matters should not, however, be construed to mean that Symmachus's relationship with his father lacked affection; *Letters* 1.7–8 express Symmachus's longing for his father's presence, and 1.1 similarly emphasizes his love and respect for his father.[20] The later letters in book 1 fill out this image of the "dutiful son" by emphasizing Symmachus's engagement in public affairs in the 370s and early 380s; these later letters depict Symmachus, though not officially holding office,

15. On the managerial hierarchy on his estates, see Vera 1986, 231–76.

16. For more on their movements, see Seeck 1883, l–li; Lizzi Testa 2004, 376–77.

17. For this attitude, see Salzman 2004, 81–94. For Symmachus's landholdings, see Seeck 1883, xlv–xlvi; Vera 1986, 231–76.

18. Bowes 2008, 128–29.

19. Bowes 2008, 129 and n. 17 for bibliography.

20. For mutual affection joined to considerations of patrimony, see Salzman 2006a, 357–75; Vera 1986, 231–76.

still engaged in public affairs and debates, on embassies and as a member of the college of priests of the state cult, and remaining influential through the patronage that he exercised in support of friends and clients.

Letter 1.1: Symmachus to His Father
Date: 375[1]

The setting for this first letter is of central importance to Symmachus's self-representation; Symmachus writes about his time spent at a villa at Bauli on the Campanian coast that belonged to famous owners and then came into the possession of his wife's family, the well-connected relatives of Memmius Vitrasius Orfitus. Symmachus includes poetry intended to accompany the images of famous past owners, family members, and in-laws, as well as his own accomplishments. Though the quality of these verses is unimpressive to the modern reader, Symmachus's reputation for eloquence and for letter writing remained high among contemporaries.[2]

In this letter and throughout this book, Symmachus demonstrates how important property was in establishing aristocratic status and social networks.[3] This prestigious villa had come under his control through his wife, yet in *State Paper* 34.11, dated to 384, Symmachus claimed that his wife had not inherited anything from her father. The issue was not about the legality of a daughter inheriting property from her father; as Julia Hillner has shown, in Rome in the fourth to sixth centuries C.E., family property such as villas could be transmitted to younger sons or even daughters.[4] In this case, there was another issue. Rusticiana's father, Orfitus, had foreseen the possibility that his heirs would be held liable for repayment of public funds that he, as urban prefect, had been held accountable for, so Orfitus had made sure that his daughter was not his legal heir.[5] Yet if Rusticiana had inherited nothing from her family but an illustrious name, Symmachus's usufruct of her family's estate at Baiae, so lovingly described in this letter, would indicate that some legal machinations had been performed that enabled her to pass on this villa to her husband before her father's demise. Indeed, houses and villas regularly passed from one family to another or from one family member to another, as was the case in *Letter* 1.6; sale, inheritance, or gift were strategies used by late Romans to maintain their social and economic status in society.[6]

Without a doubt, Symmachus's emphasis on this property and its famous inhabitants, including his wife's ancestors, at the beginning of his first book of letters was intended to enhance his reputation, even as his high offices (section 3) and his literary efforts (sections 3 and 5) linked him to a long line of accomplished aristocrats, such as the previous inhabitants of this villa and of Baiae (section 5). Symmachus ends with a request for his father's aid in polishing his own poetry, an artful albeit conventional appeal that serves here also to dedicate this book of letters to his father.[7]

Text

1. Ne mihi vitio vertatur intermissio litterarum, malo esse promptus officii quam longa expectatione vicissitudinis desidere; tum quod parentibus non ad lancem neque ad demensum verba tribuenda sunt. Iniurius videar, si summo vobiscum iure contendam; nam praeter aequum censet, qui inter dispares obsequium par requirit. Itaque vester sermo ex beneficio proficiscitur, noster ex debito. Haec me atque alia huiusmodi oppido perpulerunt scribendi munus insuper non habere. 2. Nunc vobis actuum nostrorum ordo pandendus est: libet enim non minus otii quam negotii praestare rationem. Baulos Lucrina sede mutavimus; non quod eius deversorii nos ceperit satias, quod cum diutius visitur, plus amatur, sed quod metus fuit ne si Baulorum mihi inolevisset adfectio, cetera, quae visenda sunt, displicerent. Ibi Acindyno conditori eiusque maioribus emmetra verba libavi et picturae licentiam, quae vestitum disparem singulis tribuit, in rationem coegi. Protelarem te paululum, ni vererer ne dilatione expectatio nutriatur. Quare elaboratam soloci filo accipe cantilenam:

3. Attica palla tegit socerum, toga picta parentem:
praefuit iste sacris, hic dixit iura Quiritis;
at mihi castrensem quod mordet fibula vestem,
Aurorae in populis regum praetoria rexi,
sed fasces pictura tacet: tu respice fastus.

4. Scio te, simul atque haec legeris, actutum poetica plectra moturum. Nullus feceris ne mei periculo gloriere! ego te nostri vatis exemplo quasi quadam lege convenio: liceat inter olores canoros anserem strepere. Silentium mihi, nisi praestiteris, imperabis. Quam nihil abs te metuam, vis probare? En tibi aliud alucinationis meae prodo secretum, adhuc sollicitus de priore. Audi versus ad Baulorum historiam pertinentes:

5. Huc deus Alcides stabulanda armenta coegit
    eruta Geryonae de lare tergemini.
Inde recens aetas corrupta boaulia Baulos
    nuncupat occulto nominis indicio.
Ab divo ad proceres dominos fortuna cucurrit,
    fama loci obscuros ne pateretur heros.
Hanc celebravit opum felix Hortensius aulam,
    contra Arpinatem qui stetit eloquio.
Hic consul clarum produxit Acindynus aevum
    quique dedit leges Orfitus Aeneadis.

Hos inter iuvenile decus, sed honore senili,
bis seno celsus, Symmache, fasce cluis.
Sed te Baulorum necdum lenta otia quaerunt;
cura habeat iuvenem publica pervigilem.

6. Nempe derides, quod de me aliqua iusto indulgentius praedicavi? Est haec vera et digna reprehensio. Omnis quippe ostentatio non caret suspicione mendacii, quia quidquid adsumitur, proprium non putatur, dehinc quod iactantia avara laudis multum decoquit de pudore. Posse me dices, si quis inrepserit externus auditor meos esse versiculos diffiteri, ut verecunde in nos cadat ab altero profecta laudatio. Sed video opusculum non esse paenitendum. Ita res crepera atque anceps dubium me habet, utrum verecundiae praemetuendum sit discrimen an gloriae. Tibi igitur, qui prudentia antistas ceteris, optionis huius delego provinciam. Quid facto usus sit, ipse videris; ego et infantiae et inprudentiae meae patrem conscium non inprudenter elegi. Vale.

Translation

1. To avoid being blamed for the interruption in our correspondence, I prefer to promptly fulfill my responsibility rather than to sit by in prolonged anticipation of a reply; besides, one ought not apportion words to one's parents as if rationed or weighed on a scale. I would seem unjust if I should take issue with you according to the strict letter of the law, for the man who asks for equal deference between unequals is unreasonable in his expectation. And so your words[8] arise from generosity, mine obligation. These considerations and others of this sort have strongly impelled me not to neglect my duty to write.

2. Now I must lay out the order of my activities for you, for it is no less pleasing to offer an account of leisure than of work.[9] We left Bauli for our home on the Lucrine Lake[10] not because we were tired of lodging there—for the longer it is visited, the more it is loved—but because I was afraid that, if my affection for Bauli became established, the other places that I must visit would displease me. There I poured out a poetic libation of words to Acindynus,[11] the founder of the house, and to his ancestors, and I corrected the liberties taken in their painted portraits, which assigned inappropriate attire to each figure.[12] I would put you off a little while longer, if I were not afraid that anticipation is fed by delay. Therefore, accept a slight poem, labored over though still rough in texture:

3. An Attic *palla* clothes my father-in-law, a *toga picta* my father;[13]
the one presided over sacred rites, the other pronounced on Roman law.
But as evidenced by the clasp that fastens my military attire,

among the peoples of the East I ruled as the emperors' prefect.[14]
About my *fasces*,[15] though, the painting is silent; look to the *fasti*.[16]

4. I know that as soon as you have read these verses, you will immediately set in motion your poetic plectrum. Do not do so lest you glory at my expense. I beseech you, on the authority of our bard, as if by a kind of law: "Let a goose be allowed to honk among melodious swans."[17] You will command me to silence, unless you agree to be silent yourself.

Do you want to put to the test how little I fear you? Look, I am revealing to you another of my secret ramblings, even though I am still worried about the first. Listen to my verses on the history of Bauli:

5. Here the god Alcides gathered a herd to be stabled,
snatched from the home of the three-bodied Geryon.[18]
Subsequently a more recent age, corrupting "Boalia," called it "Bauli,"[19]
disguising the meaning of its name.
Fortune has descended from this god to distinguished masters,
so that the fame of this place should not endure obscure owners.
Hortensius, fortunate in his wealth, lived in this hall,
who competed in eloquence against the man from Arpinum.[20]
Here the consul Acindynus lived out his outstanding life
and here, too, Orfitus,[21] who prescribed laws for the heirs of Aeneas.
Among these, the glory of the youth, but senior in office,
you, Symmachus, win lofty fame with your twelve *fasces*.[22]
But the languid pastimes of Bauli do not yet call you.
May public service keep you, young man, ever vigilant!

6. No doubt you are mocking me because I made some claims for myself more complacently than is justified? This is a true and appropriate reproof. Indeed, all display is not without some suspicion of falsehood, since whatever is claimed is thought not to be one's own, and again boastfulness that is eager for praise greatly detracts from one's modesty. You will say that, if some outside listener steals in, I can deny that these little verses are mine, so that the praise, as if coming from another, falls on my ears with my modesty intact. But, as I see it, I should not regret my little poem. Thus, uncertainty and suspense leave me in doubt whether I should fear more the hazard to my modesty or to my renown. To you, therefore, who exceed everyone else in prudence, I delegate the authority for this choice.[23] You yourself will see what needs to be done; I was not unwise in choosing to make my father privy to both my lack of articulateness[24] and my lack of wisdom. Farewell.

Notes

1. See 2 nn. 6 and 7.
2. See the introduction, xxiii–xvi.

3. For the importance of the *domus* in a late Roman aristocrat's identity and status, as well as in securing political and social ties, see Machado 2006; Hillner 2003, 129–45.

4. See Hillner 2003, 130 and n. 5 for the city of Rome. This villa is at Baiae, but the property laws were the same.

5. See Barrow 1973, 178–79; Vera 1986, 243–52.

6. See Hillner 2003, 130–45.

7. On the circulation of written drafts for evaluation, see Starr 1987, 213–23. For more on this among Symmachus's peers, notably Ausonius, see Sivan 1992, 86 and 96.

8. "Words" translates the Latin term *sermo*, or "conversation." In using this word, Symmachus is following the convention in Latin and Greek epistolography that writing a letter is like speaking to an absent friend; see Cicero, *Letters to Atticus* 9.10.1; 12.53; *Letters to Friends* 16.16.2; Julius Victor, *Ars Rhetorica* (*The Art of Rhetoric*) 27. However, Symmachus's letters are not colloquial in style, as are many of Cicero's letters.

9. The sentiment is quoted by Cicero, *Pro Plancio* (*On Behalf of Plancius*) 66, who attributes it to Cato. This phrase became proverbial, and so it appears also in Pliny, *Letter* 1.3.3. Cato's notion of "leisure" (*otium*) emphasized literary and rhetorical productivity; see Bruggisser 1993, 51–54.

10. Bauli is south of Baiae on the Campanian coast in Italy, in the direction of Cape Misenum. The Lucrine Lake is north of Baiae, southeast of Cumae between Avernus and the Mediterranean Sea. This area of Campania had long been the preferred retreat of the Roman elite; see especially D'Arms 1970. The distance between the two villas was not great.

11. Symmachus imitates Cicero and Pliny by including some Greek in his letters, in this case *emmetra*, "metrical" or here, "poetic." However, Symmachus's habit of quoting on occasion just one or two words derived from Greek differs greatly from the practice of Cicero and Pliny, who quote full sentences from Greek authors. This suggests that Symmachus's familiarity with the Greek language and its literature was somewhat limited; see the introduction, xxi. For Acindynus, see 10 n. 13 below.

12. Symmachus does not explain how he corrected the attire in these pictures. He is referring to the painted portraits in the house that he had inherited through his wife's family. Painted portraits (in fresco) were one of the four types of *imagines* or depictions of Roman ancestors noted by Pliny, along with wax portraits, "portraits" with trophies, and shield portraits (*Natural History* 35.6). Flower (1996, 40–47) notes that ancestral portraits were considered part of the house by Roman law, and hence they would have come into Symmachus's wife's family and then into his possession. Presumably Symmachus had these portraits repainted, since they were not wearing clothing appropri-

ate to their rank or office. Such confusion in the portraiture or the identities of the person depicted was common; Pliny (*Natural History* 35.4) reports that Romans would change the heads on marble busts, thereby losing any possibility of realistic representation. This reference to painted ancestral portraits indicates the continued vitality of Roman aristocratic traditions of self-presentation among Rome's fourth-century elite and argues against the views of scholars, notably Badel (2005, 116–18), that ancestral portraits (*imagines*) were no longer relevant in late Roman society. For more on the political and social importance of the senatorial aristocratic *domus* and of statues in general, see Machado 2006.

13. Symmachus's poem is composed as if recited by Septimius Acindynus = Acindynus 2, *PLRE* 1:11, consul in 340. Septimius evidently wed an Athenian woman, whose father-in-law wore the Greek cloak, or *palla*, whereas Septimius's father was a Roman magistrate of high enough standing to wear the ornate Roman *toga picta*. For a discussion of the associations of the *palla* and *toga picta*, see Bruggisser 1993, 82–86; Salzman 1990, 34–35.

14. "I ruled as the emperors' prefect," literally, "I ruled the praetorian office of the kings." The reference is to Acindynus's office as praetorian prefect of the east from 338 to 340; see Acindynus 2, *PLRE* 1:11.

15. The *fasces* were the bundle of rods of elm or birchwood to which was tied a single-headed axe; these were held by the attendants (*lictors*) who preceded Roman magistrates and signified the legitimate authority and power of the officeholder; see *OCD*, s.v. *Fasces*. The *fasces* here refer to the consulship of Septimius Acindynus in 340.

16. *Fastus*, a form of the accusative plural of the Latin word for "calendar," is the same word used for the lists of consuls; see *OCD*, s.v. *Fasti*.

17. The idea that swans make melodious music in competition with cackling geese is proverbial; see Otto 1890, 104 no. 2, under *cycnus*. Symmachus has in mind Vergil's rendition of this proverb (*Eclogues* 9.35–46: "... videor ... argutos inter strepere anser olores," "I seem ... a goose honking among melodious swans,") "Our bard" is Vergil.

18. Alcides, i.e., Hercules, grandson of Alcaeus. In one of his labors, Hercules robbed the three-bodied monster Geryon of his cattle.

19. According to Symmachus, the name *Bauli* derives etymologically from *Boaulia*, "cow pen," an etymology also found in Servius, *In Aeneidem* (*Commentary on the Aeneid*) 6.107 and 7.662, where it is connected with exploits of Hercules; see Callu 1972, 214 n. 1.

20. The "man from Arpinum" refers to the Roman orator and statesman Marcus Tullius Cicero, who was born in this town in Latium.

21. Memmius Vitrasius Orfitus signo Honorius was an eminent senator from a noble family. He twice was urban prefect of Rome, 353–356 and

357–359; for his career in full, see *PLRE* 1:651–53. He was Symmachus's father-in-law.

22. The twelve *fasces* here symbolize Symmachus's proconsulship of Africa in 373; proconsuls received this honor as well as consuls and praetors; see *C. Th.* 6.4.15. Since Symmachus did not attain the consulship until 391, and since his father was still alive, i.e., before 376, this letter must refer to his earlier honor. The notion of a "youthful old age" was a late Roman convention; see Curtius 1953, 98–101; Bruggisser 1993, 80–81. For more on this notion in Symmachus's letters, see Sogno 2007, 85–102.

23. The Latin word *provincia* is translated here as "authority." It is the standard word to indicate the sphere of authority of a Roman magistrate. Since Symmachus was already a provincial governor, he seems playfully ironic in delegating his "authority" (*provincia*) over his literary efforts to his father.

24. Symmachus's claim of "inarticulateness" (*infantia*) and modest literary ability in this opening letter to his father is repeated with slight modifications in *Letter* 1.14.1 ("paupertini ingenii mei conscius … infantiae meae maciem"), in his second letter to Ausonius, his metaphorical father and literary mentor. Such thematic echoing underscores the functional similarities between these two "father" figures.

Letter 1.2: Symmachus's Father, Avianius, to Symmachus
Date: 375[1]

In response to his son's letter, the elder Symmachus, still in voluntary exile, sent the epigrams he had written in his spare time on the great men of his generation. In this, the elder Symmachus imitated Varro, the great scholar of the first century B.C.E. who in exile had composed epigrams and whose importance for this book is fundamental. Moreover, poetic composition was a traditional activity for Rome's elites, and there seems to have been a resurgence of interest in the epigram in the fourth century, judging in part from the extant poetry of Ausonius and from that of other of Symmachus's contemporaries, such as Naucellius.[2]

The inclusion of the elder Symmachus's letter is almost unique in this book; the letter of only one other of Symmachus's correspondents—the poet and Symmachus's "spiritual father," Ausonius—was felt worthy of inclusion here (*Letters* 1.25). By comparing his father to Ausonius, one of the most distinguished poets of the age, Symmachus added to his father's literary reputation. Through his father's comments on own poetry, Symmachus demonstrates, in a cleverly indirect fashion, that his own literary endeavors are praiseworthy. Finally, the contents of these epigrams on famous men elegantly convey the traditional senatorial values and virtues that both Symmachi want to exemplify.[3]

Text

1. Hoc est munus, quo se non sola possit iactare Campania, sed prae ceteris Roma aut Athenae, si in Graecum loquendi honorem huiusmodi lingua vertatur. Quid enim concinnius epistula tua, quam nuper accepi? quid versuum admixtione iucundius? Vere dicam tibi, plura legere volentibus celeriter terminata est. Quod utinam sensus aliquis eorum supersit, quorum imaginibus praescripta videmus epigrammata! Facile laudabunt tales successores laborum suorum, qui picturae nitorem pulchrioribus versibus inluminarint. Et ego igitur gratulor non magis ostreis et peloridibus abdomen quam pectus tibi eloquio esse satiatum; 2. et quoniam pudorem meum ipse ordiendo solvisti, a nobis quoque accipe bonorum aetatis meae exarata nuper elogia. Nam quia nihil est quod agam et, si nil agam, subit me malorum meorum misera recordatio, inveni quod illis libellis, quos nuper dictaveram, possimus adicere. Scis Terentium, non comicum, sed Reatinum, illum Romanae eruditionis parentem, hebdomadon libros epigrammatum adiectione condisse. Illud nos, si fors tulerit, conamur imitari. Sed quae prima conpegi, interim pauca misi, obtestatus te per deos, ut si quid in his displicebit, emendes. Quod mihi pudendum non est; nam sive <quid ex me sive> ex te placuerit, mea laus est nec vito consortium, in quo talem non erubesco consortem.

3. Aradius Rufinus
Princeps ingenio, fortunae munere princeps
aetatis, Rufine, tuae, cui prospera quaeque
admiranda tuis aequabat gloria rebus.
Unus amor cunctis et praesidium trepidorum,
principibus, quorum viguisti tempore, doctus
aut calcaria ferre bonis aut frena tyrannis.

4. Valerius Proculus
Cum primis, quos non oneravit gloria patrum,
ponemus Proculum, vitae morumque decore
haud umquam indignum magnorum Publicolarum.
Olli semper amor veri et constantia, simplex
caelicolum cultus. Non illum spernere posses,
et quamquam reverendus erat, non inde timeres.

5. Anicius Iulianus
Cuius opes aut nobilitas aut tanta potestas,
cedenti cui non praeluxerit Amnius unus?

Acer ab ingenio cunctisque adcommodus idem
hic et carus erat, conferre iuvare paratus;
nam dives, tum celsus honoribus, et tamen illis
grandior, aeterno conplebat nomine Romam.
6. Petronius Probianus
Iactet se Fortuna aliis, quos iudice nullo
lucem ad Romuleam sua sola licentia vexit;
te, Probiane, pudor, te felix gratia teque
Itala simplicitas morum et sollertia iuvit.
Adsidue quocirca, Augustis notus et hospes,
praemia magnorum tetulisti dignus honorum.
7. Verinus
Virtutem, Verine, tuam plus mirer in armis,
Eoos dux Armenios cum caede domares
an magis eloquium morum vitaeque leporem,
et—nisi in officiis, quotiens tibi publica curae—
quod vitam innocuis tenuisti laetus in agris?
Nullum ultra est virtutis opus, nam si esset, haberes.

8. Octoginta personis nescio an solus occurram, et ideo in socerum atque avunculum nostros tibi delegamus epigrammata. Nam et Varronis libri diversis notantur auctoribus. Vale.

Translation

1. This is a gift about which not only Campania could boast but above all Rome, or even Athens, if such words were translated into the glory of the Greek language! For what is more harmonious than your letter, which I recently received? What more pleasing than the intermingling of verses?[4] To tell you the truth, your letter ended too quickly for its readers, who wanted more. But would that some sensation remained for those above whose images we see epigrams inscribed![5] They will readily praise these successors of their deeds, who are illuminating the luster of the painting with even more beautiful verses. I therefore rejoice that your stomach is not more replete with oysters and mussels than your soul is with eloquence. 2. And since you yourself have loosened my inhibition by making a beginning, accept from me, too, these eulogies[6] of the honorable men of my age that I just recently penned. For since there is nothing for me to do, and since if I do nothing the wretched recollection of my troubles overtakes me, I have found how I can add to those little books that I had just recently dictated. You know that Terentius—not the comic writer but the man from Reate, that parent of Roman erudition—seasoned the books of the *Hebdomades* by the addition of

epigrams.[7] I am trying to imitate that work, if Fortune will allow. But for the present, I have sent the few verses I composed first, beseeching you, by the gods, to emend anything in these that displeases you. But there is nothing for me to be ashamed of in this, for if anything of mine[8] or of yours finds favor, the glory is mine, nor do I avoid an association in which I do not blush at having such an associate.

3. Aradius Rufinus[9]
First of your age in talent, first in the gift of Fortune
among your peers, Rufinus, your extraordinary glory
matched your prosperity to your deeds.
One person beloved by all, protection for the fearful,
you knew both how to spur on good princes,
and how to rein in tyrants in whose time you flourished.[10]

4. Valerius Proculus[11]
Among the first men of his age, whom the glory of his ancestors did not overburden,
we will place Proculus; in the dignity of his life and character
he never was unworthy of the great Publicolae.[12]
That man possessed always a love for truth, steadfastness, and a sincere
worship of the gods above. You could not scorn him,
and although he was a figure of awe, you would not for that reason fear him.

5. Amnius Anicius Iulianus[13]
Whose wealth, nobility, or power was so great,
that he did not yield to Amnius, who, alone, outshone all?
He was penetrating in mind, yet also obliging
and dear to all, ready to bring aid and assistance.
For he was rich and eminent because of his offices, but still
transcending these he filled Rome with an eternal name.[14]

6. Petronius Probianus[15]
Let Fortune boast about others whom her wantonness alone,
for no reason, has brought to brilliance in Romulus's city.
You, Probianus, were helped by your modesty, by your happy charm,
by your Italian sincerity of character and resourcefulness.[16]
For this reason you, an attentive familiar and guest of emperors,
rightly secured the rewards of great honors.

7. Verinus[17]
Should I admire more your virtue in arms, Verinus,
when as a general you subdued by bloodshed the Armenians in the East,
or your eloquence, the charm of your character and life,
and—except when in office and in charge of public affairs—

the fact that you lived your life happily in the innocent countryside? There is no further scope for virtue; for if there were, you would claim it.

8. I do not know whether I can account for eighty people all by myself, and for that reason I delegate to you the epigrams about my father-in-law[18] and my maternal uncle.[19] For the books of Varro also contain writing by various authors.[20] Farewell.

Notes

1. See 2 nn. 6–7.

2. For Iulius (?) Naucellius, see *PLRE* 1:617–18. For more on epigrams and Varro in the fourth century, see 15 n. 7.

3. For more on the ideology of these epigrams, see Bruggisser 1993; Lizzi Testa 2002, 187–99; Salzman 2006a; Weisweiler forthcoming; and 15–16 n. 9 below.

4. This is a reference to Varro's *Menippean Satires*, which included both verse and prose; see *Letter* 1.4.1.

5. The elder Symmachus is referring to the inscribed epigrams that accompanied the depictions of the past owners of the house who were eulogized in his son's *Letter* 1.1.5.

6. Eulogies translate the Latin word *elogia*, which Avianius uses to describe his commemorative poems. These, he continues, were inspired by the epigrams (*epigrammata*) composed by Varro (see 15 n. 7).

7. The elder Symmachus took as his model the lost *Hebdomades vel de imaginibus* of Marcus Terentius Varro. Composed ca. 39 B.C.E., Varro's collection of seven hundred portraits of celebrated men was arranged in seven categories of Greeks and Romans; each picture was accompanied by an epigram and a short biographical notice, following the example of the *Pinakes* of Callimachus. Pliny the Elder (*Natural History* 35.1) recorded seeing this work with portraits, but Aulus Gellius (*Noctes Atticae* 3.10.1) mentions only the epigrams, not the portraits. Apparently the elder Symmachus had already dictated some books of epigrams in imitation of Varro, to which he was now adding the recently composed epigrams included in this letter. The thematic importance of Varro for the elder Symmachus was noted by Bruggisser (1993, 95–97), but the allusion to this particular work by Varro may also, as I have suggested (see lxiv–lvi), explain publication of Symmachus's letters in seven books. Inscribing epigrams on private objects or for pubic display, as well as on funerary monuments, was very much a Roman habit; see Niquet 2000 27–46; Weisweiler forthcoming.

8. I follow Callu (1972, 64) in accepting the emendation "<ex me sive>" proposed by Mommsen.

9. Aradius Rufinus can be identified with Rufinus 10, *PLRE* 1:775, urban

prefect in 312–313 and consul in 311. Aradius was among the leading men in Rome in the early decades of the fourth century, hence a generation older than the elder Symmachus.

10. Aradius Rufinus was appointed urban prefect from 29 November 312 to 8 December 313 by the victorious emperor Constantine. Aradius served as consul in 311 and also urban prefect from 9 February–27 October 312, under the usurper Maxentius. Since Maxentius had the misfortune of losing a civil war, he is called "tyrant" in accord with fourth-century usage and pro-Constantinian sources. For Maxentius, see M. Aur. Val. Maxentius 5, *PLRE* 1:571–72.

11. Valerius Proculus can be identified as L. Aradius Valerius Proculus signo Populonius 11, whose career is detailed in *PLRE* 1:747–49. Aside from his pagan priesthoods—*augur*, *pontifex maior*, *quindecimvir sacris faciundis*, and *pontifex flavialis*—he was twice urban prefect (337–338, 351–352), as well as consul in 340. Symmachus's epigram emphasizes Proculus's religious affiliation with the striking phrase "sincere worship of the gods." He also focuses on Proculus's noble ties that extend back to the republican period, when his family name was synonymous with opposition to unfair rulers. It is noteworthy that Proculus's second urban prefectureship was held under the usurper Magnentius. Some scholars have suggested that Proculus was a symbol of the traditional civic and religious virtues of the Roman elite; see Bruggisser 1993, 102–7. But this symbolic role did not necessitate hostility to the emperor. Weisweiler (2010) rightfully notes that this man and his family proudly linked themselves to the Constantinian dynasty when he was honored with a commemorative statue, inscription, and epigram in the Forum of Trajan; see *CIL* 6:1693 = *ILS* 1242. This is reinforced by Proculus's priesthood in the imperial cult (*pontifex flavialis*). But contra Weisweiler, imperial favor did not mean that Proculus could not also represent traditional civic and pagan values, as he does in this epigram.

12. The Publicolae were a noble Roman family in the republican period. The Valerii Publicolae, a branch of this family, owned a home on the Caelian Hill that was acquired by Valerius Proculus, according to *PLRE* 1:748–49. Hence, the claim to continuity is reinforced, though the veracity of the claim that one family existed for over four centuries is open to some doubt.

13. Amnius Anicius Iulianus was proconsul of Africa, later consul in 322 and urban prefect in 326–329; see Iulianus 23 in *PLRE* 1:473–74. His family, the Anicii, were among the most powerful in fourth century Rome; see too Niquet 2000, 123 n. 79, for their distinctive nomenclature.

14. The last line of the epigram alludes to Anicius's reputation in Rome. The elder Symmachus may also here be suggesting Anicius's benefactions to the city; by providing games or monuments, he also added to his reputation.

15. Petronius Probianus can be identified with Probianus 3 in *PLRE* 1:733–34. He was consul in 322 and urban prefect in 329–331. Symmachus's allusion to merit, not Fortune, as the source of his success suggests that Probianus was not someone who had inherited his honors and wealth but had risen from nonelite origins to achieve his offices. Such praise is conventional for a man new to the aristocracy. For more on the attributes of such men, see Salzman 2002, 97–106.

16. Probianus's Italian sincerity (*simplicitas*) of character is described in a positive light; similarly, Proculus's sincerity (*simplicitas*) in his religiosity (*Letter* 1.2.4, verse 4) was also seen as a virtue.

17. This epigram provides good reason to think that Locrius Verinus should be identified with Verinus 1 and Verinus 2 in *PLRE* 1:950–52. Like the others eulogized here, Verinus 2 held the office of urban prefect (323–325). He had an unusual career for an aristocrat in this period, for he had seen military as well as civic service. The reference to his being a "royal praetorian" in the East suggests that he held the office of *praeses* (governor) of Syria, attributed to Verinus 1 by *PLRE* 1:950–51. His *praenomen*, Locrius, is unusual and suggests an Etruscan origin to Martindale 1967; see Verinus 2, *PLRE* 1:951.

18. The elder Symmachus's father-in-law was probably the distinguished Fabius Titianus, consul in 337 and twice urban prefect of Rome, 339–341 and 350–351; see Fabius Titianus 6 in *PLRE* 1:918–19.

19. Chastagnol (1960, 113) suggests that the elder Symmachus's maternal uncle was Av(ianius?) Maximilianus 1 in *PLRE* 1:575, prefect of the watch (*vigiles*) in the early fourth century, because he reconstructs his distinctive first name as the same as that of the elder Symmachus. However, this office, though of clarissimate status under Constantine, was not part of the normal senatorial career pattern; hence, this identification is suspect.

20. When the elder Symmachus says that the *Hebdomades* of Varro "contain writing by various authors" (*notantur*), he is referring to some of the epigrams (or prose) added to that work by others; see 15 n. 7.

Letter 1.3: Symmachus to His Father
Date: 375[1]

In this chatty letter filled with proverbs, Symmachus expresses gratitude for his father's praise of his literary abilities. In section 3, the younger Symmachus turns to his most recent travels along the Bay of Naples. He notes with pride his visit to the town of Beneventum (modern Benevento), which, according to Symmachus, honored him as a patron at great expense despite a recent earthquake. The town citizens were hoping that he would contribute to the city's rebuilding, an expectation that he tactfully avoided by leaving town.[2]

Text

1. Summa adficior gratia quod animadverto litteras meas tibi insubidas non videri, et in gravi dono habeo hanc apud vos esse de nostris epistulis censionem. Laudari quippe ab laudato viro rara est messis ingenii. Verum ut hoc mihi laetitiae fuit, ita illud ludificandi gratia opinor adiectum, si quid in tuis versibus sorduisset, id ut mei stili cura limaret. 2. Ne ego sum stultus ac nihili, si os sublitum mihi esse non sentio. Quid enim corrigi vel a me potest, vel in te fas est? Unus aetate nostra monetam Latiaris eloquii Tulliana incude finxisti. Quidquid in poetis lepidum, apud oratores grave, in annalibus fidele, inter grammaticos eruditum fuit, solus hausisti, iustus heres veterum litterarum. Ne mihi verba dederis. Novi ego, quid valeat adagio, sus Minervam. Adprime calles epicam disciplinam, non minus pedestrem lituum doctus inflare. Ain tandem? Orandi aeque magnus et canendi meae te opis indigum mentiare? Haud aequum facis, neque me iuvat falsa lactatio. 3. Interea si nobis utendas aures datis, dicam quid diebus superioribus egerimus. Bais remotis arbitris otiabar. Eo postquam rumor adlatus est, terrae filios convenire, oppido cavimus ne sobriam solitudinem nostram sodalitas plebeia fuscaret. Ac primo Neapolim, dehinc brevi intervallo Beneventum me recepi. Ibi summo cultu civium plausuque susceptus tanto honore celebrabar, ut iam gravarer officiis. Sedulitas enim, quae non conpensatur, onerosa est. 4. Et urbs cum sit maxima, singuli eius optimates visi sunt mihi urbe maiores, amantissimi litterarum morumque mirabiles. Deos pars magna veneratur; privatam pecuniam pro civitatis ornatu certatim fatigant. Nam postquam terra movit, nihil paene illis reliqui factum est, sed fractae opes infractos animos reppererunt. Pro se quisque operam boni civis adfectat; nox diei iungitur ad laborem. Unde nobis summa cura fuit abire ocius quam volebam, ne aut mihi diu dediti ab opere desiderent aut eos occupatio geminata distenderet. 5. Itaque Baianum sinum rursus accessi; nam Baiae id temporis iam silebant. Hinc vos munere salutationis impertio doque nuntium propere nos diis volentibus esse redituros. Fors fuat huiusce promissi. Vestra tamen indulgentia adfatum saepe tribuat, quasi diutius abfuturis. Vale.

Translation

1. I am very grateful that, as I can tell, my letter does not seem foolish to you, and I consider the fact that you have this opinion of my letter a great gift, for "to be praised by the praiseworthy"[3] is a rare reward for talent. But even as I was happy about this, I still think you were joking when you added that the application of my pen should smooth out any rough spots in your verses. 2. Truly, I am stupid and worth nothing at all, if I do not notice that

you are making fun of me.[4] For what can be corrected by me or what right to correct do I have in your case? You alone of our age have stamped the coin of Latin eloquence on a Ciceronian anvil. Whatever is delightful in the poets, whatever is of consequence in the orators, whatever is trustworthy in history, whatever is learned in the grammarians—all this you alone have absorbed; you are the true heir of the literature of the ancients. Do not try to trick me. I know that proverb about "the pig and Minerva."[5] You are a particular expert in epic and no less adept in sounding a more pedestrian verse.[6] Oh, really? You who are as great in oratory as in poetry, are you pretending that you need my help? You are acting not at all equitably, and I have no taste for false compliments.

3. Now if you lend me your ears, I shall tell you what I have been up to in the past days. I was taking my leisure at Baiae, unnoticed by anyone. After a rumor arrived there that some "sons of the earth"[7] were approaching, I took great precautions that the plebeian company not cast a shadow on my sober solitude. So I took myself off, first to Naples, then after a brief time to Beneventum. There I was received with the greatest courtesy and enthusiasm by the citizenry, and I was feted with such great honors that I am now weighed down by obligations, for zealous attention that is not returned is burdensome. 4. And, although the city is very great, each of its leading men seemed to me greater than the city, being the most impassioned lovers of literature and possessed of admirable character. A great part of them worships the divine;[8] they exhaust their private fortunes in competition over the adornment of the city. For after the earthquake, almost nothing was left to them, but broken fortunes have found spirits unbroken. Each man strives to do his duty as a good citizen; night is joined to day in work. For this reason I took the greatest care to leave more quickly than I wished, lest by overlong devotion to me they be distracted from their work or lest the doubling of their duties overextend them.[9] 5. So I went back to the bay at Baiae, for Baiae was then silent. From here I bestow on you a dutiful greeting and send the news that I will return soon, if the gods are willing.[10] May Fortune make this promise come true! Just the same, indulge me often with your reply, as though writing to someone destined to be away longer. Farewell.

Notes

1. This date is traditionally based on the identification of the earthquake and destruction mentioned in section 3 before the death of Valentinian I in November 375. But that identification is unlikely; see 2 n. 6 above. References to *Letters* 1.1, 1.2, and 1.4 suggest a similar date of 375.

2. For the expectations and patronal obligations of late antique office holders, see Brown 1992, 35–70; Weisweiler 2010.

3. Symmachus is citing a well-known phrase that first appears in Naevius 18 (Ribbeck 1897, 9): "laetus sum laudari me abs te, pater, a laudato viro." Later writers, notably Cicero, *Letters to Friends* 5.12.7 and 15.6, reiterate this as a commonplace.

4. The translation conveys the meaning since, literally, Symmachus says that "his face has been smeared" ("os sublitum mihi esse"), alluding to the practical joke that Romans played on one another by smearing the face of a sleeping person; see Nonius, 45.21.

5. The proverb is explained well by Festus, p. 408, 14–17 L: "sus Minervam in proverbio est, ubi quis id docet alterum, cuius ipse inscius est," "The pig and Minerva is proverbial for when someone teaches someone else something about which he himself is ignorant." Otto (1890, 224) assumes the proverb derived from some fable. Its appearance in Cicero's letters (e.g., *Letters to Friends* 9.18.3) is indicative of the conversational epistolary style that Symmachus is here emulating.

6. "Pedestrian verse" translates the Latin *pedester lituus*, literally a "pedestrian trumpet" (see *OLD*, s.v. *pedester* 3.b). The elder Symmachus is praised as skilled in verse "less lofty than epic." This could include epigrams, but the kind of verse is not specified.

7. The phrase "the sons of the earth" is proverbial for those of humble, i.e., plebeian, status; see Callu 1972, 67 n. 3.

8. Seeck (1883) corrected the manuscript reading of the singular "god" (*deum*) to plural "gods" (*deos*) on the grounds that a Christian scribe had made this change here and in *Letter* 1.3.5, as also in numerous other letters (e.g., 1.6.2, 4.54, 5.13, and 5.17.) I follow Seeck's correction, as did Callu (1972, 67) but translate as "the divine" to convey the message, central here, that this is a pious city not deserving of its destruction. See 20 n. 10.

9. Harries (2003, 125–141) underscores that the local elites often strove to find a wealthy patron for their city to help with civic projects not supported by the imperial government.

10. I follow Seeck (20 n. 8 above) and substitute the plural, "gods willing," "diis volentibus" for the manuscripts that read the singular, "god willing," "deo volente." Cameron (2011, 377–82) has proposed that Symmachus calibrated his usage of the singular "god" versus "gods" in response to the religious sensibility of his correspondent. In this case, that would justify the plural reading of "gods." However, since in book 1 Symmachus also uses the plural "gods" in addressing letters to the Christians Ausonius and Probus (1.14.5; 1.21), this attention to singular versus plural does not appear to consistently match the religion of the recipient. See my discussion, xlvii–xlviii.

Letter 1.4: Symmachus to His Father
Date: 375[1]

Symmachus praises the epigrams that his father composed, a sample of which appeared in *Letter* 1.2. The son alleges that, because of his far inferior literary talents, he cannot provide the editorial assistance his father has asked of him.

Text

1. Studium quidem Menippei Varronis imitaris, sed vincis ingenium. Nam quae in nostrates viros nunc nuper condis epigrammata, puto hebdomadon elogiis praenitere; quod haec <et illa> aeque sobria, haec tamen castigata sunt, illa bono metallo cusa torno exigi nescierunt.

2. Et duriorem materiam, nisi fallor, adniteris. Ille Pythagoran, qui animas in aeternitatem primus adseruit, ille Platonem, qui deos esse persuasit, ille Aristotelen, qui naturam bene loquendi in artem redegit, ille pauperem Curium, sed divitibus imperantem, ille severos Catones, gentem Fabiam, decora Scipionum totumque illum triumphalem senatum parca laude perstrinxit; tu rutuvam proximae aetatis inluminas. Difficile factu est, ut honor angustis rebus addatur.

3. Me quoque iubes versibus tuis nonnulla subnectere. Haud ita Flaccus tuus praecepit in illis poeticae artis edictis, quorum hoc memini esse principium, ne humano capiti cervix equina iungatur. Malo itaque tibi contumacia negati officii quam inprudentia promissi operis displicere. Plura de hoc coram loquemur, quando hanc epistulam sequi paramus aut consequi. Tu coepta perage et tam sollertis eloquii esto munificus; ego tibi ut linguae obsequia nego, ita aurium commodabo. Vale.

Translation

1. You imitate the project of Varro, author of the Menippeans, but surpass him in talent, for I think that the epigrams that you have just now composed about the great men of our age outshine the eulogies of the *Hebdomades*. Both works are equally serious, but your epigrams have been subject to correction, while his, although struck from good metal, did not experience finishing on the lathe.[2]

2. And, unless I am deceived, you are working with more resistant material. That man briefly addressed with scanty praise Pythagoras, who first asserted that souls are eternal; Plato, who made the case that the gods exist; Aristotle, who reduced the nature of speaking well to an art; Curius,[3] a poor man who nevertheless ruled the wealthy; and the severe Catos, the Fabian

race, the honors of the Scipios, and that whole triumphal Senate. You, however, illuminate our recent, unsettled times.[4] It is difficult to add honor to such narrow subjects.[5]

3. You urge me also to weave something into your verses. Your beloved Flaccus[6] made no such a recommendation in those precepts in "The Art of Poetry," whose beginning is, as I recall, that "a horse's neck not be joined to a human head."[7] I prefer, therefore, to displease you by my obstinacy in refusing my duty rather than by my folly in undertaking such a task. I shall say more about this in person, since I am preparing to follow soon after this letter or even to catch up with it. For your part, continue as you have begun, and be generous with your refined eloquence. Although I refuse you the compliance of my tongue, I place my ears at your disposal.[8] Farewell.

Notes

1. See 2 nn. 6–7; this is written when the elder Symmachus was in exile.

2. See the introduction, lxiv–lxvi, and 15 n. 7.

3. Curius is Manius Curius Dentatus, Roman soldier and statesman, consul in the third century B.C.E., famed for his incorruptibility and frugality. He was idealized by Cato, whose influence on the younger Symmachus has been discussed; see 9 n. 9.

4. "Unsettled times," *rutuva* in Latin, is otherwise unattested. It is probably a variant spelling of *rutuba*, "perturbation," attested by Nonius, 167M. The word also appears in Varro, *Menippean Satires* 488: "nunc sumus in *rutuba*." It seems to be an archaic term, intended to give an elevated tone to this letter.

5. The phrase "to add honor to unpromising subjects" derives from Vergil, *Georgics* 3.290: "angustis … addere rebus honorem."

6. That is, Q. Horatius Flaccus, the Augustan poet Horace.

7. Adapted from Horace, *Ars Poetica* (*The Art of Poetry*) 1–2.

8. The Latin words *obsequium*, "compliance," and *commodo*, "lend, put at one's disposal," are common terms of patronage. Symmachus writes here as if he were a client of his father.

Letter 1.5: Symmachus to His Father
Date: 375[1]

Symmachus turns to the theme of work (*negotium*), since that, along with the proper use of leisure (*otium*), is required to meet the Catonian ideal proclaimed in *Letter* 1.1. Symmachus complains that in these "degraded times" he has to invest in his agricultural properties to ensure their continuing productivity; such a sentiment might seem to imply that Symmachus had only a modest income. That impression would be wrong, for Symmachus was very well off; he owned at least thirteen estates in central Italy, as well as land in Samnium, Apulia, Sicily, Mauretania, and perhaps Lucania.[2] Indeed, his expenditure on his son's praetorian games, reported at 2,000 pounds of gold, indicates that he was among the richest men of his age.[3]

Text

1. Nequiquam taciturnitatis incessimur, quibus summa cautio est officii persequendi, fere ut nulla statio fuerit tot locorum, in qua huius muneris ferias egerimus. Et sane iuvat animum pia sermonis exactio. Dulcis est enim querella, quae nascitur ex indulgentia. Vos modo facite noveritis hanc stimulationem religiosam magis esse quam iustam.

Interea loci de Praenestina secessione siluisti, cuius fama mihi fecit indicium. Quam vellem deliciis vestris inprovisus obrepere! Licet Campaniae amoena praeniteant, mihi tamen esset adcommodatius agitare vobiscum et spiraculis regionis illius aestivam flagrantiam temperare.

2. Sed res familiaris inclinat et nobis usque quaque visenda est, non ut quaestuum summa ditescat, sed ut spes agri voluntariis dispendiis fulciatur. Namque hic usus in nostram venit aetatem, ut rus, quod solebat alere, nunc alatur. Verum haec missa facio, ne salutatio in querellam versa minuat officii voluptatem. Date operam valetudini et adloquio crebriori, quae cum petimus, sedulo pollicemur. Vale.

Translation

1. I am being reproached for my silence without good reason, since I have taken the greatest precautions to carry out my duties, so much so that in almost none of the many places where I stopped did I take time off from this obligation. Admittedly an affectionate request for communication pleases the spirit, for even a complaint is sweet if it arises from fondness. But you should know that your insistence[4] shows your correctness more than your reasonableness.

Meanwhile, you have been silent about your Praeneste retreat, about which rumor has informed me. How I would love to sneak up on your refined haunt there unexpectedly! Although the charms of Campania may outshine them, it would nonetheless be more agreeable to me to spend time with you and to temper the summer heat with the cool breezes of that region.[5]

2. But family affairs are taking a downward turn, and we have to be attentive to them everywhere, not so that the sum of our revenues may grow greater, but that the expected harvest from our fields be supported by volun-

tary expenditures. For this custom has grown up in our age, that land that used to provide nourishment now receives it![6] But I leave this aside, lest my greeting turn into a complaint and diminish the pleasure of my service to you. Take care for your health and be sure to write more often; these requests that I make, I earnestly promise you in return. Farewell.

NOTES

1. This letter was probably written when the elder Symmachus was away from Rome, still in exile, and so dated to 375; see 2 nn. 6–7.

2. See Salzman 2002, 25–26; Vera 1986, 243–52; and introduction, xvii–xx.

3. See Cameron 1999a, 477–505; and the introduction, xvii–xx.

4. Following Callu 1972, 216 n. 5, we emend the manuscript reading of *stipulationem*, the demanding of a guarantee from a prospective debtor, to *stimulationem*, translated here as "insistence." There is a slight tone of reproach that makes the father-son relationship come alive in this line.

5. Praeneste, modern Palestrina, was a city just 23 miles southeast from Rome on a spur of the Apennines. Its cool breezes had attracted Roman aristocrats to build villas in this area for centuries.

6. Symmachus's complaint about the decreasing viability of his land should not be taken at face value; he drew rental from his estates, whether or not they produced crops. Hence, the value of his properties remained high, for prestige purposes as well as income, despite such complaints. See Whittaker and Garnsey 1998, 282–83; Wickham 2005, 270–71.

LETTER 1.6: SYMMACHUS TO HIS FATHER
DATE: BEFORE 375/376[1]

The elder Symmachus inherited an estate at Ostia from an unidentified kinswoman. He then bequeathed the estate to Symmachus, who hoped to pass it on to his heir (1.6.2). At the time of this letter Symmachus did not yet have any children. Indeed, it is even possible that he was not yet married, although this is unlikely, since it would mean the letter is earlier than all the others to his father except *Letter* 1.12. The emphasis on family and the wish for a successor suggests that he is already planning a family.

TEXT

1. Solent inpatientes dilationis esse, qui sperant in se aliquid muneris conferendum; hoc vero a vobis recens ortum videmus, ut suarum rerum munifici moram non ferant largiendi. Nunc nuper ad vos praedium lege venit, cuius me iure donastis. Cucurrit quaestus vester in meum commodum, et meliore

voto fortunam estis imitati. Nam quod ex propinquae bonis cum maestitia sumpseratis, cum laetitia tradidistis.

2. Quid quod hanc liberalitatem cumulastis amplissimo testimonio? Cuius ego honestamentum praeopto muneribus, nam qui opibus inlaudatus iuvatur, necessarium magis donum quam iustum praemium videtur adipisci. Ago igitur iudicio vestro atque habeo gratias, quantae sunt maximae, quod mihi honorem utrumque fecistis et deos precor, ut datis in commune omnes longum fruamur sintque ex nobis quibus Ostiense praedium nostro iudicio, vestro tradatur exemplo. Vale.

Translation

1. Those who expect some gift to be conferred on them are usually impatient with delay. But in your case we see this fresh innovation, that those generous with their wealth cannot bear a delay in bestowing their generosity. A little while ago an estate came to you by legal inheritance, the title to which you gave to me. Your gain passed rapidly on to my benefit, and you imitated Fortune, but in happier circumstances, for what you received in grief from the possessions of a kinswoman, you handed over to me in joy.

2. What shall I say of the fact that you have added to this liberality a most splendid commendation, the distinction of which I prefer to the gift of the estate, for whoever receives material benefit but no praise appears to be receiving a gift out of necessity rather than as a deserved reward. Thus, I express and feel gratitude for your judgment to the fullest extent possible, because you have bestowed upon me a double honor. I pray to the gods[2] that we all may enjoy for a long time what has been given us in common and that I may have offspring to inherit this Ostian estate in accordance with my judgment and your example. Farewell.

Notes

1. I date the letter to sometime before 375–376, when Symmachus's daughter was born; see the introduction, xxviii–xxix n. 85. In this I disagree with Callu (1972, 71 n. 2), who dates Symmachus's daughter's birth, incorrectly, in my view, to 371.

2. See 20 nn. 8 and 10 for the plural "gods" instead of the singular "god" that appears in the manuscript. See also the introduction, xlvii–xlviii.

Letter 1.7: Symmachus to His Father
Date: 375[1]

Symmachus is in Campania, where he is awaiting the arrival of his father and his father's friends. It is now early autumn, and Symmachus dwells on the enticements of Campania at this time of year in part to encourage his father to hasten to join him. Such descriptions were also valued as literary tours de force in their own right. See also *Letter* 1.8.

Text

1. Bono animo sumus, cum viam promissi memores inchoastis. Nunc properato opus est, ut, dum anni tempus calet, autumni bona raptim fruamur. His quippe mensibus Campania nitet agri ubere et arbusti honore, Baiae imbre raro, sole modico temperantur, mensae ab edulibus copiosae sunt, quibus tu amicorum catervas minaris. 2. Sed mihi honestae multitudinis nulla minatio est et, si bis tanto plures quam scribis adfuerint, frugem bonam feceris. Non deerit quo famem polluant; nam comitibus vestris utpote sobriis caedundae saginae cura posterior est. Quousque longum loquor? Mitto verba, rem flagito. Occasionem rapere prudentis est. Si quid dilationis itineri demitur, mora otii rependatur. Vale.

Translation

1. We are in good spirits, since mindful of your promise you have begun your journey. Now there is need for haste, so that we may speedily enjoy the rewards of autumn while the weather is still warm. Indeed, Campania is radiant in these months with its fertile fields and its fine trees; Baiae is temperate, with infrequent rain and moderate amounts of sunshine; tables, which you threaten with hordes of friends, are laden with foods. 2. But an honorable multitude is no threat in my eyes; even if twice as many come as you write, you will have acted properly. There will be no lack of food here to break your fast, for "killing the fattened animal"[2] is for your companions, temperate as they are, the furthest thing from their minds. How long am I going to speak? I am sending words, but I look for action! It is the mark of a wise man to "seize the moment."[3] If any time is lost by delay on your journey, let it be repaid by the length of your leisurely retreat. Farewell.

Notes

1. See 2 nn. 6–7.

2. The idea is close to the English proverbial "killing the fattened calf." The Latin proverb does not specify the animal but simply indicates "killing the fattened animal" (*saginam caedere*); see Callu 1972, 72 n. 1.

3. An allusion to Horace, *Epode* 13.3–4: "Rapiamus, amice, / Occasionem de die..." ("Let us seize, friend, the opportunity from the day...").

Letter 1.8: Symmachus to His Father
Date: 370/371–375[1]

In this playful letter, Symmachus encourages his father to come visit Campania by including a poem in praise of the region. The meter is iambic dimeter catalectic. Symmachus presents an artful imitation of lines 208–212 from Ausonius's *Moselle*, where the poet likens the sports of dwellers on the Moselle to "the games that Liber views on the Cumaean water, when he roams over the cultivated ridges of sulfurous Gaurus and through the vineyards of smoking Vesuvius, when Venus joyful at Augustus's Actian triumph bids the lascivious Cupids play at fierce battle."[2]

Text

Iamdudum vestri cupiunt Lucrina tacita et liquida Baiana et Puteoli adhuc celebres et Bauli magnum silentes. Vos apud Coram rusticam vel apud steriles Formias desidetis. Tandem, si operae est, contendite viam atque animadvertite meliora terrarum, ubi alte turbis quiescitur, ubi fruendis feriis modus nullus est,

ubi corniger Lyaeus
operit superna Gauri,
Volcanus aestuosis
medium coquit cavernis,
tenet ima pisce multo
Thetis et Baiae sorores.
Calet unda, friget aethra,
simul innatat choreis
Amathusium renidens,
salis arbitra et vaporis,
flos siderum, Dione.

num vobis videor quasi multae luxuriae ebrius mentis insipere atque ideo in poetas nomen dedisse? Nihil moror hanc litteraturam; loci potius quam ingenii mei munus exercui. Sed si invitantia loquor, gradum tollite, ut et vos sitis laeti praesentium et nobis potiundi quae volumus fortuna succedat. Vale.

TRANSLATION

For a long time now the quiet of the Lucrine Lake, the clear waters of Baiae, Puteoli, still crowded, and Bauli, with its vast silences, have desired your presence. You sit idle in your rustic retreat at Cora or at barren Formiae.[3] If you have the chance, hasten to make your way here at long last and view more pleasing regions, where there is a deep peace removed from the crowds and where there is no limit to your enjoyment of a holiday,

Where horned Lyaeus
covers the summits of Gaurus,
Vulcan heats in steamy caverns
what lies between,
and the sisters Thetis and Baiae[4]
possess the depths with a wealth of fish.
The water is warm, the air is cool;
together with her company swims,
with the radiance of Amathus,[5]
ruler of sea and balmy sky,
flower of the stars, Dione.[6]

Surely you think I am of unsound mind,[7] as though intoxicated by indulgence, and for this reason I entered my name among the poets? I make no claims for this composition; I have relied on the endowments of the place more than my talent. But if my words are inviting, pick up your pace, so that you may enjoy what is at hand and that we may have the good fortune to possess what we desire. Farewell.

NOTES

1. Most scholars date Ausonius's *Moselle* to 370/371 or see this year as the *terminus post quem*. For further discussion, see the introduction to *Letter* 1.14, pp. 43–44. Hence, this letter must postdate that poem but be written before the elder Symmachus's recall to Rome.

2. Ausonius *Moselle*, 208–212: quales Cumano despectat in aequore ludos / Liber, sulphurei cum per iuga consita Gauri / perque vaporiferi graditur vineta Vesuvi, / cum Venus Actiacis Augusti laeta triumphis / ludere lascivos fera proelia iussit Amores.

3. Cora, Terracina, and Formiae were cities on the road from Rome to Campania; see *Letter* 2.3.

4. Thetis was a sea divinity, wife of Peleus and mother of Achilles. Symmachus here invents a sister of Thetis, Baiae, the eponymous sea divinity of the town of Baiae (see *ThLL* 2:1683.53–55).

5. Amathus is a town in Cyprus sacred to Venus.

6. Dione, i.e., Venus.

7. "To be of unsound mind" translates the Latin "insipere mentis." This is a back formation from the adjective *insipiens*, and its use here with a genitive of respect reflects Late Latin tendencies as well as Symmachus's archaizing taste; see Haverling 1988, 184, 190, 195.

Letter 1.9: Symmachus to His Father
Date: 375[1]

This brief note shows the perils of travel as Symmachus, once more, expresses his desire for his father to visit.[2]

Text

In metu fuimus, ne vos imber inhiberet. Sed verum illud est, quod poeta noster scriptum reliquit, iter durum vicisse pietatem. Quare adventum vestri in diem placitum praestolamur. Dii modo auctores sint, ut, quae animo destinatis, nullis causationibus obstrepantur. Vale.

Translation

We were afraid that the rain would delay you. But the lines our poet left us are true, that "dutifulness has overcome a hard voyage."[3] For this reason, we expect your arrival on the appointed day. May the gods only guarantee that no objections interfere with what you have set your heart on. Farewell.

Notes

1. See 2 nn. 6–7.
2. For Symmachus's reservations about travel, see Salzman 2004, 81–94.
3. Symmachus alludes to Vergil, *Aeneid* 6.688: "vicit iter durum pietas."

Letter 1.10: Symmachus to His Father
Date: 375[1]

The younger Symmachus's attention to repairing and maintaining his family properties was typical of the land-owning elite. His activities in this regard would naturally be of interest to his father who as *paterfamilias* was legally in control of the properties.

Text

Hanccine mihi esse fortunam, ut quoquo versum pedem gradumque contulero, exaedificandum aliquid offeratur? Velut me nunc Capuani praetorii instauratio in graves cogit expensas, cuius pars fatiscit incuria, pars neglegenti dudum celeritate reparata inbecillum praestat habitaculum. His nisi properata cura subvenerit, aut pecuniae postea dispendium cumulabitur aut ruinae. Nam quisquis haec opera intermittit, amittit. Quare animus est amoliri aedium senectutem. Ita desiderato et expetito otio ad negotium concessimus sumptuosum. Quid rerum geramus, audistis. Facite vicissim vestrae salutis atque actuum prospera noverimus, ut hoc pauxillum tempus, quod in Campania paramus absumere, sine offensa vestri silentii transigamus. Vale.

Translation

Just my luck! Wherever I turn my foot or direct my path I come across a construction project! Now, for example, the rebuilding of the villa at Capua involves me in heavy expenditure. Part of it is falling down due to neglect and part repaired with speed but insufficient care some time ago provides an unsound place to live. Unless I attend to these matters right away, my loss will increase in the future, either financially or with the collapse of the villa. For whoever postpones this sort of work loses out.[2] For this reason, I intend to do away with the signs of the building's old age. And so, I have given up my much-desired and much-sought leisure time for this expensive business. You have heard what I am doing. Tell me, in turn, the good news about your health and activities so that I may pass the brief time I am preparing to spend in Campania without resentment for your silence. Farewell.

Notes

1. See 2 nn. 6–7.
2. We have not been able to represent in our translation the paronomasia in the Latin "intermittit, amittit," but compare the English "you snooze, you lose."

Letter 1.11: Symmachus to His Father
Date: 375[1]

The "daughter" (*filia*) referred to in the opening line of this letter is Symmachus's wife, Rusticiana. This usage is intentional. When the younger Symmachus refers to his wife as the elder Symmachus's daughter (*filia vestra*), not daughter-in-law (*nurus vestra*), he suggests the elder Symmachus's affection for Rusticiana, as if she were the same as a daughter. Moreover, the omission of his wife's name is typical of Symmachus's letters to and about female family members especially, although even Symmachus's brother is named only in the letter headings and not directly in the letters to him (*Letter* 1.62–74) or in the letters discussing Symmachus's grief at Titianus's demise.

The anonymity of the women in Symmachus's family is a striking feature of his letters as a whole. There are eighty-one letters in book 6 to his daughter and her husband, and all are addressed to the "his children, the Nicomachi." In these letters Symmachus depicts his daughter as possessed of traditional female virtues, notably chastity and modesty, and engaged in conventional matronly pursuits such as weaving (see *Letter* 6.67.) Not once does he address her directly. Nor does Symmachus address his wife directly or give outward expression to his feelings for her, as Pliny did in his letters to and about his wife, Calpurnia. Symmachus does not even allude to his wife's health or discuss her activities at all. Yet his wife, Rusticiana, was well-regarded by Sidonius Apollinaris, who tells us that she even helped Symmachus with his literary endeavors (Sidonius Apollinaris, *Letter* 2.10.5). The anonymity of the women in his family, in conjunction with his depictions of his daughter and his silence about his wife, suggest that Symmachus is presenting himself as having a conservative and traditional view of the role of women in Roman society.

Text

1. Cum iam filiae vestrae dies natalis adpeteret, commodum aderant, quae muneri miseratis. Ea nobis inmane quantum cara et gravia fuere. Nam si quid in absentes bene consulas, inpensu maiore gaudetur. Ilico amplexi litteras, quae prosequebantur oblata, in expectatione esse coepimus, quam mox vobis capessendum iter Appiae scriberetis. Nihil horum pagina nuntiabat. 2. Percontor tabellarium num constantiam decreti rerum subita turbassent. Ait sententiam nihil claudicare, sed placita differri, donicum statio Formiana multa fruge et aliis hoc genus in usum necessariis instruatur. Tunc mihi animus ab aegritudine remigravit. Do fidem nihil herili mensae, nihil servitiis aut pecori defuturum. Ne mihi sit dicti huius posthac negatio, en vobis chirographi instar litteras meas. Sponsionem meam stipulat adfectio. Neque enim patiar decipi, quos opto conplecti. Vale.

Translation

1. As your daughter's birthday[2] was already approaching, the gifts that you had sent arrived in a timely manner. They were, in my opinion, extraor-

dinarily precious and significant, for to show any consideration for those who are absent brings all the greater joy.[3] I immediately embraced the letter that accompanied your gift, and we began to anticipate how soon you would write us that you would be traveling on the Appian Way. But nothing of this was in your letter.

2. I asked the messenger whether something unexpected had disturbed your firmness of purpose. He said that there was no faltering in your resolution but that your plans were being deferred until the staging-post at Formiae was supplied with abundant grain and with other practical necessities of this sort. Then my mind recovered from its agitation. I give you my word that the gentlemen's table here shall lack for nothing, nor shall the household or the animals.[4] In order that I not deny these promises hereafter, consider my letter the equivalent of a formal contract. Affection guarantees my promise, for I will not allow those whom I hope to embrace to be deceived. Farewell.

Notes

1. See 2 nn. 6–7.

2. Symmachus is referring to the birthday of his wife, Rusticiana (see *PLRE* 1), whom he calls the "daughter" of the elder Symmachus. For the status of late Roman aristocratic women in general, see Clark 1993.

3. Haverling (1988, 64) observes that Symmachus's use of *impensu*, i.e., "extraordinarily," is a rare archaism, occurring only twice in Symmachus's extant works; here its usage would seem to augment the antique virtues attributed to his father.

4. "Gentleman's table" is the translation of Haverling 1988, 127, for *herilis mensa*. She notes that the word *herilis* is one of the "more frequent archaisms in late Latin." Symmachus's use of it is a sign of his conservatism in literature.

Letter 1.12: Symmachus to His Father
Date: Before 377[1]

This letter opens playfully with a comparison between the censors' role of overseeing public works and Symmachus's designation by his father to oversee the work on one of the family's houses. One would like to know more about the location and layout of the house described in this letter. It was not the main ancestral residence of the Symmachi on the Caelian Hill, for that property was designated as Symmachus's *lares* (*Letter* 7.18).[2] Indeed, the Caelian house, one of the largest in the fourth-century city, was identified as belonging to the Symmachi on the basis of inscribed finds (two statue bases, a brick stamp, and a gold glass cup);[3] it was renovated in the early fourth century, when cut-marble slabs (in a style known as *opus sectile*) were added to certain rooms and one of its apsidal rooms was altered to allow for more mosaic work.[4] As this letter shows, Symmachus and his father placed great value on such cut-marble floors, a preference that fits well with the archaeological evidence from other fourth-century Roman homes, such as that of the rich urban prefect Iunius Bassus.[5]

Julia Hillner suggested that the house referred to in *Letter* 1.12.2 as being rebuilt was the one across the Tiber in Rome, the home of the elder Symmachus that had been destroyed by an angry mob (see the introduction to *Letters* 1.1–12).[6] This would be poetic justice, as well as provide a fitting conclusion to this sequence of letters to his father. Unfortunately, there is little in the letter to pin this notion down. We do not know the location of this house, nor is it clear that only the elder Symmachus will reside there. Rather, Symmachus is working under his father's guidance on a house that he considers part of his patrimony, as emerges from his reference to it as "our house" (1.12.1: *aedibus nostris*). Indeed, this recalls *Letter* 1.6, where a house bequeathed to the elder Symmachus was handed over to Symmachus and that he hopes to use "in common" (1.6.2: *in commune*) until the younger Symmachus can pass it along to "our" children (1.6.2: *ex nostris*) in a seemingly unbroken line of Symmachi and their property.

Text

Censorum notio fuit spectare opera, quae locassent; hoc me negotium curare voluisti. Mos gestus est imperatis, vel quod tibi dicto audiens esse debui, vel quod studio meo congrue mandatum munus agnovi. Audi igitur quantum in aedibus nostris cura promoverit. Scalis subpectus est honor marmoris; superiora conclavia crustis teguntur ea operis levitate, ut conpago solidum mentiatur. Columnas nihilo amplius mercatus es, quam si tibi muneri contigissent. Eas Bithyno lapide caesas, si bene oculis utor, existimo. Hactenus est, quod scire debueris. Deinceps tantum adiciemus cognitioni tuae, quantum aedificationi viderimus accedere. Vale.

Translation

It used to be the censors' responsibility to examine all those works that they had contracted out;[7] you have requested me to oversee this business. I have followed your instructions because I must obey what you say and because I have recognized that the task enjoined on me conforms to my own inclinations. So listen to how much my efforts have accomplished in our house. Fine marble has been laid on the stairs. The upper rooms have been covered with a veneer of such delicacy that, despite the joints, it gives the illusion of being made of one solid piece. You paid no more for the columns than if they had come to you as a gift. If I can trust my eyes, I think they were cut from Bithynian marble.[8] So much for what you ought to know. From now on, I will add as much to your information as I see is added to the building. Farewell.

NOTES

1. Since there are no indicators of the elder Symmachus's exile, this letter could date to any time before his death in 376.

2. A senator had to declare his main residence and establish his *lares* (household gods) officially in order to allow the state to know where he would attend court and where he would pay taxes (the *aurum oblaticium*); see *C. Th.* 6.2.13; 6.2.16.

3. See Carignani 2000, 149–51, for the house and the finds consisting of two statue bases (*CIL* 6.1699: to Symmachus by his son; 6.1782: to Flavianus), a brick stamp with the inscription "Sym(machus)," and a fragmentary gold glass cup, inscribed "Summachus consul o(rdinarius)" and below it (reconstructed) "Q. F(abius) S(ummachus) Iu[n]ior?" Carignani (1993, 494) estimates the size of the house at ca. 6,500–8,500 square meters.

4. The renovations included laying cut marble, *opus sectile*, and changing an apsidal niche so that a single large apse replaced seven niches in the curve of the wall used for statues; see Carignani 1993, 486–92, 496–502.

5. For the use of cut marble (*opus sectile*) in the houses of Iunius Bassus and Symmachus, see Machado 2006, ch. 6.

6. Hillner 2003, 136. Hillner argues that the Transtibertine house was where Symmachus was raised and that he moved his household gods (*lares*) to the house on the Caelian Hill when he wed. But it is also plausible that he was raised in the Caelian house and that his father moved his *lares* to another house even more grand across the Tiber; see Ammianus Marcellinus, *Res Gestae* 27.3.4.

7. Symmachus uses the past tense to describe what the job of the censor was once, i.e., in the late republic or early empire. This was not, apparently, fourth-century practice; the title "censor" is not noted even once in Jones's magisterial work, *LRE*. The point of the quip is to compare their role in public building with his obligation for private work.

8. Bithynia, a territory in northwestern Aisa Minor, was the source of expensive marbles, some black in color; see Mango 1986, 86 n. 149. The point here is that these inexpensive columns look as good as costly ones.

Book 1, *Letters* 13–43: Symmachus to Ausonius

The letters that Symmachus wrote to Ausonius and the one that Ausonius wrote in response (Ausonius *apud* Symmachus, *Letter* 1.32) are among the most elegant, witty, and engaging in the collection.[1] In addition to vividly depicting a deepening friendship between two well-educated men of high literary attainments, these letters underscore Symmachus's growing public influence as senator and patron, as well as that of his correspondent. Indeed, the dated letters to Ausonius included in book 1 belong to the decade when Ausonius was at the height of his career and influence, between 369/370 and 380; no other letter can be securely dated after 380.[2] Ausonius's prominence explains why most of Symmachus's letters to him are recommendations (*commendationes*) for friends, family, and clients.[3]

Ausonius's success in the imperial bureaucracy provides a good example of the upward mobility of provincials and of the value of rhetorical education in the fourth century. Born in Bordeaux in 310 to a curial family, Decimius Magnus Ausonius was educated in what was, at the time, a leading center for rhetorical training. Although he initially practiced at the bar, he soon turned to rhetoric and earned a reputation for teaching and poetry. His standing, along with his strong family connections in Gaul, convinced Valentinian I

1. The letter that Ausonius sent to Symmachus as a dedication to his poem, the *Riddle of the Number Three* (*Griphus Ternarii Numeri*, poem 15 in the edition by Green 1991), survives only in manuscripts of Ausonius and was not included in Symmachus's correspondence. This *Letter* of Ausonius to Symmachus is dated by Green (1991, 445) to a year or two after Symmachus's departure from Trier in 370 but before *Letter* 1.14. For Ausonius's letter to Symmachus asking for editorial advice for the *Griphus*, see Green 1991, 111–12.

2. Bowersock (1986, 11) has argued that the relationship between Symmachus and Ausonius continued later than this date, as evidenced by the bond between Symmachus and Ausonius's son Hesperius; he dates *Letter* 1.86 (to Ausonius's son) to 384 because he identified the Hesperius mentioned in Symmachus's *State Paper* 23 with Ausonius's son. However, Bowersock's arguments for the date of *Letter* 1.86 are not compelling (see 157 n. 1).

3. On the importance of letters of recommendation, see Roda 1986, 177–207; and Rees 2007, 149–68.

to offer him the position of tutor for his son Gratian, probably in 366–367.[4] Valentinian appreciated Ausonius's rhetorical training, for he appointed him quaestor of the sacred palace likely in 375, after having bestowed upon him the honorary title of *comes*, or count.[5] As quaestor, Ausonius drafted laws and imperial texts.

When Gratian became senior Augustus in 375, Ausonius's influence grew even greater, for he was now in position not only to present but also to shape the young emperor's policies. As quaestor of the sacred palace, he had crafted some of Gratian's legislation,[6] but his elevation to the office of prefect brought with it greater powers. Ausonius was appointed prefect of Gaul no later than 377, but by January of 378 he held this office with his son, Hesperius. Ausonius then was appointed co-prefect of Gaul, Italy, and Africa with his son from 378 to 379.[7] This illustrious career culminated in 379, when he obtained the much-coveted honor of consul.

After this successful sequence of offices, Ausonius's public career ended. He may well have retired to his estates for a while, but in 383 we find Ausonius at court in Trier once again, possibly involved in negotiations concerning Gratian's restoration after the revolt of the Roman general Magnus Maximus. These proved futile; Gratian died in Lyons at the hands of Magnus Maximus's forces (Ausonius, *Letter* 20) in 383, making Ausonius's position as supporter of the dead emperor precarious.[8]

Under the circumstances, it seems likely that Ausonius then left Trier. His son Hesperius seems to have remained active at the court of Valentinian II in Milan at least until 384; he has been identified as the Hesperius recorded in Rome on public business in that year.[9] Ausonius may well have gone to Milan in this period, for he would have been in an uncomfortable situation if he had remained in Gaul, given his close ties to Gratian. No wonder Ausonius

---

4. Coşkun 2002a, 37–43, argues for the summer of 368, although others date his appointment between the years 364 and 367; see Sivan 1993, 101 n. 33, who persuasively dates his appointment to 366–367. For more on these early years, see Coşkun 2002a, 41; Sivan 1993, 49–96, 115–41.

5. See *PLRE* 1:140. Coşkun's (2002a, 56–58) proposed start date of 374 on stylistic evidence is not compelling, though Ausonius was quaestor into 377.

6. For Ausonius's role as quaestor, see Green, 1992, 695; Sivan, 1993, 119–41.

7. For the dates of Ausonius's offices, see *PLRE* 1:140–41. Coşkun (2002a, 140, 145) suggests that their joint prefectureship be dated to spring 377, but see the introduction to *Letters* 75–88 (pp. 145–46) for reservations about this earlier dating.

8. See Bowersock 1986, 1–12.

9. Symmachus, *State Paper* 23.1, talks of a man on this embassy who has been identified with the son of Ausonius, Hesperius. See Vera 1981, 166–67; *PLRE* 1:428; and Bowersock 1986, 10.

rejoiced in the demise of Magnus Maximus in 388 (Ausonius, *Ordo Nobilium Urbium* [*Order of Noble Cities*], 71–72). At his by now advanced age of seventy-seven or seventy-eight, he was unwilling to engage in an active political life or to be court poet under Theodosius (Ausonius, *Praefationes Variae* [*Various Prefatory Pieces*] 3). After this date, Ausonius and his family recede from public life. Ausonius is last attested as alive in 393 (Ausonius, *Epistulae* [*Letters*] 27–32); he probably died soon thereafter.[10]

If we see that Symmachus's letters to Ausonius in book 1 were chosen in part to publicize his ties to one of the most accomplished and prominent figures of the age of Gratian, it is not surprising that Symmachus omitted what has been identified as the earliest letter in their correspondence, *Letter* 9.88. It was written by a youthful Symmachus who expressed great pleasure at the recognition he received from an unnamed but established teacher at court on whom Symmachus lavishes fawning praise. Although the letter lacks an addressee, Sergio Roda has argued convincingly on the basis of internal evidence that its recipient was Ausonius; of special import is Symmachus's praise for this "imperial teacher" and the Gallic school to which this teacher belonged.[11] If Roda's arguments are accepted, as I think they should be, *Letter* 9.88 indicates also that Ausonius had initiated the correspondence after he had read and admired something written by the young Symmachus. This in itself suggests something of Symmachus's status, since this imperial teacher considered this young aristocrat from Rome important enough to include in his friendship network. As was typical, a letter paved the way for a personal encounter; the two met when Symmachus went to Valentinian I's court at Trier to deliver the Senate's vows of allegiance and crown gold to the emperor, and also present his speech on the occasion of the emperor's *quinquennalia* on 26 February 368 (*Oration* 1).[12]

However, if *Letter* 9.88 was their earliest extant correspondence, Symmachus chose to begin his published book of letters with a very different image of himself and of his relationship to Ausonius. *Letter* 1.13 opens the correspondence by focusing on a public moment, the optimism of a new reign

10. For more on his life and career, see Decimius Magnus Ausonius in *PLRE* 1.140–41; Sivan 1993; and Coşkun 2002a, especially 1–11.

11. Roda 1981a, 219–22; 1981b, 273–80. Coşkun (2002b, 120–28) has argued against Roda's identification of the recipient as Ausonius because identifies the *imperialis magister* as a high official. But the Latin must mean "an imperial teacher," that is, the teacher of the emperor. Hence, *Letter* 9.88 supplies good evidence to identify the letter's addressee as Ausonius.

12. Symmachus's *First Oration* was delivered in honor of Valentinian's *Quinquennalia*, correctly dated to 368 by Chastagnol 1987, 255–68. Symmachus's *Second Oration* is securely dated to the third consulship (*Oration* 2.9) of Valentinian in January 370. For meeting Ausonius while both were in imperial service, see Symmachus, *Letter* 1.14.3–4.

and the reading of the accession speech of Gratian in 376. In place of the fawning youthful admirer of *Letter* 9.88, Symmachus depicts the relationship as one between two friends, not at all equal in age or literary abilities, but bound by a shared interest in political events, literature, and family. Theirs is a friendship that exhibits mutual respect and common values—*unanimitas*, in Symmachus's terms (e.g., *Letter* 1.34). Ausonius is cast in the supportive role of Symmachus's mentor and spiritual intimate, a bond likened to that of father and son, a point made poignant by the familial language that Symmachus and Ausonius employ to address each other. Ausonius calls Symmachus his "son" or *filius* (Ausonius *apud Symmachum, Letter* 1.32.4), a term of endearment typically used in Latin epistolography when older men address their younger "friends." Symmachus addressed Ausonius as "my lord" (*dominus, Letter* 1.15), a sign of the latter's high social and political position, but not a master-slave relationship by any means.[13] Rather, this term fits standard epistolographic vocabulary to indicate respect. But what is not typical is the use of the term *parens*, that is, "relative" or "parent" (*Letter* 1.33; Ausonius *apud Symmachum, Letter* 1.32.4), to express Ausonius's mentoring of Symmachus, a unique expression of what Bruggisser has rightly seen as indicative of the depth of the bond between the two men.[14] This intimate, paternalistic tie is accentuated, too, by the placement of these letters to Ausonius directly after those to Symmachus's natural father.

Given the closeness of the relationship that Symmachus depicts in these letters that I date no later than 379, it is somewhat surprising that there are no subsequent letters to Ausonius in the Symmachan corpus as a whole. Some scholars have suggested that this silence reflects a tension in their relationship; Symmachus had delivered a panegyric to the usurper Magnus Maximus in 388, an act that would have created tensions with Ausonius, Gratian's former teacher and backer.[15] But we have little to indicate Symmachus's support for Maximus before 388, and it is unlikely that Symmachus had taken any overt action in support of Maximus until the latter had moved into Italy, that is, after 387. This leaves some six or seven years without any extant correspondence, and none after 388, when Maximus fell. It is just as likely that Symmachus and Ausonius continued to correspond after 380 but that their later exchanges were less frequent; the political uncertainties of the time may have contributed to the difficulties of keeping up their correspon-

---

13. See *OLD*, s.v. *dominus*, 4. On *unanimitas*, see 51 n. 3.

14. Bruggisser 1993, 152–55, 418–420. He records (154 n. 25) the use of the term *filius* by Symmachus for young men whom he wants to nurture but points out how rare it is for him to call another *parens*, as he does Ausonius (*Letter* 1.33). See also 51 n. 4.

15. For Symmachus's panegyric and the circumstances, see introduction, xxxvi–xxxvii.

dence.[16] So, too, their communications would have naturally diminished after 380 in large part because of Ausonius's reduced influence in the politics of patronage; after 380 Ausonius was no longer in public office, and hence the necessity of sending him letters of recommendation was gone. Their subsequent silence thus underscores one of the key motivations for publishing this book; Symmachus selected letters to Ausonius in book 1 to represent himelf not only as a prominent literary talent in his own right in conversation with the leading poet of the age, but even more to advertise his influence as patron and political actor in the age of Gratian.

Letter 9.88: Anepigraphic but Probably Written to Ausonius[1] Date: Probably 366–367[2]

As was the norm in late Roman society, a letter such as *Letter* 9.88 paved the way for a personal meeting (cf. Symmachus, *Letter* 4.1, to Stilicho). Since in my view this letter is part of the correspondence between Ausonius and Symmachus, I include *Letter* 9.88 here by way of contrast with *Letter* 1.13, the letter chosen by Symmachus to depict their relationship. *Letter* 1.13 represents the two men as equals but emphasizes Ausonius's greater political influence and literary abilities.

Text

Olim te mihi fecit optabilem cultu fama litterarum tuarum, sed diu officium scribendi per verecundiam distuli, ne in aula positum viderer ambire; cuius morbi ita crebra est adfectatio, ut diligentes existimationis viri pro alienis vitiis erubescant. Iam remota est causa haesitantiae, postquam me prior salutatione dignatus es. Patentes amicitiae tuae fores benigne accitus intrabo et compensare meditabor pudentis silentii moras crebrioribus paginis. 2. Tu tantum bona venia respice obsequium linguae inopis et paulisper imperialis magistri submitte iudicium. Indicasti certe meorum te aliqua legisse; eandem posco patientiam. Novus tibi non ero nec inexpertum formidabo arbitrum; omnia mea ferre didicisti. Accessit etiam nobis familiaritas, quae te mihi aequiorem iudicem faciat. Gratiosa quippe est amicitia et a severo examine in blandiores sensus caritate mutatur. 3. Quodsi ego deposito ingenii pauperis metu adsiduas tibi epistulas spondeo, vides quanto amplius sperem de promptuario largiore.

Fatendum tibi est amice: Gallicanae facundiae haustus requiro, non quod

16. Coşkun 2002a, 93 n. 238, emphasizes the difficulties in communication.

his septem montibus eloquentia Latiaris excessit, sed quia praecepta rhetoricae pectori meo senex olim Garumnae alumnus inmulsit, est mihi cum scholis vestris per doctorem iusta cognatio. 4. Quidquid in me est, quod scio quam sit exiguum, caelo tuo debeo. Riga nos ergo denuo ex illis Camenis quae mihi lac bonarum artium primum dederunt et, si te in meis scriptis aliquid offenderit, auditorem quondam popularis tui aut silentio tuere aut tu quoque rursus institue. Vale.

TRANSLATION

Long ago your literary reputation made me wish to pay my respects to you, but I put off the task of writing for a long time out of modesty, lest I seem to be ingratiating myself with someone at court; so frequently do men show themselves afflicted by this illness that those who are careful about their reputations blush in shame over this vice in others. But now the reason for my hesitation has been removed, after you have taken the lead and considered me worthy of greeting. Since I have been kindly summoned, I will now enter through the open doors of your friendship, and I will plan to compensate for the time lost in timid silence with more frequent letters. 2. Of you I only ask that you regard the devotion of an impoverished tongue with kindly forbearance and abate your judgment, as an imperial teacher, for a brief while. You have indicated, I know, that you have read some of my writing; I seek the same patience. I will not be new to you, nor will I fear an unfamiliar judge; you have learned to permit me to send everything. Added to this is our intimacy, which makes you a judge more favorable to me, for friendship is obliging and out of affection changes from a harsh examination to more sympathetic feelings. 3. But if, after having put aside my concern about my poor ability, I promise a continual flow of letters to you, you see how much more I hope for from your far richer repository!

I must declare to you in a friendly fashion: I need drafts of Gallic eloquence, not because Latin eloquence has withdrawn from these seven hills, but rather because an old man, a nursling of the Garonne, once poured into my heart the precepts of rhetoric, and so I have a legitimate attachment to your school through my teacher.[3] 4. Whatever talent I have—and I know how slight it is—I owe to your part of the world. So, let me drink again from those Camenae who first offered me the milk of the liberal arts,[4] and, if anything in my writing offend you, either protect a former student of one of your compatriots with silence, or take your turn, too, in instructing me. Farewell.

NOTES

1. Roda 1981a, 219–22; 1981b, 273–80.

2. Roda (1981a, 219) dates *Letter* 9.88 to 367, but this depends on the date of Valentinian's appointment of Ausonius as imperial tutor. This letter is certainly prior to Symmachus's trip early in the winter of 368 to the court at Trier, after Ausonius's appointment as the imperial teacher. See 36 n. 4 and 37 n. 12.

3. Scholars generally identify Symmachus's teacher with Tiberius Victor Minervius, following Seeck (1883, xliv n. 106 = Minervius 4, *PLRE* 1:603–4). This is the same grammarian who taught Ausonius (*Commemoratio professorum Burdigalensium* [*Poems Commemorating the Professors of Bordeaux*] 1, Green 1991, 41–42). This identification is not certain because of the number of teachers of rhetoric in Bordeaux in the mid-fourth century with this name.

4. The Camenae, the Italian goddesses of a spring, meadow, and grove below the Caelian Hill in Rome, had long been identified with the Muses; see, e.g., the republican poetry of Livius Andronicus, *Odyssia* (*Odyssey*) *Fr.* 1. The Camenae reappear in Symmachus's other letter to Ausonius, *Letter* 1.20.1.

Letter 1.13: Symmachus to Ausonius
Date: 376[1]

Symmachus chose to make this the first letter to Ausonius in the official version of their friendship that was promulgated with the publication of book 1 of the letters. Here the status of the two men appears relatively equal as Symmachus relays the senatorial reaction to the emperor Gratian's speech in the Roman Senate house. Interestingly, there are similarities in vocabulary (e.g., Camenae) when comparing *Letters* 1.13 and 1.20 and that of *Letter* 9.88. But unlike *Letter* 9.88, which is devoted to private matters, *Letter* 1.13 emphasizes the public mood of hopeful expectation at the beginning of the reign of Gratian, and the Senate's optimism that the excesses of Gratian's father, Valentinian, have come to an end (see Symmachus, *Oration* 5.3 *Pro Trygetio* [*On Behalf of Trygetius*]; Ausonius, *Gratiarum actio* [*Speech of Thanksgiving for the Consulship*] 1.3). Section 3 of *Letter* 1.13 underscores that the Senate's response was important to Ausonius and also, at the beginning of this new rule, to the emperor.

Text

1. Solet facunda esse laetitia et angustias clausi pectoris aspernata gestire; tibi, amice, scribendi oblivionem peperit res secunda. Id mihi imitationi esse non potuit, quem domini nostri Gratiani caelestis oratio bonae spei et hilaritatis inplevit. Ultro igitur adloqui residem non peperci vel officii vel gaudii mei gratia, quorum alterum familiaritas nostra, alterum felicitas publica suggerebat. 2. Nunc si operae est, utendum mihi tantisper animum fac remittas. Primores Kalendas Ianus anni aperibat. Frequens senatus mature in curiam

veneramus, priusquam manifestus dies creperum noctis absolveret. Forte rumor adlatus est, sermonem desiderati principis multa nocte venisse. Et erat verum, nam tabellarius vigiliarum fessus adstabat. Nondum caelo albente concurritur; luminibus accensis novi saeculi fata recitantur. quid multa? Lucem, quam adhuc opperiebamur, accepimus. 3. Dic mihi, inquies—nam id praestat audire—quid nostri patres super ea oratione senserunt? Rerum tibi natura respondeat quibus suffragiis exoptata pietas audiatur. Novimus bona nostra conplecti. Si credis, etiamnum illius gaudii mei quandam patior cruditatem. Bonus Nerva, Traianus strenuus, Pius innocens, Marcus plenus officii temporibus adiuti sunt, quae tunc mores alios nesciebant: hic in laude est natura principis, ibi priscae munus aetatis. Cur verso ordine ista optimarum artium putemus exempla et illa de saeculo priore vestigia? 4. Beneficium suum fortuna tutetur et has saltem Romano nomini velit servare delicias! Nullo fascino felicitas publica mordeatur! Audisti omnia sed summo tenus ore libata; monumenta curiae nostrae plenius tecum loquentur. Ubi cum plura scripta reppereris, aestima quanto uberiora unius mens optaverit, quam plausus effuderit. Vale.

Translation

1. Joy is usually eloquent and exultant, spurning the narrow confines of a closed heart; in your case, friend, happy events have made you forget to write. I have not been able to imitate you in this now that the celestial speech of our Lord Gratian[2] has filled me with great hope and cheer. Thus, despite your inactivity, I have not refrained from communicating with you, moved by my sense of duty or of happiness, the former inspired by our friendship, the latter by the public good fortune. 2. Now, if you have the time, let me have your attention for the moment. Janus was opening the doors for the first Kalends of the year.[3] We, a full Senate, had come early into the Senate House, before the full light of day had removed the darkness of night. By chance a rumor came to us that an oration of our much beloved emperor had arrived late at night. And it was true, for a letter carrier, tired from his wakeful nights, was standing before us. Although the sky had not yet fully brightened, we hurried together; after the torches were lit, the fates of the new age were recited. What more to tell? We received the light that we were waiting for until that moment. 3. Tell me, you will say—for that is an important matter to hear—what was the opinion of our fathers concerning that oration?[4] Let the nature of the events tell you with what approval his dutifulness—so ardently hoped for—was heard! We know how to embrace our good fortune. If you believe it, even now I suffer some agitation from that joy I experienced! The good Nerva, the energetic Trajan, the irreproachable Pius, the ever responsible Marcus were all aided

by their times, which knew no other morality.[5] But now praise is due to the character of this emperor, whereas then it was a gift of the former age. Why should we reverse the situation and think that those are examples of the highest virtue, while the present ones are but the traces of an earlier age? 4. Let Fortune guard her benefactions, and may she be willing at least to guard this special favorite for the name of Rome! Let no evil eye look askance on the general felicity. You have heard all but have had only the slightest taste; the records of our Curia will speak more fully to you. When you have consulted further accounts, imagine how much more abundant the wishes of any one person were than the flood of applause expressed.[6] Farewell.

Notes

1. The dating is based on the delivery of Gratian's oration at the beginning of the year and of his reign.

2. To refer to the emperor as "our lord" (*dominus noster*) was standard practice.

3. Janus is the Roman god of doors and entryways, so is often depicted as a double-headed, bearded man looking in two directions at once. He is associated with beginnings, hence his name, appropriately, is the source for the first month of the year, *Ianuarius*, or January.

4. "Our fathers" (*nostri patres*), refers to the members of the Senate at Rome. Symmachus would naturally emphasize the importance of their reaction to changes in imperial policy. However, it is also true that the Senate of Rome in the fourth century had grown in independence and prominence as the emperors left more of the task of governing the city to it; see Salzman 2002, 19–68.

5. The list of good emperors is formulaic, and Symmachus has used the same figures before. See his *Oration* 1.16; cf. the various uses of Trajan by Ausonius in his *Speech of Thanksgiving for His Consulship* 16; and Ammianus Marcellinus, *Res Gestae* 16.1.4.

6. This is a reference to the *Acta Senatus*, the *Acts of the Senate*, and to the Roman custom of recording the number of acclamations after imperial proclamations; see Matthews 2000, 31–54. The urban prefect was supposed to send an account of senatorial *Acta* each month to the emperor; see Callu 1972, 77 n.7.

Letter 1.14: Symmachus to Ausonius
Date: after 370/371[1]

This playful letter displays Symmachus's wit, as well as his close ties to Ausonius. Although this is one of the longest letters in the book, Symmachus alleges a preference for Laconic brevity to mask his literary failings. Symmachus claims that he has not yet received his personal copy of Ausonius's celebrated poem, the *Moselle*, and is thus, as a friend, hurt by this oversight. Despite this claim, Symmachus has seen or heard the poem and alludes to its content in his letter. For example, he remarks on the varieties of fish it contains (*Letter* 14.4), a reference to the catalog of some fifteen varieties of fish described in the *Moselle* (82–149).[2]

The dating of *Letter* 1.14 depends in part on the dating of Ausonius's *Moselle*, an issue that has been much discussed of late. Certainly the poem was composed after 368; it records the victory of Valentinian I and Gratian over the Alamanni at Solicinium in this year (lines 422–424) as a recent occurrence. The *Moselle* presents an admiring vision of the emperor Valentinian and a flattering view of his achievements across the Rhine but is most praised for its descriptions of the countryside and of villa life in the Moselle Valley.[3] Most scholars would date the *Moselle*'s *terminus ante quem* to 370/371, at least for its initial publication.[4] Indeed, the poem shares some of the same political ideology as attested by Symmachus in his *Second* and *Third Orations*, delivered at the imperial court in 369–370.[5] Beyond that, the use of common imagery suggests that the two probably read and responded to each other's works.

Symmachus's *Letter* 1.14 was written after Symmachus had left court, sometime in 370. It seems to have had an effect on Ausonius. In an apparent attempt to normalize relations after this gaffe, Ausonius sent to Symmachus his poem the *Griphus* or *Riddle on the Number Three*, with a dedicatory letter that not only requested Symmachus to emend and improve Ausonius's poem but also claimed that if he had any choice, Ausonius always asked Symmachus for such assistance.[6] Their interaction also explains the pointed but playful language in Ausonius's *Prefatory Letter* dispatched with the *Griphus* that echoes language in Symmachus's *Letter* 1.14; of special note is the reiteration of the Greek word ἀμουσότερος, "deaf to the Muses," used both by Ausonius in *Griphus* (*Carm.* 15, Green 1991, 111 line 6), and Symmachus, *Letter* 1.14.2. In any case, since Symmachus had left Trier in 370, and since *Letter* 1.14 indicates that the *Moselle* has already been in public circulation, this *Letter* must date to late in the year 370 or, more probably, to 371.

Text

1. Petis a me litteras longiores. Est hoc in nos veri amoris indicium. Sed ego qui sim paupertini ingenii mei conscius, Laconicae malo studere brevitati quam multiiugis paginis infantiae meae maciem publicare. Nec mirum, si eloquii nostri vena tenuata est, quam dudum neque ullius poematis tui neque pedestrium voluminum lectione iuvisti. Unde igitur sermonis mei largam

poscis usuram, qui nihil litterati fenoris credidisti? 2. Volitat tuus Mosella per manus sinusque multorum divinis a te versibus consecratus, sed tantum nostra ora praelabitur. Cur me istius libelli, quaeso, exortem esse voluisti? Aut ἀμουσότερος tibi videbar, qui iudicare non possem, aut certe malignus, qui laudare nescirem. Itaque vel ingenio meo plurimum vel moribus derogasti. Et tamen contra interdictum tuum vix ad illius operis arcana perveni. 3. Velim tacere quid sentiam, velim iusto de te silentio vindicari; sed admiratio scriptorum sensum frangit iniuriae. Novi ego istum fluvium, cum aeternorum principum iam pridem signa comitarer, parem multis, imparem maximis: hunc tu mihi inproviso elatorum versuum dignitate Aegyptio Melone maiorem, frigidiorem Scythico Tanai clarioremque hoc nostro populari Tiberi reddidisti. Nequaquam tibi crederem de Mosellae ortu ac meatu magna narranti, nisi certo scirem quod nec in poemate mentiaris. 4. Unde illa amnicorum piscium examina repperisti quam nominibus varia tam coloribus, ut magnitudine distantia sic sapore, quae tu pigmentis istius carminis supra naturae dona fucasti? Atqui in tuis mensis saepe versatus, cum pleraque alia, quae tunc in praetorio erant esui obiecta, mirarer, numquam hoc genus piscium deprehendi. Quando tibi hi pisces in libro nati sunt, qui in ferculis non fuerunt? 5. Iocari me putas atque agere nugas? Ita me diis probabilem praestem, ut ego hoc tuum carmen libris Maronis adiungo. sed iam desinam mei oblitus doloris inhaerere laudibus tuis, ne hoc quoque ad gloriam tuam trahas, quod te miramur offensi. Spargas licet volumina tua et me semper excipias, fruemur tamen tuo opere sed aliorum benignitate. Vale.

Translation

1. You seek from me a longer letter. This is proof of your true affection for me. But being aware of the poverty of my talent, I prefer to pursue Laconic brevity rather than to make public my feeble inarticulateness by writing page after page. Nor is it surprising if the vein of my eloquence has grown thin, since you have not helped it for some time now by sending me any of your poetry or even any of your prose works to read. How can you ask that my letters pay you generous interest when you have advanced none of your literary efforts to my account? 2. Your *Moselle*, hallowed by immortal verses, flits through many hands, from one pocket to another,[7] but I can only watch it drift by. Why, I wonder, did you wish to deprive me of your little book? Did I seem to you so "deaf to the Muses"[8] that I could not judge it or so vindictive that I did not know how to praise it? So you have cast serious aspersions either on my intellect or my character. Yet still, despite your ban, I have gained access with difficulty to the secrets of that work. 3. I would like to be quiet about what I feel; I would like to avenge myself on you by a righteous silence,

but my admiration for your writing breaks down my sense of injury. I came to know that river, when a long time ago I accompanied the standards of the eternal emperors.[9] It is the equal of great rivers, but not of the very greatest. But, unexpectedly, the dignity and eminence of your verses rendered it greater than the Egyptian Nile, colder than the Scythian Don, and more celebrated than our native Tiber.[10] I would not believe your lengthy account of the source and course of the Moselle at all, if I did not know for certain that you do not lie, not even in your poems.

4. Where did you find those schools of river fish, as varied in their colors as in their names, as different in their taste as in their size, which you depicted with the colors of your poem so vividly as to surpass even nature's gifts? And yet I, who was often present at your table, never discovered that type of fish, although I marveled at many other things that were at that time served in the military headquarters.[11] When were these fish—which have never been served on platters—born in your book? 5. You think that I am joking and talking trivia? May the gods be my witness; I rank your poem alongside the books of Maro.[12] But I shall stop dwelling on your praises, forgetful of my grievance, lest you interpret this, too, to your credit, that I admire your work even though my feelings have been hurt. Even if you distribute your volumes widely and always leave me out, I will nonetheless enjoy your work, but it will be through the kindness of others. Farewell.

Notes

1. My dating is based on the dating of the *Moselle*; see 44. Evelyn-White prints the letter in the LCL edition of Ausonius: 1919, 1:265–67.

2. That Symmachus read the *Moselle* or heard parts of it recited is clear from this and other substantive remarks, such as a reference to the source of the Nile, *Moselle* 470–471, and the common echoes of Ennius in the *Moselle* and in this letter; see 47 n. 7 below. Hence, I do not find Shanzer's remarks (1997, 289) on the "impossibility" of Symmachus's familiarity with the *Moselle* convincing. In his letter Symmachus is asking specifically for his own personal copy of a poem with which he is already familiar.

3. For commentary on the *Moselle*, see Green 1991, 456–63. Ausonius's support for imperialism and military conquest was muted by his appreciation of nature and civil society, or so it has been argued by Scafoglio 2003, 521–39; and O'Daly 2004, 152.

4. See Shanzer 1997, 284–305, for discussion and suggested composite dating, with an initial publication in 371 and a second edition in 378/379. Sivan (1993, 383–94) would date it even earlier, to 368, but this is not widely accepted.

5. *Oration* 2 is dated to January 370 and *Oration* 3 to either April 369 or

January 370; see Callu 2009b, x n. 1. For both men's positive assessment of Valentinian's campaign as well as fortifications, see *Moselle* lines 2, 9, and 457; cf. Symmachus, *Oration* 2.28–31; and 47 n. 9 below.

6. For this dating of the *Griphus*, see Ruggini 1989a, 167–76. Her chronology is more compelling than the argument of Bowersock (1986, 3), who reverses the chronology of the *Griphus* and *Letter* 1.14 on the grounds that it would have been extremely tactless for Symmachus to write *Letter* 1.14 after Ausonius had sent the *Griphus* with its accompanying dedicatory letter. For Ausonius's letter to the *Griphus*, see Green 1991, 111–12.

7. Callu (1972, 78) notes that the verb *volitat* ("flits") alludes to a famous line of Ennius, reused by Vergil, *Georgics* 3.9, which Shanzer (1997, 290) suggests is also alluded to by Symmachus, *Oration* 2.31, and Ausonius, *Moselle* 475. This shared allusion may reflect shared texts or simply a common literary tradition.

8. See the introduction to this letter for the Greek word ἀμουσότερος.

9. After Symmachus was at the court of Valentinian I, he went on a campaign of the emperor against the Alamanni, as he notes in *Oration* 2.2 and 18. Given the evidence, it seems most likely that the campaign was that of 368; see xxv nn. 64 and 66. For the alternative view, that it was Valentinian's campaign of 369, see Salzman 2006b, 363.

10. Symmachus cites the famous rivers of the ancient world. He refers to the Nile as *Melo*, the archaic Latin name for the river, another indication of his archaizing tendencies. Ausonius, *Moselle* 470–471, discusses the source of the Nile, another indication that Symmachus has read the poem but does not possess a personalized copy of it.

11. The word here, *praetorium*, indicates the tent of the general or the imperial body guard. It suggests that Ausonius was also present on the same imperial campaign of Valentinian I as Symmachus, probably in 368; see 47 n. 9.

12. P. Vergilius Maro, the Augustan poet Vergil, was so familiar to educated Romans that Symmachus uses only his cognomen.

Letter 1.15: Symmachus to Ausonius
Date: before 379[1]

Symmachus writes a letter of recommendation for the Athenian rhetorician, Palladius, who practiced in Rome. After Palladius was summoned to court at Trier in 379 (Symmachus, *Letters* 1.94, 3.50; Sidonius Apollinaris, *Letter* 5.10.3), his abilities quickly won him advancement. Under Theodosius, Palladius became count of the sacred largesses in 381 and master of offices at the eastern court between 382 and 384.[2] This letter shows Symmachus as a powerful patron, willing and able to use his friends at court to aid his own friends/clients and protégés. It is interesting that Symmachus's support ignored Palladius's religious affiliation; Palladius has been identified as the Christian philosopher who corresponded with Gregory of Nazianzen (*Letters* 103 and 170).

Text

1. Paene evenerat, ut tecum succincta brevitate loqueremur, quoniam deerant digna memoratu et in defectu rerum nihil operae est indulgere verbis, sed tempestive Palladii rhetoris nostri declamatio auxit paginam meam. Ea conplacita summatibus litterarum clam te esse non debuit. Itaque cum et meo officio et tuo studio talis relatio conveniret, vix soluto coetu necdum eventilatam auribus nostris auditionis meae fidem iudicio calente dictavi. 2. Movit novus Athenaei hospes Latiare concilium divisionis arte, inventionum copia, gravitate sensuum, luce verborum. Opinionem meam dico: tam probus est oratione quam moribus. Tunc nostrates viri, qui inter se aliarum rerum saepe dissentiunt, concordem sententiam super huius laude tenuerunt. Credo plane, nec fides cassa est, rhetorum hanc esse prosapiam; nam plenum ingenio genus noscitur. Non solus vultus aut colos adserit posteros in honorem parentum: certiores habet natura vindicias. Bene sentiendi ac bene loquendi gignuntur, non scribuntur, heredes. Quod alii docentur, hic natus est. 3. Haec apud te, mi domine, silenda non credidi, et quod prae tui amore nihil habeo pensi, et quod vicissim, quanti a te fiam, numquam me paenitebit, et quod Palladio factum volo, ne lateant honesta prolatu. Cura ut valeas et quia tibi facultas scribendi praesto est, adhibe voluntatem. Vale.

Translation

1. I almost wrote a brief and succinct letter to you, since I had nothing worth mentioning, and in the absence of events there is no value in indulging in wordiness. But in a timely way the declamation of our teacher of rhetoric, Palladius, has increased the letter's length. That declamation, which pleased the most eminent literati, ought not be unknown to you. So, since such a report would satisfy both my sense of responsibility and your interests, I dictated a faithful account of what I had heard before his words had escaped from my ears, when the meeting had just broken up and my judgment of it was still fresh. 2. The recent guest moved Latin listeners at the Athenaeum[3] by the artfulness of his division, by the richness of his invention, by the gravity of his thoughts, and by the brilliance of his words. I declare my own opinion; he is as distinguished in oratory as in character. At this time our fellow countrymen, who often disagree among themselves about other matters, reached a

unanimous judgment in praise of this man. I really believe, nor is my faith misplaced, that he comes from a line of rhetoricians, for his stock is recognized as full of talent. It is not only appearance or complexion that marks descendants as doing honor to their ancestors; nature has more certain grounds for making such claims. Thinking and speaking well are inherited by birth, not by a legal document. Others are taught this skill; this man was born with it. 3. I did not believe that I should be silent about these matters, my lord,[4] because I consider nothing of greater importance than my affection for you and because I in turn will never regret the esteem in which you hold me and, finally, because I am promoting Palladius's interests so that his noteworthy talents may not lie hidden from public view. Take care of your health, and since you have the ability to write at your disposal, show also the willingness. Farewell.

Notes

1. According to Symmachus (*Letters* 1.94, 3.50) and Sidonius Apollinaris (*Letter* 5.10.3), Palladius was summoned to court at Trier in 379. Hence, this letter preceded that summons.

2. For more on Palladius, see Palladius 12, *PLRE* 1:660.

3. I print the emendation of the text supported by Cameron 2011, 537. The text printed by Seeck introduces an unattested Greek word (λόγος) into the corrupted passage. The Athenaeum is an odeum in Rome where recitations took place.

4. For *dominus* in fourth-century usage, see 38 n. 13 above.

Letter 1.16: Symmachus to Ausonius
Date: 376–380[1]

In a bantering manner, Symmachus complains that he has been slighted by Hesperius, Ausonius's son; a rumor, not a private letter, had informed Symmachus of Hesperius's announced promotion to an office, probably proconsul of Africa (376–377) or possibly praetorian prefect of Gaul (378). Hesperius, whose full name is Decimius Hilarianus Hesperius, had a successful career in state government, aided in large measure by his father's influential connections. Symmachus, for his part, was eager to be on good terms with Hesperius as well as Ausonius, as shown by this letter and the inclusion of Symmachus's correspondence with Hesperius (*Letters* 1.75–88) in book 1.[2]

Text

1. Saepe unanimitatis tuae sermone convenior, ut epistulis quas ad me cura propensiore misisti, vel sero rescribam. Quibus ego, ut quaequae mihi

redditae sunt, actutum pari religione respondi, quia neque rescriptorum ratio neque amoris vicissitudo sinebat me diutius desidere. Nunc quoque agere me gratias atque habere protestor, quod prospera nuntiorum clam me esse non pateris. Haec et talia prioribus quoque litteris tecum fueram conlocutus; sed si te tabellarii sermonis mei conpotem reddiderunt, congesta non onerant. Malo quippe aures tuas iterando obtundere quam fraudare reticendo. 2. Fratris mei Hesperii honore exulto, taciturnitate convulneror. Nam si me sui amantem usu rerum probavit, scriptis debuit famam praevenire, quae diu incerta fluxam fidem gaudiis exhibebat. Ipse igitur nuntius communis boni esse debuerat, ut epistulae adsertio nihil relinqueret opinionis ambiguo. Sed dicis eum pudore praestrictum successuum suorum vitasse iactantiam. Quisquamne, cum de se apud se ipsum loquitur, erubescit? Quid quod eam rem mihi supersedit ingerere quam iuste ad utrumque noverat pertinere? Verum ego, ut religiose ista conqueror, ita libenter omitto, quia nec amori in vos meo convenit silere quod doleam, nec amicitiae incussi doloris transire mensuram. Vale.

Translation

1. Often by the expression of your devotion[3] I am compelled to write back, even if belatedly, to the letters that you, with more urgent care, have sent me. Every time a letter has been handed to me, I have responded immediately with equal conscientiousness, for neither the practice of our correspondence nor the mutuality of our affection allowed me to defer action longer. Now, too, I declare that I am grateful and appreciative because you do not allow good news to be kept secret from me. I had also spoken with you of these and other such matters in an earlier letter, but even if the letter carriers have apprised you of my words, reiteration is not burdensome. Indeed, I prefer to buffet your ears by repetition than to defraud them by silence. 2. I rejoice in the office of my brother Hesperius,[4] but I am wounded by his silence. For if he has confirmed through experience my affection for him, he ought to have forestalled with a letter the rumor that, long uncertain, offered only unreliable assurance of the happy news. He himself ought to have been the messenger of shared good fortune, so that the affirmation of a letter would leave nothing to the uncertainty of conjecture. But you say that, constrained by modesty, he had avoided boasting about his successes. Who, when he speaks about himself among his own family, blushes? Why did he refrain from telling me about a matter that he knew rightfully concerned both of us? But, although I complain about those things in good conscience, yet I stop doing so willingly, since it neither suits my affection for you to be silent about what causes me pain, nor my friendship for you to exceed due measure in the grief that has been inflicted. Farewell.

Notes

1. See the introduction to *Letters* 1.75–88 (pp. 145–46) for the contested dating of Hesperius's prefectureships. His earliest office was held in 376 and his last attested office in 380, hence the dating for this letter is 375–380.

2. For more on Ausonius's son Decimius Hilarianus Hesperius, see Hesperius 2, *PLRE* 1:427–28, and the introduction to *Letters* 1.75–88 (pp. 145–46).

3. "Devotion" is used here to translate the Latin term "unanimitas," which means, literally, "oneness of feeling" or "unity of purpose." It is frequently used as a title of address in the fourth century; see Souter 1997 s.v.; Bruggisser 1993, 155–58, who notes that Symmachus uses this word fifteen out of nineteen times for members of his family by blood or by marriage. As Callu (1972, 218 n. 4) observed, the frequency of this term in Symmachus's letters demonstrates that it is not a word reserved for Christian discourse.

4. Symmachus's reference to Hesperius, Ausonius' son, as "brother" or *frater* is not a sign of kinship but rather standard epistolary vocabulary to indicate close friendship. For other examples of *frater* to indicate close friendships in book 1, see *Letters* 1.43 for a certain Iulianus; 1.70 for Magnus and Magnillus; and 1.90 for Marius. There are no less than two pages listing "brothers" in V. Lomanto's *Concordance* to Symmachus's works (1983). Nonetheless, Symmachus's usage of *frater* has misled some scholars to posit family ties where none exist. So, for example, in *Letter* 1.63, when Symmachus addresses Syagrius in this way, Callu (1972, 82, ad loc.) sees it as evidence that Syagrius was a relative of Symmachus; so also Barnes 1992, 7–13. In *Letter* 1.16, the word *frater* has taken on an added metaphorical meaning, since Ausonius is represented as Symmachus's "spiritual father," thus making Hesperius his "spiritual brother." This metaphor is not, however, developed; see *Letters* 1.75–88.

Letter 1.17: Symmachus to Ausonius
Date: Probably 377–379[1]

This letter provides a fascinating glimpse at how private friendships influenced public policy in the late Roman Empire. Symmachus recommends to Ausonius a certain Ambrosius,[2] who was sent as a legate to the imperial court by the provincial assembly of Sicily. Ambrosius did not feel as if his local ties were enough, so he turned to an influential patron, Symmachus, to advance his case even before arriving at court or presenting his arguments. Symmachus often took on this role as intercessor for cities or provinces with the imperial court. Acting as broker for local elites in places where Symmachus had property enabled Symmachus to exercise control over his distant estates as well as augment his influence.[3]

Text

Ambrosium de summatibus provincialis fori ad dominos et principes nostros Siciliae commune legavit variis instructum mandatis, quae spectare visa sunt bonum publicum. Huic si fautor accesseris, futurum reor ut illi pro labore fructus adcommodet. Quaeso igitur vel legationis merito vel meo nomine in optimum virum bene consulas, qui satis animi confirmatus est, suffragio tuo successuram facilitatem petitionibus promovendis. Vale.

Translation

The Assembly of Sicily[4] has chosen Ambrosius, one of the foremost men in the public courts of the province, to send to our lords and rulers, with various injunctions judged to concern the public good. If you will support him as his patron, I think that he will obtain a fruitful outcome for his efforts. So I ask that you show favor to this excellent man, either because of the merit of his embassy or because he has my name to support him, for he is convinced that your patronage will facilitate the promotion of his petitions. Farewell.

Notes

1. This dating is based on the likelihood that Ausonius held high office in these years and could thus aid Symmachus's request.

2. Ambrosius is Ambrosius 5 *PLRE* 1:52–53; although he may have been an advocate, as the *PLRE* claims, the Latin does not state this.

3. See on this phenomenon Weisweiler forthcoming.

4. The earliest attestation for the assembly of Sicily comes from the reign of Constantine (*CIL* 6:31961 = *ILS* 8843, 312–324). Cecconi (1994, 83–106) and Jones (1986, 1:336–337, 763–66) have described how in the fourth century the political and religious functions of provincial assemblies changed as a result of the expansion of government undertaken by Diocletian and Constantine. The religious duties of these assemblies were also altered over time, as the emperors embraced Christianity. So, for example, the games associated with the imperial cult and organized by provincial assemblies were increasingly justified as "entertainments" and celebrated without animal sacrifice; this seems the intent of Constantine's rescript about the imperial cult in Italy (*CIL* 11:5265 = *ILS* 705). Italian local elites sent representatives to communicate with the imperial court as well as to cement ties to senatorial patrons such as Symmachus, to whom they turned for aid.

Letter 1.18: Symmachus to Ausonius
Date: 377–379[1]

Symmachus complains of Ausonius's silence, the reason for which is his undertaking a new and important office at court. According to Symmachus, Ausonius's office allows him "to make judgments about the most important matters" (*summa iudicia*), a phrase that is reminiscent of one used by the historian Ammianus Marcellinus (*summa rerum*, 17.3.4) for the office of praetorian prefect, as Callu (1972, 83 n. 1) observed. If this interpretation is correct, then Symmachus could be referring to Ausonius's appointment either as praetorian prefect of Gaul in 377 or as praetorian prefect of Gaul, Italy, and Africa, a position that he held from 378 to 379. The date of the letter depends on which appointment is in view.

Text

Ego etsi continuis litteris honorem tuum celebrare possem, non satis mihi viderer, proquam res postulat, fungi debitum meum: tantum abest ut operam tibi adsiduitatis exprobrem. Sed ut hoc meae verecundiae conpetit, item tuae humanitatis est studium nostrum pari gratia sustinere. Animadverte quo tendat summa verborum meorum: iamdudum nihil tribuis quod legamus. Totum me, inquies, emancipavit sibi cura praetorii. Verum est: potiris merito summa iudicia, sed maximas ingenii tui vires fortuna magna non onerat. Proinde etiam his rebus adtende, quae ita occupatis nihil molestiae adferunt, ut ipsas molestias plerumque solentur. Vale.

Translation

Even if I were able to celebrate the honor of your appointment by a succession of letters, I would not be satisfied that I was sufficiently fulfilling my obligation as the occasion demands; so far am I from reproaching you for your diligent efforts in your new office.[2] But, as such a course befits my sense of propriety, so it is due to your generosity to support my devotion with equal goodwill. Notice where the gist of my words is leading; for some time now you have given me nothing to read. You will say, "The concerns of the praetorian prefecture have claimed me entirely for themselves." It is true; you deservedly have the right to make judgments about most important matters. But great good fortune does not weigh heavily on the very great resources of your talent. Be attentive, then, to these matters, which are no trouble for busy people but often in fact provide solace from troubles. Farewell.

Notes

1. The dating is based on Ausonius's high office, as discussed in the introduction to this letter (p. 53).

2. The sequence of ideas is somewhat hard to follow because of Symmachus's formal and oblique style. His point is that he is not writing to reproach Ausonius; on the contrary, he cannot write often enough in praise of him. But it would be a failure of epistolary etiquette if Symmachus were not to write and seek a letter in response from Ausonius.

Letter 1.19: Symmachus to Ausonius
Date: 378[1]

This letter is typical of Symmachus's vagueness about specific details when writing letters; he leaves out both the reason and purpose of Potitus's[2] visit to Ausonius. Like Symmachus, Potitus owned property in Rome. He was an influential and wealthy man in his own right, as is indicated by Symmachus's reference to him as a "brother" (*frater*), a term he used also for Hesperius (*Letter* 1.16.2), and by the "different" circumstances of the recommendation Symmachus provides for him. As this letter shows, Potitus was a member of Symmachus's circle of friends in Rome.[3]

Text

Qui sua fiducia deseruntur, epistulas meas in usum commendationis accipiunt. Id nunc aliter est. Nam fratri meo Potito hac condicione litteras dedi, ut eas ipse commendet. Est enim nihilo secus atque ego sum de summatibus amicorum tuorum. Qui ubi te conpotem fecerit praesentiae suae, vereor ne excusatio mea ignoscenda non sit. Sed si mihi placabilitas tua experiundo probe cognita est, futurum reor, non ut me, qui resedi, conlatione venientis alterius incessas, sed ut illum magis pro utroque suscipias. Vale.

Translation

Those who lack confidence in themselves receive my letters to use as recommendations. This case now is different, for I have given a letter to my brother Potitus on this condition, that he himself should recommend it. For he, no less than I, is one of your greatest friends. And when he has made you party to his presence, I fear that my excusing myself will not be forgivable. But if by experience I have rightly assessed your good nature, I think that you will not find fault with me for remaining behind in comparison with this other one, who has made the journey, but that you will rather receive that man in place of both of us. Farewell.

Notes

1. This letter looks to Ausonius's consulship in 379 and makes no mention of Potitius's position as vicar of Rome, from 379 to 380.

2. For laws addressed to Potitus as vicar, see Potitus 1, *PLRE* 1:721.

3. The Potitus in this letter has been identified as the owner of a house on the Aventine Hill in Rome that was large enough to have slaves, one of whose collars noting the house and owner was discovered; see *CIL* 15:7181.

Letter 1.20: Symmachus to Ausonius
Date: 378[1]

The occasion for this letter is Ausonius's invitation to Symmachus to attend the inaugural ceremonies for his consulship that were to be held on 1 January 379 in Milan.[2] According to the rules of late Roman society, it was important for Symmachus to explain his absence in such a way as to avoid offending Ausonius. Hence, Symmachus's extended flattery of Ausonius, taking up more than two thirds of the letter, must be understood as serving this key social function. Section 2 is of special note, for here Symmachus praises Ausonius as the teacher of the future emperor Gratian by comparing this duo to other famous pairs of teachers and students. Lists of such examples may well have been in circulation, and Symmachus's instances, drawn from Roman republican and Greek history, are not extremely recondite. In fact, not all of his examples are apt, as the notes indicate. Symmachus favored these cases and reused them in another work (*Oration* 3.7), but there were obviously other examples that were commonly used, as shown by Ausonius's selection in his *Speech of Thanks for Receiving the Consulship* 7, delivered after receipt of this letter. Only in section 3 does Symmachus turn to justifying his absence from the consular inauguration by alleging ill health and the difficulties of travel in winter. Although both of these reasons may be true, they are, as Symmachus himself notes, conventional excuses.[3]

Text

1. Bene ac sapienter maiores nostri, ut sunt alia aetatis illius, aedes Honori atque Virtuti gemella facie iunctim locarunt conmenti, quod in te vidimus, ibi esse praemia honoris, ubi sunt merita virtutis. Sed enim propter etiam Camenarum religio sacro fontis advertitur, quia iter ad capessendos magistratus saepe litteris promovetur. Haec parentum instituta consulatus tui argumenta

sunt, cui morum gravitas et disciplinarum vetustas curulis sellae insigne pepererunt.

2. Multi posthac adnitentur artes bonas ut laudis germina et matres honorum, sed cui eveniet aut tam felix discipulus aut tam memor debitor? An ignoramus magnum illum, cui supra votum fortuna fluxit, Stagiritae suo nihilum commodasse? nisi quia Ennio ex Aetolicis manubiis captiva tantum chlamys data Fulvium decolorat? enim vero neque Panaetio Africanorum secundus neque Opillo Rutilius vel Cineae Pyrrhus aut Metrodoro suo Mithridates Ponticus liberalium disciplinarum pretia solverunt. At nunc eruditissimus imperator et opum largus et honorum, quasi pro usura tibi prima detulerit, insuper ad sortem fenoris redit.

3. In hac tanta laetitia mea, quibus verbis diluam, quod adesse non possum? Nimis vereor ne, male interpretatus excusationem meam, quantum tibi gratuler, parum credas. optavi ad oculos tuos raptim venire, sed fessus virium, quas diu morbus exhausit, itiones longas et mansiones asperas, tum accessiones frigorum et decessiones dierum quaeque alia inportunitati sunt opportuna vitavi. Si sum tibi spectatus ab animo, quaeso ut aequus sis mihi atque has adlegationes boni consulas. Fors fuat an optineamus apud te veterem gratiam; nunc quod satis est, eluctemur offensam. Vale.

Translation

1. Our ancestors acted well and wisely in this, as in other affairs of that time, when they situated the temples to Honor and Virtue together with a twin façade,[4] recognizing, as we see in you, that wherever the merits of virtue are found, there are the rewards of honor. But, in fact, the cult of the Camenae with its sacred spring is also found nearby, since often the path to obtaining office is advanced through literature.[5] These practices of our ancestors are the hallmarks of your consulship, for weight of character and long experience in the liberal arts have won you the distinction of the curule chair.

2. Many men hereafter will strive to acquire liberal learning as the seedbed of praise and the mother of honors, but what teacher will ever have either so fortunate a student or so mindful a debtor?[6] Do we not know that that great man, whom fortune favored beyond his fondest prayer, gave nothing to his Stagirite?[7] Was not Fulvius also disgraced by his gift to Ennius of just a captured *chlamys* from the spoils of Aetolia?[8] What is more, the second Africanus never made payment to Panaetius for his liberal education, nor did Rutilius to Opillus, nor Pyrrhus to Cineas, nor Mithridates of Pontus to his Metrodorus.[9] But now, our most learned emperor, generous with both wealth and offices, as if he has conferred the highest rank in payment of interest, in addition turns his attention to the principal of the debt.[10]

3. In the midst of my great joy, with what words am I to explain away the fact that I cannot be present? I am very much afraid that you, misinterpreting my explanation, will not sufficiently believe how much I congratulate you. I wanted to come into your sight with all haste, but because I am exhausted and a long illness has drained away my strength, I have avoided long journeys and uncomfortable lodgings, likewise the onset of cold weather and the reduction of daylight and everything else to occasion discomfort. If I am truly esteemed by you, I beg you to be fair to me and to favorably receive these representations. It may be that I will regain my former favor with you; for now, let me strive not to give offense—that is enough. Farewell.

Notes

1. The letter is just prior to the inauguration ceremonies for Ausonius's consulship.

2. See p. 36 above.

3. For Symmachus's attitudes toward travel in general, see Salzman 2004, 72–85. For Symmachus's attitudes toward his health, see Cecconi 2002a, 466–76.

4. The double temple has been traced to the fulfillment of a vow in 222 B.C.E. by M. Claudius Marcellus for victory in the Battle of Clastidium; his son dedicated this double temple in 205 B.C.E. inside the Porta Capena at Rome, near the spring of the Camenae. The double temple of Honor and Virtue and the spring of the Camenae remained venerable sites in the fourth century; the last mention of this temple is in the regionary catalogues of the fourth century. For more on this temple, see Richardson 1992, 190, s.v. Honos et Virtus, Aedes; 64, s.v. Camenae.

5. The cult of the Camenae or Muses, normally associated specifically with poetry, here stands for literature more broadly. Symmachus notes the value of literature (*litterae*) for a public career. His correspondent, Ausonius, used his rhetorical expertise to compose not just literary works but also documents for the imperial bureaucracy. For more on the fourth-century emphasis on rhetorical training and the high status of the grammarian, see Kaster 1988, 97–134.

6. Symmachus refers to Ausonius's student Gratian, whom Ausonius tutored at the imperial court, probably from the summer of 368; see the introduction to *Letters* 13–43, pp. 35–36 and n. 4.

7. The "great man" is Alexander the Great. Symmachus refers to his tutor, Aristotle, by his city of origin, Stagira. He can assume that the learned Ausonius would know the reference.

8. Ennius (239–169 B.C.E.) came to Rome from the Messapii in 204 B.C.E. and was granted citizenship in 184 B.C.E. by Q. Fulvius Nobilior (consul in

153 B.C.E.) as a reward for his literary services. Ennius's reputation rested on his epic poem, the *Annales*, but he was a writer of remarkable versatility, also composing tragedies and satires.

9. Not all the examples Symmachus cites of teacher-pupil relationships are analogous to Ausonius's tutorship of Gratian. The second Africanus, P. Cornelius Scipio Aemilianus Africanus (Numantinus), was a hero in the Numantine war in the second century B.C.E. and patron of writers and philosophers, including the Greek Panaetius. Their bond is generally depicted as a positive one, especially by Cicero (see Cicero, *Tusculan Disputations* 1.81; *Republic* 1.34), but Panaetius was not Scipio's tutor. Aurelius Opillus (late second, early first century B.C.E.) taught philosophy, rhetoric, and grammar and accompanied his patron, P. Rutilius Rufus, into exile at Smyrna (Suetonius, *On Grammarians* 6), ca. 92 B.C.E. There is insufficient evidence to describe the nature of the relationship between Cineas, a Thessalian orator and diplomat, and King Pyrrhus of Epirus. Symmachus's final example is perhaps the most apt, albeit ironic. Metrodorus, identified as the friend of Mithridates VI, king of Pontus, changed sides in a time of war and lent his support to Tigranes II, Mithridates' enemy; to avenge this infidelity, Mithridates had Metrodorus killed, quite the opposite of a reward. This may be the same Metrodorus whom Cicero praised for his memory system (Pliny, *Natural History* 7.88); if so, we see once more the influence of Cicero's writings on Symmachus's letters.

10. The monetary metaphor is a little contrived. Symmachus's point is that Gratian has honored Ausonius with the consulship as if in payment of interest on a loan, but the emperor still feels himself indebted to his former tutor for the principal.

Letter 1.21: Symmachus to Ausonius
Date: late 378–379[1]

Symmachus thanks Ausonius for securing him passes to use the public post for his own purposes. This letter reveals how the late Roman elite used their influence with important people in the imperial administration to advance their interests. Ausonius, as praetorian prefect of Italy, Africa, and Gaul, had such favors at his disposal.[2]

Text

Gaudeo pluris me tibi esse quam ceteros, quando ita animatus es, ut sponte in rem meam consulas nec opperiaris petitiones, sed solam voluntatis meae famam sequaris. Accepi evectiones quattuor inmane quantum commodas in excursus et recursus meorum. Dii te pro tanta gratia munerentur et, quia perfectis atque elatis in cumulum bonis nihil adici potest, velint tuta erga te et propria, quae dederunt. Vale.

Translation

I rejoice that you value me more than all others, since you are so disposed that without prompting you look out for my best interests nor do you wait for my petitions, but pursue only the report of my wishes. I have received four passes for the public post, which are extraordinarily useful for the goings and comings of my people. May the gods reward you for such great beneficence, and, since nothing can be added to your good fortune, which is perfect and at its highest eminence, may they be willing to keep the prosperity they have bestowed upon you safe and sound.[3] Farewell.

Notes

1. Symmachus's remark that Ausonius's fortune has reached its "highest eminence" may indicate that had already been designated for or entered on the consulship. If so, the letter can be dated to late 378/379.

2. For more on the public post system in the late Roman Empire, see Kelly 1998, 162–75.

3. Symmachus invokes the plural "gods" (the unanimous reading of the manuscripts) in his letter to the Christian Ausonius without any hesitation. On this, see 20 nn. 8 and 10 and xlii–xlviii.

Letter 1.22: Symmachus to Ausonius
Date: 378[1]

Although this letter heralds the news of the consulship of Ausonius, which he entered on 1 January 379, its primary purpose is to provide a recommendation for one Patruinus, a client whose business is only vaguely described.[2] Symmachus's protests that his endorsement could add little to Ausonius's evaluation of the man should not be taken literally; they sound formulaic, and the next sentence indicates that, should Patruinus not have such a letter, his request would have been less favorably viewed.

Text

Abundo gaudio, cum te consulem novus annus expectat. Sed nunc transcurso est opus; plenius enim secundis litteris contestabor huiusmodi de te gratulationem. Alius in praesentia mihi sermo sumendus est. Patruinus v. c.

accitu tuo iter adornans in rem suam fore existimavit, si meo testimonio niteretur. Huic ego nihil per me accessurum putavi et tamen deesse nolui, sciens iudicio erga illum tuo nihil adici posse, si scriberem, decessurum tamen aliquid meo officio, si tacerem. Unum est igitur, quod oratum a te atque exoratum volo, ut ineat gratiam suscepti laboris praeter eum fructum, qui illi ex tuo conspectu, tuo congressu, tuo honore proveniet. Vale.

Translation

I am filled with rejoicing, since a new year looks forward to you as consul! But I must be brief here; I will testify to my joy at the news about you more fully in a second letter. For the moment I must take up another topic. Patruinus, a *vir clarissimus*, when preparing to set out at your summons, thought that it would be to his advantage if he had my endorsement to support him. I thought that I would be of no benefit to him at all. Nevertheless, I was unwilling to fail to do this, knowing that nothing could be added to your opinion of him if I were to write, and yet, if I were to remain silent, I would be somewhat delinquent in my duty. So there is one thing that I wish to ask from you and to ask insistently, and that is that he win your goodwill for the task he has undertaken, over and above the benefit he will have from appearing before you, from meeting you, and from honoring you. Farewell.

Notes

1. The date is based on Ausonius's consulship for the following year, 379.

2. The identity of Patruinus is uncertain. He is identified as Patruinus 2, *PLRE* 1:674, but he may also be identical with Patruinus 1, a governor (*consularis*) of Picenum in 355. There is another mention of a Patruinus, perhaps this same man, in Symmachus, *Letters* 8.18 and 8.19, where he is recorded as living in the country in 397.

Letter 1.23: Symmachus to Ausonius
Date: before 375–377[1]

Symmachus complains with some frequency about the shortness of Ausonius's letters. This epistolary brevity can be explained by Ausonius's duties at court, especially the writing demands placed on him as quaestor of the sacred palace (see section 1 below). However, Symmachus's insistence on longer letters is an epistolary commonplace that also intimates how close the correspondents are; only intimates could joke and complain so openly. As befits such a bond, Symmachus's letter is rather long and concludes with an ironic reference to Ausonius's unwillingness to even read this much!

Text

1. Post longum silentium tuum non minus desiderabam quam sperabam litteras largiores. Namque his vicibus humana variantur, ut defectui succedat ubertas. Ea me opinio frustra habuit; siquidem brevis in manus meas pagina recens a te profecta pervenit. Erat quidem illa Atticis salibus aspersa et thymo odora sed parcior, quae magis fastidium detergeret quam famem frangeret. 2. Quid? Si ego cenas dapales et saliare convivium, tum viscerationes atque epulum postulassem, tu mihi mensas secundas et scitamenta exiguae lancis adponeres? Fac veniat in mentem quid Graeca super hoc dicat oratio: parvis nutrimentis, inquit, quamquam a morte defendimur, nihil tamen ad robustam valetudinem promovemus.

3. Putasne me de occupationibus tuis esse taciturum? Quaestor es, memini; consilii regalis particeps, scio; precum arbiter, legum conditor, recognosco; adde huc alia mille rerum, numquam eveniet ut ingenium tuum labor deterat, benignitatem cura flectat, facundiam usus exhauriat. Si diurna negotia numquam distingues quiete, certe antelucano somno nullus indulseris. Detur aliquod tempus officiis! An tibi parum exempli videtur in comico, cum ait: quam vellem etiam noctu amicis operam mos esset dari! 4. Sed cur ego diutius sermonis pauper obgannio? Imitanda est mihi epistula recens, ut cetera morum tuorum. Forte occupatus recusas litteras longiores. Id ita esse, rite coniecto. Video enim quam nolis multa legere, cui vix otium est pauca dictare. Vale.

Translation

1. After your long silence, I was expecting as much as desiring a fuller letter from you, for the cycle of human affairs is such that abundance follows dearth. In that opinion I was deceived, for a short missive recently sent by you has come into my possession. It was indeed sprinkled with Attic wit and scented with thyme but was rather meager, able rather to dispel fastidiousness than assuage hunger.[2] 2. What then? If I had requested a sacrificial meal and a feast fit for the Salii[3] or servings of meat and a public banquet, would you have put out only dessert and delicacies on a little platter? Keep in mind what a Greek oration says about this: although a little nourishment guards us against death, it does not contribute to robust health.[4]

3. Do you think that I will be quiet about your affairs? You are the quaestor, I remember; you are a participant in the imperial council, I know; an arbiter of requests, a drafter of laws, I understand; add to this a thousand other things; never will it happen that your tasks wear away your intellect, that your cares deflect your kindness, that constant use exhausts your eloquence. If you never

take a rest during the business of the day, certainly you will not indulge in sleep in the predawn hours! Let some time be given to your personal obligations! Or do not the words of the comic poet seem enough of a lesson for you, when he says: "How I wish that it were the custom to attend on friends even at night!"[5] 4. But why do I, a man poor in words, go on badgering you any longer? I ought to imitate your recent letter, as I should the rest of your character. Perhaps, as you are so busy, you refuse to receive a longer letter. That is the case, I am not mistaken. Indeed, I see how unwilling you are to read much, since you have scarcely the time to dictate a few words. Farewell.

Notes

1. The dating of this letter depends on Ausonius's position at court; for his career, see the introduction to *Letters* 1.13–43, pp. 35–39.
2. Symmachus plays on this food metaphor, indicating that Ausonius's letter is more like a dainty tidbit rather than a substantial meal.
3. The Salii are priests originally associated with Mars. During March and April, the Salii processed through Rome, performing elaborate ritual dancing and singing. They were known, too, for their banquets; see *OCD*, s.v. *Salii*; and Van Haeperen 2002, 23–24 and 269, on the activities of and references to the Salii after 382, when the emperor Gratian removed public monies from a number of public pagan state cults and priesthoods.
4. See Demosthenes, *Olynthiaca* (*Olynthiac*) 3.39.
5. This is a quotation from Terence, *Adelphoe* (*The Brothers*) 532. Symmachus expects Ausonius to know to which poet he is referring.

Letter 1.24: Symmachus to Ausonius
Date: 370–379[1]

Symmachus's frustration at the failure of the scribe to copy his texts accurately is echoed by other ancient writers, pagan and Christian. This particular scribe had a tall order; Pliny's *Natural History*, an encyclopedia of contemporary knowledge on animals, vegetables, and minerals, comprises thirty-seven books. This letter elucidates how books were produced and circulated; Symmachus describes the practice of hiring scribes as copyists. It is interesting that, despite his own dissatisfaction with the finished product, he is not willing to undertake the corrections on his own.[2]

Text

Si te amor habet Naturalis Historiae, quam Plinius elaboravit, en tibi libellos, quorum mihi praesentanea copia fuit. In quis, ut arbitror, opulentae eruditioni tuae neglegens veritatis librarius displicebit. Sed mihi fraudi non erit emendationis incuria. Malui enim tibi probari mei muneris celeritate, quam alieni operis examine. Vale.

Translation

If you love the *Natural History* that Pliny composed, see here are the books, which I just now have got at my disposal. In them, as I think, the scribe's careless inaccuracy will displease a man of your rich erudition. But neglect of emendation will not be held against me, for I preferred to gain your approval by the speed of my gift rather than by the correction of the work of someone else. Farewell.

Notes

1. There is no certain indication of dating other than that the letter was written after Symmachus had left Gaul, i.e., after 370, and before the last dated letter to Ausonius in the book, i.e., 379.

2. For the practice of emendation (*emendatio*), see Zetzel 1981, *passim.* Hedrick (2000, 183–214) has argued that the production and correction of texts containing classical literature was a significant cultural activity, with political and religious dimensions. This view has not been accepted by all; see, most explicitly, Cameron 2011, 421–526.

Letter 1.25: Symmachus to Ausonius
Date: soon after January 379[1]

Symmachus writes to praise Ausonius's son-in-law, Thalassius. This young man, identified as the son of Severus Censor Iulianus and Pomponia Urbica, came from a landed Gallic family.[2] Thalassius was the second husband of Ausonius's daughter but is perhaps best known as the father of the poet Paulinus of Pella, whose long poem, the *Eucharisticos* (*Thanksgiving*), gives us much information about Thalassius's life and career.[3] Thalassius, who had been *vicarius* of Macedonia in 376/377, became proconsul of Africa in 377/378. He had left this office and was passing through Rome on his way home to Bordeaux in the summer of 379. Thalassius no doubt expected that his father-in-law, now consul, would help him to advance his career, but, as far as we know, Thalassius held no further office, although he did live a good many more years in Bordeaux. As his son Paulinus indicates, Thalassius lived through the political upheavals and Gothic invasions in the early fifth century but died in 407, when his home was raided by barbarians (Paulinus of Pella, *Eucharisticos* 236).

Symmachus's *Letter* 1.25 was preserved in certain of Ausonius's manuscripts, which explains why it is also printed in certain modern editions of Ausonius's *Letters*.[4] This is noteworthy, since the survival of this letter with Ausonius's works suggests that Ausonius valued Symmachus's letters and so retained them in his papers or even circulated some of his responses, just as Symmachus kept and then included Ausonius's letter to him in his first book of letters.[5]

Text

Etsi plerumque vera est aput parentes praedicatio filiorum, nescio quo tamen pacto detrimentum meriti sui patiatur, dum personarum spectare gratiam iudicatur. Quaero igitur incertus animi quae mihi nunc potissimum super viro honorabili Thalassio genero tuo verba sumenda sint. Si parce decorem morum eius adtingam, liventi similis existimabor, si iuste persequar, ero proximus blandienti. Imitabor igitur Sallustiani testimonii castigationem: habes virum dignum te et per te familia consulari, quem fortuna honoris parti maiorem beneficiis suis repperit, emendatio animi et sanctitas potioribus iam paravit. Vale.

Translation

Although praise of children in the presence of their parents is generally truthful, in some degree nevertheless it suffers a loss of value when it is judged to be directed at winning the favor of the interested parties. So I am uncertain and wonder how best to express myself now about your son-in-law, the distinguished man Thalassius. If I touch sparingly on the beauty of his character, I will be thought to be acting like a jealous person; if I pursue it as it deserves, I will border on the flatterer. I will therefore imitate the succinctness of Sallust's commendation: "You have a man worthy of you" and, through you, of a consular family; [6] a man whom Fortune, in bestowing her honor, has found greater than her rewards; a man whose upright character and personal integrity have prepared him for greater things. Farewell.

Notes

1. This letter is dated on the basis of Ausonius's consulship.

2. Thalassius 3, *PLRE* 1:887–88, is identified with the father of Paulinus of Pella; see 64 n. 3 below.

3. For Paulinus of Pella, see Paulinus 10, *PLRE* 1:677–78. The *Eucharisticos* was written ca. 459/460, when Paulinus was eighty-three years old.

4. See, for example, Ausonius, *Letter* 18.3 (Evelyn-White 1919, 2:10–11). Green (1991, xlx) notes that it is found in manuscripts V and H, but he does not include Symmachus's *Letter* 1.25 in his now-definitive edition of Ausonius's *Letters*.

5. For discussion of the manuscripts of Ausonius's *Letters*, see Green 1991, 606–7; 1980, 191–211; Sivan 1993, 148–58.

6. Symmachus is citing Sallust, *Bellum Iugurthinum* 9.2: "En habes virum dignum te et avo suo Masinissa" ("You have in him [Jugurtha] a man worthy of yourself and of his grandfather Masinissa").

Letter 1.26: Symmachus to Ausonius
Date: 377–379[1]

The man to whom Symmachus entrusted this letter is called a *familiaris*, a word that can mean either a friend or client, as was Barachus in *Letter* 1.29. Friends typically acted as letter carriers (e.g., Julian, *Letter* 1.1; 1.32, Wright 1913–1923).[2] Often, especially when a friend was conveying the letter, he relayed personal information from the sender orally, as *Letter* 1.28 makes clear.

Text

Utor apud te fiducia, quam dedisti. Dudum parcus es litterarum, sed non imitabor exemplum, ut qui noverim viro in specula honorum locato et ideo varia et magna curanti non tam studium deesse quam copiam. Ea quippe natura rerum est, ut quae praeter industriam negleguntur ignoscenda ducamus. Ego tamen securus, ut soleo, amoris tui officium sollemne non renuo in summa gratia et honore positurus, si familiari meo, qui has tibi litteras dabit, fructus aliqui pro tanta in nos sedulitate responderit. Vale.

Translation

I am relying in your case on the confidence that you have inspired in me.[3] For a long time now you have been sparing in your letters, but I will not imitate your example, since I know that a man placed at the pinnacle of office[4] and therefore concerned with various and important matters lacks not so much the desire to write as the opportunity. For it is in the nature of the case that we think unintentional negligence should be forgiven. Still secure, as always, in your affection, I do not shirk my customary duty, and I will consider it the highest favor and honor if, out of your devotion to me, some benefit should accrue to my friend who delivers this letter to you. Farewell.

Notes

1. The reference to Ausonius's holding the "pinnacle of office" provides the evidence for the dating at any point during one of his high offices, likely the prefectureship or consulship in 379.

2. On the role of the letter carrier, see Gorce 1925, 205–47.

3. Symmachus's point seems to be that, although Ausonius has not written recently, their past relations inspire confidence in a sustained friendship.

4. The phrase *in specula honorum locato*, "placed at the pinnacle of office," is identified as a Plinian metaphor by Callu (1972, 90 n.1), who cites as parallels Pliny, *Letters* 2.12.3, 3.18.3; *Panegyric* 86.4. Some echoes of Pliny's language are to be expected in Symmachus's letters; see the introduction, xxi–xxii and lxii–lxiii.

Letter 1.27: Symmachus to Ausonius
Date: probably 378[1]

Text

Quid agam, scire postulas. Opperior in dies litteras, quales nunc mihi facultas tua promittit, amor semper exhibuit. Sum vero praesentium laetus, ut qui sciam nihil insidiatori meo loci relictum atque insuper tibi, cui factum semper volo, meritam polliceri fortunam. Ergo quando ita res tulit, ut sollicita mutarentur, optati sermonis tui fructum feramus, qui animum mihi exaugeat atque indicet pro tanta retro familiaritate mei te oppido esse cupientem. Vale.

Translation

You ask to know what I am doing. I am waiting from day to day for a letter from you of the kind that you now have the capacity to promise me and that expresses the affection you have always shown. But I am truly joyful at the present news, as I know that no opportunity is left for my assailant[2] and, moreover, that you are promised the outcome I always desire for you, the good fortune you merit. So, since it has come about that our anxieties have changed, let me win the benefit of a much-desired letter to bolster my spirits and to show that in accordance with our great and long-lasting friendship you are thoroughly devoted to me. Farewell.

Notes

1. The letter has been dated to the period after Ausonius's departure from the office of praetorian prefect of Gaul, Italy, and Africa in 378–379

and before his consulship in 379, on the assumption that the "good fortune" to come is his consulship. This is probable, but the lack of specifics does not allow certainty.

2. It is not at all clear who or what Symmachus is referring to when he talks of "his assailant."

Letter 1.28: Symmachus to Ausonius
Date: 375–379[1]

This letter makes explicit why Symmachus so often omits details from his correspondence: it was typical for the letter carrier to deliver personal news orally.[2] Here the carrier is a certain Claudius. The tone suggests that Claudius was a young man. This may be the same Claudius who was subsequently consular of Tuscany in 389 and perhaps, too, father of the poet Rutilius Claudius Namatianus.[3]

Text

Facis pro mutua diligentia et antiquitate amicitiae nostrae, quod honorem tuum vires meas esse confirmas. Convenit dictum cum fide morum tuorum nec umquam te dissimilem scriptis talibus dies arguit. Modo fortuna munifica prosperorum secundet optata. Longum de his loqui cautio est, ne blanditiae longiores corrumpant veri dignitatem. Si quid de me scito opus erit, frater meus Claudius et cultui tuo deditus et studii mei gnarus expediet. Vale.

Translation

You act in accordance with our mutual regard and the long duration of our friendship in assuring me that your office means power for me. This sentiment is consistent with the loyalty of your character, and never has the passage of time shown you untrue to expressions of this kind. Let Fortune only be generous with prosperity and favor your vows. But I must take care not to speak at length on these matters, lest overlong compliments destroy the high standing of truth. If you need to know anything about me, my brother Claudius, a man dedicated to your service and well aware of my devotion to you, will inform you. Farewell.

Notes

1. This letter is certainly after Ausonius held a high office, either that of quaestor or prefect of Gaul, Italy, and Africa, and consul. It was sent before Ausonius left office in 379.

2. For more on this convention, see the introduction, liii–liv.
3. For more on this man, see Claudius 5 and 6, *PLRE* 1:208.

Letter 1.29: Symmachus to Ausonius
Date: 370–379[1]

This is an amusing letter of recommendation. Symmachus makes the claim that he does not need to be a practitioner in order to judge philosophy, art, indeed, all cultural accomplishments, and he demonstrates his cultural literacy with references to several well-known works of classical Greek art. Such allusions were well-known to Ausonius, who had written epigrams on philosophers and no less than eight epigrams on a famous work of art, the heifer sculpted by Myro.[2] But Symmachus undercuts his claim to cultural connoisseurship with his ironic conclusion to this letter; even if his claim to being a judge of all culture is suspect, his recommendation is not. We know nothing about the subject of this recommendation, the philosopher Barachus, other than what Symmachus tells us about him.[3]

Text

Nihil moror ceteros, vulgus ignobile, qui philosophiam fastu et habitu mentiuntur. Paucos et in his praecipue familiarem meum Barachum nostra aetas tulit, quorum germana sapientia ad vetustatem vegeret. Tune, inquies, audeas de philosophis iudicare? Licet alienas spectare virtutes. Nam et Phidiae Olympium Iovem et Myronis buculam et Polycliti canephoras rudis eius artis hominum pars magna mirata est. Intellegendi natura indulgentius patet. Alioqui praeclara rerum paucis probarentur, si boni cuiusque sensus etiam ad inpares non veniret. Concede igitur mihi de Baracho testis officium et amicitiam viri prudentis amplectere, cuius exploratio brevi faciet, ut mihi de omnibus quae scio facile credas, cum videas me nec in his falsum esse quae nescio. Vale.

Translation

I pay no regard to everyone else, an ill-bred crowd, who in their pride and manner of comportment ape philosophy. Our age has brought forth few philosophers, and among these in particular my friend Barachus, whose true wisdom has the vigor of ancient times. So, you will say, do you dare to make judgments about philosophers? A man may judge skills he does not himself possess. A great majority of humankind is ignorant of the art of sculpture yet has admired the Olympian Jove of Phidias, the heifer of Myro, and the Canephorae of Polyclitus.[4] It is the nature of human intelligence to extend itself with some latitude. Otherwise, if a sense of some special excellence did not also affect those unequally gifted, objects of particular distinction would be appreciated by only a few. So, allow me to serve as witness for Barachus and you embrace the friendship of this wise man. Your acquaintanceship with him will soon make you readily believe me about everything that I know, since you see that I am not untruthful even concerning things that I do not know. Farewell.

Notes

1. See 63 n. 1 above.

2. For epigrams on philosophers, see Ausonius, *Epigrams* 30, 31 (Green 1991, 74); for the Heifer of Myro, see Ausonius *Epigrams* 63–68 (Green 1991, 82–83).

3. See Barachus, *PLRE* 1:146.

4. These great works of art were widely known through Roman copies and much discussed. For the collecting of such works in late antiquity, with special reference to Ausonius, see Stirling 2005, 138–64.

Letter 1.30: Symmachus to Ausonius
Date: 370–379[1]

The subject of this letter, a certain Rusticus, was detained in Rome for reasons that are left vague. It is possible, but not certain, that this Rusticus can be identified with Septimius Rusticus, consular of Campania in the late fourth/early fifth centuries.[2] Although Ausonius cultivated friendships with Symmachus and other aristocrats in Rome such as Sextus Petronius Probus, he had not yet visited the city, and most scholars agree that he probably never did.[3]

Text

En tibi Rusticum vix urbanis negotiis absolutum, cui volo pro nostra amicitia morarum culpam remittas. Neque enim laboris fuga indulsit quieti. Difficile est hinc abire, cum veneris; adeo si contemplari maiestatem urbis nostrae velis, cito tibi Rusticus videbitur revertisse. Sed de hoc non laboro, quando ita es ingenio placabili inter reliqua virtutum, ut boni consulas errata leviora. Illud me orare inpensius convenit, tanta ut animo tuo scribendi cura sit, quanto me amore dignaris. Vale.

Translation

Here I give you Rusticus, just now freed from his business in the city. I hope on the strength of our friendship that you will forgive him his fault in being late. It is not that he fled from hard work and abandoned himself to ease. It is difficult to leave here once you have come, so much so that if you were willing to contemplate the majesty of our city, Rusticus will seem to you to have returned quickly. But I do not want to belabor this point, since among your other virtues you are of such an agreeable nature that you interpret charitably slight faults. It is fitting that I beg you with special urgency that your concern for writing to me match the affection in which you think right to hold me. Farewell.

Notes

1. See 63 n. 1 above.

2. See Rusticus 3, *PLRE* 1:787.

3. For some of the implications of Ausonius's not visiting Rome, see Salzman 2002, 71–73. For more on Sextus Petronius Probus, see the introduction to *Letters* 56–61, pp. 117–19.

Letter 1.31: Symmachus to Ausonius
Date: 370–379[1]

Symmachus's *Letter* 1.31 is also printed in certain editions of Ausonius's works as *Letter* 1 because it was included in some manuscripts with Ausonius's works.[2] However, in the most recent and authoritative edition of Ausonius's writing by R. P. H. Green, Symmachus *Letter* 1.31 appears only in an appendix; there is no evidence that Ausonius circulated *Letter* 1.31 with his own letters, and the inclusion of *Letter* 1.31 in just three of Ausonius's manuscripts does not suggest that it was a standard part of subsequent editions either.[3] In contrast, Symmachus explicitly and intentionally included both his *Letter* 1.31 and Ausonius's response to it (Ausonius *apud Symmachum*, *Letter* 1.32) in the book of letters that he published.[4]

Symmachus *Letter* 1.31 is interesting in no small part for the insights it provides into the circulation, publication, and ownership of ancient texts. Symmachus states that he received a "little book" of Ausonius's poems but defends himself against a complaint by Ausonius (in a letter we do not have) that he (Symmachus) had divulged these poems before Ausonius had been willing to allow them to circulate. Symmachus's position—that a work of art once circulated has a life of its own—should not be taken to mean that ancient works, once circulated, were viewed as copyrighted in any modern sense of the term (see Gaius 2.73, 77). Indeed, readers could change texts, as could scribes, and authors could revise and recirculate works, especially poems, often adding new dedications. So Ausonius, for example, added a preface written for a general reader to his eulogy for his father in his poem *Epicedion in Patrem*. He also revised and rededicated poems, as he seems to have done for his poem the *Technopaegnion*.[5]

Unfortunately, Symmachus does not indicate which book of poetry he has received from Ausonius. Since this letter (1.31.1) contains language found also in Ausonius's *Technopaegnion*, a work that Ausonius also refers to as a "little book" (*libellus*; Ausonius, preface to *Technopaegnion*), some have thought that the poetry book mentioned here by Symmachus was an early version of that poem.[6] More probably, as L. Cracco Ruggini has proposed, this letter refers to the poem *Griphus ternarii numeri* or *Riddle on the Number Three*, dedicated to Symmachus, by Ausonius.[7] The distinctive Greek word ἀμουσότερος in the prefatory letter to that poem (*Riddle on the Number Three* line 6, Green 1991, 111) was echoed by Symmachus, *Letter* 1.14.1, a point that suggested to Cracco Ruggini that Symmachus had already received Ausonius's dedicatory letter and poem. There are other echoes in Symmachus's letter of the complimentary language used by Ausonius to address Symmachus in the dedicatory preface to the *Griphus*. So, when considering the recipient of the *Griphus*, Ausonius chose Symmachus "alone of all men" ("ex omnibus … unum semper elegerim," line 8, Green 1991, 111). Symmachus returned the compliment when here he declared "there is no human being whom I esteem more than you" ("neminem esse mortalium quem prae te diligam," *Letter* 1.31.1).[8]

Even if the poem alluded to in Symmachus's *Letter* 1.31 cannot in the end be identified with complete certainty as the *Riddle on the Number Three*, the inclusion of this letter in this book helps establish Symmachus's literary credentials as an equal of Ausonius, one of the foremost poets of the age.

Text

1. Merum mihi gaudium eruditionis tuae scripta tribuerunt, quae Capuae locatus accepi. Erat quippe in his oblita Tulliano melle festivitas et sermonis mei non tam vera quam blanda laudatio. Quid igitur magis mirer, sententiae incertus addubito, ornamenta oris an pectoris tui. Quippe ita facundia antistas ceteris, ut sit formido rescribere, ita benigne nostra conprobas, ut libeat non tacere. Si plura de te praedicem, videbor mutuum scabere et magis imitator tui esse adloquii quam probator. Simul quod ipse nihil ostentandi gratia facis, verendum est genuina in te bona tamquam adfectata laudare. Unum hoc tamen a nobis indubitata veritate cognosce: neminem esse mortalium quem prae te diligam; sic vadatum me honorabili amore tenuisti.

Sed in eo mihi verecundus nimio plus videre, quod libelli tui arguis proditorem. 2. Nam facilius est ardentes favillas ore comprimere quam luculenti operis servare secretum. Cum semel a te profectum carmen est, ius omne posuisti. Oratio publicata res libera est. An vereris aemuli venena lectoris, ne libellus tuus admorsu duri dentis uratur? Tibi uni adhoc locorum nihil gratia praestitit aut dempsit invidia. Ingratis scaevo cuique proboque laudabilis es. Proinde cassas dehinc seclude formidines et indulge stilo, ut saepe prodaris. Certe aliquod didascalicum seu protrepticum nostro quoque nomini carmen adiudica. 3. Fac periculum silentii mei, quod, etsi tibi exhibere opto, tamen spondere non audeo. Novi ego quae sit prurigo emuttiendi operis quod probaris; nam quodam pacto societatem laudis adfectat, qui aliena bene dicta primus enuntiat. Ea propter in comoediis summatem quidem gloriam scriptores tulerunt; Roscio tamen adque Ambivio ceterisque actoribus fama non defuit. Ergo tali negotio expende otium tuum et novis voluminibus ieiunia nostra sustenta. Quod si iactantiae fugax garrulum indicem pertimescis, praesta etiam tu silentium mihi, ut tuto simulem nostra esse, quae scripseris. Vale.

Translation

1. Your erudite writings brought me pure joy when I received them at Capua. They possessed a certain gaiety, coated in Tullian honey,[9] with some praise of my language, more flattering than truthful. So I hesitate in my opinion what to admire more: the distinction of your art or your heart.[10] Indeed, you so excel all others in eloquence that I am fearful of writing back, yet you speak so generously of my writing that it is a pleasure not to remain silent. If I say more about you, I will seem to be "engaging in mutual back-scratching" and to be more an imitator than an admirer of your words.[11] At the same time, because you yourself do nothing just for show, I must beware of praising your authentic good qualities as if they were affectations. Nevertheless, be assured by me of this one indisputable truth: there is no human being whom I esteem more than you, and so you have me bound to you with a love that brings me honor.

But you seem to me much too modest in accusing me of betraying your little book. 2. For it is easier to hold burning coals in one's mouth than to keep hidden this brilliant work. Once a poem has left you, you have abandoned all rights.[12] Words once made public are free property. Or do you fear the venom of a jealous reader lest your little book smart at the gnawing of a harsh critic's tooth?[13] You alone so far have acquired nothing because of favoritism and lost nothing because of envy. Like it or not, the malicious and the honest all consider you praiseworthy. So from now on put aside your baseless fears and give free rein to your pen so that you may often be betrayed. At least assign to my name some didactic or hortatory poem, too.[14] 3. Put my silence to the test; even though I wish to show that I can do it, yet I do not dare to guarantee it. I know how great is the itch to blurt out a work that you have admired, for somehow that man aspires to a share in the praise who first proclaims another's fine compositions. For that reason writers of comedies have received the greatest renown, yet Roscius and Ambivius and other actors have had no lack of fame.[15] So, spend your free time on such business and nourish our hunger with new volumes. But if in your avoidance of self-promotion you fear a garrulous informer, then grant me, too, your silence so that I may safely pretend that what you have written is my own. Farewell.

Notes

1. See 76 n. 2.

2. So Peiper 1886, followed by Evelyn-White 1919, 2:2–5.

3. For the *Letters*' manuscript traditions, see Green 1991, 606–7, 707–8; Ausonius *apud Symmachum*, *Letter* 1.32 = *Letter* 2 in Evelyn-White 1919, 2:6–11; printed as *Letter* 12 in Green 1991.

4. See liv–lxii.

5. For more on Ausonius' method of circulating, revising, and publishing, see the lucid comments by Sivan 1993, 157–58; Green 1991, xlv–xlvii, 273–274 on the *Epicedion*, 584 on the *Technopaegnion*.

6. See Ruggini 1989b, 167–76 for bibliography and 73 n. 11 below.

7. Ruggini 1989b, 167–76.

8. See Green 1991, 444–56.

9. Tullian honey is a reference to Marcus Tullius Cicero, the preeminent orator of the late republic. Cf. Ausonius's intentional echoing of the imagery, Ausonius *apud Symmachum*, *Letter* 1.32.1.

10. "Your art or your heart" is an attempt to represent the common play on words between *oris* and *pectoris*. Symmachus admires both Ausonius's intellect and his kindness in praising his writing.

11. Symmachus uses the proverb "mutuum muli scabunt," "mules scratch each other" (Varro, *Satires*, frag. 321, Astbury 1985), i.e., "you scratch my back, and I'll scratch yours." Ausonius uses this same phrase in *Technopaegnion* 4.

12. The idea recalls Horace, *Epistle* 1.18.71.

13. The language recalls Vergil, *Georgics* 2.378–379.

14. Ausonius responds to this request in his reply, Ausonius *apud Symmachum*, *Letter* 1.32.5. He will send another work, presumably also with another dedicatory letter, hence "assigning" it to Symmachus.

15. Symmachus refers to actors of the republican age who were proverbially talented. Q. Roscius Gallus, a freedman of Lanuvium, was raised to equestrian rank by Sulla and defended by Cicero in the *Pro Roscio* (see Horace, *Letter* 2.1.82). Ambivius was an actor and theater director who produced all the plays of Terence (Terence, *The Mother-In-Law*, prologue 2).

Letter 1.32: Ausonius to Symmachus[1]
Date: 370–379[2]

Ausonius's *Letter* replies directly to Symmachus's *Letter* 1.31 and is filled with praise for Symmachus's eloquence. His admiring tone explains in part why Symmachus chose to include it in his first book of letters. *Letter* 1.32, from Symmachus's mentor and "literary" father, thus neatly parallels the letter by Symmachus the elder to his son, *Letter* 1.2, which similarly praised the younger man's eloquence. By including these two letters from his two "fathers" (note the word "parent," *parens*, in section 4) to testify to Symmachus's eloquence, this book augments the younger Symmachus's literary reputation, a view that these mentors shared with many contemporaries as well as fifth- and sixth-century Roman elites [3]

Text

1. Modo intellego quam mellea res sit oratio, quam delenifica et quam suada facundia. Persuasisti mihi quod epistulae meae apud Capuam tibi redditae concinnatio inhumana non esset, sed hoc non diutius quam dum epistulam tuam legi, quae me blanditiis inhiantem tuis velut suco nectaris delibuta perducit. Ubi vero chartulam pono et me ipsum interrogo, tum absinthium meum resipit et circumlita melle tuo pocula deprehendo. 2. Si vero, id quod saepe facio, ad epistulam tuam redii, rursus inlicior; et rursum ille suavissimus, ille floridus tui sermonis adflatus deposita lectione vanescit et testimonii pondus prohibet inesse dulcedini. Hoc me velut aerius bracteae fucus aut picta tabula non longius quam dum videtur oblectat chamaeleontis bestiolae vice, quae de subiectis sumit colorem. Aliud sentio ex epistula tua, aliud ex conscientia mea.

3. Et tu me audes facundissimorum hominum laude dignari? tu, inquam, mihi ista, qui te ultra emendationem omnium protulisti. Haut quisquam ita nitet, ut conparatus tibi non sordeat. Quis ita Aesopi venustatem, quis sophisticas Isocratis conclusiones? Quis ita ad enthymemata Demosthenis aut opulentiam Tullianam aut proprietatem nostri Maronis accedat? Quis ita adfectet singula, ut tu imples omnia? Quid enim aliud es quam ex omni bonarum artium ingenio collecta perfectio? 4. Haec, domine mi fili Symmache, non vereor ne in te blandius dicta videantur esse quam verius. Et expertus es fidem meam mentis atque dictorum, dum in comitatu degimus ambo aevo dispari, ubi tu veteris militiae praemia tiro meruisti, ego tirocinium iam veteranus exercui. In comitatu tibi verus fui, nedum me peregre existimes conposita fabulari; in comitatu, inquam, qui frontes hominum aperit, mentes tegit, me tibi et parentem et amicum et, si quid utroque carius est, cariorem

fuisse sensisti. 5. Sed abeamus ab his, ne ista haec conmemoratio ad illam Sosiae formidinem videatur accedere.

Illud quod paene praeterii, qua adfectatione addidisti, ut ad te didascalicum aliquod opusculum aut sermonem protrepticum mitterem? Ego te docebo docendus adhuc, si essem id aetatis, ut discerem? Aut ego te vegetum adque alacrem commonebo? Eadem opera et Musas hortabor, ut canant et maria, ut effluant et auras, ut vigeant et ignes, ut caleant admonebo, et si quid invitis quoque nobis natura fit, superfluus instigator agitabo. 6. Sat est unius erroris, quod aliquid meorum me paenitente vulgatum est, quod bona fortuna in manus amicorum incidit. Nam si contra evenisset, nec tu mihi persuaderes placere me posse. Haec ad litteras tuas responsa sint. Cetera quae noscere aves, conpendii faciam. Sic quoque iam longa est epistula. Iulianum tamen familiarem domus vestrae, si quid de nobis percontandum arbitraris, tibi adlego, simul admoneo, ut, cum causam adventus eius agnoveris, iuves studium quod ex parte fovisti. Vale.

Translation

1. Now I understand what a honey-sweet thing speech is, how soothing and persuasive a thing is eloquence. You convinced me that my letter that reached you at Capua was not a monstrous compilation, but I believed this only as long as I read your letter, which, as though soaked in liquid nectar, led me astray as I avidly fixated on your compliments. For when I put down the paper and examine myself, then I taste my own bitter wormwood, and I realize that my cup has been smeared round with your honey.[4] 2. If indeed, as I often do, I return to your letter, I am again ensnared, and again that most enticing and flowery scent of your speech fades away as soon as I stop reading and prevents its sweetness from carrying the authority of evidence. Like the shimmering luster of gold leaf or a colored mist, this letter delights me just as long as I see it, in the manner of that little creature, the chameleon, which takes its color from the objects beneath it.[5] I feel one thing from reading your letter but another from my knowledge of myself.

3. And do you dare to deem me worthy of the praise that belongs to the most eloquent men? You, I say, state this to me, you who have advanced yourself beyond the criticism of all men! There is no one so brilliant that he does not seem tarnished when compared to you. Who so approaches the charm of Aesop, the rhetorical periods of Isocrates? Who so approaches the logical arguments of Demosthenes, the richness of Tully, or the precision of our Maro?[6] Who can pretend to any one of these qualities as fully as you achieve them all? For what else are you than the perfection gathered from every gifted practitioner of the liberal arts?

4. My lord,[7] my son Symmachus, I am not afraid that I may appear to have spoken more flatteringly than truthfully. You have already experienced my trustworthiness in thought and speech when we both, although of unequal age, spent time at court, where you, a fresh recruit, earned the rewards of a veteran, whereas I, already a veteran in years, saw service as a recruit.[8] At court I was truthful to you; still less should you think that I would make up stories when apart; at court, I say, which reveals the faces of men but conceals their thoughts, you recognized that I was both a parent and friend to you, and even dearer, if there is something dearer than those two. 5. But let us leave off these matters, lest the recollection of them seem to come close to the fear felt by Sosia.[9]

Under what pretense did you add that request, which I almost passed over, that I send to you some little didactic work or hortatory text? Shall I teach you, I who still must be taught, if I were still of the age to learn? Or shall I urge you who are quick and alert? I might as well urge the Muses to sing, the seas to surge, the breezes to blow, and fires to grow hot and be the unnecessary instigator to action of whatever else happens in nature without our willing it!

6. One error is enough: that a work of mine was made public to my regret, which by good fortune fell into the hands of friends. For if the reverse had been the case, not even you could persuade me that I was able to win approval. Let this be my response to your letter. I shall dispense with the remaining matters that you wish to know. Even so, this letter is already long. Still, I am dispatching to you Julianus, an intimate of your household, if you think that you have any questions concerning me.[10] At the same time I urge you, when you understand the reason for his coming, to aid him in a pursuit that you have partially encouraged. Farewell.

Notes

1. = Ausonius, *Letter* 2, in Evelyn White 1919 = *Letter* 12, in Green 1991, 207–8.

2. Seeck (1883, 16–18) dated *Letters* 1.31 and 1.32 after 378 on the grounds that Ausonius imitates the unusual vocabulary (such as *delenifica* and *suada* in section 1) found in *Letter* 3.6 of Symmachus, dated to 379/380. But, as Green (1991, 625) points out, it is more probable that it was Symmachus who imitated Ausonius, since it is unlikely that Ausonius saw Symmachus's *Letter* 3.6 to a Julianus, not the same Julianus mentioned in this letter. Moreover, Ausonius's letter could have been written long before Symmachus, *Letter* 3.6. Alternatively, Symmachus and Ausonius may have imitated a third shared source. Hence, we can only be certain that *Letter* 1.32 was written after Symmachus left the emperor's court, i.e., after 370, and in response to Symmachus,

Letter 1.31, also written after 370. Both letters were likely written before Ausonius left office, hence by 379.

3. For more on Symmachus's reputation, see lxvi–lxviii.

4. These are allusions to Lucretius, *On the Nature of Things*, 1.936–950 and 4.11–25.

5. Ausonius has expressed this analogy clumsily. His point is that, just as the chameleon (according to Ausonius) takes its color from the object on which it is sitting and holds on to the color only as long as it is in contact with the object, so he believes Symmachus's compliments only as long as he has the color and charm of Symmachus's eloquence before him; when no longer in visual contact with the words, Ausonius comes to a less positive assessment of his abilities. For the ancient beliefs underlying this analogy, see Green 1991, 626.

6. Like Symmachus, Ausonius evokes great writers to make his point. Among the Greeks he lists are the writer of fables Aesop, the rhetorician Isocrates, and the orator Demosthenes. Among the Romans, Ausonius repeats Symmachus's allusion to Cicero, again using his family name, Tullius, and adds Maro (i.e., Vergil).

7. Ausonius, like Symmachus (e.g., Symmachus, *Letters* 1.15; 2.83; 3.69), uses the word *dominus* as a polite title for a landowner. For the emphasis on *domini* as property owners, see Cooper 2007, 131–42.

8. For the first encounter of Symmachus and Ausonius at the imperial court, see the introduction, xxiii–xxvi. This metaphor is appropriate because the Latin word for service at court was the same as for military service, *militia*.

9. This is an allusion to the fear felt by the slave Sosia in Terence, *Andria* (*The Girl from Andros*) 43–44: "this retelling is like a reproach for a forgotten kindness" ("istaec conmemoratio / quasi exprobatiost immemoris benefici").

10. Julianus may be the advocate noted in *Letter* 1.43. Here Ausonius is recommending him to Symmachus.

Letter 1.33: Symmachus to Ausonius
Date: 375–379[1]

This letter demonstrates that Symmachus was able to be playful. Symmachus jokes with Ausonius on the subject of snails, a delicacy among the Romans, in an attempt to inspire Ausonius to write a letter.[2]

Text

Aiunt cocleas, cum sitiunt umoris atque illis de caelo nihil liquitur, suco proprio victitare. Ea res mihi usu venit, qui desertus pastu eloquii tui meo adhuc rore sustentor. Diu scribendi operam protulisti et vereor ne forte in nos parentis claudat adfectio. Si falsa me opinio habet, facito ut ceteris negotiis tuis respondendi cura praevortat.

Translation

They say that snails, when they thirst for moisture and have none from the heavens, keep themselves alive with their own juices. That fact comes in handy for me, who, bereft of the sustenance of your eloquence, feed myself up to now on my own dew. For a long time you have put off the effort of writing to me, and I fear that perhaps your paternal affection toward me is failing. If I hold a false opinion, ensure that your concern for replying to me takes precedence over your other affairs. Farewell.

Notes

1. The last line suggests that Ausonius holds a high office, such as quaestor or praetorian prefect. Hence the letter is dated to 375–379.

2. Callu (1972, 98 n. 1) cites Plautus, *Captivi* (*The Captives*) 80–81, to show that it was a common belief among the Romans that snails fed themselves on dew.

Letter 1.34: Symmachus to Ausonius
Date: 375–379[1]

Symmachus cleverly incorporates metaphors of work, using the language of business and contract law, to vary his complaint about Ausonius's dilatoriness in writing. The reference to Ausonius's friendship as "interest-bearing" (section 2) provides a memorable last line. This letter should not, however, be taken literally to suggest that Symmachus is truly concerned with the financial rewards of his friendship with Ausonius. Rather, this is a witty variant on an epistolary commonplace that serves to underscore his professed reticence about expressing his feelings. But even as Symmachus articulates his eagerness to maintain their friendship, we should also note that this was a highly advantageous relationship for him. This letter dates to the years when Ausonius was in high public office and so could be of most benefit to Symmachus and to his family and friends.

Text

1. Plenum laboris negotium gero, qui conpellare totiens tacitum persevero. Contra nisi instigare pergo atque exculpere a te aliquid litterarum, gliscet oblivio. Sive igitur hoc officium meum sedulum iudices seu molestum,

stat sententia honorem tuum celebrem praestare colloquiis; adeo mihi veteris in te amoris nulla discessio est. Et merito, nam amicitiae operam nusquam locavi aeque bene. Propterea silentium tuum conqueror. 2. Facit enim tenerior adfectio, ut sit querella proclivior. Mollis est animus diligentis et ad omnem sensum doloris argutus. Si neglegentius tractes, cito marcet ut rosa, si durius teras, livet ut lilia. Legisse me memini vultu saepe laedi pietatem. Quid ille tam serius arbiter super continuo silentio ac dissimulato scribendi munere censuisset? Tecum haec pensius aestimabis, sed mihi religio fuit tegere quae dolebant. Nam ut in te animi usque pendeo, ita opere maximo usuram tuae unanimitatis expecto. Vale.

Translation

1. I am shouldering a burdensome task by persisting so often to address silence. On the other hand, unless I continue to goad you and to extort some letter from you, your forgetfulness will grow. Thus, whether you consider my performing this duty conscientious or annoying, I am determined to maintain frequent communication with you despite your public office, so true is it that there is no break in my old affection for you. And appropriately so, for I have nowhere invested the effort of friendship as well. For these reasons, I complain about your silence. 2. For the more tender the affection, the readier the complaint. The spirit of a loving friend is soft and sensitive to every feeling of pain. If you treat it too neglectfully, it quickly fades, like a rose; if you handle it too harshly, it bruises, like a lily. I remember reading that "dutifulness is often injured by a glance."[2] What would that so severe judge have thought about continued silence and the neglect of the obligation to write? You will reflect on this more carefully yourself, but I felt obliged to conceal what pained me. For, as I continue to depend on you in spirit, so I look forward with the greatest eagerness to the interest from your devotion to me. [3] Farewell.

Notes

1. See 78 n. 1.

2. This echoes of Cicero, *Pro Sexto Roscio Amerino* 13.37: "vultu saepe laeditur pietas." The intent is to defend the conscientious performance of one's duty.

3. For the Latin word *unanimitas*, see 51 n. 3 above. Since it is so often used by Symmachus for members of his family, usage of it here when addressing Ausonius emphasizes the intimacy of their relationship.

Letter 1.35: Symmachus to Ausonius
Date: 375–379[1]

This letter reverses the usual roles of the correspondents, for here Symmachus mentions his time spent at leisure in one of his villas in Campania as partial justification for his own failure to write Ausonius. To a certain degree, this letter balances out the power relations in their depicted relationship by reinforcing the importance of reciprocity. But there is some irony, for while Ausonius attributes his failure to write to the burdens of high office (e.g., *Letter* 1.34), Symmachus has been delinquent on his end because he has been at leisure. Still, as Symmachus observed in his first letter to his father (1.1), leisure time well spent is as important as work in assessing the life of an aristocrat.[2]

Text

Diu in Campaniae secessibus otiatus occasione carui scriptionum. Ideo paulisper sermonis mei circa te munus intepuit, sed, ubi in patriam pedem retuli, antiqua mihi fuit instaurandi officii diligentia. Ergo debito te honore salutationis inpertio utrumque deposcens ut et silentio superiori venia iusta praestetur et praesenti obsequio vicissitudo respondeat. Vale.

Translation

For a long time in retreat in Campania I was at leisure and had no occasion to write. For that reason, my sense of responsibility to write to you cooled for a little while, but when I set foot in my fatherland again,[3] my old diligence in renewing my duty returned. So I am sending you the respectful greetings that I owe you, and I ask for two things: that a deserved pardon be granted for my previous silence and that a response be returned for my current attentions. Farewell.

Notes

1. See 78 n. 1.

2. The theme of *otium/negotium*, leisure/work knits together this first book of letters; see Bruggisser 1993, 51–55.

3. Symmachus's use of the word *patria*, "fatherland," to refer to his home in Rome recalls Pliny the Younger's usage of this word for his area of origin in Italy; see Pliny, *Letter* 7.32.1; and Champlin 2001, 121–28. For more on the relationship of Symmachus's letters to Pliny's letters, see the introduction, lxii–lxiii. Here Symmachus expresses a traditional aristocratic attitude to his

natal home in Rome; for more on his attachment to his ancestral home on the Caelian Hill, see Hillner 2003, 129–45.

Letter 1.36: Symmachus to Ausonius
Date: 375–379[1]

Letter 1.36 tells us that Ausonius traveled, but it omits a key fact: where he traveled to. Most scholars argue, rightly, in my view, that he never visited Rome. Hagith Sivan, Ausonius's biographer, noted that, when Gratian's court left Gaul for Milan, Ausonius went into retirement, moving between Bordeaux and Trier in the years between 379 and 383.[2] Most likely, Symmachus's reference to Ausonius's travels is to his movement in Gaul rather than to some unidentified mission to Milan, as Callu suggests (1972, 100 n. 1), largely on the basis of a reference to Gorgonius's stopping in Ancona (Picenum) before bringing a letter to Ausonius (*Letter* 1.39). This line of argument is far from conclusive. Finally, it is worth noting that Symmachus attributes to Ausonius his own dislike for travel and his own view of it as tedious and tiring.[3]

Text

Interpello occupationes tuas adsiduitate colloquii. Nam et ipse huiusmodi pascor officio et peregrinationem tuam solaciis talibus credo recreari. Tuas autem vicissim litteras expecto, non exigo. Iniurium quippe est magnopere flagitare quod speres, ne, quod est voluntarium, videatur extortum. Sane fratri meo Innocentio gratulor amicitias tuas, priusquam scriberem, contigisse, quia facilior mihi esse coepit eius commendatio quem probasti, quam fuisset incogniti. Itaque hoc unum beneficii loco postulo, ut, qui sui commendatione iam nititur, testimonii nostri gratia cumulatius diligatur. Vale.

Translation

I am interrupting your work by the persistence of my correspondence both because I derive sustenance from duties of this kind and because I believe your travels are refreshed by such comforts. As to a letter from you in return, I anticipate it but do not demand it. For it is inappropriate to ask insistently for what you hope for lest what is given voluntarily appear to have been extorted. Certainly I congratulate my brother Innocentius for having gained your friendship even before I wrote, since a recommendation for a man whom you have already approved of is an easier undertaking than it would have been for a man you did not know.[4] So I ask you for this one kindness, that the man who already has the support of his own recommendation be held in greater esteem because of my endorsement. Farewell.

NOTES

1. The reference to Ausonius's duties in office suggests he was in high office, hence 375–379 is the suggested dating for the letter.

2. Seeck (1883, lxxx) believed that Ausonius never left Gaul, as does Sivan (1993, 139–41); Symmachus, *Letter* 1.30, would suggest that as well.

3. For more on Symmachus's professed disdain for travel, see Salzman 2004, 81–94.

4. The identity of this man, Innocentius, is not known, nor is he noted in *PLRE* 1. Symmachus's letter appears somewhat redundant, as Ausonius is said to have already approved of the man recommended. The artfulness of this letter thus resides in Symmachus's recommendation for a man who has arrived before his recommendation of him.

LETTER 1.37: SYMMACHUS TO AUSONIUS
DATE: 375–379[1]

Symmachus's praise for Ausonius's trustworthiness in section 1 sounds somewhat ironic, given the frequent complaints of earlier letters in the sequence.

TEXT

1. Non frustra praedicant mentes hominum nitere liquido die, coacta nube fatiscere. Meus animus fidem fecit exemplo. Nam quotiens tibi ex sententia <fit>, verbis, quorum mihi alias supellex desit, indulgeo. Quippe laetitia loquax res est atque ostentatrix sui; adeo magnae parti hominum nulla ab hoc morbo cautio est. Patere igitur me, quae ad laudes tuas pertinent, obloquentem, vir quantum hominum in terris est spectatissime, qui et summis copiis vigiliam pro meis rebus adniteris et amicitiam diligentia stabili perseveras. Si fides seria cuiquam fuit, tibi puto esse; quam plerique verbo ostentant, opere deserunt. Quod genus nulli rei est, nisi ad loquendum. 2. Merito processus tuos in meo aere duco, quando iuxta magnae curae sum tibi atque cum maxime fui. Superest tamen aliquid quod huic in me studio adici velim. Nolo memineris quod animo tuo aliquando suscensui. Amor fiduciam nutrit. Quid tam liberum quam amicitia? Negotiis plerumque adposita est expostulatio sine labe concordiae. Ita verum est, quod hodie tibi gratias ago, ut illud non potuerim dissimulare, quod dolui. Cassa fide sunt, qui iugiter blandiuntur. Sed quid diutius ea retexo quorum te oblivisci volo? esto, ut es, benigna semper in me voluntate, quod ego sperandum magis a te sentio quam petendum. Vale.

Translation

1. Not without reason do they say that the minds of men are brilliant on a clear day but grow weak when clouds gather.[2] My mind by its example gives proof of this, for whenever things go to your liking, I find a ready supply of words, which fails me at other times.[3] For, in fact, joy is loquacious and makes an exhibition of itself, so much so that for most people there is no guarding against the disease. Bear with me, then, as I speak about matters that relate to your merits, you who are the most distinguished of all men on earth, who both strive with all your powers to keep watch over my affairs and who maintain our friendship with steadfast constancy. If anyone possesses real trustworthiness, I think it is you. How many parade their trustworthiness in words but fall short in deeds. Trustworthiness of that kind has no substance but is just talk. 2. With good reason I reckon your advancement to be to my profit, since your concern for me is as great as it ever was. Still there remains something that I would like to be added to this zealousness on my behalf. I do not want you to remember that I was at times angry with your state of mind. Love nourishes trust. What is as open as friendship? In public affairs remonstrations are often leveled without destroying concord. It is just as true that I am grateful to you today, as it is that I was not able to hide that fact that I was aggrieved. They can inspire no trust who continually flatter. But why do I any longer go back over what I wish you to forget? Be, as you are, always of goodwill toward me, a sentiment that I realize I should expect from you rather than request. Farewell.

Notes

1. Ausonius's advancement, noted in section 2, suggests he held a high office, hence the dating.

2. This notion is found in other texts, as Callu 1972, 100 n. 2, observes; see, for example, *Collatio Alexandri cum Dindimo* (Kübler 1888, 188,5–7).

3. I follow here the reading suggested by Callu 1972, 101: "… ex sententia <fit>." However, this sentence remains somewhat obscure and may be corrupt in the manuscripts.

Letter 1.38: Symmachus to Ausonius
Date: 375–379[1]

Symmachus's description of Fortune as just, not blind and arbitrary, was a *topos* in letter writing that Symmachus has expressed, echoing the opening lines of Sallust's *Bellum Iugurthum* 1.1.[2] As such a generic notion, this deity could appeal to even a Christian writer such as Ausonius.

Text

Falso creditur, nesciam iudicii esse fortunam; illa vero et praeteritorum memor et praesentium diligens et prudens futuri tibi rependit, quidquid ceteris praestitit. Non ergo vaga neque erratica est, a qua scimus alios donum cepisse, te praemium. Quis tibi honoris, inquies, nostri fecit indicium? Celebritas Famae, cui iusta narranti statim creditur. An opperirer super hoc tuas litteras quas verecundia differebat? Minime; siquidem difficilis est patientia gaudiorum. Fungor igitur, ut vides, partibus tuis et, quae debui cognoscere, malui quodammodo nuntiare. Sed nolo ista properatio litterarum mearum tuum munus inpediat. Scire me, quod nunc scribo, dissimula et tribue quasi novum nuntium, quem ego gratulabor iteratum. Vale.

Translation

People falsely believe that Fortune is incapable of judgment. But truly, mindful of the past, careful about the present, and with foresight for the future, she pays you as your due all that she has given the rest. Fortune, therefore, is not random or erratic, for we know that others have received a gift from her, but you a reward! "Who told you about my honor?" you will ask. The wide currency of Rumor, which because her story was just was instantly believed. Should I, then, wait for your letter about this, which your modesty delayed? Not at all, for patience is hard in the midst of joy. Therefore, as you see, I am playing your role and have chosen, in a certain way, to bring you the news that I should have learned from you. But I do not want the haste of my letter to obstruct the course of your obligation. Pretend ignorance of the fact that I know the things that I now write about and share your news with me as if it were new, at which I, hearing it repeated, will rejoice again. Farewell.

Notes

1. The dating revolves in large measure about the identification of the office (*praemium*) attained by Ausonius. As usual, Symmachus does not specify which honor Ausonius had attained, but his discussion of the office as granted by Fortune suggested to Seeck (1883, lxxxiii) that it was more likely one of Ausonius's earlier offices, and hence he dated it to the years 370/375–378. Callu (1972, 102) dates the letter to the period 373–376 without any explanation. It seems more likely to me that it was one of his later offices. Hence, I suggest a dating of 375–379.

2. Bruggisser 1993, 191–93. M. Marcos suggested this echo of Sallust's *Bellum Iugurthum* 1.1.

Letter 1.39: Symmachus to Ausonius
Date: 375–379[1]

Text

Scio quidem litteras meas tibi sero reddendas, vel propter occupationes quae te in procinctu aliquantisper tenebunt, vel quod frater meus Gorgonius admirator virtutum tuarum diutinae apud Picentes indulgebit quieti. Utut est tamen ista condicio, supersedendum officio non putavi. Fors fuat an haec mature in manus tuas scripta ventura sint. Ego tamen, quantum per commeantes licebit, istius muneris operam non reparcam. Vale.

Translation

I know well that my letter will have to be given to you late, either because of the activities that will occupy you for some time in service or because my brother Gorgonius, an admirer of your virtues, will treat himself to a long break in Picenum.[2] Still, whichever is the case, I did not think that I should neglect my duty. May this letter soon reach your hands. I will still spare no effort in this task, insofar as the travels of letter carriers allow. Farewell.

Notes

1. See 82 n. 1.

2. One reason for the late arrival has to do with the delay of the letter carrier in Picenum, modern Ancona. This letter carrier has been identified with the Flavius Gorgonius 7, *PLRE* 1:399, who held the court office of *comes rei privatae* in 386 and whose sarcophagus, *CIL* 9:5897 = *ILS* 1290, was found in Ancona (Picenum), which was most likely his home. He is one of the many Christians with whom Symmachus maintained friendship ties.

Letter 1.40: Symmachus to Ausonius
Date: 376–377[1]

Letters of recommendation could be somewhat formulaic and repetitive. Hence, it is understandable that several lines of this letter of recommendation for Victor duplicate those in a letter about a certain Eusebius (*Letter* 9.59), with only some slight variation (e.g., Victor is called *sanctus*, "virtuous," but Eusebius is not.) Such doublets are, however, rare in the Symmachan corpus, a testament to the care with which Symmachus approached even standard letters of recommendation and especially those chosen for publication.[2]

Text

Non novum aut incognitum sed conpertum iam fide et sedulitate militiae sanctum Victorem amicum meum promptus commendator insinuo, quem adhoc aevi nulla actuum culpa fuscavit; sed fortunae licentia, quae interdum optimos decolorat, spes eius paulisper infregerat. Quae in integrum saeculi beatitudo restituet, si innocentiam supplicis secundo favore respexeris. Vale.

Translation

I am eager to introduce to you with my recommendation a virtuous[3] man, my friend Victor,who is not a new acquaintance or unknown but proven already in loyalty and zeal of service, a man whose reputation, until this day, no blameworthy action has darkened; but the caprice of Fortune, which at times stains even the best of men, had shattered his hopes for a while.[4] These the happiness of the age will restore to him intact, if you will look with a favorable glance on the innocence of the petitioner. [5] Farewell.

Notes

1. The date of this letter is suggested by the inclusion of the phrase "the happiness of the age" (*saeculi beatitudo*). It seems, as proposed by Callu (1972, 223 n. 6), to be a reference to the expectant times of 376–377, when Gratian had just become Augustus and inspired great hopes for the future as a student of Ausonius.

2. Bruggisser 1993, 320–22, makes this point. It is not coincidental that *Letter* 1.40 is most similar to a letter from book 9, one of the later books that was drawn from the family archives by a later editor; see the introduction, lviii–lxiv.

3. The adjective *sanctus*, "virtuous," is frequent in Symmachus's correspondence and need not imply Christian belief; see Symmachus, *Letters* 1.93; 2.11; 5.16; 8.101. Victor may perhaps be identified with the *agens in rebus* mentioned in Symmachus, *State Paper* 23.8.

4. By invoking the notion of blind Fortune to explain Victor's misfortunes, Symmachus expresses a sentiment about Fortune that is at odds with that used in *Letter* 1.38. Such versatility in the adoption of this *topos* in a letter just two letters after 1.38 indicates the writer's skill as well as his playfulness with the convention.

5. Symmachus speaks of the restoration of Victor's hopes but does not specify the nature of the reversal that Ausonius is in a position to grant.

Letter 1.41: Symmachus to Ausonius
Date: after 370[1]

Text

Facio rem cum tuis moribus tum meo studio congruentem, ut praestantissimo viro amicitias optimi cuiusque conciliem; velut nunc tibi a me traditur philosophiae candidatus, cuius pudorem vel prima facies, cetera bona longus usus expediet. Hunc ego abs te nollem diligi, ni mereretur probari. Sed si bene aestimo, actutum merebitur atque ideo diligetur. De hoc nihil amplius. Neque enim praeiudicio meo debet astringi, cuius ego expecto iudicium. Illud te potius oratum volo, ut in nostri diligentia perseveres. Quod cum efflagito, vereor ne me iniurium putes, qui a te postulem quod sponte praestatur. Vale.

Translation

I am acting in a manner that agrees both with your character and with my own desire in uniting all the best men in friendship with you, the most distinguished of men; so now I introduce to you an aspiring philosopher whose sense of decency will be apparent even at first glance but whose other good qualities a longer familiarity will reveal. I would not wish this man to win your affection, unless he were deserving of your approval. But if I judge him rightly, he will earn this quickly and in this way win your affection. About this, nothing more. For your decision about him, which I await, ought not to be constrained by my prejudgment. Rather, I want to make this request of you, that you continue to hold me in your affection. When I ask for this, I am afraid that you think me unjust in asking for what is granted spontaneously. Farewell.

Note

1. This letter of recommendation for some unnamed philosopher makes no mention of any office held by Ausonius. It may be as early as 370, after Symmachus's return from Gaul.

Letter 1.42: Symmachus to Ausonius
Date: 377–379[1]

Symmachus attributes to Ausonius the aristocrat's traditional profession of distaste for public office.[2] In doing so, Symmachus is including Ausonius as one of "us aristocrats," despite Ausonius's provincial origins and elevation to senatorial status by virtue of his rhetorical abilities and imperial service; these latter accomplishments are emphasized in Symmachus's *Letter* 1.43.

Text

1. Conpensasti longum silentium gemina scriptione. Pariter enim mihi binas litteras praebuisti, ut desiderium meum officio largiore conpleres. Ex quo adverti non voluntatem tibi hactenus sed baiulum defuisse. Neque enim aliter potuisset accidere, ut me tam diu sermonis tui honore fraudares. Merito apud nos in dies singulos tui cultus augescit et iusto cumulo crescit adfectio. Namque ita usu conparatum videmus, ut amicitia bene locata experiundo cottidie provehatur. Sed de ista parte verbis supersedendum est; neque enim me oportet haec dicere quae te malo sentire.

2. Conperi sane ex litteris tuis, quanto opere publici muneris absolutionem requiras et stupere me fateor tantum tibi administrationis eius esse fastidium, cui fructus optabiles ex omnium amore respondet. An est aliquid tenacius gloria, quae laudem adiecit voluptati? Haec tamen cura non deerit, ut libens patiaris. Tu tantum peregrinationem solare iusto amore provinciae. Vale.

Translation

1. You have compensated for your long silence by a double post, for you have furnished me with two letters at the same time to satisfy my desire by this unusually generous courtesy. From this I realized that up to now you lacked not the desire to write but the letter carrier. Indeed, there could have been no other reason for depriving me for so long of the honor of your conversation. Veneration of you deservedly grows day by day in me, and my affection rightly increases to overflowing. For we see that it is established by practice that friendship well-invested progresses daily by experience. But I must refrain from speaking of that matter, for it is not fitting for me to discuss things that I prefer you to feel.

2. Certainly I discovered in your letters how much you seek freedom from your public duties, and I confess that I was dumbfounded that you were so weary of your official responsibilities, responsibilities that win you enviable rewards through the love of everyone. Is anything more lasting than a glory that has joined praise to pleasure? Nonetheless, I shall spare no effort to see that you endure cheerfully. As for you, only seek consolation for your absence from home in proper devotion to your office.[3] Farewell.

Notes

1. Ausonius's burdensome office is probably the praetorian prefectureship, hence the date of 377–379.

2. Salzman 2002, 49–53.

3. "In proper devotion to your office" (*iusto amore provinciae*) translates the Latin term *provincia*, the standard word to indicate the sphere of influence or special assignment of a Roman magistrate. The term is here probably a reference to Ausonius's praetorian prefectureship, but Symmachus has utilized this word to grant a metaphorical *provincia* to his own father in *Letter* 1.1.6; this verbal echo only reinforces the paralleling of these two paternal figures in Symmachus's life as in his correspondence.

Letter 1.43: Symmachus to Ausonius
Date: 370–379[1]

Symmachus concludes his letters to Ausonius with a letter of recommendation for an otherwise unidentified orator, Julian, who was probably an advocate in the legal system, one of many such men whom Symmachus, as the foremost orator of his day, took on as protégés. Symmachus expands on this personal reference by incorporating Quintilian's notion (*Institutio oratoria* [*Orator's Education*] 10.1.33) that an orator be "a good man experienced in speaking." This man's recommendation is further supported by Symmachus's affectionate reference to him as a "brother."[2]

Text

1. Vetus sententia est artes honore nutriri. Eam nostrae aetatis confirmavit usus. Nemo enim belli notus aut domi clarus exortem praemii sensit industriam. Ita cum dignis fructus tribuitur, eandem viam capessentibus spes paratur. Glisco igitur gaudio, cum propter alios quibus fortunam sollers vita conciliat, tum maxime Iuliani fratris mei gratia, quem sic a te diligi volo, ut probari posse confido.

Scis nempe, in illo forensi pulvere quam rara cognatio sit facundi oris et boni pectoris, dum aut modestum ingenium verecundia contrahit aut successu eloquens insolescit. 2. Haec in meo familiari ac necessario ea societate viguerunt, ut neque obiectu pudoris areret nec cum detrimento frontis adflueret. Numquam in mercedem linguae ornamenta corrupit ac fortunis tenuis opulentiam fide, quaestum laude mutavit. Merito hunc tibi in manum vel magis in animum libens trado. Nam mihi summa curatio est, ut amicitiam tuam boni uberent. Te quoque idem velle habeo conpertum. Semper enim natura aequalibus gaudet et familiare sibi est omne quod simile est. Sed ne prolixo testimonio suspicionem laudatoris incurram, quaeso ipse de eo iudices examine pensiore. Ita cum illius institutum probaveris, periculum iudicii mei feceris. Vale.

Translation

1. It is an old saying that the arts are nourished by honor.[3] The practice of our age has confirmed it. For no one of military distinction or civilian repute has seen his efforts go unrewarded. Accordingly, since rewards are given to the deserving, hope is engendered in those who take up the same career. Thus I swell with joy for the others whose industrious life attracts the favor of Fortune, but most of all because of my brother Julian, whom I wish you to love, even as I am confident he can win your approval.

You are aware, I know, how rare is the association of eloquent speech and moral character in the arena of the courts, since either diffidence constrains the temperate character or the eloquent man grows arrogant with success. 2. In my friend and associate, these qualities are so powerfully combined that he neither runs dry checked by inhibition nor flows abundantly to the erosion of his modesty. Never has he corrupted the charms of his speaking for gain, and, though of humble fortune, he has preferred trustworthiness to wealth, praiseworthiness to profit. With good reason I happily entrust this man to your hands, or rather to your heart, for I take the greatest pains to ensure that good men enrich your friendship. I know full well that you wish the same, too. Indeed nature always rejoices in equals, and all things that are alike are friendly to each other. But to avoid suspicion of being a eulogist because of my overlong endorsement, I ask you to decide about him after a more searching examination. In this way, when you put his conduct to the test, you will make trial of my judgment. Farewell.

Notes

1. This letter was written after Symmachus left court and likely before Ausonius's retirement from public life in 379.

2. See 51 n. 4 above on the term "brother" (*frater*) as a sign of friendship.

3. Symmachus reiterates this maxim in *Letters* 1.79 and 1.96. It is a proverbial notion that he may have taken from Cicero, *Tusculanae disputationes* (*Tusculan Disputations*) 1.4: "Honor nourishes the arts" (*Honos alit artes*).

Book 1, *Letters* 44–55: Symmachus to Praetextatus

Although Vettius Agorius Praetextatus belonged to the generation of Symmachus's father, he was one of Symmachus's closest friends as well as one of Rome's most successful senators. Like Symmachus's previous correspondent, Ausonius, Praetextatus was well-positioned to mentor the younger man as he advanced in late Roman society. Further, despite the difference in their ages, the two shared similar interests in literature, politics, and religion.

Praetextatus's public career is well-known. He had been quaestor, praetor, governor (*corrector*) of Tuscia and Umbria in central Italy, and consular of Lusitania in Spain before 362; he was then appointed proconsul of Achaea in 362–364 under the pagan emperor Julian, with whom he shared religious as well as literary interests. Praetextatus's public career flourished under the tolerant Christian emperor Valentinian I; he attained the much sought after position of urban prefect of Rome in 367–368.[1] In this post he won praise for effective governance and earned a reputation for integrity; an active pagan, as urban prefect Praetextatus was lauded for mediating between two opposing Christian parties in Rome in 367–368, as he restored civil order by supporting Damasus for the papacy.[2]

In the 370s, Praetextatus's public stature continued to grow even though he, like many other senators, spent long periods of time out of public office. He acted in a variety of capacities, including taking on the role of legate on several senatorial embassies to emperors.[3] He was eventually rewarded with another high office, that of praetorian prefect of Italy, Illyricum, and Africa by

1. For more on Vettius Agorius Praetextatus's career, see Praetextatus 1, *PLRE* 1:722–24; for a full biography, see Kahlos 2002.

2. Ammianus Marcellinus, *Res Gestae* 27.9.9; *Collectio Avellana* (*Avellana Collection*) *Letters* 5–7; and Sozomen, *Hist. eccl.* (*Church History*) 6.23.2.

3. See, for example, Praetextatus's embassy to Valentinian in 370/371, described by Ammianus Marcellinus, *Res Gestae* 28.1.24–25. Although Vera (1981, xli, xlix–l) sees this hiatus as a sign of political disfavor, that is not necessarily the case. Extended periods of time out of office were normal practice in a senatorial career; see Salzman 2002, 110–14; Kahlos 2002, 43–44. For the importance of embassies, see Gillett 2003, 17–35.

May 384. His public career was at its zenith when in in October or November of 384, as consul designate for the following year, he died just as he was on the verge of attaining the highest civic honor of all.[4]

It may seem somewhat surprising, then, that the funerary monument set up in Rome to honor Praetextatus and his wife, Paulina, proclaimed that the former deemed trivial his secular honors and offices compared to wearing "priestly headbands" and serving the gods.[5] Indeed, after his death, as this monument attests, Praetextatus was lauded especially for his engagement with and expertise in cult ritual. Inscriptions record that he was augur, priest of Vesta, priest of the Sun, *quindecimvir*, curial of Hercules, as well as consecrated to Liber, a participant in the Eleusinian Mysteries, a high priest (*hierophanta*), temple overseer (*neocorus*), an initiate of the *taurobolium* (in honor of the Great Mother) and Father of the Fathers (the highest priesthood of the Mithras cult).[6] Praetextatus's commitment to pagan cults went beyond ritual practice. As proconsul of Achaea between 362 and 364, he intervened to persuade Valentinian I to allow the continuance of the Eleusinian Mysteries (Zosimus, *New History* 4.3.3). As urban prefect from 367 to 368, he restored the Portico of the Consenting Gods in the Roman Forum and took action to protect statues of and monuments to the gods from the encroachments of private individuals.[7] Well after his death, Praetextatus's reputation as a learned pagan persisted; Macrobius, writing his *Saturnalia* in the 430s, represented Praetextatus as uniquely qualified to discourse on the origins of the festival of the Saturnalia and of the traditional cults and rituals associated with the Roman calendar, as well as on Vergil's knowledge of pontifical lore.[8]

Given this posthumous image of Praetextatus, Symmachus's portrait of this eminent senator is somewhat surprising. Among other things, we find in Symmachus's letters to Praetextatus criticism, albeit muted, of Praetextatus's procrastination in performing religious duties (e.g., *Letters* 1.47, 1.51). Moreover, Praetextatus is portrayed at times as playful and fully apprecia-

---

4. Cameron (2011), 185 argues persuasively for the death of Praetextatus after September 4, 384, likely in October or November, before Damasus's death on December 11, 384. He was praetorian prefect by May 384; see *PLRE* 1:723.

5. *CIL* 6:1779 = *ILS* 1259, lines 18–22 on the back panel.

6. *CIL* 6:1779 = *ILS* 1259.

7. *CIL* 6:102 = *ILS* 4003. For a possible polemical point in the restoration of the Portico of the Consenting Gods, see Nieddu 1986, 37–52. For his actions preserving statues and pagan monuments, see *Letter* 1.46 and Kahlos 2002, 91–96.

8. Macrobius, *Saturnalia* 1.7–10; 1.12–23 (Praetextatus on the Saturnalia and the Roman calendar); 3.4–14 (Praetextatus on Vergil's knowledge of pontifical lore). Macrobius calls Praetextatus "sacrorum omnium unice conscius" (1.7.17). For more on his image in Macrobius's *Saturnalia*, see Kahlos 2002, 180–200; Liebeschuetz 1999, 185–205.

tive of Symmachus's humor. So, for example, Symmachus teases Praetextatus about his preference for reading over hunting (*Letter* 1.53). Such levity was apparently appreciated by Praetextatus, despite his reputation as a serious scholar not only of religion and literature but also of philosophy. We know, for instance, that Praetextatus translated Themistius's paraphrases of Aristotle's *Analytica* (*Analytics*), along with perhaps composing a Latin commentary on Aristotle's *Categoriae* (*Categories*).[9] Symmachus certainly respected Praetextatus's learning and literary abilities, as is evident by his desire for Praetextatus's evaluation of a speech he delivered in 376 (*Letter* 1.44).

Symmachus's Praetextatus is thus depicted as an engaging individual, erudite and rather witty. This is a man whom one could easily see bantering with Pope Damasus, as in his famous remark: "Make me bishop of Rome, and I will become a Christian overnight."[10] Like Symmachus, Praetextatus was imbued with a passion for literature as well as for politics (see *Letters* 1.44, 1.48, and 1.53). Their shared interests provided the foundation for their friendship, which Symmachus's letters depict as growing increasingly close. One sign of their intimacy, expressed in the conventions of letter writing, is Symmachus's reiterated demands for longer and more frequent letters (see *Letters* 1.45, 1.50).

Praetextatus's friendship for the younger Symmachus extended to offering him political as well as personal support; in *Letter* 1.55 Praetextatus offers to act as a mediator in a dispute with a third, unnamed party. Indeed, if we accept the proposed date of *Letter* 1.55 as 384, then their relationship advanced from hopeful beginnings, perhaps as early as 360/365 and into the early years of the reign of Gratian in 376 (*Letter* 1.44), extending into the more difficult, politically charged, and increasingly intolerant period in Roman society circa 384, where this sequence of letters ends.[11] The political circumstances, as well as his personal feelings of loss at Praetextatus's death in 384, contributed to Symmachus's decision to step down early from the office of urban prefect; without his friend and confidant (*State Paper* 10.3: *consortis*), Symmachus felt increasingly unwilling to face the challenges of office (*State Papers* 10, 11).

Symmachus's humanizing portrayal of Praetextatus may have also been somewhat polemical. After his death, Praetextatus was widely mourned and honored for his piety as well as his learning, perhaps nowhere more elo-

9. See Boethius's second commentary on Aristotle's *De interpretatione* 1.289; see *PLRE* 1:723.

10. Jerome, *Contra Joannem Hierosolymitanum* (*Against John of Jerusalem*) 8; for discussion, see Kahlos 2002, 201–5.

11. For this movement in these letters, see Bruggisser 1993, 346, 370–73. Symmachus's pagan priesthood is as early as 360/365; see xxiii.

quently than on his funerary monument in Rome: "[you illuminate] your country, the Senate, and your wife by your integrity of mind, your character, and your scholarship all at once.... You, a holy man and priest of the mysteries, conceal in the secret places of your heart what you discovered in the sacred initiations."[12] Praise of his piety, however, fueled Christian animosity.[13] After he died, Praetextatus's piety became a contested matter even among pagans. The chief Vestal, on behalf of the Vestal Virgins, requested from the college of priests the extraordinary right to set up a statue in Praetextatus's honor. Symmachus opposed this privilege on the grounds that it went against religious tradition; never before had a Vestal proposed such a distinction even for a *pontifex maximus*, not even for such luminaries as Numa Pompilius or Metellus, *pontifex maximus* for twenty-two years (*Letter* 2.36.2–3).

Symmachus's religious reservations were tied to his political concerns; he argued that he did not want to establish a precedent that would open the way for even greater competition among his peers or for the possible degradation of this honor. [14] Rather, Symmachus claimed, he wished to honor Praetextatus in accordance with traditional norms. Following the vote of the Senate, Symmachus, as urban prefect, requested from the emperor Valentinian II permission to erect statues to Praetextatus in a public space (Symmachus, *State Paper* 12.3). The emperor did not acquiesce at once but requested copies of Praetextatus's speeches.[15] Eventually, however, the request was granted, judging from fragmentary inscriptions to Praetextatus found in the Roman Forum.[16] Indeed, if the find site is to be trusted as the location of the original statue, its placement in the Roman Forum rather than the Forum of Trajan

12. CIL 6:1779 = *ILS* 1259, D lines 5–8 and 13–15. See also Kahlos 2002, 124–79. For learning as a mark of status, see Salzman 2002, 47–49.

13. Kahlos (2002, 23–24, 160–71) considers the Christian invective against Praetextatus, including Jerome, *Letter* 23.2–4, and the *Carmen contra paganos*, which in my opinion is best understood as an attack on Praetextatus. For this poem, see especially Ruggini 1979; Cameron 2011, 273–319.

14. As Kahlos (2002, 156) observes, there is no reason to see Symmachus's opposition to Paulina and the Vestals' request as aimed at preventing Roman aristocratic women from gaining too much influence; rather, it was a question of tradition and, I would add, intrasenatorial competition. See also Frei-Stolba 2003, 281–315. For the opposing position, see Ruggini 1979, 114.

15. Polara (2000, 107–26, esp. 111) argues that this was a delaying tactic to ease tensions within the city.

16. *CIL* 6:1778 and 1779a. For interpretation of these fragments associated with a statue, see Niquet 2000, 238; Kahlos 2002, 155. For detailed discussion of this incident, see Frei-Stolba 2003, 281–315, esp. 285.

was in itself a signal honor for Pratextatus.[17] Yet before this public honor was realized, the college of priests granted to the chief Vestal, Coelia Concordia, the extraordinary right to erect a statue to Praetextatus, probably in the house of the Vestals.[18]

Among those lobbying for Praetextatus's honorific statue was his widow, Fabia Aconia Paulina, whose health is a cause of concern for Symmachus in his *Letter* 1.48. As the daughter of the distinguished aristocrat Aco Catullinus, Paulina was in a position to protect and augment Praetextatus's reputation, even in the face of his Christian detractors.[19] Paulina's devotion to her husband and their shared engagement in pagan cults are well-attested. Paulina shared her husband's religiosity: she was consecrated to Ceres, to the Eleusinian Mysteries, and to Hecate; in addition, she was an initiate of the *taurobolium* in honor of the Magna Mater and a high priestess.[20] As these activities, noted on the couple's funeral monument, attest, theirs was a marriage in which involvement in pagan cult was part of their public identities. Hence gratitude to the Vestal who championed her husband's honor led Paulina to erect a statue of the priestess in the couple's home in Rome.[21]

In these posthumous attempts at image-making, Paulina and the chief Vestal Coelia Concordia appear to have won what Maijastina Kahlos has called the "war of the statues": Praetextatus received unique honors, and Paulina demonstrated her influence.[22] However, Symmachus may have had the more long-lasting success; his humanizing image of Praetextatus as a witty but somewhat delinquent pagan undermines attempts at representing this eminent senator as a virtual "holy man." Rather, Praetextatus is portrayed, like Ausonius, as a powerful member of Symmachus's circle of friends, willing to

17. For the topographical implications, see Chenault 2008, 106–35. For the implications of such political statues, see Machado 2006, ch. 4. For statues and Roman society in general, see Stewart 2003.

18. *CIL* 6:2145 = 32408. The Vestals' statue was erected before the public statue, based on reading *prius* in the inscription to honor Coelia Concordia as her success in erecting a statue "before," i.e., the public statue was granted; for the argument, see Kahlos 2002, 156; Frei-Stolba 2003, 281–315; and Polara 2000, 107–26.

19. For more on Fabia Aconia Paulina, see *PLRE* 1:675. For his Christian detractors, see 94 n. 13 above.

20. For the inscription, see *CIL* 6:1779 = *ILS* 1259. For the religious role of late Roman, pagan aristocratic women, see Salzman 2002, 155–58; more generally, Clark 1993. For bibliography and a study of the conversion of aristocratic women, see also Disselkamp 1997.

21. *CIL* 6:2145 = *ILS* 32408. For this view of Paulina, see especially Kahlos 2002, 156; Frei-Stolba 2003, 281–315.

22. Kahlos 2002, 156; Frei-Stolba 2003, 281–315.

share in public duties associated with the state cults but more eager to share literary witticisms than to come to meetings of the pontifical college.

Letter 1.44: Symmachus to Praetextatus
Date: 376

In *Letter* 1.2.2, Symmachus talks only vaguely about the civic disturbances that led an angry mob to burn down his father's house in Rome and forced his father's exile from the city. In marked contrast to that allusiveness, here he explicitly relays the honors conferred on his father and, consequently, on himself by the Senate of Rome. Symmachus describes (section 2) how he delivered a speech of gratitude to the Senate on 9 January, taking advantage of the opportunity offered by a previously scheduled speech on behalf of a certain senator, Trygetius, who had requested that his son be designated for the praetorship.[1] Unfortunately, only fragments of that oration, *Oration* 5, *On Behalf of Trygetius*, survive, but they include several words of gratitude about his father (*Oration* 5.1). *Letter* 1.44 indicates that it was this oration that Symmachus sent to Praetextatus (who had been absent from the 9 January Senate meeting). A longer version of a speech of gratitude, *Oration* 4, *On Behalf of His Father*, was delivered by Symmachus after his father's designation as consul, somewhat later in this same year, likely in June, 376; that speech is also fragmentary.[2]

Symmachus was eager to learn Praetextatus's reaction to this oration. Evidently, Symmachus was confident of this speech's success, for he sent it to several other friends, including Hesperius, Syagrius, Rusticus Iulianus, and Neoterius.[3] Symmachus's *Letter* 1.52, which records Symmachus's joy that Praetextatus had made a positive assessment of one of his orations, probably refers to the oration mentioned here in *Letter* 1.44. It is all the more disappointing that Symmachus did not include the letter that Praetextatus must have written in response to this oration; only reply letters from his father and Ausonius were included in book 1, signs of their special status.

Text

1. Meretur diligentia in me tua, ut ea quae proxime laudi mihi fuerunt clam te esse non patiar. Credo indicium fecisse tibi Famam, quod parentem meum ruri atque in secessu amissae domus iniuriam decoquentem frequentibus suffragiis, denique oratoribus missis novo honore senatus acciverit. Qua causa ubi primum facultatem loquendi apud collegas adtulit dies, egit pater senatui gratiam ea facundiae gravitate, qua notus est. Kalendae tunc erant quibus annus aperitur.

2. Brevi intervallo, cum familiaris mei Trygeti filio praetorio candidato

operam spopondissem, animum religio convenit, ut occasione destinati officii obirem munus adhuc a me patri debitum sed, ut dixi, ab illo senatui iam solutum. Ergo a. d. quintum Idus Ianuarias verba feci in amplissimo ordine; quae ubi in manus tuas venerint, ex tuo animo conicies iudicia ceterorum. Ego sub incerto examinis tui aliorum sententias occulendas putavi, ne te praeiudicio tanti ordinis viderer urguere. Vale.

Translation

1. Your affection for me warrants that I not allow you to remain in ignorance of those matters that have won me praise most recently. I believe that Rumor has given you some notice that my father, who was in seclusion in the country digesting the injury he received from the loss of his house, was summoned by the Senate with repeated votes and finally the dispatch of a delegation—a novel honor indeed![4] Because of that, on the first day that offered an opportunity of speaking before his colleagues, my father gave a speech of thanks to the Senate with that dignified eloquence for which he is known. It was then the Kalends, which begin the year.

2. After a brief interval, since I had promised the assistance of a speech on behalf of my friend Trygetius's son,[5] who was a candidate for the praetorship, my sense of responsibility impelled me to decide to use the opportunity provided by this undertaking to meet the obligation I still owed for my father, an obligation, as I said, already paid by him to the Senate. Therefore, on the 9th of January I gave a speech before this most splendid order; when it comes into your hands, you will form a conclusion on your own account about the judgments of the rest. Since I am uncertain about your assessment, I thought that I should conceal the opinions of others lest I seem to be influencing you by the previous judgment of so great an order. Farewell.

Notes

1. Trygetius 1, *PLRE* 1:923.

2. Symmachus, *Oration* 5, *Pro Trygetio* (*On Behalf of Trygetius*), in Seeck 1883, 335–36, and in Callu 2009b, 34–35. Callu (1972, 224) notes that Symmachus makes frequent mention of his orations in his letters; see *Letters* 1.52, 1.78, 1.96, 1.105, 3.7, and 5.43. For Symmachus's *Oration* 4, *Pro Patre* (*On Behalf of His Father*), see Seeck 1883, 332–35, and Callu 2009b, 28–34, with a date for this speech of June 376. Avianius's designation as consul is a sign of the harmony between the Senate and the new emperor at the beginning of his reign.

3. Symmachus, *Letters* 1.78, 1.96, 1.105; 3.7; 5.43.

4. For discussion of Symmachus's father's problems, see the introduction to *Letters* 1.1–12, pp. 1–5.

5. The son is not named. For the father, see 97 n. 1.

Letter 1.45: Symmachus to Praetextatus
Date: before Fall 384[1]

Symmachus's request for longer letters parallels those he made to Ausonius for more substantial and more frequent letters. Such demands are indicators of intimacy, in accord with the norms of epistolary etiquette, but they should not be taken too literally; when the occasion called for it, Symmachus was happy enough to write brief notes. His preference, however, was for the more ornate, more developed letter, composed in a "rich and flowered" style that Macrobius noted as a hallmark of his writing.[2]

Text

1. Auctus sum gaudio, quod valetudo tecum revertit in gratiam; nam semper incolumitas tua voti mei summa est. Nunc si diis volentibus reconciliatae vires animi tui integraverunt vigorem, facito epistulae tuae multiiugis paginis augeantur. Odi parsimoniam verborum bonorum. Scribendi quippe brevitas magis fastidio quam officio proxima est. Nolo litteras stillantes de summo ore; illas peto, quae arescere nesciunt, quae ex intimo pectoris fonte promuntur.

2. Memini brevitatem Spartanam laudi quondam fuisse; sed ego Romanis tecum legibus ago et, si ita vis, Atticis, quibus tantum decus a facundia fuit, ut mihi videantur Lacones metu collationis in diversum studia destinasse. Vellem plura, sed tuo modo conpungendus es. Simul cautio est mihi, ne te sermo multus offendat. Instituto igitur meo calcem pono, dum tuo pareo. Qua ex re intellegis eo te invidiae et condicionis adductum, quasi a me pauca scribi velis, nisi multa rescripseris. Vale.

Translation

1. I am enriched with joy because your health has returned, for your well-being is always the first of my prayers. Now if, with the gods willing, your restored strength has renewed the vigor of your spirit, ensure that your letters are increased to many pages. I hate economy in fine language. Indeed, brevity in writing is closer to disdain than to courteousness. I do not want a letter that drips off the tip of your tongue. Rather, I seek one that cannot run dry, that wells up from the innermost springs of the heart.

2. I recall that Spartan brevity was once cause for praise. But I treat with you according to Roman law, and, if you so wish, according to Attic, too, in

which so great was the glory arising from eloquence that the Spartans seem to me to have chosen different pursuits from fear of comparison. I would like to say more, but I must spur you on in your own style. At the same time, I am cautious lest a long letter offend you. Therefore, I put a stop to my usual habits, while I comply with yours. In this way you understand that you have been brought to such an invidious situation that if you do not write back at length, it is as if you want me to write briefly. Farewell.

NOTE

1. This letter is dated before the death of Praetextatus in fall 384.

2. Macrobius, *Saturnalia* 5.1.7, states that Symmachus luxuriates in the same prose style as Pliny and other classic authors, namely, "the rich and flowered" ("pingue et floridum [genus dicendi], in quo Plinius Secundus quondam et nunc nullo veterum minor noster Symmachus luxuriatur"). Robert Kaster (in private correspondence) has observed that since Macrobius, as most readers until the fourteenth century, confused the elder and younger Senecas, Macrobius may also have confounded the two Plinys. Indeed, many readers did that as well, and since the elder Pliny's style is in truth closer to the "rich and flowered" style than that of his nephew, that may explain Macrobius's comment.

LETTER 1.46: SYMMACHUS TO PRAETEXTATUS
DATE: 360/365– 380[1]

This letter is frustrating for the historian in search of specific details about controversies in fourth-century Rome in large part because the particulars were conveyed in person by the letter carrier, who in this case was Symmachus's brother Celsinus Titianus. Symmachus does not specify what happened that prompted the public priests to hand over "care of the gods to the guardianship of the people for an act of public observance." Moreover, the imperial edict referred to at the end of section 2 is not specified, nor is it clear if that edict was tied to the priests' turning over the "care of the gods."

There are no less than four different interpretations of what this letter and this edict describes. Hans Peter Kohns proposed that the imperial edict under question was that of 380 that proclaimed "Catholic" Christianity the religion of the empire.[2] There is, however, nothing beyond the possible date of the letter to support this identification. Jean Pierre Callu proposed a second explanation, that the edict in question, now lost, had ordered the restitution of temple goods to sacred buildings. Along these same lines, other scholars have suggested that Praetextatus had obtained this edict from the emperor, perhaps when urban prefect in 367–368, but enforced it only later, for its application is attested only in 384, when he was praetorian prefect and Symmachus was urban prefect. The statues that Praetextatus had recovered, referred to at the end of the letter, were thus those taken from public temples by private individuals.[3] Rita Lizzi Testa has proposed a third scenario, suggesting that the edict under question was an earlier one, dated to 376, that restricted building in Rome; the restored statues were those linked to temples.[4] The fourth interpretation, by Otto Seeck, proposes that the reference to the statues began a new statement, not linked at all to the edict, which he did not identify. According to Seeck, Symmachus was referring to the public statues that honored Praetextatus in his own lifetime that were threatened with destruction as a result of popular anger created by food shortages.[5] It is true that such hostility over food shortages was directed at officials with some frequency although, as Callu observed, no such food shortage is attested for the year 380. However, the date of the letter is not secure (it could be earlier than 380), and, in any case, popular hostility could well have been aroused for other reasons, for instance, as in the case of Symmachus's father.[6]

Given the state of our information, there can be no certainty about the content of the emperor's edict or the meaning of the incident with the statues. It seems most plausible to me that Symmachus's concern for public cult at the beginning of section 2 is tied to the restoration of the statues from temples. This was an issue with which Symmachus as urban prefect had been actively concerned.[7] Finally, the reference to popular acclamations (section 2) does lend some support, not often noted, to the opinion that the recovered statues were in a public place. Plausibility, however, is not proof, so these must remain hypotheses only.

Despite these uncertainties, this letter is nonetheless invaluable. It provides significant information about the mechanisms of state cult and its continued performance by public priests in Rome. Indeed, the letter reveals an independent college of public priests (section 2) that is still actively directing rituals in Rome in the last quarter of the fourth century. This self-governing, self-sustaining group is a vivid reminder of the bureaucratic difficulties Christian emperors faced as they sought to dismantle centuries-old institutions of pagan state cult.

Text

1. Potui facere scripta conpendii, cum tibi germanus meus verbis suis satisfacturus uberius videretur quam meis literis, sed in maiore lucro officia honesta quam otia muta ponenda sunt. Ergo neque tacito opus est, ut honor amicitiae mihi feratur accepto, neque omnia mandanda sunt litteris, ut illi ad

narrandum aliquid relinquatur. Accipe tamen rerum capita et summas negotiorum quibus frater admonitus quaesita latius exequatur.

2. Convenit inter publicos sacerdotes, ut in custodiam civium publico obsequio traderemus curam deorum. Benignitas enim superiorum, nisi cultu teneatur, amittitur. Ergo multo tanto ornatior quam solebat caelestis factus est honor. Expectare mihi videris omnia quae supersunt. Titianus meus fungetur indicium, cui indulgentius narrandi quod velis opera legata est. Edictum principum, nisi iam notum est, idem tibi adsertor expediet. Et iam statuas recepistis iisdem paene populi adclamationibus quibus amiseratis. Ride si libet. Ut rideas, afuisti. Plura desino, ne, qui strictim meliora detexui, amaris videar inmorari. Vale.

Translation

1. I could have saved myself the trouble of writing, since my brother's[8] conversation seemed likely to satisfy you more fully than my letter, but the performance of honorable obligations must be considered of greater profit than speechless repose. Therefore, I must neither be silent, in order that the honor of friendship redound to my credit, nor must everything be entrusted to a letter, so that something be left for him to tell. Receive nevertheless a summary of these matters and the chief points of the affair concerning which my brother is instructed and will handle any questions at greater length.

2. An agreement was reached among the public priests that we should hand over care of the gods to the guardianship of the citizens for an act of public observance, for the goodwill of the gods is lost, unless it is maintained by cult.[9] Therefore, honor was paid to the gods very much more lavishly than was customary. You seem to me to be waiting for all the rest. My dear Titianus will serve as your informant, to whom the task has been delegated of telling you more fully whatever you want. This same man will explain to you the edict of the emperors, unless it is already known to you. Now, too, you have got back those statues with almost the same popular acclamations as when you had lost them. Laugh if it pleases you. You were away, so you can laugh. I say no more lest, after recounting better news cursorily, I seem to linger over the bitter. Farewell.

Notes

1. Symmachus is already one of the public priests, hence this letter can be between 360 and 365 (see xxiii). It is no later than 380 because the letter carrier, Celsinus Titianus, Symmachus's brother, died in late 380. See the introduction to *Letters* 62–74, pp. 129–30.

2. Kohns 1961, 157, identified it with *C. Th.* 16.1.2 and 16.2.25 (= *Cod. Just.* 1.1.1).

3. Callu 1972, 109 and 224 n. 4. Symmachus refers to these activities in *State Paper* 21. This is also the view proposed by Vera 1981, 159–60.

4. Lizzi Testa 2004, 373–74, referring to *C. Th.* 15.1.19 (376).

5. Seeck 1883, lxxxviii–ix.

6. Callu 1972, 224 n. 5. For riots, see 2–3 and n. 9; Ammianus Marcellinus, *Res Gestae* 27.3.3–4; and Kohns 1961.

7. See 102 n. 3.

8. Symmachus's brother by birth, identified by name in section 2, is Celsinus Titianus; for more on this man, see the introduction to *Letters* 1.62–75, pp. 129–30.

9. What precipitated handing over this public ceremony and what this public ceremony consisted of is not specified. But Symmachus articulates here a key concept of Roman religion: the necessity of maintaining the "goodwill of the gods" (in Latin, the *pax deorum*, described here with the phrase *benignitas superiorum*). This desire helps to explain why Romans went to such great lengths in the correct performance of cult ritual. It is an idea that recurs in Symmachus's letters (see 1.48, 1.49) and in his well-known *State Paper* 3. For more on Symmachus's religiosity, see the introduction, xxxi–xxxv, and Salzman 2011, 167–83. For the notion of the *pax deorum* in traditional Roman religion, see Rüpke 2007, 80 and 130.

Letter 1.47: Symmachus to Praetextatus
Date: 360/365–before Fall 384[1]

As *pontifex maior*, literally a "greater priest," Symmachus was a member of the college of priests and had particular responsibilities in the cult of Vesta. He had attained this honor no later than 360/365 (see the introduction, xxiii–xxiv). As *Letter* 1.47, along with *Letters* 1.49 and 1.51, shows, he took the demands of this priesthood seriously. Hence, these letters also shed unique light on how the public priesthoods functioned in the late fourth century. Symmachus's devotion to his office reflects, on one level, his personal beliefs. It was also a prestigious honor at least in certain senatorial circles in Rome. Yet, as Symmachus later remarked with some bitterness, some ambitious men stay away from the altars for fear of hindering their advancement under Christian emperors (*Letter* 1.51). As I have argued elsewhere, this is the first stage in the gradual conversion of the aristocracy, since some pagans removed themselves from religious offices out of concern for their status.[2]

The prestige of a priestly office lived on into the late fourth century; even Christian emperors still officially held the title of "chief priest" (*pontifex maxi-*

mus), although they no longer performed animal sacrifices to the gods. The late fifth-century historian Zosimus claimed that the emperor Gratian was the first to refuse this title when he turned down the pontifical robes in 382, but this does not seem likely; Alan Cameron has demonstrated that there is no evidence for such a ritual and that Gratian and later emperors continued to use the title of "priest" (*pontifex*), now deemed "renowned" (*inclitus*), into the fifth century.[3]

Finally, as noted in the introduction (li), Symmachus's depiction of Praetextatus as a man unwilling to give up his leisure to attend to his priestly duties goes against the widespread view of him held by ancient writers as well as modern scholars. Rather than appearing as a dedicated polytheist, Pratetextatus is revealed to be a far more typical aristocrat, eager to be at leisure in his villa at Baiae. But like Symmachus's father and in accord with Cato's notions, Praetextatus knew how to use his leisure correctly by pursuing his interest in literature and philosophy (see 9 n. 9).

Text

1. Silentii nostri ratio diversa est, sed unus effectus. Me inpedit pontificalis officii cura, te Baiani otii neglegentia. Neque enim minus residem facit remissio animi quam occupatio. Nec mirum, si te illa ora totum sibi vindicat, cum ipsum Hannibalem fides certa sit bello invictum manus dedisse Campaniae. Non illius caeli aut soli illecebram retinax advenarum lotos arbor aequaverit et suada Circae pocula et tricinium semivolucrum puellarum. 2. Neque ego te pingues ferias agere contendo aut virtutem puto friguisse deliciis. Sed dum tibi legis, tibi scribis et urbanarum rerum fessus ingentem animum solitudine domas, amicitiarum munia nullus exequeris. Quin adripis stilum nostraeque in te adfectioni honorem mutuum facis? Nisi mavis auctoritatem pontificis experiri: multa nobis in collegio sunt deliberanda; quis tibi has indutias publici muneris dedit? Senties ius sacerdotis, nisi inpleveris ius amici. Vale.

Translation

1. The reasons for our mutual silence are different, but the effect is the same. Concern for my pontifical duties constrains me, whereas the carefree leisure of Baiae constrains you. For relaxation of the mind makes one no less remiss than preoccupation. Nor is it surprising if that shore claims you entirely for itself, since it is well-established that Hannibal, although unconquered in war, surrendered to Campania.[4] Neither the lotus tree, that entrapment for travelers, nor the seductive potions of Circe nor the trio of half-bird girls could equal the enticements of that climate and soil.[5] 2. I do not contend that

you are spending your holidays in luxury nor think that your virtue has grown cold from sensory delights. But while you read for yourself, write for yourself, and, tired out from urban affairs, tame your great spirit in solitude, you perform none of the obligations of your friendships. Why do you not seize your pen and honor with a like response my affection for you? That is, unless you prefer to make trial of a pontiff's authority? We have many things to deliberate in the college;[6] who gave you this leave of absence from public service? You will feel the rightful claim of a priest, unless you satisfy the rightful claim of a friend. Farewell.

Notes

1. Callu (1972, 110) dates *Letter* 1.47 to around 383 because he would place it in the same period as Praetextatus's travels noted in *Letter* 1.51. But *Letter* 1.47 locates Praetextatus in Baiae, while 1.51 places him in Etruria. *Letter* 1.47, then, can only be dated broadly to the period after 360/365, when Symmachus held the office of *pontifex*; see xxiii. The *terminus ante quem* is the death of Praetextatus in fall 384. Bruggisser (1993, 344–45) dates this letter and the other letters that contain no references to specific datable events, notably 1.47, 1.48, and 1.83, to after the first letter in the collection to Praetextatus, i.e., *Letter* 1.44, which is securely dated to 376. However, this also relies on a false assumption, since the letters are not always in strict chronological sequence.

2. For a two-step model of conversion, see Salzman 2002, 135–37.

3. Zosimus, *New History* 4.36. For the standard view of Gratian as the last *pontifex maximus*, see Croke and Harries 1982, 30. For a strong and convincing counter to this view, see Cameron 2007, 341–84.

4. For Campania as the home of aristocrats, see 5 and 9 n. 10.

5. The words *retinax*, "entrapment," and *tricinium*, "trio (of singers)" are attested nowhere else before Symmachus. This unusual language serves to convey how extraordinary the delights of Campania were.

6. The college of pontiffs included the major priests of Rome who advised on religious traditions and sacred law; they were under the guidance of the *pontifex maximus*, or chief priest, the position held by all emperors after Augustus; for a lucid account of the Roman system of pontifical colleges, see Scheid and Lloyd 2003, 132–44. For an excellent account of changes to the Roman pontifical college in late antiquity, see Van Haeperen 2002.

Letter 1.48: Symmachus to Praetextatus
Date: before Fall 384[1]

Symmachus's concern about Praetextatus's wife, Paulina,[2] is further sign of his close attachment to Praetextatus. His reference to Praetextatus's wife is especially striking, since he cites so very few women by name, not even his wife or daughter. This is also a sign of her status.

Text

Dii boni, quam nihil homini tutum atque exploratum est! Certe levandi animi causa Baias concesseratis. Quis oculus fascinavit destinatam quietem? Paulina ergo cura communis extremum salutis accesserat. An vester pro illa tantus est metus, ut omne eius incommodum periculi instar habeatur? Quidquid horum est, spectare animo licet, quas aerumnas dierum, quas noctium vigilias duxeritis. Sic nati sumus, ut saepius adversa fungamur. Fugiunt voluptates et bonae cuiusque rei tam brevis usus quam levis sensus est. Verum haec philosophorum disputationibus relinquantur. Nunc habitum laetiorem mentibus suadeamus, quando Paulinae nostrae valetudinem rursus locavit in solido pax deorum. Vale.

Translation

Good gods! How nothing is safe and secure for mankind! No doubt you had withdrawn to Baiae to ease your mind. What evil eye enchanted your intended rest?[3] So Paulina, our shared care, had approached the brink of death? Or is your fear for her so great that every one of her ailments is considered a crisis? Whichever of these is the case, one can imagine the daily distress and sleepless nights you have suffered. It is a condition of our birth to suffer adversity frequently. Pleasures are fleeting, and the enjoyment of every good thing is as brief as the sensation is slight. But let these things be left to the disputations of philosophers. Now let us persuade ourselves to a happier frame of mind, since the peace of the gods has securely established our Paulina's health. Farewell.

Notes

1. See 99 n. 1.

2. For more on Fabia Aconia Paulina, see *PLRE* 1:675 and 94 with n. 14 above.

3. The presumption that the evil eye can cause illness was universally accepted in antiquity. Callu (1972, 111 n. 1) aptly compares this reference with Vergil, *Eclogues* 3.103: "I do not know what evil eye bewitched my tender lambs" ("Nescio quis teneros oculus mihi fascinavit agnos").

Letter 1.49: Symmachus to Praetextatus
Date: 360/365–before Fall 384[1]

There is no explanation of the "disturbing matter" mentioned by Symmachus at the opening of this letter. Seeck associated this letter with the Roman defeat at Adrianople. [2] However, Symmachus's letter expresses only concern about the rumors of failed sacrifice and the prodigy itself and gives no hint of military defeat. So, while the opening sentence echoes official slogans—Praetextatus is called a citizen "born for the common good"—the point of the letter is to call attention to the importance of appeasing Jove and Public Fortune with acceptable public sacrifice.

Traditionally, expiations for prodigies were occasioned by some natural event that defied Roman notions of normalcy (e.g., excessive rain, an animal born with two heads, crop failure), and public authorities performed sacrifices to appease the angry deities.[3] Hence this letter is of special interest because it indicates quite clearly that, despite imperial legislation that prohibited public sacrifice, such sacrifices continued in Italy and Rome.[4]

Text

Quaeris ut civis ad bonum commune genitus, quid super rebus anxiis vero proximum nuntietur. Certis indicibus secunda cognovimus; dehinc multi silentii suspicio sollicitis rumoribus locum fecit. Sed mihi opinionum talium quae sine auctore prodeunt nulla curatio est. Inpendio angor animi, quod sacrificiis multiplicibus et per singulas potestates saepe repetitis necdum publico nomine Spoletinum piatur ostentum. Nam et Iovem vix propitiavit octava mactatio et Fortunae publicae multiiugis hostiis nequiquam undecimus honor factus est. Quo loci simus, intellegis. Nunc sententia est in coetum vocare collegas. Curabo ut scias, si quid remedia divina promoverint. Vale.

Translation

You ask as a citizen "born for the common good"[5] what is the news that is closest to the truth about this disturbing matter. From reliable sources we received favorable reports; thereafter the suspicion caused by a long silence gave rise to anxious rumors. But I am not concerned about such opinions that arise without any attribution. I am intensely distressed because, despite numerous sacrifices, and these often repeated by each of the authorities, the prodigy of Spoleto has not yet has been expiated in the public name. For the eighth sacrificial victim scarcely appeased Jove and for the eleventh time honor was paid to Public Fortune with multiple sacrificial victims in vain.[6] You know now where we are. The decision now is to call the college to a meeting. I will make sure you know if the divine remedies make any progress. Farewell.

Notes

1. See 104 n. 1.

2. Seeck 1883, lxxxix.

3. The repetition of sacrifice was required if the internal organs (*exta*) showed unacceptable markings, which the *haruspices* (specialists trained in reading divine signs) interpreted as a sign of divine displeasure. In this case such signs were especially sinister because the sacrifices were undertaken in expiation of some prodigy; see Beard, North and Price 1998–1999, 1:36–37.

4. The *Theodosian Code* contains a number of laws against public sacrifice. The earliest extant one, dated to 341 C.E., is directed to the vicar of Italy and Africa, *C.Th.* 16.10.2. See also Salzman 1990, 205–7; 2011, 167–83.

5. Callu (1972, 111, 225 n. 5) cites similar official titles to elucidate this phrase; cf. the inscription on coinage of Constantine from 308, which reads: "To the Prince of Youth, born for the good of the State" ("Principi Iuvent(utis) B(ono) R(ei) P(ublicae) N(ato)").

6. Symmachus's reference to Public Fortune suggests this deity had its own cult at Spoleto.

Letter 1.50: Symmachus to Praetextatus
Date: before 377[1]

It is interesting that Symmachus's willingness to chide Praetextatus for a breach of epistolary etiquette is couched in friendly terms, in contrast to his note of annoyed superiority when correcting the bishop Ambrose for similarly failing to meet epistolary norms by writing one letter of recommendation for two men (Symmachus, *Letter* 3.32, 398). *Letter* 1.50 also shows Symmachus's desire to assert his own tie to Praetextatus, apart from that of his father.

Text

1. Ego quidem securus amicitiae tuae aequi bonique facio, si quid in me ab amante peccatur; sed tuos mores, quibus nihil desit ad laudem, dedecet officii neglegentia. Queri me opinaris, quod nihil scribas, et refellere mendacium paras, quia te aliquid scripsisse meministi. Ego vero minimum animi angerer, si taceres, prae ut hoc est, quod mihi et patri unas atque eas oppido

breves litteras detulisti. Ita tibi ambo digni singulis paginis non videmur? 2. Tui, inquies, honoris interfuit, ut iungereris parenti. Alia sunt, quae cum illo nobis vel communia opto vel paria; amor mihi meo nomine deferatur. Abstine igitur epistulis quae sunt instar edicti; facessat omne fastidium, ex quo nascitur cura conpendii. Sed longum de his loqui cautio est, ne tibi molestior sit prolixitas querellae nostrae quam mihi brevitas epistulae tuae. Quod superest, deos quaeso, ut nos plenos gaudii quam primum revisas. Facile erit angustias scriptorum tuorum multiloquio repensare. Vale.

Translation

1. I am secure in your friendship, and I accept without offense whatever wrong is committed by a friend against me.[2] But neglect of duty does not become your character, for which my wish is that nothing praiseworthy be lacking. You think that I am complaining because you write nothing, and you are getting ready to dispute this lie since you remember that you wrote something. Truly, I would be pained very little if you were silent, in comparison with this, that you sent me and my father just one letter, and a very brief one at that. Do we two then not seem to you worthy of a single page each? 2. You will say: "It served your honor to be associated with your father." There are other things that I wish to share with him or hold equally; love should be shown to me under my own name. So, abstain from a letter that is like an edict; let all fastidiousness be gone, from which arises a concern for brevity. But I must beware talking at too great length about these matters, lest the prolixity of my complaint annoy you more than the brevity of your letter did me. For the rest, I beseech the gods that you visit us again as soon as possible, filling us with joy. It will be easy to requite the scantiness of your writing with abundant conversation. Farewell.

Notes

1. *Letter* 1.50 was written when Symmachus's father was still alive, i.e., before 377.

2. For this archaism, *aequi bonique facio*, see Haverling 1988, 200. For Symmachus's fondness for archaism in the letters of book 1, see the introduction, xlvii.

Letter 1.51: Symmachus to Praetextatus
Date: 360/365–before Fall 384[1]

This letter provides important information about the structure and duties of the late Roman public priesthoods. Françoise Van Haeperen has proposed, based in large part on this letter and Symmachus, *Letter* 2.53, that by the late fourth century the state priests (*pontifices*) routinely divided the priestly tasks between them, with a minimum of two priests being required to perform their religious tasks in any given month.[2] This responsibility, according to Symmachus, was seen increasingly as a problem by upwardly mobile senators who were eager to satisfy Christian emperors.[3]

Text

Statueramus in externis adhuc morari, sed labantis patriae nuntius destinata mutavit, cum mihi in communibus malis decolor videretur securitas mea. Ad hoc sacri pontificalis administratio curam de me et officium stati mensis exigit. Neque enim fert animus in tanta sacerdotum neglegentia sufficere collegam. Fuerit haec olim simplex divinae rei delegatio; nunc aris deesse Romanos genus est ambiendi. Vos Etruria quousque retinebit? Iam querimur esse aliquid quod tamdiu civibus praeferatur. Sit licet ruris status mitior, non potest bene defrui otio, qui suis absentibus timet. Vale.

Translation

We had decided still to remain outside the city, but a messenger with news of our wavering fatherland changed our plans, since my own security seemed to me a dishonorable concern in the midst of common ills.[4] In addition, the priestly administration of the sacred requires my attention and makes me responsible for my appointed month.[5] I do not intend a colleague to take my place when there is such negligence among the priests. Once this sort of delegation of religious affairs was straightforward; now to desert the altars is, for Romans, a kind of careerism. As for you, how long will Etruria[6] detain you? We are now beginning to complain that there should be something that takes precedence over your fellow-citizens for so long. Granted, staying in the countryside is more peaceful, but he cannot well enjoy his leisure who fears for absent friends. Farewell.

Notes

1. Symmachus does not explain the reason for the "wavering fatherland" and "common ills." Callu (1972, 113) and others have pointed to food shortages throughout the Mediterranean, and in particular, the one noted by Symmachus in 383 (*State Paper* 3. 15) as the likely cause of concern. Hence, Callu dates this letter to ca. 383. That a shortage of food was the occasion for *Letter* 1.51 seems likely, but there is no indication whether this is the shortage of 383 or another one. Consequently, the letter can be dated only to some

point after Symmachus's priesthood, i.e., from 360/365 until the death of Praetextatus, fall 384.

2. Van Haeperen 2002, 209–10.

3. See Salzman 2002, 64–65.

4. I follow here the manuscript reading *adhuc*, instead of adopting with Callu (1972, 113) the emendation *ad K. Oct.*, i.e., "until the first of October."

5. This reflects the division of tasks on a monthly basis noted in the introduction to this letter (108–9). Van Haeperen (2002, 209–10) would date this reorganization to the fourth century, but others, including Jörg Rüpke (private correspondence), would date this change to Aurelian's reforms in the late third century.

6. Praetextatus's connections to Etruria, which are evidenced by provincial governorship of Tuscia and Umbria in 362, are strengthened by the identification by Berti and Cecconi (1997, 11–21) of a marble epigraph and large funerary monument from Etruria to honor Praetextatus.

Letter 1.52: Symmachus to Praetextatus
Date: 376

Symmachus had previously sent the oration (*Oration* 5) that he had delivered on January 9 for Praetextatus's approval (see *Letter* 1.44, p. 96). Here he notes his pleasure at Praetextatus's lost reply. Simultaneously, Symmachus venerates the reaction of the Senate of Rome presumably to that same *Oration* 5, and this, too, is much in keeping with his attempt to maintain and strengthen the prestige of this traditional aristocratic Roman institution. Indeed, changes in the senatorial order from Constantine's time onward had expanded its size, but the status and influence of the Senate of Rome in Italian and local matters had increased over the course of the fourth century, as the emperor rarely resided in the city.[1]

Text

Orationem meam tibi esse conplacitam nihilo setius gaudeo, quam quod eam secunda existimatione pars melior humani generis senatus audivit. Adiecisti sacramenti pondus et in bona verba iurasti, ut qui scires in suspicionem gratiae venire amantium iudicata. Nam ubi certa est amicitia, ibi fides laudis incertior. Ergo securus examinis tui nihil moror sententias ceterorum. Quid si adfuisses, tam bonae voluntatis auditor? Ne ego digito, ut aiunt, supera convexa tetigissem. Erit alias fortasse nobis optatior praesentiae tuae copia. Nunc testimonio epistulae tuae fruimur, tunc adiumento favoris utemur. Vale.

Translation

I rejoice that my oration was pleasing to you no less than that the Senate—the better part of the human race[2]—heard it with favor. You added the weight of an oath and swore in solemn form, since you knew that the judgments of friends incur suspicion of favoritism. For where friendship is secure, there the credibility of praise is less secure. So, freed from concern about your judgment, I pay no regard to the opinions of others. What if you had been present, as so well-disposed an audience member? I would certainly, as they say, have touched the arching heavens with my finger![3] Perhaps there will be a more convenient opportunity for your company at some other time. For now we derive pleasure from the evidence of your letter, but then we shall put to good use the benefit of your favor. Farewell.

Notes

1. Salzman 2002, 19–68; Weisweiler 2011, 346–75.

2. This praise for the Senate echoes that found in the *Panegyrics*. See, for instance, that of Nazarius on Constantine, 4.35.2; Nixon and Rodgers 1994, 380 and n. 157.

3. For this proverb, see, e.g., Cicero, *Letter to Atticus* 21 (2.1.7). Otto (1890, 63) cites numerous examples where the head touches the heavens as a sign of joy, for instance, Horace, *Odes* 1.1.36, and Ovid, *Metamorphoses* 7.61. The notion that one can touch the sky with one's hands is far less frequent, but it does appear in Ovid, *Letters from Pontus* 2.2.9; Propertius 1.8.43. Shackleton Bailey (1965, 1:349), Cicero's *Letters to Atticus*, notes that the expression of such joy is a favorite example of an impossible condition in the jurists, e.g., Gaius, *Institutiones* (*The Institutes*) 3.98.

Letter 1.53: Symmachus to Praetextatus
Date: before Fall 384[1]

This is one of the most delightful letters in the book. Symmachus playfully mocks Praetextatus's description of his leisure (*otium*) as a time devoted to hunting and exposes his true passions: literature and "ruminating over the books of ancient authors." Praetextatus's literary and philosophical learning has been earlier remarked (see 92–93), but here Praetextatus's writings are specifically praised for displaying "novelty of content" but "archaism of language" (1.53.2: "sensuum novitas, verborum vetustas"). This reference to Praetextatus's fondness for archaism may have suggested Symmachus's comparison of Praetextatus with the early Greek poet Hesiod.

Text

1. Otio et venatibus gloriare. Est haec quidem iucunda iactatio sed ludo magis a te prolata quam serio. Nam remissa tempora et ab negotiis publicis feriata libris veterum ruminandis libenter expendis. Aliis igitur dabis verba, qui te congressu primore noverunt. Ego actus, quos pernox et perdius curae tibi habes, tum cotidiana ingenii tui pabula de litterarum, quas mihi tribuis, sapore coniecto. 2. Nisi forte in silvis Apollinem continaris, ut ille pastor Hesiodus, quem poetica lauru Camenalis familia coronavit. Nam unde est haec in epistulis tuis sensuum novitas, verborum vetustas, si tantum nodosa retia vel pinnarum formidines et sagaces canes omnemque rem venaticam meliorum oblitus adfectas? Quare cum scribis, memento facundiae tuae modum ponere. Rustica sint et inculta, quae loqueris, ut venator esse credaris. Vale.

Translation

1. You pride yourself in your leisure and hunting. This is certainly a pleasant boast, but it is made more jokingly than seriously, for by preference you spend your free time and your holidays from public affairs ruminating over the books of ancient authors.[2] So, you will deceive others, who know you only from a superficial encounter, but I, from the flavor of your letters to me, infer the activities that keep you busy day and night and the daily nourishment that your intellect receives. 2. That is, unless, perhaps you meet Apollo in the woods, like that shepherd Hesiod, whom the family of the Muses crowned with poetic laurel.[3] For from where comes this novelty of content in your letters, from where this archaism of language, if, forgetful of loftier pursuits, you are concerned only with knotted nets and feathered snares, with keen-nosed dogs and the entire habit of hunting? For this reason, when you write, remember to put a limit on your eloquence. Let your language be rustic and unsophisticated, so that you make a credible hunter. Farewell.

Notes

1. See 99 n. 1.

2. These words suggest Praetextatus's general enthusiasm for ancient literature and philosophy, although some have argued the reference is specifically to the emendation of texts; see Kahlos 2002, 129. Symmachus makes the same charge in *Letter* 8.69, where he claims that a friend Valerianus has pretended to spend his time gardening instead of in literary pursuits.

3. Symmachus's reference to Hesiod's receiving a laurel crown is true to the text of Hesiod's *Theogony* 30, as remarked by Bruggisser 1993, 397–98. Symmachus may also have been familiar with this image of Hesiod from his

reading of Vergil, *Eclogues* 6.69–70, or from the correspondence of Fronto, *Epistula* (*Letter*) 1.4.6 (van den Hout 1954).

Letter 1.54: Symmachus to Praetextatus
Date: 380–381[1]

Symmachus's brother Celsinus Titianus died in the late spring or summer of 380. The letter bringing this news to Praetextatus precedes the letters to Titianus (1.62–74) in the book. The order of the letters in the collection is not strictly chronological, even in the groupings by correspondent. *Letter* 1.54 registers the impact of his brother's death on Symmachus and prepares the reader for hearing more about their relationship. That Symmachus turns to Praetextatus for consolation is one more sign of the intimacy of their friendship.

Text

Maestitiae meae solacium grande tribuisti. Nam ut dudum tibi fama fecit indicium, fratris obitu vulneratus continuo animi dolore discrucior. Non mediocre tamen inter praesentes curas levamen accepi, quod te conperi secundum communia optata salvere. Superest ut tu istiusmodi officiis frequentem operam digneris inpendere, quae perspicis medicinam quandam mihi infortunii et maeroris adferre. Vale.

Translation

You have given me great solace in my grief. For, as rumor has already made you aware, wounded by the death of my brother, I am tormented by an incessant pain in my heart. Nevertheless, in the midst of my present preoccupations, I have received no slight relief because I discovered that you, in accordance with the wishes of all, were in good health. It remains for you to consider it worthwhile to expend your energy frequently on duties of this sort, which, as you see, bring some remedy to me for my misfortune and grief. Farewell.

Note

1. See 129–30.

Letter 1.55: Symmachus to Praetextatus
Date: Probably 384[1]

The specifics are missing, but the dynamics of the situation described in this letter are discernible. Praetextatus has offered to act as a mediator between

Symmachus and an unknown person whose actions had insulted Symmachus. The elaborate second sentence reflects the difficulty that Symmachus has in bringing himself to reconcile with this individual. The allusion to Symmachus's "circumstances" suggested to Domenico Vera that this individual wanted to reconcile because Symmachus was about to take up the position of urban prefect, which he had done by June of 384, and the allusion to Praetextatus's work for the public safety reinforces the notion that Praetextatus had already taken up the office of praetorian prefect, which he had done by May of 384.[2] Given these factors, it seems probable that this letter be dated to 384 and hence that it is one of the latest letters in the book.

This letter is an artful conclusion to this correspondence with Praetextatus. Indeed, being in the position of the friend in need is something of a role reversal for Symmachus; in his letters to Ausonius he presented himself as the one who was most often brokering favors for his friends/clients but in no need of such intervention himself. In this letter, it is he who has benefited from the aid of a more powerful friend, and Praetextatus, like a brother, is more than willing to act on his behalf.

Text

Scio germani amoris esse, quod suades. Sed reconciliatio eum requirit auctorem, quem habuit iniusta dissensio, ne noxam meruisse videatur, qui abiuratas amicitias quasi nihil passus adfectat. Quare oblatam concordiam non refuto, <sed> sequestrata consideratione fortunae redeat in gratiam, qui movit offensam.

Tibi pro nostra amicitia satis gratulor, cuius labor saluti publicae commodabit. De quo interim parcius loquar; res enim, quae ad omnes pertinet, numquam uno teste contenta est et mihi magnopere convenit ita meminisse gloriae tuae, ne verecundiae oblitus existimer. Vale.

Translation

I know that what you advise arises from brotherly[3] love. But reconciliation requires the initiative of the one who was the cause of the unjust rupture lest the one who strives to resuscitate a disavowed friendship, as if he had suffered nothing, seem to have deserved injury. For this reason, I do not refuse the peace offered, but let the one who caused the offense restore good relations, without any regard to circumstances.

As befits our friendship, I heartily congratulate you for your hard work that will benefit the public safety. About this for the time being I shall speak rather briefly, for a matter that pertains to all is never satisfied with a single witness, and it is highly appropriate for me to recall your glory in this way, lest I be thought forgetful of your sense of honor. Farewell.

Notes

1. Callu (1972, 116) follows Seeck (1883, xc) and dates this letter to 384. Both see references to Praetexatus's work for the public safety (*saluti publicae*) as alluding to Praetextatus's actions as praetorian prefect in 384. In my view, this suggestion is reinforced by Symmachus's reference to Praetextatus's "glory," an allusion to his attainment of high office, probably the praetorian prefectureship that he held from May 384 until his death in fall of 384; see *PLRE* 1:723. See, too, 115 n. 2.

2. Vera 1981, lix n. 49. See also Bruggisser 1993, 370–72.

3. Again, familial language is indicative of intimacy; see 51 n. 4.

Book 1, *Letters* 56–61: Symmachus to Probus

Symmachus's correspondence with Sextus Claudius Petronius Probus affirms among his friends one of the most distinguished and well-connected Christian aristocrats in Rome. Indeed, Seeck proclaimed that no civic aristocrat held so many offices and for as long as did Probus, and extant inscriptions proudly confirm that Probus held no less than four prefectureships in his lifetime.[1] Ammianus Marcellinus (*Res Gestae* 27.11.3) describes Probus as driven to hold office at least in part to meet the demands of family, friends, and clients. Symmachus's correspondence supports this view of Probus as unusually active in public office, even as he is depicted as imbued with traditional aristocratic concerns for leisure (*otium*) devoted to classical literature to balance work (*negotium*). So *Letter* 1.58 surprises by depicting Probus as an aristocrat who prefers private life and has to be convinced to take up the burdens of office.

If there is agreement among scholars about the illustriousness of Probus's career, there is no such consensus in reconstructing it. Indeed, the dates and locations of his offices have been much disputed, largely due to the conflicting nature of the evidence provided by the inscriptions. Since certainty on these points is not possible given the status of the evidence, the best I can do is to present the most likely chronology. Probus was probably born in 328 in Verona.[2] He had ties to Rome and attained the quaestorship and urban praetorship before being appointed proconsul of Africa, probably in 358. He then held the praetorian prefectureship four times (*CIL* 6:1752 = *ILS* 1268; *CIL* 6:1753 = *ILS* 1267). It is the sequence and dates of these that are problematic. According to the account in the *PLRE*, Probus was prefect in Illyricum in 364, prefect in Gaul in 365/366, and prefect in Illyricum, Italy and Africa for an extraor-

1. Probus 5 in *PLRE* 1:736–740. All the documents for Probus's career were published also by Seeck 1883, xc–ci.

2. In this reconstruction of Probus's career, I am presenting the dates and offices recorded for Probus 5 in *PLRE* 1:736–40, only diverging with regard to his death. There are problems with the dates and locations of the prefectureships, especially that of Illyricum, usually dated to 364. The evidence is complicated, but the date cannot be determined without new information. For discussion and bibliography, see Lizzi Testa 2004, 316–19.

dinarily long time, from 368 to 375. In 371, he was *consul posterior* (junior consul) with the emperor Gratian. It is to 370 or 371 that Seeck ascribed Symmachus's first contact with Probus; an anonymous *Letter* 9.112 is identified by some scholars as Symmachus's initial contact with Probus, but certainty on this letter, its date, or the recipient is not possible.[3]

Like Praetextatus and Symmachus himself, Probus spent almost a decade out of office. But he was pressed back into service, for he attained his fourth praetorian prefecture, most likely in 383 and probably that of Illyricum, Italy, and Africa; he remained in that position at least until the spring of 384.[4] Throughout his career, he served the family of Valentinian loyally; he was among the supporters of Valentinian II who fled to Thessalonica with this emperor in 387 before the approach of the usurper Maximus. In doing this, he was taking a position at odds with that taken by Symmachus, who lent his support to Maximus; this period marked a real divergence between the two men.[5] After this point Probus's movements are unknown; Probus probably returned to Rome after the demise of Maximus in 388 and died by 394.[6]

After his death, Probus was honored in Rome with a large funerary mausoleum housing an epitaph set on marble panels attached to a column behind the altar of St. Peter's Basilica. His epitaph addressed Probus's accomplishments: "rich in wealth, of noble family, exalted in office and distinguished in your consulship … these noble titles you rose above when in time you were presented with the gift of Christ. This is your true office, your nobility."[7] This inscription has been variously interpreted, but in my view it is best understood as a statement of Probus's continuing adherence to traditional aristocratic senatorial ideals of nobility and service, now seen as compatible with attaining Christian glory.[8] These are the same values ascribed to Probus in Symma-

3. Seeck (1883, xxv n. 49) and Roda (1981a, 247–49) argue that *Letter* 9.112 was sent to Probus when he was designated consul or was holder of the consulship, thus in or after 370. Many scholars accept this as the beginning of their relationship, even though this cannot be verified, as Roda correctly observes.

4. Lizzi Testa (2004, 318 n. 418) argues that Probus was in office in October 384 based on *C.Th.6.30.6*, but this date is unreliable. We should end his prefecture in May 384 to allow for his replacement by Praetextatus; see Cameron 2011, 309–10, 364

5. For Symmachus's support for Maximus, see Sogno 2006, 67–71.

6. For further discussion of Probus, see also Seyfarth 1970, 411–25; with critical remarks by Schmidt 1999, 99–116, who dates the death of Probus between 390 and 394. *PLRE* 1:739 dates his death to ca. 388 but with no justification. See also Schlinkert 1996, 182–87; and Giardina 1983, 170–82.

7. *CIL* 6:1756 = *ILCV* 63, vv. 5–24., trans. Croke and Harries 1982, 116.

8. For discussion and bibliography on the inscription from Probus's funerary monument in St. Peter's, see Salzman, 2002, 59–60, 202–3, 214–15; Matthews 1975, 195–97.

chus's letters. Symmachus's emphasis on their common values diminishes the differences between the two men, including religious ones. Indeed, Symmachus feels comfortable enough to direct a conventional wish to Probus: "May the gods only bless our desires" (*Letter* 1.57).

Although Symmachus portrays Probus as a powerful and respected friend, the tone and the brevity of their correspondence indicates that theirs was not an intimate relationship of the sort that Symmachus enjoyed with Ausonius and Praetextatus. There is, for example, no indication of concern for Probus's family and no mention of Probus's wife, even though she was an influential woman in Rome and a member of the large and well-connected Christian family, the Anicii, and his sons, consuls in 395, would later be correspondents.[9] Nor does Symmachus dwell on their shared literary interests, even though we know that Probus was himself a patron of poets. It was almost certainly this Probus to whom Rufius Festus Avienius dedicated his poem *Ora maritima* (*The Seacoast*).[10] Indeed, Probus's knowledge of Greek was far greater than Symmachus's. Thus, while Symmachus's relationship with Probus was cordial and mutually beneficial at the time these letters were sent, theirs was not a deep bond. If the families fell into conflict, as some have argued, and if Symmachus himself was not overly fond of Probus as an individual nor of his father-in-law (whom he would act against when urban prefect), none of that animosity emerges in these early letters.[11]

LETTER 1.56: SYMMACHUS TO PROBUS
DATE: AFTER 364[1]

TEXT

Et tibi publicis negotiis occupato breves litterae demunt fastidium lectionis et mei officii adsiduitas, quidquid scribendum videbatur, exhausit. Merito salutatione librata frugi epistulam necessario stringo conpendio. Alia est

9. Probus's wife was Anicia Faltonia Proba = Proba 3, *PLRE* 1:732–733. Probus's sons, Olybrius and Probinus, were included in Symmachus's fifth book of letters, *Letters* 5.67–71.

10. See Festus 12, *PLRE* 1:336–37. Cameron (2011, 365–66) has demonstrated that Sextus Petronius Probus was not the author of the poems from the *Anthologia Latina* (*Latin Anthology*) 783, as was once proposed by, for one, the *PLRE* 1:740; these poems were by a fifth-century calligrapher named Probus to the emperor Theodosius II.

11. For the identification of the unnamed man whom Symmachus disliked with Probus in Symmachus, *Letter* 3.88, see Matthews 1986, 174. For the circumstances of Symmachus's actions against Probus's father-in-law, see li n. 189. The two men did take opposite sides during the usurpation of Maximus, another cause for hostility; see, too, Pellizzari 1998, 242.

enim protestatio amoris, alia linguae ostentatio. Atque ideo mihi antiquior fuit obsequendi opera quam loquendi. Copiosi videbimur, si abunde seduli iudicemur. Vale.

Translation

Since you are so busy with public affairs, the brevity of my letter spares you any tedium in reading it, and my conscientiousness in fulfilling my duty has exhausted whatever it seemed I should write about. With good reason I send you this economical and necessarily abridged letter with its measured greeting, for protestations of love are one thing, a display of language quite another. And for that reason it was more important to exert myself to show deference than eloquence. I will seem fluent enough, if I am deemed fully attentive to you. Farewell.

Note

1. Callu (1972, 116) dates this letter after 370, based on the assumption that Symmachus, *Letter* 9.112, was sent to Probus and can be dated to 370 (see 118 n. 3). But this is not certain. Hence I date this letter after Probus's first office, i.e., after 364.

Letter 1.57: Symmachus to Probus
Date: 364–375/384[1]

The reference to Probus's workload suggests that he is holding a high office, but Symmachus does not specify which one of the four praetorian prefectureships he is likely referring to. Since the praetorian prefect was in charge of food supplies, Seeck suggested that food shortages in Rome and Italy in 380 or 383 are being alluded to when Symmachus mentions events creating concern about "the safety of the state"; Seeck thus dates the letter to 383, as does Callu, who interprets this remark as a possible allusion to the political uncertainties surrounding the usurpation of Maximus, 383–388. [2] This latter interpretation seems less than likely, given Symmachus's later involvement in support of Maximus that led to his alienation from the court in the later 380s and early 390s, the period in which he likely published this first book of letters.[3] Reading this remark in the light of an earlier prefectureship seems more likely, since it would not raise these issues for Symmachus's reputation.

As noted in the introduction to these letters (p. 119), Symmachus's use of a commonplace phrase, "May the gods only bless our desires," is as formulaic as saying "God bless you" in contemporary parlance. He felt no compunction in using it here, just as he did not refrain from using it in addressing the Christian Ausonius (*Letter* 1.21). The linguistic conventions of polytheism were still acceptable within elite society, even in addressing powerful Christians, though more often in this book Symmachus used polytheistic phrases in letters to known pagans.[4]

Text

In praesentia, quantum satis visum est amicitiae munerandae, cum tuas occupationes tum festinationem tabellarii contemplatus exhibeo; alias mihi et usus veniae et cura non deerit epistulae longioris. Dii modo optata fortunent, salutem reipublicae in solido locent! Tum mihi voluntas promptior erit et ad scribendum quae tu libenter accipias, et ad legenda quae tu animo vacante rescripseris. Vale.

Translation

For the moment, in light of your preoccupations and also the haste of the letter carrier, I am communicating just what seemed to me sufficient to repay the duties of friendship; at another time I shall have no lack either of the exercise of indulgence or the effort needed for a longer letter. May the gods only bless our desires and set the safety of the state on a firm footing! Then I will be more ready and willing both to write what you will gladly receive and to read what you will write back to me with a heart free of care. Farewell.

Notes

1. The reference to workload and "the security of the state" suggests that Probus held a praetorian prefectureship, the earliest of which is 364 according to my dating; see 117–18. His last office makes the year 384 the *terminus ante quem*.
2. Seeck 1883, cvi and 27; Callu 1972, 117 n. 1.
3. See Sogno 2006, 67–71; and liv–lviii.
4. See xlvii–xlviii in the introduction and 20 nn. 8 and 10.

Letter 1.58: Symmachus to Probus
Date: 364–384[1]

The letter includes a reference to "a second set of labors," indicating another one of Probus's praetorian prefectureships, be it his second, third, or fourth (hence the dating). But what is most surprising is the content, for Symmachus depicts Probus as experiencing the traditional reluctance of the senatorial aristocrat to give up private leisure (*otium*) for work (*negotium*). Yet it is the responsibility of the true aristocrat to serve the state, as Symmachus's exempla from Rome's republic make vivid. Probus was reluctant to halt his building projects on his estates, an activity in which Symmachus was himself deeply engaged (see *Letter* 1.12).

Text

Sit tibi animus aequus et patiens muneris imperati. Saepe usu venit, ut in secundos labores virtus probata reparetur. Quid? Tu libenter Atilio factum putas, quod fascibus aratra mutavit et in medio sementis opere anhelos boves statuit rusticus magistratus? Quisque bonae frugis est, in publicum commodum vindicatur. Pone illas interim cogitationes felicis otii tui: 'Quam bene urbana opera novis fastigiis excitabam! Ubi ager noster, vel ille autumno omnis copiae ferax, vel ille hieme apricus, aut qui vere anni primus rosas exuit, aut qui sub aestivo sole de nemore et fonte frigescit?' Sed quid a proposito excidi? Dum medicinam facio querellis tuis, ultro desideranda suggessi. Esto, ut es, curarum omnium tolerans et debitam operam solve principibus, qui rationem magis meriti tui quam voluntatis habuerunt. Vale.

Translation

Let your spirit calmly and patiently endure the task that has been assigned to you. Often it happens that virtue once demonstrated is restored to perform a second set of labors.[2] What? Do you think that Atilius was happy to exchange his plough for fasces and, a rustic turned magistrate, to stop his panting oxen right in the midst of the labor of sowing?[3] Everyone who is of any real worth is claimed for public service. Put aside for the time being those thoughts of your pleasant leisure time. "How nicely I was just fixing up my city place with a new roof! Where is my property, either the estate where the land is fertile with every abundance in fall, or the one that is sunny in winter, the one that first releases the roses from the earth in spring, or the one that with its woods and fountains remains cool under the summer sun?" But why have I strayed from my subject? Even as I supply an antidote to your complaints, I have given you more to long for. May you be, as you are, tolerant of all burdens and pay the service owed to the emperors,[4] who have taken into account your merits more than your desires. Farewell.

Notes

1. Seeck (1883, cvi) proposed that this letter refers to the second prefectureship of Probus, but this is too literal a reading of Symmachus's statement about a second stage of labors. Callu (1972, 117) proposed that Symmachus's

reference to undertaking new honors after a period devoted to leisure fits Probus's acquisition of the office of praetorian prefect in 383, but this would make the letter among the latest in the book, coming after what some have seen as a long period of animosity; see Cameron 2011, 378. No certainty is possible beyond the period of Probus's time in high office, 364–384.

2. Symmachus does not make explicit what he means by "a second set of labors." See 122–23 n. 1.

3. Atilius is a stock example of the virtuous farmer of the Roman republic who, like Cincinnatus, was called from his plow to serve the state and then won a victory that earned him a triumph; see Cicero, *Pro Sexto Roscio Amerino* (*On Behalf of Sextus Roscius Amerinus*) 50; Valerius Maximus, *Factorum et dictorum memorabilium libri ix* (*Nine Books of Memorable Deeds and Sayings*) 4.4.5; Pliny, *Natural History* 18.50; Claudian, *De IV consulatu Honorii* (*On the Fourth Consulship of Honorius*) 438–441. There is still disagreement as to which triumph and which Atilius this story refers to, but most scholars identify these allusions with A. Atilius Calatinus, consul in 257; see Brennan 2000, 1:80–84. Atilius came readily to Symmachus's mind, for he refers to him at least twice more in his correspondence: *Letters* 5.68 and 7.15.

4. The emperors (*principibus*) here noted depend on the dating of this letter. If the letter dates to 365–366, the emperors would be Valentinian I in the west and Valens in the east, since appointments involved nominally the approval of the eastern and western emperors; see Sogno 2006, 55. If this letter is dated to 383, the emperors would be Gratian (still alive until August 383) and Valentinian II, both in the west at the time, and the eastern emperor Theodosius.

Letter 1.59: Symmachus to Probus
Date: 364–373 or 374–376[1]

This letter illuminates the ways in which letters traveled and the distinct advantages office-holders enjoyed in maintaining epistolary networks. Symmachus continues his ongoing contrast of work (*negotium*) and leisure (*otium*) well-spent, the theme with which he opened this book (see pp. 5–6). He concludes this letter with a graceful compliment to Probus's office, which also gives him greater access to letter carriers and more opportunities to practice epistolographic eloquence than Symmachus, the man of leisure.

Text

Mones, ut amicitiae bonum scriptis frequentibus excolamus. Placet hortatio invitatrix religionis et, ut verum fatear, decus mihi est haec voluntas tua:

amor enim maximus plus requirit. Sed quod ais, me potius, qui sim vacuus publicae rei, istiusmodi vigiliam debere sortiri, aequum esse dissentio. Iamprimum quod homo licentis otii scrutari vices commeantium non laboro, tuus honor vecturam litteris, nisi invenit, facit; dehinc quod mihi iners desuetudo oblimat ingenium, tibi inpigro iamdiu negotio levatur usus loquendi. Ergo quo tu ad scribendum maiore copia, hoc ego dignior venia raritatis. Satisne videar his causis munitus in posterum? Memineris volo, quidquid a me sermonis acceperis, obsequii esse, non otii. Vale.

Translation

You urge me to cultivate the virtue of friendship by writing frequently. Your injunction, an invitation to conscientiousness, is pleasing, and, to confess the truth, this wish of yours brings honor to me, for the greatest love is more demanding. But I do not agree that it is fair when you say that, because I am free from public business, I ought rather to have the responsibility for vigilance of this kind. First of all, as a man with the liberty of leisure, I do not exert myself in keeping track of the comings and goings of those traveling, whereas your office creates a means of transporting letters, if you do not find one ready to hand. Second, inactivity and disuse have silted up my talent, whereas the habit of communicating is made easier for you by your longstanding engagement in affairs. Therefore, the greater the opportunity you have for writing, the more worthy I am of pardon for infrequency. Do I not seem sufficiently protected for the future by these explanations? I wish you to remember, whatever letter you receive from me will be the product not of leisure but of respect. Farewell.

Note

1. The dating of this letter is based on the fact that Symmachus was out of office, while Probus was in office; for Symmachus's offices, see the introduction, xxiii–xxxviii.

Letter 1.60: Symmachus to Probus
Date: after 364[1]

This is a letter of recommendation for one Romanus whose low birth is suggested by Symmachus's first line. Romanus was in service at court, yet he is here recommended by Symmachus, who also wrote *Letter* 1.104 on his behalf to Syagrius in 379 and *Letter* 1.73 to Titianus circa 379–380. Two letters in Symmachus's second book also refer to a Romanus, possibly the man noted here. If so, he was at some point adlected into the ranks of the senatorial order as *clarissimus* (Symmachus, *Letters* 2.20, 2.15, dated ca. 390).[2] In any case, Romanus clearly benefited from having Symmachus as a patron. Romanus's career demonstrates how porous the imperial and senatorial elites were and how Symmachus acted as broker in both worlds.

Text

Scio te non fortunarum sed meritorum habere dilectum. Romanus familiaris meus aulicis etiam nunc paret officiis utpote sacri administer aerarii, sed instrumenta probitatis in quemvis usum publici honoris excoluit. Quare dignitas illi est promiscua cum plurimis, honestas aequa cum paucis. Quod eo memorandum putavi, ut a te quoque pro ratione vitae, non pro gradu militiae censeatur. Fac periculum maximis in negotiis, fac in seriis remissisve muneribus: reperies hominis tectam fidem, patentem religionem, prudentiam liberam, verecundiam liberalem. Cui ego propterea factum volo, ut mei testimonii fides clareat, tibi amicus limatae probitatis accedat. Vale.

Translation

I know that you have affection not for circumstances but for merit. My friend Romanus even now is employed in the service of the court as an administrator of the imperial treasury, but he has cultivated the qualities of integrity appropriate to any position in public office. For this reason, although he shares his rank with many, his character is equal to few. I thought I ought to mention this so that he should be evaluated by you, too, for the manner of his life and not his rank in imperial service. Put him to the test in the most important affairs, in weighty or casual tasks; you will find that he is a man of discreet loyalty, of obvious conscientiousness, of untrammeled intelligence, and of gentlemanly modesty. For these reasons I am promoting his interest so that the reliability of my endorsement be clear and that you gain a friend of perfect honesty. Farewell.

Notes

1. Callu (1972, 119) dates this letter to before 375, but he does not give his reasons. More likely, this letter can be dated to a period when Probus was in office, i.e., after 364.

2. The Romanus of the letters of books 1 and 2 is identified with Romanus 4, *PLRE* 1:769. Although some scholars would identify this Romanus with a man of the same name who was count of Egypt in 391, I concur with *PLRE* that this was another man, Romanus 5. However, *PLRE* wrongly identifies Romanus 4 as the brother of Magnus and Magnillus (*Letters* 1.70, 2.20) on the

basis of a misunderstanding of the term *frater*, "brother." In the language of *amicitia*, this word does not necessitate a family tie; see 51 n. 4 and Cecconi 2002a, 189–91.

Letter 1.61: Symmachus to Probus
Date: 364–366; 368–375; 383–384[1]

Symmachus's complaint is the standard one among friends: write more often, even if you have tasks to fulfill, because our friendship is important. The style of the letter is rather clipped and suggests notions of obligation rather than intimacy.

Text

Ais te multiiugis necessitatibus impediri, quo minus naviter amicorum carissimos adloquaris. Notae rei cesset adsertio. Nam et qui procul absumus, curas ac vigilias tuas communis patriae copiis et satietate sentimus. Mutasti igitur officium, non negasti. Antiquior enim tibi fuit, ut esse debuit, salus civium quam salutatio. Nunc sane et desideramus et exposcimus litteras tuas largiter congesta fruge in proximae hiemis inpendium; quamquam scio necdum tibi hanc partem nimis tutam videri. Numquam enim securus est amor patriae et, quamvis magna remedia conquirat, semper illud putat imminere quod timuit. Vale.

Translation

You say that you are prevented by many demands from writing diligently to the dearest of your friends. No need to insist on what is already known. Even those of us who are far away appreciate from the fullness of provisions your concern and vigilance for our common fatherland. So you have exchanged your responsibility, not denied it. For the well-being of citizens was more important to you than sending a greeting, as it should be. But now at any rate we long for and lay claim to your letter since the harvest has been abundantly stored up for distribution next winter; however, I know that this task does not yet seem quite secure to you. For love of country is never carefree, and, however great the remedies a person collects, he always thinks that what he feared is imminent. Farewell.

Note

1. This letter was written at a time when Probus held the office of praetorian prefect, since it was in this capacity that he was responsible for the

collection and transport of the grain supply. Callu (1972, 120) follows Ruggini in seeing no great famine before 376 and so dates this letter before 375, to his praetorian prefectureship in Italy. However, this is not a compelling argument, since the letter does not indicate a food shortage, only Probus's efforts to avert one.

Book 1, *Letters* 62–74: Symmachus to His Brother Celsinus Titianus

Celsinus Titianus was, like his brother Symmachus, set on a senatorial career. He had already attained the office of vicar of Africa by January of 380.[1] As vicar, Titianus administered a diocese, a responsible position held in the early stages of a civic career. Symmachus's professed joy at the news of the appointment of a "brother" to high office has been identified as an allusion to Titianus (*Letter* 3.19), and since Symmachus was already embarked on the next stages of the civic career, we can assume that Titianus was younger than Symmachus. But Titianus died before advancing any further, and his successor is recorded in his position by February 381.[2]

Symmachus's grief over Titianus's death was intense; it prompted him to avoid attending Syagrius's consular inauguration, which was held on 1 January 381.[3] Yet Symmachus's letters to Titianus do not openly express any of Symmachus's strong feelings for this brother.[4] Eleven of the thirteen are letters of recommendation, probably sent to Titianus in 380, when he held office. This is in itself noteworthy. Since Symmachus has selected these letters to portray his relationship, he has chosen to honor the memory of his brother in traditionally Roman fashion by focusing on his brother's public office and influence. At the same time, these letters reveal the ways in which

1. For the date of his office, see *C. Th.* 14.3.17. The manuscript reading of July is incorrect. Seeck changed it to January, as noted by Roda (1981a, 255) and Lepelley (2003, 285 n. 1), because the emperor Gratian issued this law in Trier and he had left Trier by the spring of 380. A January dating would also allow time for news of Titianus's death to reach Symmachus, who mentioned it to Syagrius in a letter written in the fall of 380 (*Letter* 1.101); see 179–80. For Symmachus's brother, see Titianus 5, *PLRE* 1:917–18.

2. *C. Th.* 12.1.84, dated to February 381.

3. Symmachus, *Letter* 1.101, to Syagrius. Symmachus mentions his grief concerning the loss of his brother several times; see *Letters* 1.54, 1.83; 3.6.2; and 9.113. *Letter* 3.6.2 mentions the loss of three "brothers," one of whom was probably Titianus. For the extended use of the term *frater* to nonfamily correspondents, see 51 n. 4 and Pellizzari 1998, 77.

4. This is comparable to his correspondence to his father; see Salzman 2006a, 357–75.

elite families used their social networks to advance friends and clients. Hence Symmachus's letters to Titianus, like those to his father, furthered their family's reputation. In this regard, it is worth noting that all three men had the same religious affiliation and public cult office, since all were supporters of the traditional Roman state cults. Like Symmachus the elder and his brother, Titianus held a public priesthood, almost certainly that of Vesta and the Sun God (see *Letter* 1.68).

Letter 1.62: Symmachus to His Brother Celsinus Titianus
Date: before 380[1]

This letter concerns a family matter. Symmachus is urging Titianus to hasten the advance of some relatives (*parentes*). Callu imagines that he was escorting his parents, while Symmachus, with his other brothers, Avianius Valentinus and Avianius Vindicianus, was awaiting their arrival.[2] This family scene is pleasing, but there is little in the letter to pin this idea down.

Text

Bonae spei plenus, postquam mihi adventus vestri fecistis indicium, calcar quoddam subpingo properantibus et in eam rem tuum munus inploro, ut parentum studia hortator adceleres. Stabit apud me memoria beneficii tui nec unquam tacita erit, si fratrum delegata curaveris. Vale.

Translation

Full of high hopes after you gave me notice of your arrival, I am setting, as it were, a spur to the speed of your party and for this purpose beg your assistance, to hasten by your exhortations the endeavors of our relatives. I will hold fast the memory of your kindness, nor will it ever lapse into silence if you give your attention to this fraternal assignment. Farewell.

Notes

1. Callu (1972, 120–21) follows Seeck (1883, cvii), noting that Titianus was close by in Italy, posits a family reunion and dates this letter before the death of the other brothers, i.e., before 377. However, I agree with Seeck (1883, 29) that there is no evidence for this. But since Symmachus describes Titianus as nearby and since there is no reference to his leaving office, it seems unlikely that he was on his way back from Africa. Hence, it seems more likely that we date this letter before Titianus's departure for his position as vicar in Africa and thus before 380.

2. See 130 n. 1.

Letter 1.63: Symmachus to His Brother Celsinus Titianus
Date: before 374–378[1]

It may be at first surprising (see also *Letter* 1.64) that the man whom Symmachus recommends here, a certain Saturus, is probably Uranius Saturus, brother of the bishop Ambrose.[2] Although a Christian, Symmachus describes him as *frater communis*, "our mutual brother." Since Symmachus frequently called friends and clients brothers (*fratres*), this is no indication of any familial relationship. This is significant: it means the letter cannot be used to argue, as some have done, that Symmachus and Ambrose were related by blood.[3]

Text

Longum loquantur pro incognitis aut alienis verba facturi; mihi haec opera desinenda est, cum litteras nostras Saturus frater communis accipiat, quas non commendationi eius praestiti, sed nostro circa vos amore functus emisi. Vale.

Translation

Let those who have to speak about unknown or foreign people do so at great length; in my case I should abandon this task, since Saturus our mutual brother is taking my letter, which I have provided not as a recommendation for him but to demonstrate my love for you. Farewell.

Notes

1. This letter is dated before 374–378, since the Saturus in question, if identified with Uranius Saturus, had died by that date; see 131 n. 2 below.

2. See Uranius Saturus, *PLRE* 1:809. *PCBE* 2:1995–1996 n. 17 notes that his death could fall anytime between 374 and 378, depending on the identification of the barbarian invasion mentioned by Ambrose, *De excessu fratris Saturi* (*On the Death of His Brother Saturus*) 1.32, with either the Gothic invasion of 378 or that of the Quadi and Sarmatians in 374–375.

3. For this usage of *frater*, see 51 n. 4. Moreover, as Neil McLynn (1994, 263) rightly observed, Symmachus would not need to commend a real cousin in such terms to his brother Titianus. Hence, this letter does not support the view proposed by Barnes (1992, 7–13) of a blood link between Ambrose and Symmachus. Nor is the reference in Ambrose's funeral oration for his brother good evidence for a family link. When Ambrose talks of Symmachus as Ura-

nius's *parens*, or "relative" (*On the Death of His Brother Saturus* 1.32), again the term can indicate a metaphorical rather than blood bond; see, e.g., Ausonius *apud Symmachum*, *Letter* 1.32.4.

Letter 1.64: Symmachus to His Brother Celsinus Titianus
Date: 380[1]

Symmachus is aware of the potential for confusion and the potential irony of his writing in support of a bishop. He refers to Christianity as a *secta*, which is here translated as "affiliation." In doing so, he likens it to a philosophical school, a positive assertion in Symmachus's classically oriented worldview. Moreover, the actions of the bishop, Clemens, in defending his home town Caesarea (modern Cherchel, Algeria) against the rebel Firmus earn him Symmachus's praise and provide some of the background to the letter.

Firmus, a Moorish prince, son of Nubel and brother of Gildo and of Mascezel, rebelled against Rome because the governor in Africa refused to listen to his protests about the exaction of monies. The revolt was a serious threat, for some of the army and likely some Donatists supported him.[2] Firmus remained in Africa from 372/373 to 375, causing great devastation, until he was defeated by the general Theodosius (father of the Augustus Theodosius) and committed suicide in 375.[3] In the course of the war, the city fisc of the town of Caesarea was captured.

Symmachus wanted his brother, as *vicarius Africae* in 380, to intervene on behalf of this bishop and the leading men of Caesarea. Clemens had already obtained imperial assent to his request that the leading citizens, presumably the *curia*, not be forced to make good the losses the city fisc had suffered. Symmachus's language (he describes the gold and silver of Mauretania as "broken up," *lanciatum*) and the text of Ammianus Marcellinus, *Res Gestae* 29.5.16, suggest that the material that was seized by Firmus was metal plate and precious objects, not money (i.e., the golden crowns) offered by cities to the emperor. Replacing these objects would have presented a significant financial burden especially for the decurions. Since Clemens had already obtained the approval of his request from the imperial court, probably in a rescript, the point of this letter would seem to be to facilitate a local judicial decision. Claude Lepelley has observed that it was the case since the time of Hadrian that imperial rescripts were required to be reviewed at the local level to verify the facts of the request.[4] If this is so, then, Symmachus's letter was intended to advance Clemens's request at the local level, before the *vicarius*, his brother Titianus. Symmachus probably met Clemens, a man of some standing in Caesarea, when he had been proconsul in Africa. Symmachus would have been happy to advance Clemens's request, for he certainly would want to maintain his local ties with Mauretania Caesarea, where he had clients and friends as well as property (see, e.g., *Letter* 7.66). For Symmachus and his brother to be seen acting on behalf of these clients would benefit their reputation and that of their family.

Text

1. Commendari a me episcopum forte mireris. Causa istud mihi, non secta persuasit. Nam Clemens boni viri functus officium Caesaream, quae illi patria est, conciliata maximorum principum pace tutatus est. Fando acceperas rebellione barbarica, quod auri, quod argenti, privati et publici, sacri et profani Mauretaniae fuit, direptione hostium lancinatum. 2. Evenit ea tempestate, ut etiam fisci depositum belli iure raperetur. Quod a summatibus civitatis, quos reliquos fuga fecerat, ius aerarii reposcebat. Misera et acerba condicio, nisi iustitiam temporum Clementis cura movisset, quem ego non minus famae saeculi quam civium securitati dixerim commodasse. Quid enim praeter invidiam referret aerarium, si opes ab inopi curia poscerentur? Habes ordinem rei. Quod restat enitere, ut voti tui adspiratio vela faciat impetratis. Vale.

Translation

Perhaps you are surprised that I am recommending a bishop. His cause has persuaded me to do so, not his affiliation. For Clemens[5] performed the duty of a good man in guarding Caesarea, which is his homeland, and gaining the goodwill of the greatest of princes.[6] You had learned by report that in the barbarian rebellion, whatever gold or silver, public or private, sacred or secular, there was in Mauretania had been broken apart in the plundering of the enemy. 2. It happened at that time that even the holdings of the fisc were carried off in the name of the war.[7] The treasury was seeking by right the return of these holdings from the leading men of the city, whom flight had made survivors. It would have been a pitiful and bitter state of affairs, had not Clemens's commitment advanced the justice of our times and in so doing, I would say, promoted no less the glory of our age than the security of its citizens. For what would the treasury gain except hatred, if money was sought from a moneyless council? You have the sequence of events. As to what remains, take pains that the favorable breeze of your support fill his sails for a successful trip. Farewell.

Notes

1. This letter was sent to Titianus when was *vicarius* in Africa.

2. Firmus was proclaimed Augustus by the *equites quartae sagittariorum cohortis* and the *pedites Constantianorum*; see Ammianus Marcellinus, *Res Gestae* 29.5.15 and 20. He courted Donatists; see testimony for Firmus 3, *PLRE* 1:340.

3. Firmus chose suicide over captivity; see Ammianus Marcellinus, *Res Gestae* 29.5.54; Orosius, *Historiarum adversum paganos* (*History against the Pagans*) 7.33.5–6 (Zangemeister 1967); *PCBE* 1:457–58.

4. Lepelley 1981, 2:517–518; 2003, 285–97.

5. For more on Clemens, see *PCBE* Clemens 1, 1:212–13.

6. In 380, the princes would have been Gratian, Valentinian II, and Theodosius, but Clemens probably made his request to Gratian, either at Trier or Milan.

7. In the fighting, the fisc that was taken by Firmus's troops was more than likely a local imperial fund set aside for the municipal authorities, not one of the *thesauri maiores* or large imperial funds; see Lepelley 2003, 290–91.

Letter 1.65: Symmachus to His Brother Celsinus Titianus
Date: 380[1]

Symmachus's enemy is not named nor the "attack" specified. That information would be delivered orally. The letter does serve, however, to maintain contact with his brother.

Text

Scire postulas, quid de lacessentibus sentiamus. Nolo consilium suscensentis expectes neque in eius noxam labores, quem vides abundare peccatis. Ipse causas dabit, quas non videaris optasse. Sed de illo satis habeo dictum. Veniam quo me ducit adfectio. Inmane quantum a litteris desidetis neque metuitis ne vos talione silentii mordeamus. Quid hiems faciet quae terra et mari morabitur commeatus? Cogitate vestri officii necessitatem, nostrae sollicitudinis vicem eamque adripite diligentiam quam de nobis mutuo flagitatis. Vale.

Translation

You ask to know what I feel about those who are on the attack. I do not want you to wait for some expression of my anger nor to strive to harm that man whom you see commits no shortage of wrongs. He himself will furnish opportunities, which you should not seem to have invited. But about him I think enough has been said. I shall proceed to the topic to which affection leads me. You slack off terribly in your letter writing and have no fear that

I will retaliate in kind against you with silence. What will the winter bring, which will delay communications on land and on sea? Think of the necessity of your obligation, our mutual concern for one another, and seize that zeal to write that you ask from me in return. Farewell.

Note

1. See 133 n. 1.

Letter 1.66: Symmachus to His Brother Celsinus Titianus
Date: 380[1]

Gelasius was given an imperial post, which Symmachus, with characteristic vagueness, does not specify. *PLRE* suggests that Gelasius was to oversee imperial property in Africa and so tentatively assigns him the office of *rationalis rei privatae fundorum domus divinae per Africam*.[2] Gelasius's office was not necessarily given to him on the basis of experience, for prior to this he was a doctor to important men at court.[3] Clearly, the nature of one's recommendations and one's connections in society were of far more importance in advancing in the state than merit in the modern sense of the word. That Symmachus's recommendation would matter in this sphere is further indication of how interconnected late Roman society was and how closely aristocrats were tied to imperial bureaucrats as well as to each other (see also *Letter* 1.67).

Text

Gelasius, cui factum volo, imperialis domus curam recepit, quod negotium ei aliquid adtulit dignitatis, etsi plus habet honoris in moribus. Medicinam cum primis nostrae aetatis exercuit. Inde est illi via facta meritorum. Nam summates aulae, quibus iuvanda salute profuerat, testes potius habuit quam patronos. Absit ut tibi usus veniat artis eius, cum cetera honestamenta sanctissimi viri possint pro illo ferre suffragium. Ergo ama Gelasium mihi iam dudum placitum, tibi me spondente placiturum. Vale.

Translation

Gelasius, whose interest I am promoting, has received charge of the imperial household,[4] an office that has brought him some prestige, although he possesses more honor for his character. He was among the foremost of our age in the practice of medicine. From this a path was made for his merits. For the most powerful men at court, whom he had helped by promoting their health, served rather as witnesses for him than as patrons. May you have no need to call on his medical skills, seeing that the rest of this most respectable man's distinctions are able to cast a vote in his favor. Therefore, love Gelasius, a man who has long pleased me and one who, I promise, will please you, too. Farewell.

Notes

1. See 133 n. 1.

2. *PLRE* 1:387. For the title, see *Notitia Dignitatum* (*List of Offices*), western Empire 12.16; Jones 1986, 1:425–26.

3. Similarly, for Helvius Vindicianus, a career in medicine led to imperial office; see Helvius Vindicianus 2, *PLRE* 1:967.

4. See 136 n. 2.

Letter 1.67: Symmachus to His Brother Celsinus Titianus
Date: before 381[1]

Anysius has been tentatively identified as the man who served as assessor to the powerful Rufinus in the period 388–392, that is, before Rufinus held the influential office of praetorian prefect of the East from 392 to 395.[2] If this is the man, then this is another case of a protégé of Symmachus who was able to advance into the imperial bureaucracy, presumably in part through the latter's support. These lower-level officials reinforce the view that Symmachus's influence extended into imperial court circles, as shown by his letters not only to Ausonius (*Letters* 1.13–43) but also later to this same powerful Rufinus.[3]

Text

Commendarem tibi Anysium laudabilem virum, nisi in amicitiam meam te auctore venisset. Quando igitur nihil est quod illi meus sermo conciliet, beneficii loco habebo, si in eum sancti animi tui gliscat adfectio. Nam ubi amoris rudimenta praeventa sunt, secundae gratiae locus est, ut augmenta poscantur. Vale.

Translation

I would commend Anysius to you, a praiseworthy man, if he had not entered my friendship at your instigation. Since there is no respect in which my words can commend him, I will consider it a kindness if the love of your virtuous soul for this man increases. For where the beginnings of affection have been anticipated, there is room for a second favor, to request their increase. Farewell.

Notes

1. There are no indications of dating for this letter. Thus, it must be dated before Titianus's death.

2. Anysius 2, *PLRE* 1:79; Rufinus 18, *PLRE* 1:778–81.

3. See Symmachus, *Letters* 2.22; 3.91–101; and Cecconi 2002a, 210–11.

Letter 1.68: Symmachus to His Brother Celsinus Titianus
Date: 380[1]

The identity and status of Rufus are not known, but his task was to protect the properties of the pontifical college in Africa. Symmachus does not specify the nature of the threats to this property, but most often such problems were caused by seizures, contested succession, or the intervention of Christian bishops. Symmachus reminds Titianus of his duty to maintain the public well-being by preserving the college's lands. Titianus would have been receptive to this view, since he was public priest of two cults, probably those of Vesta and Sol, and hence would naturally be in favor of securing the college's holdings.[2]

Text

Rufus pontificalis arcarius prosequitur apud te mandata collegii, cui prae ceteris retinendi Vaganensis saltus cura legata est. Effice, oro te, ut divinitus videatur oblatum tui honoris auxilium et utriusque te sacerdotii antistitem recordare. Quidquid publicus vigor aut privata poscit industria, oratus exequere. Multum in gratiam tuam publica utilitas promovebit. Habes summam petitionum. Singula autem tibi vel commonitorii series indicabit vel Rufus expediet, cui maturum praestabis effectum, ut sequestratum paulisper officium regressus adripiat. Vale.

Translation

Rufus, the treasurer of the pontiffs, is pursuing with you the instructions of the college; to him the responsibility has been delegated before all else to retain the upland pastures of Baga. Make sure, I beg you, that the assistance of your office seem heaven-sent, and remember that you are a high priest in both priesthoods. Whatever official force or private industry demands, the request has been made, see it through. Serving the public good will do much to advance your influence. You have the gist of my requests. However, either itemization in a memorandum will indicate the details to you, or Rufus will explain them, for whom, I trust, you will help bring about a speedy resolution so that he may return and take up the duty that he set aside for this brief time. Farewell.

Notes

1. See 133 n. 1.

2. Titianus was a priest in two cults, identified by Seeck (1883, cvi) as Vesta and Sol because of their frequent conjunction in the fourth century; see also Leppelley 2003, 286.

Letter 1.69: Symmachus to His Brother Celsinus Titianus
Date: 380[1]

Acutianus is not otherwise identified; he is acting on behalf of his associates, Nicasius and Rogatianus, who are similarly not securely identified.[2] They desire to resolve this lawsuit in Africa and would prefer Titianus, acting in his position as *vicarius*, to be the judge in what is a private but unspecified suit. Titianus is their preferred judge because they have a letter of recommendation from his brother Symmachus.

Text

Potuit frater meus Acutianus suo nomine quod poscit adipisci, ut qui sit non minus tibi quam mihi familiaris, sed interfuit officii mei, ut ei voluntariam operam commodarem. Iuvat autem desiderium illius iustitia postulati. Nam germanos suos Nicasium et Rogatianum negotium commune curantes, vel ad disceptationem Numidici consularis remitti postulat, vel quod ei antiquius est, te potissimum cognitore, mavult quam primum molestiam litis absolvi. Quare si et illius apud te grande momentum est et a legibus causa non discrepat et interventus meus libram tui favoris inclinat, adniti aequum est, ut optimo viro ex sententia procedat optatum. Vale.

Translation

My brother Acutianus could have obtained what he wants on his own account, as he is no less a friend to you than to me, but it was important to my sense of responsibility to freely offer my services to him. Moreover, the justice of what he asks furthers his request. He asks either that his brothers Nicasius and Rogatianus, who are associates in business, be returned for judgment by the consular of Numidia or, what is more to his liking, that the annoyance of the lawsuit be resolved as soon as possible, with you preferably as judge. Therefore, if that man carries any weight with you and if his case is not inconsistent with the law[3] and if my intervention tips the scales of your favor, it is right that you exert yourself so that the desire of an excellent man progress according to his liking. Farewell.

Notes

1. See 133 n. 1.

2. Nicasius and Rogatianus are not otherwise attested, unless we identify the latter with the A....us Rogati(an)us 2, *PLRE* 1:767, who dedicated an inscription to an unidentified emperor, possibly around the time of Valentinian I (*PLRE* Anonymus 72).

3. Symmachus's concern that the requests of friends and family not lead Titianus to disregard the legal and just action is a noteworthy aim and an epistolary *topos*. However, certain Romans, it would appear, did overlook legal and ethical issues in their desire to cement personal ties with more powerful men. For a variation on this idea, see *Letters* 1.72 and 1.77.

Letter 1.70: Symmachus to His Brother Celsinus Titianus
Date: 380[1]

This is another letter of recommendation and a request for Titianus's intervention, this time on behalf of two men: Magnus and Magnillus. The former was possibly a rhetor, but the latter was apparently set on a civic career, for he is identified with one of Titianus's successors as *vicarius* of Africa from 391 to 393.[2] Both appear to be men of some standing, at least on the local level, for they are here acting on behalf of an otherwise unattested woman of senatorial rank (hence noted as *clarissima* in Latin), Eutychia. That senatorial women required the aid of intercessors in court appears a recurring problem; see *Letter* 1.74.

Text

Fratrum nostrorum Magni atque Magnilli petitio est, quam prosequendam recepi, quibus inpendio curae est, ut homines Eutychiae clarissimae feminae iudiciorum praesidio fulciantur. Intellegis eas esse personas, quibus haec gratia magis ex suo merito quam ex meis litteris debeatur. Nec mireris ipsos super ea re scribere noluisse, cum reverentia mei fecerit, ut nostro suffragio potius uterentur. Vale.

Translation

I have received a request from our brothers Magnus and Magnillus that should be followed up on. They are deeply concerned that the dependents of the *clarissima* Eutychia should be supported by the protection of the courts.[3] You understand that they are persons to whom this favor is owed more by their own merit than because of my letter. And do not be surprised that they themselves were not willing to write you about that matter, since their respect for me prompted them to use my support instead. Farewell.

NOTES

1. See 133 n. 1.

2. The identification of these two men as brothers and of the Romanus (= Romanus 4, *PLRE* 1:769) of *Letter* 1.60 as a third brother is incorrect, depending on a misunderstanding of the word *frater* (see 51 n. 4). The identification of this Magnus is made more difficult by the fact that it is such a common name. So there are several possible people with whom this Magnus can be identified, including the rhetor attested by *CIL* 6:9585: Magnus 6, *PLRE* 1:534, or Fl. Magnus = Magnus 10, *PLE* 1:535, who received Jerome, *Letter* 70, in 397, or some unattested or some unknown person. Magnillus is identified as the *vicarius Africae* by *PLRE* 1:533.

3. The dependents were legally tied to Eutychia. What is desired from the courts is not specified.

LETTER 1.71: SYMMACHUS TO HIS BROTHER CELSINUS TITIANUS
DATE: 380[1]

Caecilianus is not otherwise attested, but his duties as *defensor civitatis* would primarily involve acting as a judge in local matters. He was, thus, part of the imperial administration of a province.[2] Symmachus asks Titianus for assistance in some "family business" (*negotium familiare*), perhaps in a lawsuit involving property in Africa; as *vicarius*, Titianus had oversight over appeals from provinces and was also charged with monitoring the investigations of governors into officials associated with taxes.[3]

TEXT

Caecilianum virum honestum Laurentum Lavinatium defensorem susceptum commendat officium. Cui si nihil conciliationis cetera vitae honestamenta praestarent, interventus meus gratiam tuam deberet adquirere. Ama ergo hominem placitum mihi et religiosae civitatis commodis obsequentem. Amoris autem tui sumemus indicium, si eos quibus negotium familiare mandavit adiuveris. Vale.

Translation

The duty I have undertaken recommends the honorable Caecilianus, *defensor* of the Laurentines of Lavinium. If the other distinctions of his life have provided nothing to commend him to you, my intervention ought to win your favor. So, embrace this man, a man who has pleased me and is attentive to the interests of a sacred city.[4] Further, I will take it as a sign of your affection, if you help those to whom he has entrusted his personal business. Farewell.

Notes

1. Symmachus probably wrote Titianus when he was *vicarius*.
2. Frakes 2001, 119–20. Frakes (84) proposes that Constantine was responsible for creating "a new kind of *defensor civitatis* sometime between November 326 and 330/331 in lost legislation that curtailed local corruption by providing a new means of accessible justice to smaller landowners."
3. On the legal stipulations, see *C. Th.* 1.15.2.1; 1.15.3; 1.15.5–6.
4. By describing Lavinium as a "sacred city" (*religiosa civitas*), Symmachus echoes a longstanding Roman reverence for a city allegedly founded by Aeneas (see Vergil, *Aeneid* 1.258–259, 270–271), venerated for its Trojan origins, and considered the home of the household gods of Aeneas, the Penates. Macrobius (*Saturnalia* 3.4.11) reiterates this association. Symmachus's letter suggests that the religious reputation of this city continued in the fourth-century elite's *mentalité* and perhaps practice. The late fifth-century pope Gelasius's decision to build a basilica to Santa Maria delle Vigne on the site of the pagan altars associated with Aeneas at Lavinium would support this view; see Lavinia in *PECS*.

Letter 1.72: Symmachus to His Brother Celsinus Titianus
Date: 380[1]

This is another letter of recommendation, but rather less enthusiastic than many, as shown by comparison with *Letter* 1.73. This Bassus[2] may be the man whose sister owned territory in Africa (see *Letters* 4.36 and 4.48, dated after 395), which would then explain why Symmachus is writing to Celsinus about him.

Text

Amicorum desideriis operam non negamus, dum iusta credimus quae petuntur; ut nunc mihi usu venit, qui Bassum optimis viris placitum non putavi suffragio deserendum. Salva igitur mea existimatione, qui bonis credidi, meritum tibi hominis dies longior indicabit. Mihi satis est, si illi primus aditus spem tui dederit pleniorem. Vale.

Translation

We do not deny our services for the wishes of friends, so long as we believe what they seek is just; this is now my experience, for I have concluded that Bassus, a man pleasing to the best of men, ought not to be deprived of support. So, setting aside my estimation of him, for which I took the word of good men, the passing of time will show you the merit of this man. For me, it is enough if his first audience with you gives him some fuller hope of your support. Farewell.

Notes

1. The association of this man with Africa suggests that the dating is the year that Titianus was in office.

2. Bassus may be identified with Bassus 8, *PLRE* 1:151.

Letter 1.73: Symmachus to His Brother Celsinus Titianus
Date: Probably 381[1]

This recommendation for Romanus is fuller and more animated than the previous one. For another recommendation for this man, see *Letter* 1.60.

Text

Quando eam dii potestatem dederunt, ut amicis ac necessariis meis usui esse possis, confido Romano optimo viro, quocum mihi iam diu familiaritas est, in tuo praesidio paratam bonae spei copiam. Duabus enim commendationibus, quarum tibi antiqua cura est, adiuvatur, mei testimonii praerogativa et sui meriti conscientia. Nam sedulo audeo iudicare dignum esse quem pensi habeas et, ne longum loquar, cuius amicitia non graveris. Spectata mihi est in eo quies animi, officii diligentia; nemo in amicos fide utitur promptiore. Haec ita esse, si quid mihi tribuis, velim credas, si haeret animus, hortor examines. Vale.

Translation

Since the gods have given you the power to be able to be of service to my friends and associates, I am confident that an abundance of high expectations is in store under your protection for Romanus, an excellent man with whom

I have for a long time now been friendly. For he benefits from two recommendations for which you show particular regard: the special claim of my testimony and knowledge of his own merit. For, in all sincerity, I dare to judge that this man is worthy of your esteem and, not to speak at length, a man by whose friendship you will not be burdened. I have scrutinized the serenity of his soul, his diligence in his duties; no one shows a more ready loyalty toward friends. I would like you to believe this is so, if you grant me any credence; if your mind is hesitant, I urge you to put him to the test. Farewell.

Note

1. This letter probably dates to Titianus's vicariate in 380.

Letter 1.74: Symmachus to His Brother Celsinus Titianus
Date: 380[1]

The case here is typical in certain regards. Fasgania is a member of the senatorial order with property in Africa. However, while senatorial women (*clarissimae*) were independent in certain regards and had some control over their property, they often needed to go to a powerful male patron to protect their rights; this sort of dispute over property was frequent enough that not only senatorial friends and family but local bishops were willing to intervene to resolve such conflicts.[2] In this letter Symmachus is again asking for Celsinus to intervene, probably in his official role as *vicarius* of Africa.

Text

Est aliquid in querellis Fasganiae filiae meae, quod mihi ex voto fateor accidisse; nam nisi futuras sibi usui litteras poposcisset, ad scribendum mihi defuisset occasio. Praelibo igitur salutationem quae meum spectat officium; reliqua pars paginae ad causam clarissimae feminae pertinebit, quae sibi ab hominibus tuis nescio quid agrorum deflet ereptum. Id ego loci et meriti tui conscius servili ausu clam te opinor admissum atque ideo filiae meae correctionis facilitatem spopondi, si ad te familiaris conquestio genus iniuriae pertulisset. Quaeso igitur, ut temeratae possessionis statum iubeas reformari. Si quid autem controversiae est, in pignoris nostri praesentiam differatur, quae secura iustitiae tuae recusat alios cognitores. Vale.

Translation

There is something in the complaints of my daughter Fasgania[3] that, I confess, came about in accordance with my wishes, for if she had not asked for a letter that would be of use to her, I would not have had the occasion to write. So, I offer first my greeting, which fulfills the duty I owe you; the remaining part of the page will take up the case of this *clarissima* who laments that some of her land has been taken from her by your men. Being familiar with your status and your merits, I think that the crime was committed by some act of servile daring without your knowledge, and for that reason I promised my daughter ease of redress, if a friend's complaint reported to you the nature of the wrong. I ask, therefore, that you order the rights to this violated property to be restored. If, however, there is any controversy about this, let it be put off until the arrival of our child, who, confident in your justice, refuses other judges.

Notes

1. See 142 n. 1. The African connection suggests the date.

2. See, for example, the *Sermons* of Ambrose, discussed by Ruggini 1995, 25–29; and Evans Grubbs 2002, 9, 43–55, and 65–66. Disselkamp (1997, 44–45) considers Fasgania a pagan solely on the basis of her inclusion in this letter. This assumption about religious affiliation is misguided, for it ignores how religiously open were Symmachus's patronage networks, as demonstrated by his willingness to support even a bishop (*Letter* 1.64)

3. Symmachus adopts familial language by calling Fasgania his "daughter," *filia*, indicating his close support for her.

Book 1, *Letters* 75–88: Symmachus to Hesperius

Decimius Hilarianus Hesperius was the second son of the poet Ausonius (Ausonius, *Parentalia* 11). His successful career was the result, in no small part, of his father's influence. Hesperius was in office without a break during the period of his father's political ascendancy under Valentinian I and Gratian, between 375 and 380. The precise dates of his offices are contested, but they are important in as much as they bear upon the dating of Symmachus's letters.

The traditional view, proposed by the *PLRE*, makes Hesperius proconsul of Africa from 376 to 377; with his father as colleague he then was the praetorian prefect of Gaul by 378, praetorian prefect of Italy and Gaul from 378 to 379, and then held this same office in Italy and Africa between 379 and 380. The last prefectures are disputed. The *PLRE* entry for Ausonius alleged that their joint prefectureship held from 378 to 379 extended to Italy, Gaul, and Africa.[1] Altay Coşkun has raised objections to the traditional date of 378 for Hesperius's first prefectureship; on the basis of laws addressed to Hesperius as praetorian prefect as early as 376, Coşkun has argued that Hesperius held the prefecture by the end of that year. Yet these laws disagree with others addressed to Hesperius as proconsul of Africa as late as 377.[2] Given the often-confused dating of laws in the Theodosian Code, it seems most likely that the traditional dating of Hesperius's prefectureship as beginning no earlier than 378 should remain in place.

While Hesperius's last-attested office was that held with his father in 380, his political career continued after the demise of Gratian in 383; it has been argued that Hesperius was the *comes*, or count, at the court of Valentinian II who came to Rome and met with Symmachus while on public business there

1. The conventional dates are noted for Hesperius 2, *PLRE* 1:427–28; for Ausonius, see Ausonius 7, *PLRE* 1:140–41.

2. Coşkun (2002a, 136–40) cites the laws to Hesperius as praetorian prefect: *C. Th* 16.5.4, 376/378; 8.5.34, 377; and 1.15.8, 377, 378, or 379. But these laws disagree with others to Hesperius as proconsul of Africa; *C. Th*. 1.32.2, 376/377; and *C. Th* 15.7.3, 376.

in 384.[3] Hesperius, like his father Ausonius, naturally supported Valentinian II and would have been pleased at the news of the death of the usurper Magnus Maximus in 388. But we cannot trace Hesperius's activities much after this point. Probably he, like his father, returned to the family estates in Bordeaux, since he is not attested as holding another public office after this date.

As his jointly held offices with his father indicate, Hesperius's career was intimately tied to Ausonius's political fortunes. Thus, it is understandable, in the light of the influential positions he held, that five of the fourteen letters addressed to him by Symmachus are letters of recommendation, and since Hesperius was closer to Symmachus in age than was Ausonius, their relationship held out the prospect of a long friendship. Naturally, Symmachus would wish to showcase his ties to Hesperius, and this is reflected in eight of the fourteen letters that reiterate the desirability of maintaining their friendship. But despite the greater closeness in age, the letters to Hesperius are briefer and more formulaic than those to Ausonius. These are indicators, too, that the two did not have much personal interaction. We do not hear, for instance, of Hesperius's family life, although we know, from Ausonius, that Hesperius had at least three children, including a son named Pastor (Ausonius, *Parentalia* 11). Nor does Symmachus make mention of Hesperius's wife, contrary to his practice in the case of Praetextatus. This lack of personal detail suggests that their relationship was not intimate.

Finally, it is of some interest that Hesperius, like his father, was no doubt Christian.[4] Admittedly, there is no mention of this detail in Symmachus's correspondence with him or with Ausonius. One can speculate on the reasons for such an omission. In these letters, as in the letters to Ausonius, religious affiliation was not intended to be relevant in the world of patronage and friendship. Moreover, Symmachus would not want to raise an issue that would point to differences between friends; his ideal friendship was one in which *unanimitas* reigned in all matters.[5]

3. Vera 1981, 166–67, on Symmachus, *State Paper* 23.1. This is also the position taken by the *PLRE* 1:428 and Bowersock 1986, 10. But see 157 n. 1.

4. For Ausonius's religion, see xlvii–xlviii.

5. On *unanimitas* as an ideal of Symmachus, see 51 n. 3.

Letter 1.75: Symmachus to Hesperius
Date: 376–before 381[1]

Text

Quotiens viris militiae notis testimonia deferuntur, decet operam verborum facere conpendii, quia nihili negotium est rebus cognitis inmorari. Pro Caesario nosti omnia facere quae probantur. Hunc ut pensi habeas, sperare magis debeo quam rogare. Si quid ultra expetis, in alias litteras conferemus; nunc mihi multiloquio temperandum est, cum satisfactum esse videatur et illius voluntati et tuo honori et meo muneri. Vale.

Translation

Whenever testimonials are made to men recognized for their public service, it is fitting to cut short expenditure of words, since it is a waste of time to linger over facts already ascertained. You know that all praiseworthy characteristics speak in favor of Caesarius.[2] I should expect rather than be asking that you value this man. If you seek anything more, I will postpone it to another letter; now I must restrain my loquaciousness, since it seems that I have satisfied his wishes, your honor, and my own obligations. Farewell.

Notes

1. Since Hesperius appears to be in office, Callu (1972, 128) dates this letter before 381, i.e., before he left office. He uses the same criterion to date other letters to Hesperius, notably *Letters* 1.76, 1.77, 1.80–82, 1.84, 1.87, 1.88. I agree with this *terminus ante quem* but consider it likely that the letter dates from after 376, after Hesperius's office as proconsul of Africa.

2. Caesarius is identified as Caesarius 5, *PLRE* 1:170, an official in the western empire but otherwise unattested.

Letter 1.76: Symmachus to Hesperius
Date: 376–before 381[1]

Symmachus justifies writing two separate letters of recommendation for two men who are traveling together. He has already raised this as a point of etiquette (see *Letter* 1.50).

Text

Natura rerum est, ut, qui balbutiunt, plus loquantur; adfectant enim copiam pudore defectus. Hoc exemplum me expetit, cui magna est scribendi inpatientia, cum desit oratio. Duobus enim pariter commeantibus non putavi officio convenire, ut unis litteris gemina expenderetur occasio. Erit super hoc iudicatio tua, garrulusne iustius dicar an sedulus. Vale.

Translation

It is the nature of things that those who stammer speak more, for they strive for copiousness out of embarrassment at their deficiencies. This pattern is relevant to me; although I lack eloquence, I am very impatient to write. Indeed, I did not think it in accord with my duty that when two were traveling together, this double opportunity should be afforded only a single letter. It will be yours to judge whether I am more rightly called garrulous or attentive. Farewell.

Note

1. See 147 n. 1.

Letter 1.77: Symmachus to Hesperius
Date: 376–before 381[1]

This is an interesting instance of a man of senatorial status (*clarissimus*) who claims he is unable to take on the role of guardian for his brother's children. Sabinianus is known only from this letter, but his actions aroused opposition among some who apparently lodged a petition against the request.

Text

Amicorum orata curare bonae frugis officium est, praecipue si non refragetur aequitas postulatis. Quorsum spectet hoc anteloquium breviter explicabo. Sabinianum clarissimum virum ita magnifacio, ut quos maxime colo. Huic per inpressionem nequaquam patior a fratris sui liberis tutelae munus inponi. Duobus enim privilegiis amolitur iniuriam, maturitate aevi et numero filiorum. Ea res publicis designata monumentis necdum a proposita obstinatione deducit pervicacem petitionem. Nunc quia secundante fortuna in te huius negotii spes recumbit, quaeso ut ei virtute, qua celsus es, factum velis, cui vel in meam gratiam praestandus est favor vel ad tuam gloriam iuris praerogativa servanda est. Vale.

TRANSLATION

It is the duty of an honorable man to be attentive to the prayers of friends, especially if fairness is not at odds with the requests. To what end this preamble is directed, I shall briefly explain. I esteem the *clarissimus* Sabinianus as much as those for whom I have the highest regard.[2] I cannot allow that the responsibility of guardian for the children of his brother be imposed on him by force. He wards off this injustice with two privileges: his mature age and the number of his children. That fact, indicated in public records, has not yet diverted this stubborn petition from its obstinate purpose.[3] But now, since by the favor of fortune our prospects in this affair lie with you, I ask that with the virtue by which you have risen high[4] you promote the interest of that man, for whom you should either show favor out of consideration for me or preserve the prerogative of the law and add to your glory. Farewell.

NOTES

1. See 147 n. 1.

2. This man is identified with Sabinianus 4, *PLRE* 1:790, but nothing more is known about him.

3. Senators had to declare their property holdings and family members for tax purposes, the recording of which by the palatine bureaus was established by law; see especially *C. Th.* 16.2.13, dated to 383 C.E. Such information was of interest to fellow-senators also, since there were many common burdens. If Sabinianus were to avoid responsibility for his brother's sons, the burden might fall on the Senate, and this may elucidate why some of these senators filed a petition against the granting of this concession. The details of the petition and the source of it are vague, not surprisingly, since these were likely raised by other senators.

4. *Tua celsitudo* ("your highness") is a title for a high office holder, used for praetorian and urban prefects; see, for example, *C. Th.* 1.6.6 and 9.1.15. This is echoed by Symmachus's use of *celsus*, "risen high."

LETTER 1.78: SYMMACHUS TO HESPERIUS
DATE: 376

Symmachus delivered his *Fifth Oration*, the *Pro Trygetio*, on 9 January 376, in favor of Trygetius's request that his son be designated for the praetorship. It is likely that this oration is the one he sent to Hesperius; he had already sent it to Praetextatus (see the introduction to *Letter* 1.44). Here he again describes the enthusiasm the speech aroused as if it were a recent event.

Text

1. Unus mihi adhuc supereras ex summatibus litterarum viris, cui probari orationem meam laudis avarus optarem. Res cecidit ex voto: utor teste quo volui. Iam mihi comici adulescentis voce clamandum est: quis me est fortunatior venustatisque adeo plenior? Nisi forte amor mei stilum tuum coegit in gratiam. Fit enim saepe ut iudicii severitatem frangat adfectio et amicorum facta dictaque ea indulgentia censeamus, qua plerumque singuli etiam vitia nostra diligimus. 2. Sed haec merito dicerentur, ni tecum faceret existimatio omnium, quibus sermo noster auditus est; non quo sententiae tuae ex aliorum consensu quaeratur auctoritas, sed quia non patet suspicionibus iudicatum, a quo nemo dissentit. Videro tamen, utrum fides tua an amor illas litteras scripserit. Mihi in alterutra condicione aeque summus est honor, sive ita magnifice de me iudicas, ut gratificatus esse videaris, sive ita es mei diligens, ut secus iudicare non possis. Vale.

Translation

1. From among the most eminent of literati, you alone still remained whose approval I, greedy for praise, was hoping to win for my speech. It has turned out as I wished; I have the testimony I coveted. Now I ought to shout with the voice of the youth in the comedy, "Who is more fortunate than I, who more filled with happiness?"[1] unless by chance your love for me has forced your pen to partiality. For it often happens that affection destroys severity of judgment, and we consider the words and deeds of friends with the same indulgence with which each of us generally cherishes even our flaws. 2. But this would be said with good reason, if the evaluation of all who heard my speech were not in accord with yours. Not that the authority of your judgment is derived from the consensus of others, but rather because a judgment from which no one dissents is not open to suspicion. Nevertheless, I will soon see whether your honesty or your love for me wrote that letter. In either case, the honor is equally great for me, whether you judge me so generously that you seem to have shown me favor or you are so affectionate toward me that you cannot judge any other way. Farewell.

Notes

1. This line, "Who is more fortunate than I, who more filled with happiness?" ("quis me est fortunatior venustatisque adeo plenior?") is a quotation from Terence, *Hecyra* (*The Mother-In-Law*) 848.

Letter 1.79: Symmachus to Hesperius
Date: 378–before 381[1]

Symmachus asks that Hesperius, as praetorian prefect, perform one of his duties and confirm a *salarium*, or civic pension, that the Senate had granted. Although the Senate had already determined the amount, doubts appear to have arisen on the terms of the grant.[2] The recipient was a philosopher, a certain Priscianus who has been plausibly identified with the Priscianus referred to in Symmachus, *Relatio* 16, in relation to a property dispute with a relative. The notion that literature is of benefit to the state is a traditional one, although literary attainments were indeed often a pathway for advancement in the later Roman Empire.[3]

Text

Praesumptum aut conpertum tenes, quanta mihi sit tuae laudis antiquitas. Eapropter nihil fieri patior, quod actuum tuorum gratiam devenustet. Priscianus frater meus cum primis philosophorum litteratura et honestate censendus senatu auctore salarii emolumenta consequitur. Super eius annonis dicitur orta dubitatio, cui si nihil talis conpendii optimatium voluntas ante tribuisset, eruditio tua fructum ferre deberet. Scis enim bonas artes honore nutriri atque hoc specimen florentis esse reip., ut disciplinarum professoribus praemia opulenta pendantur. Quaeso igitur ne hac inquietudine aut illius minuatur utilitas aut amplissimo ordini censendi auctoritas derogetur. Interest famae et gloriae tuae ut confirmandi magis quam negandi commodi causa de philosophi salario dubitasse videaris. Vale.

Translation

You are aware either by conviction or proven fact how much regard I have for your good fame. For that reason, I allow nothing to happen that might mar the beauty of your actions. My brother Priscianus, who deserves to be considered among the first of philosophers for his writing and his integrity, with the authority of the Senate is in possession of the advantages of a civic pension. Doubt is said to have arisen about the amount of his payment;[4] if the wishes of the senators had previously granted him no such compensation, your learning should be providing him with support. You know, in truth, that the liberal arts are nourished by honor and that it is the sign of a flourishing state that rich rewards are paid to masters in the disciplines. I ask, therefore, that because of this distress neither the advantage of that man be diminished nor the authority for decision making be removed from that most distinguished order. It is important for your reputation and glory that you seem to have hesitated about the pension of a philosopher more for the sake of enhancing a benefit than denying it. Farewell.

NOTES

1. Hesperius is addressed as praetorian prefect, so the letter dates from 378–before 381.

2. See also Callu 1972, 131 n. 1; Bonner 1965, 113–37. For more on education in Rome, see Cavallo 2001, 1:92–103; Frasca 1996.

3. For numerous examples of the value of education for provincial advancement in Gaul, see Salzman 2002, 48 n. 178, 86–90.

4. Symmachus uses the word *annona* to indicate payment; the original use of this word to indicate the allotment of free grain to the citizens of Rome had changed to refer to any payments in kind; see Bonner 1965, 124–31.

LETTER 1.80: SYMMACHUS TO HESPERIUS
DATE: 376–BEFORE 381[1]

The calculus of *amicitia* demands a certain *quid pro quo*. Desire to maintain such a bond provides the impetus for this and several subsequent letters.

TEXT

En tibi secundas litteras meas et adhuc prioribus vicissitudo debetur. Dices viandi negotio impeditam diu operam scriptionis et alia forsitan multa causabere. Ego prae tui amore hanc veniam non gravabor, sed eodem amore postulo, ut, cum erit otium, mora necessarii silentii officio voluntario suppleatur. Vale.

TRANSLATION

Here is my second letter, even though a reply is still owed to my first. You will say that the activity of writing was long hindered by the exertions of travel, and perhaps you will make many other excuses. Because of my love for you, I shall not begrudge you pardon for this, but with the same love I ask that, when you have the leisure, the hiatus of your enforced silence be compensated for by voluntary diligence. Farewell.

NOTE

1. See 147 n. 1.

Letter 1.81: Symmachus to Hesperius
Date: 376–before 381[1]

This letter indicates the value of being a broker in this social network. Symmachus and Hesperius both benefit from their being able to do a favor for a fellow senator, the *clarissimus* Vitalianus. By doing so, they reinforce their obligations to one another as well.

Text

Vitalianum clarissimum virum mei potius officii gratia quam in adiumentum suum credo litteras poposcisse. Nam cum ipsi ad promerendum tuum amorem nihil ultra possit accedere, id tantum videtur egisse, ut mihi ex hoc munere conciliatio tui uberior proveniret. Cape igitur delibatam cursim salutationem, cui, si facundia largiore responderis, in exemplum copiae ingenii mei maciem provocabis. Vale.

Translation

I believe that the *clarissimus* Vitalianus[2] asked for a letter more out of a sense of duty to me than to benefit himself, for since he can have no further recommendation to merit your affection, he seems to have pressed his case only so that your bond with me grow fuller as a result of this favor of mine. So take this greeting, only hastily touched on; if you respond with more abundant eloquence to it, you will provoke the leanness of my talent to follow in the example of your copiousness. Farewell.

Notes

1. See 147 n. 1.
2. Vitalianus 2, *PLRE* 1:969, is not known from any other source.

Letter 1.82: Symmachus to Hesperius
Date: 376–before 381[1]

Text

Sum quidem silentii tui vehementer inpatiens, quod genus querellae amantibus familiare est, sed proximis litteris tibi desiderium meum expletum esse confiteor. Itaque habeo gratiam multoque opere te obsecro ut scriptioni frequenter indulgeas. Haec enim officia nullum faciunt de adsiduitate fastidium. Vale.

Translation

I am, it is true, extremely impatient with your silence—a familiar kind of complaint among friends—but I confess that you satisfied my desire with your last letter. So I am grateful and I beseech you heartily to devote yourself frequently to writing. For these attentions breed no tedium by their repetition. Farewell.

Note

1. See 147 n. 1.

Letter 1.83: Symmachus to Hesperius
Date: after late 380[1]

This letter registers the pain that Symmachus experienced at the death of his brother Titianus.

Text

Religionis indicium est, quod me taciturnitatis incessis. Sed velim credas infortunii fuisse, non voluntatis, quod diu provocatus officio scriptionis abstinui. Nec puto ignorare te, quatenus in nos fortuna saevierit, quae me amantissimo atque optimo fratre privavit. Proinde, si dies longior sensum tanti doloris exemerit, familiaribus litteris sollemnis cura praestabitur. Vale.

Translation

It is a sign of your scrupulousness[2] that you reproach me for my silence. But please believe that it was because of misfortune, not of my own free will, that I for a long time abstained from my duty to write. Nor do I think you are unaware to what extent fortune has raged against me, who has deprived me of a most loving and excellent brother. Accordingly, if the passage of time takes away my deep feelings of grief, the customary care will be devoted to letters to friends. Farewell.

Notes

1. The death of Symmachus's brother has recently occurred; his brother Titianus died in late summer or fall of 380; see pp. 129–30.

2. For the importance of "scrupulousness" (*religio*), see xlix–l.

Letter 1.84: Symmachus to Hesperius
Date: 376–before 381[1]

Symmachus is here playing on a common *topos* in Latin epistolography, the idea that a letter is a replacement for the absent friend in an ongoing conversation.[2]

Text

Quotiens tua sumo conloquia, quaedam mihi ante oculos praesentiae tuae imago versatur atque ideo uberiorem capio voluptatem, quod et tui officii et mei meriti sentio vigere momentum. Sed ut promptior circa me huius muneris diligentia perseveret, etiam ipse curam deferendi sermonis adripui, frequenter expertus dilectum religiosi animi incentivo vicissitudinis provocari. Vale.

Translation

Whenever I start conversing with you, some image of your physical presence comes before my eyes, and for that reason I feel a richer pleasure, since I perceive that the force of your duty to me and of my merit remains strong. But, in order that your attentiveness in this duty toward me continue more promptly, I have taken upon myself the initiative to write to you, having frequently experienced that the affection of a scrupulous nature is prompted by the incentive of an exchange of letters.[3] Farewell.

Notes

1. See 147 n. 1.
2. On this and other epistolary topics, see the excellent introduction, with bibliography, to Trapp 2003, 38–42.
3. Symmachus refers to the *religiosus animus* of his friend, which echoes the language of *Letter* 1.83, attributing to Hesperius "scrupulousness," the quality called *religio*; see xlix–l.

Letter 1.85: Symmachus to Hesperius
Date: after 376[1]

Text

Tandem bonae valetudinis compos, quae a me hucusque dissenserat, nunc te societate meae commoditatis inpertio, quem praeteritae sollicitudinis participem habere vitavi; etsi scio, ne illo quidem tempore, quo officium meum morbus inhibebat, ab huiusmodi munere temperatum. Restat ut observantiam vicissitudine munereris. Ea namque res et tuam curam probabit et refectioni meae adiumenta sufficiet. Vale.

Translation

At last I am in good health, which up to this point has escaped me. Now I grant you a share in my well-being, though I avoided making you a partner in my past troubles. But still I know, even at the time when illness hindered the performance of my duty, I did not avoid my responsibilities.[2] It remains for you to reward my attentiveness by reciprocating it, for to do so will both show your concern and provide aids for my recovery. Farewell.

Notes

1. Callu (1972, 134 n. 1) dates this letter to around 378, following the suggestion of Seeck that the illness referred to here is that noted in Symmachus, *Letter* 3.47, dated to 378. But this is not at all compelling. Rather, the letter can date from any point after the correspondence begins, presumably after Hesperius's first office in 376; its *terminus ante quem* is likely before Hesperius stepped down from office, hence before 381.

2. Symmachus is here referring to the responsibilities of writing letters.

Letter 1.86: Symmachus to Hesperius
Date: 378–before 381[1]

Symmachus makes explicit the difficulties of letter writing: How is one to know exactly where to send a letter? It is a reasonable concern, given the vagaries of travel in the ancient world, even if only between Milan and Rome.

Text

Utrum Mediolani etiam nunc tibi posito pagina ista reddenda sit, in ambiguo conloco. Peccari tamen in amicitiae fidem credidi, si litteris tuis referre honorem mutuum destitissem. Nihil ergo cunctatus conmisi eventui sollemnem hanc et simplicem dictionem salutis; quae si in manus venerit, fac, oro, ut pervenisse litteras meas sermonis tui recursus ostendat. Vale.

Translation

I am in doubt whether you are still now in Milan and I should send my letter there.[2] But yet I believed that it would be a crime against the trustworthiness of our friendship if I failed to honor your letter with a like response. So without delay I entrusted this customary and sincere greeting to fortune; if it comes into your hands, make sure, I beg, that a return of your correspondence shows my letter has arrived. Farewell.

Notes

1. The dating of this letter has been contested. According to Callu (1972, 134), it should date to 378–380 during Hesperius's prefecture in Italy because of Symmachus's reference to Milan. This is plausible. Bowersock (1986, 11) identifies this letter with the mission of the *comes* Hesperius who came to Rome in 384 (Symmachus, *State Paper* 23.1). Even if the *comes* in Symmachus's *State Paper* is identified with Ausonius's son, there is no evidence in this brief letter to support Bowersock's suggestion that this letter also dates to this later visit. The letter makes no allusion to the complaint that occasioned the *comes* Hesperius's visit to Rome in 384. Moreover, dating this letter to 384 would place it later than all the other dated letters to Hesperius or to his father in book 1, all of which fall before 381. For these reasons, I would associate this letter with one of Hesperius's prefectures and hence date the letter from 378–before 381.

2. Maximinian Herculius, Diocletian's co-emperor, made Milan his imperial residence between 293 and 305. It remained an imperial residence throughout the fourth century, which explains why the praetorian prefect of Italy would naturally reside there; see Jones 1986, 133; Krautheimer 1982, 69–71.

Letter 1.87: Symmachus to Hesperius
Date: 376–before 381[1]

This letter details the typical way that information was conveyed: the letter carrier often spoke at length, whereas the written letter was often no more than a token or calling card.[2]

Text

Si facultas mihi ad seribendum saepe suppeteret, voluntas numquam deesset officio. Huius rei evidens certumque documentum est, quod, ubi primum amici communis fida adfulsit occasio, libens scribendi munus adripui. Intellexi enim iucundiores fore litteras meas, si has tibi familiarior tabellarius tradidisset, qui non solum epistulam sed insinuationem quoque actuum meorum tibi fideliter exhibebit. Vale.

Translation

If I had the ability to write to you often, I would never lack the will to do so. It is a clear and certain proof of this that, as soon as a reliable opportunity presented by a mutual friend dawned, I willingly seized the task of writing. For I understood that my letter would be more agreeable if a messenger who was quite familiar to you brought it, a man who will reliably present you not only with the letter but also with an account of my actions. Farewell.

Notes

1. See 147 n. 1.
2. See xlv–xlvi and liii–liv; Callu 1972, 135 n. 1.

Letter 1.88: Symmachus to Hesperius
Date: 376–before 381[1]

Symmachus places great value on his own correspondence, thereby indirectly complimenting himself. His emphasis on Hesperius's eagerness to receive his letter also expresses his confidence in their mutual affection.

Text

Numquam in me parcam, quin tuo animo obsequar. Novi quam sis mei sermonis exoptans. Propterea decrevi cum animo nihil supersedere litteris porrigendis nec expectare vicissitudinem, ne scribendi tardior fiam. Sed ut ipse metui, ne mihi foret flagitio, si tacerem, sic velim tu quoque caveas culpam dissimulatae familiaritatis accedere. Quod te curaturum liquido habeo conpertum, quia non minus ingenium tuum quam meritum meum cogitans nequeo tui amoris esse diffidens. Vale.

Translation

Never would I spare myself the trouble of obeying your wishes. I know how eager you are for my correspondence. For that reason, I made a solemn determination neither to refrain from sending letters nor to wait for a return lest I become too dilatory in writing. But just as I feared that it would be a disgrace to me if I were silent, so I would want you also to beware of incurring the charge of neglected friendship. That this will carry weight with you I consider clearly established, since, as I ponder your character no less than my merit, I am unable to doubt your love. Farewell.

Notes

1. See 147 n. 1.

Book 1, *Letters* 89–93: Symmachus to Antonius

Fl. Claudius Antonius, Symmachus's penultimate correspondent in this book, was an important and well-placed figure in the imperial bureaucracy. Antonius may have held the office of *magister memoriae*, the master of records from 367 until an unknown date; in this office in the palace secretariat he dictated and sent out legal annotations to imperial laws and responded to petitions. Following a typical imperial bureaucratic career path, he next attained the office of quaestor of the sacred palace, a post he held probably beginning in 370 and likely continuing until 375; in this position he had increased responsibilities, not only in dictating and composing imperial laws, but communicating imperial decisions and hence composing imperial orations.[1] Not only did this office require a high level of legal and rhetorical training; it also required political skills. Consequently, many who held this post gained higher office still. Indeed, Antonius, like Ausonius, advanced from this quaestorship to praetorian prefect of Gaul from spring 376[2] through 377, moving on to the office of praetorian prefect of Italy from 377 to 378, and even reaching the pinnacle honor, the consulship in 382.[3]

Antonius's elevation to the consulship was aided, however, by his family connections, for he has plausibly been tied, through marriage, to the emperor Theodosius.[4] While the precise nature of Antonius's link to the emperor

1. See *Letter* 1.89; Harries 1988, 159–72, on the responsibilities of the quaestor and *magister scriniorum*. He probably was quaestor of the sacred palace after Flavius Eupraxius, who left office in 370 (see *PLRE* 1:299), but before Ausonius became quaestor of the sacred palace (by 1 January 375; see Symmachus, *Letter* 1.13, and 35–39 above).

2. The earliest constitution to Antonius as prefect of Gaul is dated to 23 May 376 (*C. Th.* 13.3.11).

3. See Antonius 5 in *PLRE* 1:77 for the inscriptions and documents indicating the dates of these offices.

4. Martindale 1967, 254–56. His argument rests on Themistius's *Oration* 16.203D, which refers to the consul as a relative by marriage of Theodosius, and on a series of hypotheses identifying the consuls.

cannot be certified,[5] Antonius's position placed him at the center of the imperial bureaucracy in the western empire in the critical period at the end of the rule of Valentinian I and the beginning of that of Gratian. Antonius's influence extended also in all probability to Christian circles in northern Italy, if he is the man to whom Ambrose wrote a letter of gratitude.[6]

Given Antonius's position at court in the 370s, we see why Symmachus chose to include their correspondence. It was probably while Symmachus was at the court of Valentinian I in Trier that he first made the acquaintance of Antonius, and he continued conscientiously to maintain this useful friendship.[7] Moreover, Antonius shared with Symmachus an appreciation of literature and was himself the author of a highly regarded imperial oration (see *Letter* 1.89.1). Nonetheless, Symmachus's correspondence, while flattering, lacks the intimacy and personal allusions that characterized Symmachus's letters to Praetextatus and Ausonius.

Letter 1.89: Symmachus to Antonius
Date: 370–373 or late spring–fall 374[1]

This is an intriguing letter, for as noted above the oration described by Symmachus alludes to an imperial speech delivered to the Senate. Lizzi Testa has argued that the oration mentioned here was one that favored the senatorial prerogative to act as a court of justice for its members; this had been the cause advanced by Praetextatus in response to the case of a senator, Hymetius, who had been exiled for treason by Maximinus, vicar of Rome from 370 to 372 or 373.[2] If so positioned, it would be among the earliest dated letters in book 1.

Text

1. Non incognito quidem nobis eloquii splendore nituisti, sed magnis

---

5. Martindale (161 n. 4) offers a plausible reconstruction. He surmises that Antonius was the brother or uncle of Marius (*Letter* 1.90; *PLRE* 1:561) and was likely the brother of the Maria who later married Honorius, brother of the emperor Theodosius. This is based on a false conjecture about Symmachus's reference to Marius as a brother of Antonius; as noted earlier (51 n. 4), this term does not necessitate a familial bond. However, *Letter* 1.90.2 does suggest they were brothers. Lizzi Testa (2004, 433 n. 385) rightly observes that we do not know for certain that Antonius was Spanish, tied to the Hispanic-Gallo faction that supported the young Theodosius for the throne.

6. Ambrose, *Letter* 90 (CSEL 82.2:118–19). Although *PCBE* (1:160, s.v. Antonius 3) correctly notes that there is no way to determine if Antonius was the correspondent of both Symmachus and Ambrose, the dates and context make it appear likely.

7. For Symmachus at court, see xxiv–xxvi.

rebus adcommoda et maiestatis scriptis aptata gloriam, quam magisterio ante quaesisti, recens auxit oratio. Nam praeter loquendi phaleras, quibus te natura ditavit, senile quiddam planeque conveniens auribus patrum gravitate sensuum, verborum proprietate sonuisti. Denique etiam hi, quorum Minerva rancidior est, non negant facundiam tuam curiae magis quam caveae convenire; et illi, quos cothurnus altior vehit et structurarum pigmenta delectant, neque tristem soliditatem neque lascivum leporem consona laude celebrarunt. 2. Haec sunt enim condimenta tui oris et pectoris, quod nec gravitate horres nec venustate luxurias, sed ratione fixus ac stabilis germanos colores rebus obducis.

Nolo igitur exspectes iudicium meum, ne amore delinquam. Quid varia ingenia senserint, intimavi. Fuit enim in illa oratione quod unusquisque diligeret et pro ingenii sui qualitate laudaret. Quare sequere coepta felicia et te in omnibus aemulare. Nobis ad testimonium religionis satis est non siluisse sententiam ceterorum. Vale.

Translation

1. Certainly the brilliance that gives luster to your eloquence was not unknown to me, but this recent speech, well-suited to great matters and a fit response to the writings of imperial majesty, has added to the glory that you won previously by your administrative post.[3] For over and above the trappings of eloquence with which nature has endowed you, you spoke with a seriousness in your sentiments and precision in your language that had a certain maturity and was wholly agreeable to the ears of the senators. In sum, even those whose tastes are rather corrupted[4] do not deny that your eloquence is more suitable to the Senate House than to the stage; both enthusiasts for tragic elevation and admirers of colorful figures of speech praised with one voice a firmness that was not austere and a wit that was not indecent. 2. For these are the very flavors of your speech and of your heart, because your seriousness is not forbidding, nor is your charm uncontrolled, but fixed and stable in your reason, you depict things in their true colors.

Do not, therefore, look for my judgment, lest I err out of affection. I have shared with you the sentiments of men of varied intellects. For in that oration each man found what he loved and praised according to the quality of his intellect. Therefore, follow up on fortunate beginnings and rival yourself in all fields. For me, not to be silent about the perceptions of others is sufficient testimony to my conscientiousness. Farewell.

Notes

1. Symmachus could have heard this oration in Rome after his return to the city from Trier, ca. 370, and before he went off to his proconsulship in

Africa in 373; this is the dating proposed by Callu (1972, 136) and Lizzi Testa (2004, 233–34, 432–433). However, it is also possible that Symmachus heard this oration after he returned from Africa to Rome in late spring or summer of 374 (see xxvi–xxviii). We can be certain only that Antonius wrote this oration when he was quaestor of the sacred palace and hence before Ausonius took up this position most likely in 375; see page 36 and Symmachus, *Letter* 1.13.

2. Lizzi Testa (2004, 225–48, 432–433) contends that the imperial response, *C. Th.* 9.16.10, was prompted by the activities of Praetextatus and an earlier senatorial embassy. The imperial oration noted here was probably not the one (*Oration* 4 [*On Behalf of His Father*]) read to the Senate after the emperor Gratian put Maximinus to death for treason in the early years of Gratian's and Valentinian II's rule, i.e., June 376; Callu 2009b, x n. 1 and 28–33. See Maximinus 7, *PLRE* 1:577–78.

3. "Administrative post," translates the vague term *magisterium. PLRE* suggests that the position that Antonius held was higher than his position as master of the imperial bureaus (*magister scriniorum*) and must therefore be quaestor of the sacred palace, an office that he probably held from 370 to 373; see 161–62 above.

4. Symmachus's expression, *Minerva rancidior*, employs *Minerva* as metonymy for intellect and is a variation of proverbial expressions describing someone of weak or slow intellect as possessing a *Minerva crassa* or *pinguis*, literally "a fat Minerva." There is, however, no other attested instance of the adjective *rancidus* used of Minerva, but the sense is clearly negative, "rotten, putrid, offending good taste"; see *OLD*, s.v. *rancidus*.

Letter 1.90: Symmachus to Antonius
Date: after 370[1]

Symmachus plays on the oft-found familial metaphor in describing the fraternal similarities between Antonius and Marius. This rhetorical ornamentation of a common *topos* aims to flatter Antonius in this elegant letter of recommendation.

Text

1. Etsi amore convenior, ne sim circa te avarus officii, nunc tamen libentius quam saepe alias scribendi munus insisto; primo quod abitio fratris nostri Marii quodam viatico carere non debuit, dehinc quod litteras meas putavi plusculum commendationis habituras, si tibi per eum, quem sancte atque efflicte diligis, redderentur. Fit enim plerumque, ut levia rerum porta-

tor festivus exornet. 2. Alia quoque de causa studii mei ardor incanduit, quod tecum super talis viri laude gratulandum putavi, qui e provincia suburbana tantum reportat publici desiderii, quantum reliquit exempli. Non dicam dolo utpote subpalpandi nescius: viget in eo vena fraterna, eoque magis factum est, ut discessum eius inpatienter feramus, qui in uno frui videbamur ambobus. Vereor protelare testimonium meum, ne magis laudi eius obsecutus iudicer quam pudori; nam quorum mens honesta est, eorum inbecilla frons est. Tu conice plura de paucis, quae nunc insinuare non decuit, sed per alium scribere non pigebit. Vale.

Translation

1. Although I am impelled by love not to be miserly in paying my respects to you, nonetheless I now set about my task of writing more readily than I often do at other times; first because the departure of our brother Marius[2] ought not to lack some provisions for the journey, then because I think my letter would convey more of a recommendation if it was handed to you by that man whom you esteem so purely and with such passion. For it generally happens that a congenial letter carrier enhances trivial news. 2. Also the fire of my enthusiasm has intensified for another reason, because I thought I should rejoice with you over the praise of such a man who carries with him from a suburban province as much public longing as the exemplary behavior he left behind.[3] I will not speak to deceive, for I am incapable of flattery; a strain of likeness to his brother is pronounced in him, and for that reason I find his departure even more difficult to endure, since I seemed to enjoy both of you in just the one man. I am afraid to prolong my statement lest I be judged to have served his praise more than his modesty, for those men whose minds are honorable have a sensitive demeanor. Feel free to read more into these few words, which it was not fitting to communicate to you now, but which I will be pleased to write through another intermediary. Farewell.

Notes

1. This dating, also proposed by Callu (1972, 137), is based on Symmachus's return from Trier in 370 and assumes that Symmachus met Antonius at court and began corresponding only after he left Trier.

2. For the identification of Marius, see 162 n. 5.

3. Symmachus alludes to the division of Italy into two dioceses and their provinces or districts, with Italia annonaria and its capital in Milan comprising one diocese and the other being *Italia suburbicaria* or *suburbana*, with its

head at Rome. Hence, Marius has left from the area of southern Italy, perhaps Rome, i.e. a suburban province.

Letter 1.91: Symmachus to Antonius
Date: after 370[1]

This is a formulaic letter intended to maintain contact but otherwise including little information.

Text

Dudum te, mi frater, silentio indulgere mirabar. Ea res inpendio augebat dolorem, quod ipse minime scribendi observantiam neglegebam. Simul atque accepi litteras tuas, animum subiit laetitia, querella deseruit. Amicitia enim cito sanatur officio. Tu quoque ita paginam melle eruditissimi oris obleveras, ut quaelibet offensa tamquam Lethaeo poculo mergeretur. Verso igitur stilo gratiam fateor, qui expostulare meditabar, adiciens postulatum, ne unquam supersedere litteris perseveres. Quod si scribenda defuerint, mihi satis erit, ut tibi gratuler sospitatis. Vale.

Translation

For a long time I was surprised that you abandoned yourself to silence, my brother. The fact that I myself did not in the least neglect my attention to writing increased my pain greatly. But as soon as I received your letter, joy entered my heart, grievance departed. For friendship is quickly healed by courtesy. In addition, you had so coated your page with the honey of most learned eloquence that any offense was drowned, as it were, in the cup of Lethe. So, with a turn of my pen,[2] I, who was planning to complain, confess my pleasure, and I add this request, that you never persist in postponing your letters. If you have nothing to write, it will be enough for me to rejoice in your well-being. Farewell.

Notes

1. See 165 n. 1.

2. "With a turn of my pen" (*verso stilo*) alludes to turning the stylus used for incising letters on wax tablets round and using the blunt end as an eraser; see *OLD*, *stilus* 3.b.

Letter 1.92: Symmachus to Antonius
Date: before 378[1]

Text

Dulce certamen est familiaris officii et ideo iure ambo cavimus, ne alternis epistulis vinceremur. Gratulor igitur pares nos esse non solum adfectione mentium sed etiam vicissitudine litterarum. Curabo tamen posthac, ut obsequii mei trutina et libra praeponderet, ne videatur inertiae quoddam esse conludium semper aequa lance censeri. Itaque scribam saepius, modo facultas commeantium non desit optanti. Ita fiet ut et ipse laudem sedulitatis adfectem et te curis publicis occupatum ad rependenda conloquia adsiduitate sollicitem. Vale.

Translation

Rivalry in performing the duties of friendship is sweet, and for that reason we are both rightly careful not to be outdone in the exchange of letters. So I rejoice that we are equals not only in the affection of our minds but also in the reciprocity of our correspondence. After this I will, nevertheless, take care that the balance and scale of my allegiance incline lower, lest it seem a kind of collusion in laziness always to be weighed as being in equilibrium. [2] And so I shall write more often, provided that there is a ready supply of go-betweens when I want one. In this way I myself will strive for praise of my conscientiousness and by my persistence pressure you, occupied though you are with public cares, to repay my communications. Farewell.

Notes

1. Symmachus alludes to the public office that Antonius held, so the letter cannot postdate his last active public office in 378; his appointment as consul in 382 was an exalted office but an honorific one that was not likely to be seen as an occupying Antonius with "public cares."

2. Symmachus intends to outdo Antonius in the volume of his letters, thereby outweighing his correspondent's letters and so, metaphorically, tilting the scales of their correspondence lower on his side.

Letter 1.93: Symmachus to Antonius
Date: after 370[1]

In this letter of recommendation for one Zeno, otherwise unidentified, Symmachus is open about the workings of patronage and the benefits that he, as broker, garners from acting on behalf of his clients. He is careful to remind Antonius to tell Zeno of Symmachus's role in providing a recommendation.

Text

Sanctum Zenonem commendare non debeo, quem scio ad clientelam tuam et amicitias pertinere; sed tanta in eo morum probitas est, ut laudes eius silere non possim. Itaque virum bonis omnibus merito suae sedulitatis acceptum quaeso etiam me precante propensius fovere digneris, praestaturus et tuae famae, quae debet omnium ore celebrari et interventui meo, ut has litteras sibi intellegat profuisse. Vale.

Translation

I do not have to recommend to you the virtuous Zeno,[2] whom, I know, belongs among your clients and friends, but such is the uprightness of his character that I cannot keep silent about his praise. And so I ask that you deign to show even greater favor in response to my prayer for a man thought well of by all good men for the quality of his attentiveness; thereby you will contribute both to your own reputation, which ought to be celebrated on the lips of all, and my intervention, so that he understands this letter has benefited him. Farewell.

Notes

1. See 165 n. 1.

2. Although he is described as *sanctus*, that word in Symmachus's letters does not indicate any special religious qualities; see Lomanto 1983, s.v. *sanctus*, and its usage at 7.51.

Book 1, *Letters* 94–107: Symmachus to Syagrius

The recipient of this last group of letters has been identified with the Flavius Syagrius whose checkered career, as reconstructed in the *PLRE*, began with the military defeat in 369 reported by Ammianus Marcellinus.[1] Syagrius had been a notary in Gaul when he participated in this failed expedition; notaries, who were expert in shorthand, were charged with taking notes of the proceedings of government, and the highest members of the corps served in the emperor's consistory. As such, some notaries were designated at times to transact sensitive political matters, especially during and after the rule of Constantius II.[2] Serving in this capacity, Syagrius had been the sole survivor of a failed military expedition across the Rhine near Mount Pirus, which brought him under suspicion and caused his removal from this post by Valentinian I.[3] Syagrius, however, was able to clear his name, for ten years later, in 379, this same man is identified with the Syagrius who held a key Palatine office, that of *magister officiorum* or master of offices, a position akin to chief of staff.[4] From here, he advanced to praetorian prefect of Italy, holding this position in the years 380–382. According to the *PLRE*, in 381 this same Syagrius also attained the honor of the consulship with Flavius Eucherius; only the recent death of Symmachus's brother Celsinus Titianus (who died late in 380) prevented Symmachus from attending Syagrius's consular inauguration.[5]

Yet even this cursory overview raises problems, not the least of which is the suggestion that Syagrius held the consulship at the same time as the praetorian prefectureship of Italy. Confusion arises also because there was another

1. Flavius Syagrius is identified with Syagrius 3, *PLRE* 1:862–63. See Ammianus Marcellinus, *Res Gestae* 28.2.5–9.

2. Constantius II especially relied on the corps of notaries, as did subsequent rulers; see Teitler 1985 for the definitive survey of this office.

3. See 169 n. 1.

4. The *magister officiorum* commanded the imperial bodyguards and supervised the imperial chancelleries, the imperial couriers (*agentes in rebus*), the public post, and the reception of foreign embassies.

5. Symmachus, *Letter* 1.101; Syagrius 3, *PLRE* 1:862–63.

man, Flavius Afranius Syagrius, of Gallic origins, who had a remarkably similar career; this man also was praetorian prefect of Italy, perhaps in 382, and consul, though probably one year after Symmachus's correspondent, that is, in 382, after his prefectureship.[6]

In my discussion I follow the reconstruction of Syagrius's career found also in the *PLRE* for Syagrius 3, as it seems most probable. I differ from the *PLRE* on two points, however. First, I think it unlikely that Syagrius held the consulship at the same time as his praetorian prefectureship. So, he could have stepped down before becoming consul in 381, or, as has been proposed, he may have held the position of prefect of the city of Rome in 381, not that of the praetorian prefect of Italy in that year.[7] Second, it seems entirely plausible that the Syagrius mentioned as a friend of Ausonius was the same man who was Symmachus's correspondent, not, as the *PLRE* indicates, Flavius Afranius Syagrius.[8] Symmachus could have easily met Flavius Syagrius at the same time that he met Ausonius when at court in Trier, for Syagrius was a notary in Gaul for some of that time.[9] Indeed, such a connection would be fitting, reinforcing the ties between Symmachus and his circle of Gallic correspondents who were also at the imperial court. All of these men, including Ausonius, Hesperius, Flavius Claudius Antonius, and Syagrius, are prominently featured in Symmachus's first book of letters and have ties with each other as well as with Symmachus.

6. Flavius Afranius Syagrius = Syagrius 2 in *PLRE* 1:862, who was also consul, although a year later, in 382; this man was proconsul of Africa in 379, perhaps *comes sacri largitionis* in 381, prefect of Rome in 381 before becoming consul in 382, probably with Flavius Antonius, the recipient of Symmachus's *Letters* 1.89–93. This latter Syagrius was alleged to have a triple prefectureship and was of Gallic origin and included among his descendants the Syagrius (Syagrius 3, *PLRE* 2:1042), who was a friend and correspondent of Sidonius Apollinaris (*Letter* 8.8.3).

7. For this view, see Clauss 1981, 192–93, who would thus see Flavius Syagrius as notary, *magister officiorum* in 379–381, prefect of the city and not of Italy in 381, and consul in 381. For a succinct discussion of the possible views and reconstructions, see Pellizzari 1998, 24–25 and especially n. 12.

8. *PLRE* 1:862, identifies Flavius Afranius Syagrius as Ausonius's friend, whom he refers to at *Praefationes Variae* 2 (Green 1991, 4–5).

9. Bowersock 1986, 5 n. 17, also made this suggestion. See also Bagnall, Cameron, Schwarz, and Worp 1987, 296–99.

Letter 1.94: Symmachus to Syagrius
Date: after 379 and before 382[1]

The Athenian rhetorician recommended here was also the subject of another letter of support, sent by Symmachus to Ausonius, *Letter* 1.15; for more on Palladius's career, see the introduction to that letter, 47–48.

Text

Laudentur incogniti, ut eorum merita in occulto sita testimonii splendor inradiet; mihi inpraesentiarum supersedendum est huiusmodi scriptione, ne incepti frustra sim, si fratrem meum Palladium spectatum bonis omnibus facundiae atque eruditionis adstipuler. Dehinc cauto opus est, ne inpar tanto viro praedicatio neque eum, cui defertur, aequiperet et meam operam devenustet. Quiesco igitur has partes et hoc unum persuasum tibi volo, mereri facundiam Palladii ut doleamus, quod urbi negatus est, mereri amabilitatem eius, ut quod accitus est, gaudeamus. Vale.

Translation

Let those who are not known be praised, so that the splendor of testimony illuminate their merits that have been hidden in obscurity; in the present instance I must refrain from writing in this vein, lest my undertaking be to no purpose if I make the case for my brother Palladius, a man well-known to all good men for his eloquence and erudition. Hence I must take care that my recommendation is not unequal to so great a man nor fails to do justice to him to whom it is paid and thereby disfigures my effort. So in these respects I am silent, and I wish you only to be convinced of this one thing, that the eloquence of Palladius merits that we mourn the fact that he was denied to our city but that his lovable nature merits that we rejoice that he has been summoned to court. Farewell.

Note

1. Since Syagrius was probably succeeded as praetorian prefect of Italy by an interim official to whom laws dated 2 April 382 (*C. Th.* 7.18.6 and 8.4.13) were sent, Callu suggested that Syagrius had died before this date, i.e., before April 382. Val. Severus 29, *PLRE* 1:837, is the likely successor. See also Syagrius 3, *PLRE* 1:863. It is just as likely that Syagrius simply left office, but Symmachus likely wrote him before that date, i.e., before 382.

Letter 1.95: Symmachus to Syagrius
Date: 379 or soon after[1]

This letter begins with a reference to a noteworthy honor granted to Symmachus. Normally the urban prefect read the messages of the emperor to the assembled senators. To confer this task on another senator was a signal distinction that Symmachus had received once before in the spring or summer of 376 (*Letter* 10.2). Clearly, Symmachus was pleased at this opportunity to read a report of victory, identified as that over Goths, Huns, and Alans in 379.[2] As befits its context and content, Symmachus peppers this account with references to monuments in the Roman Forum, namely, the Temple of Castor and Pollux and the Pool of Juturna, both of which were also associated with legendary Roman military successes at Lake Regillus in 499 B.C.E. In this way, Symmachus shows off his learning as well as honors the emperors.

Text

1. Quod nullas sumpsi litteras tuas, cum mihi a principibus aeternis legenda in concilio patrum delegaretur oratio, scio non fuisse fastidii tui. Nam bonae et exploratae amicitiae, vel si cesset officium, satis tutae aestimationes sunt. Propterea talionem referre vitavi veritus, ne quod tu invitus feceras, ego offensus crederer reddidisse. Longe enim diversa condicio est fortuiti quam adfectati silentii. Res quidem una neglegitur, plurimum tamen refert, quis eam quasi occupatus, quis quasi iratus omiserit. 2. Sed de hoc satis habeo dictum.

Nunc, si me amas, vel quia me amas—nam referri mihi confido quod defero— contestare apud invictos principes gaudium meum, qui humanae voci divinas litteras crediderunt, quorum victorias ex mei oris promptario senatus audivit. Fac veniat in mentem, quis ille mihi inluxerit dies, quo ego quasi ex media profectus acie auribus et animis omnium salutarem nuntium primus infudi. 3. Olim cum res Romana adoreae militaris potita est, Polluces gemini apud Iuturnae lacum proelii secunda vulgarunt. Eos quippe priscorum voluminum fides tradidit, anhelis equis plenos sudoris et pulveris Fama belli post tergum relicta indicium adfectasse victoriae. Idem nunc mihi sacro iudicio factus est honor. Ita quantum gratiae Castores adepti sunt, tantum principes praestiterunt. 4. Haec pro me copiosius et ornatius, quantum es linguae melior, apud auctorem beneficii prosequeris. Habes summam voluntatis meae; cui si quid commendationis inspiraveris, ceteris ornamentis animi tui adicietur decus praesentis officii. Vale.

Translation

1. I know that it was not out of indifference that I received no letter from you after I was chosen by our eternal emperors to read their oration before the senatorial assembly.[3] For in the case of sound and well-established friendships, attitudes are sufficiently secure, even if obligations are neglected. For this reason I avoided retaliating in kind, fearing that I would be thought to have taken offense and returned to you what you had unwittingly done to me. Indeed, the circumstance is very different when a silence is accidental rather than purposeful. While there is neglect all the same, it nevertheless makes a very great difference whether someone fails to write because he is occupied or because he is angry. 2. But I have said enough about this.

Now, if you love me, or rather because you love me, for I am confident that what I feel for you is returned to me, testify to my joy before the unconquered emperors, who entrusted their divine letter to a human voice and whose victories the Senate heard from the ready storeroom of my voice. Bring to mind how brightly that day shone for me when, as if called forth from the midst of battle, I was the first to fill the ears and spirits of all with the news of our safety. 3. Once in the past, when the Roman state achieved glory in war, the twins Pollux and Castor[4] announced the favorable outcome of battle at the Pool of Juturna.[5] For the authority of ancient texts reported that with their horses out of breath, covered with sweat and dust, and leaving Rumor, the messenger of war, far behind, they desired to bring the news of the victory in person.[6] This same honor by sacred decision has now been granted to me. The emperors have bestowed upon me as much favor as Castor and Pollux received. 4. You will take up this subject for me before the author of this kindness with greater fluency and adornment to the degree that your eloquence is better than mine. You have the sum total of my desires; if you infuse them with some special commendation, the loveliness of this present courtesy will be added to the other ornaments of your soul. Farewell.

Notes

1. The dating of this letter is based on the identification of the victories it mentions with those of 379, proposed first by Seeck (1883, cxi), as the victories over the Goths, Alans, and Huns cited by the *Fasti Idatiani* on 17 November 379.

2. Seeck 1883, cxi.

3. As already noted, normally this honor was granted to the prefect of the city. The prefect in the autumn of 379 was Arborius, nephew of Ausonius and friend of Syagrius, as well as of Symmachus. Ausonius's influence may have convinced Arborius to allow Symmachus this honor.

4. Callu (1972, 232 n. 4) observes that Symmachus calls the twins by the less frequently used name, Pollux, in Latin, *Polluces*. More often the twins were named after Castor, in Latin, *Castores;* see Ammianus Marcellinus, *Res Gestae* 19.10.4; Pliny, *Historia naturalis* (*Natural History*) 10.121. This is part of Symmachus's stylistic striving for variation and novelty; see xliv–liii.

5. The Pool of Juturna in the Roman Forum continued in use, based on pottery finds, until the eighth century C.E.; see Richardson 1992, 230–31.

6. There were multiple versions of the story of Castor and Pollux that Symmachus could have consulted; see Valerius Maximus, *Factorum et dictorum memorabilium libri ix* (*Nine Books of Memorable Deeds and Sayings*) 1.8.1; Ovid, *Fasti* (*The Roman Calendar*) 1.708; *Panegyrici Latini* (*Latin Panegyrics*) 2.39.4, among others. The cult of the twins was especially tied to the military success of the emperors, and the Temple of Castor and Pollux is noted in the fourth-century Regionary Catalogs as still in use; see Richardson 1992, 74–75. The anniversary of this temple was celebrated with circus races on 8 April in the fourth century, another sign of the popularity of the cult; see Salzman 1990, 156.

Letter 1.96: Symmachus to Syagrius
Date: 376[1]

Symmachus has sent an oration to Syagrius for his approval. It seems likely that this was the same *Oration 5*, *On Behalf of Trygetius*, that he has sent to other correspondents and has been alluded to throughout book 1. This speech was used to express gratitude for his father's return as well as a proud demonstration of his performance before the Senate. If we keep in mind that the competitive element remained within elite circles, Symmachus's reiteration of this speech and its impact takes on added significance in the race for honor and prestige that remained an earmark of fourth-century senatorial circles.[2]

Text

Studium, quod scribendis orationibus exhibebam, praemio laudis auxisti. Vetus quippe sententia est, artes honore nutriri. Quis autem tam cumulatus est honor quam palma dicendi? Ergo etsi intellego quod amore fallaris, titulum tamen praeclari testimonii albo calculo veterum more signabo. Non enim mihi ex ore ieiuno tributa laudatio est, sed de facundiae penu boni iudicii fructus adrisit. Vereor indulgere verbis praeconii tui, ne gratificandi operam mutuam credamur adniti. Vale et, ut es nostri diligens, religiosam observantiam persevera.

Translation

You have increased the enthusiasm that I was showing for writing speeches by the reward of your praise. For it is an old saying that the arts are nourished by honor.[3] Moreover, what honor is as perfect as the palm of speaking well? Therefore, although I understand that you are led astray by affection, still, in the manner of the ancients, I will mark the distinction of this outstanding endorsement with a white pebble.[4] For the praise was not bestowed on me by an impoverished speaker, but the fruit of good judgment smiled on me from a storeroom of eloquence. I fear to abandon myself to words in your praise, lest we be thought to be engaging in a work of mutual gratification. Be well and, as you love me, continue your scrupulous attentions. Farewell.

Notes

1. See 96–97 and 97 n. 2. For further discussion, see also Seeck 1883, cxi; Callu 1972, 142.

2. For the senatorial competition in fourth-century Rome, see especially Lizzi Testa 2004, 55–92, 327–80.

3. Symmachus has used this maxim before; see *Letters* 1.43 and 1.79.

4. It was typical to use a small stone for voting: a white one for assent or approval, a black one for denial or condemnation. From here it became a common trope, as in Pliny, *Letter* 6.11.3, to signify a most positive and happy day by a white stone.

Letter 1.97: Symmachus to Syagrius
Date: before 382[1]

Text

Meae litterae, quoniam tibi acceptae sunt, crebrius commeabunt; nam ut respondeas, non laboro, siquidem videtur iniurium flagitare officia, quae sponte religiosus animus pollicetur. Vale.

Translation

My letters, since they are welcome to you, will travel more frequently, for I am not concerned about your response, since it seems wrong to demand duties that a scrupulous spirit spontaneously promises. Farewell.

Notes

1. This letter is not separated in the manuscripts from the preceding one, but following Seeck (1883, 39) we print them as two letters. There is no reference to Syagrius's offices. I suggest a possible dating before 382 because, after Syagrius left office in that year, he disappears from view and would have been of little help to Symmachus.

Letter 1.98: Symmachus to Syagrius
Date: before 382[1]

Text

Dudum mihi nullus litteris tuis honor factus est. Quererer de silentio tuo, si de religione dubitarem; sed quia amicitia usu credita et expensa documentis a periculo suspicionis aliena est, intellego quidem per occupationes publicas inhibitam diligentiam scriptionum tuarum, verum quaeso ut intermissum munus instaures. Stabit apud me gratia tributi officii, quasi nulla negati culpa praecesserit. Vale.

Translation

For a long time I have not received the honor of a letter from you. I would complain about your silence, if I were in doubt about your scrupulousness, but since a friendship endorsed by experience and certified by proofs is far from the danger of suspicion, I certainly understand that your diligence in writing has been hampered by public responsibilities, but I ask you to resume the task you have broken off. My gratitude for the performance of your duty will endure, as if no guilt for denying it preceeded. Farewell.

Notes

1. The reference to "public responsibilities" suggests that Syagrius was in office, but this does not allow more precise dating than pre-382, since Syagrius held a number of offices.

Letter 1.99: Symmachus to Syagrius
Date: before 382[1]

The Ponticianus recommended here has been identified with the man who as an imperial courtier in Trier and then Milan, circa 386–387, played a pivotal role in Augustine's *Confessions*; Ponticianus recounted the story of the conversion of St. Antony to Augustine, thus inspiring the latter to embrace ascetic

Christianity.[2] It should not be surprising to find Symmachus writing on behalf of a Christian; in addition to letters for bishops, we know that Symmachus had also written on behalf of Augustine's promotion to the chair of rhetoric in Milan.[3] Hence, given Symmachus's ties to African circles as well as his visit to the imperial court in Trier, this identification seems likely. At this date, however, it appears that Ponticianus is still at a relatively low rank, or so the bareness of this letter of recommendation suggests. A later letter of Symmachus, *Letter* 5.32, also mentions one Ponticianus, now as a *frater*, "brother," suggesting to the commentator Paola Rivolta Tiberga that by 395 he had attained a higher status, if he is the same man.[4]

Text

Si quando mihi apud amicum testimonii dictio est, cohibeo operam plus loquendi. Nam quid religio agit, ubi desideratur oratio? Fero igitur ad te nudum de familiari meo Ponticiano sed fidele iudicium, quem nisi amore nostro dignum probassem, minime tuo traderem. Mens eius in aperto est, vita spectat ad laudem. Scis certe nunquam me faciliorem favoris esse quam veri. Horum omnium fidem confirmabis, cum in illo plura reppereris. Vale.

Translation

If ever I address a recommendation to a friend, I restrain the impulse to speak at too great length. For what purpose does scrupulousness serve, if a speech is still required? So, I bring to you a simple but reliable verdict on my friend Ponticianus, whom I would not recommend to you at all if I had not approved of him as worthy of our love. His mind is without dissimulation; his life aspires to praise. Certainly you know that I am never more disposed to favoritism than to truth. You will confirm the reliability of all this when you get to know more of the man. Farewell.

Notes

1. See 176 n. 1 to *Letter* 1.97.
2. Augustine, *Confessions* 8.6.14–15; *PLRE* 1:715. See Callu 1972, 144 n. 1.
3. See Ebbeler and Sogno 2007, 230–242.
4. Rivolta Tiberga 1992, 134. The only voice against this identification of Ponticianus is that of Ensslin 1894–1980.

Letter 1.100: Symmachus to Syagrius
Date: 380[1]

Whatever Syagrius's ailment, Symmachus believes that it will respond to warm weather. The basis of his medical knowledge is not clear, nor does he specify what things (*Letter* 1.100.2) he is sending to Syagrius. There were indeed medical manuals that Symmachus could have consulted on such matters, such as the *De medicamentis* written by a certain Marcellus, another Gallic friend of Symmachus.[2]

Text

1. Instaurant dolorem sera solacia et ideo mutuum silentium calamitatibus nostris praestare debemus, ne fortunae vulnera, quae cicatricem processu temporis ducunt, intempestive contrectata crudescant. In alia potius sermo vertendus est, quae te ad curam sanitatis hortentur. Omnis quippe internus corporis dolor hiemali crescit iniuria ac, nisi iter apricis diebus et auris salubribus egeritis, male metuo ne vitium contemptus exaggeret.

2. Nunc ea quae remedio adcommoda credidisti, vel quae nobis commendavit utendi exploratio, ad te misi inter votorum summa constituens, ut remediorum talium necessitatem spontanea incolumitate praevenias, aut si quae morbi reliquiae fuerint, ut his curationibus tergeantur. Satis autem muneris communi amicitiae dabis, si eam sollicitudinem, quae mihi ex aegritudine tua oborta est, prosperiore nuntio nihil moratus exemeris. Vale.

Translation

1. Consolation, when delayed, renews grief, and for that reason we ought to cloak our misfortunes in mutual silence, lest the wounds of Fortune,[3] which scar over in the course of time, become raw again by untimely handling. Rather, my conversation should turn to other matters and that urge you to take care of your health. For every internal pain of the body increases with the harshness of winter, and unless you journey on sunny days when the breezes are healthful, I very much fear that your disregard for your illness will only increase it.

2. As it is, I have sent you what you believed conducive to a cure or what investigation of their use recommended to me,[4] while cherishing as a dearest wish that you forestall the need for such remedies by the spontaneous restoration of your health or, if any disease remains, that it be removed by these treatments. Moreover, you will do what is due to our mutual friendship if without delay you remove with happier news the anxiety that welled up in me because of your illness. Farewell.

Notes

1. The dating of this letter is based on identifying the reference to Symmachus's grief as an allusion to the recent death of his brother Celsinus Titianus, late in 380. This association is supported, too, by the explicit reference to his brother's death in *Letter* 1.101.

2. Marcellus is identified as a friend in *Letters* 2.15 and possibly 9.11 and 9.23; see also Marcellus 7, *PLRE* 1:551.

3. The "wounds of Fortune" (a literal translation) is a vague phrase, but the identification of this as a reference to the death of his brother is reinforced by the explicit statements in the next letter, 101.1, that associate Symmachus's unhappy fortune with his brother's death.

4. One would like more specifics about the nature of the remedies, but that is left characteristically vague.

Letter 1.101: Symmachus to Syagrius
Date: 380[1]

This letter, written in the fall of 380, vividly conveys the conflict Symmachus experiences over the invitation to attend the inauguration ceremonies for Syagrius's consulship, to be held on 1 January 381. The ordinary consulship was a great honor, allowing its holder to give his name to the year and coming as the culmination of a senatorial career. Being invited to a consular inauguration meant attending a series of events, for the consul arranged a banquet, distributed consular gifts, and provided public games on 1 January. An invitation to such an event was a great honor, and so not lightly refused. When he declined to attend the consular ceremonies of Neoterius (*Letter* 5.38), Symmachus also sent letters to other friends at court to express his regret (e.g., to Hephaestio, *Letter* 5.34). Here he adduces his grief at the recent demise of his brother and his concern for his family as personal reasons to excuse his absence. Of course, writing an elegant letter was an exercise in tact, but its inclusion here also serves to build Symmachus's reputation as one who was influential enough to be invited to consular ceremonies.[2]

Text

1. Video, consul amplissime, quantum mihi amor tuus honoris inponat. Iubes ut te adeam et coram defruar magistratus tui gaudio. Quo pacto istud possum negare, nisi ea religione ignoveris, qua vocasti? Nam quid agam fortunae dubius, cum hinc inviter ad obsequia honoris tui, hinc luctu amissi fratris inpediar? 2. Duae mihi simul personae dispares offeruntur. Qui fieri potest ut os unum contrariis adfectionibus induamus? Proinde animi aequus huius

operis facito mihi gratiam. Fortunati sellam tuam laeto agmine prosequantur; auspiciis tuis quivis fati integer amicus intersit; me sinito interim tempore aut ratione decoquere amissi fratris crudum dolorem. 3. Quid quod etiam parentes mihi in communi maerore solandi sunt? Quorum aerumna geminabitur, si illis tam inmaturae peregrinationis meae cura iungatur. Esto igitur promptus ad veniam. Certe si putas arguendum esse, quod desumus, fortunae meae potius irascere. Illa iniecit manum, illa ịnvitum retraxit. Ita tibi non persuadeat, ut est eadem inpotens, me noluisse proficisci. Vale.

Translation

1. I see, most distinguished consul, how great an honor your affection is bestowing on me. You order that I come to you and in person share the joy of your magistracy. How can I refuse you, unless you forgive me with the same sense of scrupulousness with which you invited me? For what am I to do, uncertain of my fortune, when, on the one hand, I am summoned to attend your inauguration, on the other, am held back by grief for the brother I have lost? 2. Two different roles are offered to me at the same time. How can I wear a single face for conflicting emotions? Accordingly, with patient understanding do me an act of kindness in this matter. Let the fortunate accompany your consular chair in joyful procession;[3] let any friend whose fate is unimpaired be present at the taking of the auspices; allow me meanwhile the time and means to digest my raw sorrow. 3. What of the fact that my family also has to be comforted in their shared grief? Their worries will be doubled, if they are augmented so soon by concern about my journey. Be therefore quick to forgive. Certainly, if you think my failing should be condemned, be angry rather at my fortune. She placed her hand on me; she held me back against my will. Let her not persuade you, such is her power, that I did not wish to set out. Farewell.

Notes

1. This letter is securely dated to the year 380, since it refers to the upcoming consular inauguration of Syagrius in January 381.

2. For the tact required for Symmachus to turn down invitations to consular ceremonies, see McGeachy 1942, 98–100. For the consulship in this period in general, see Bagnall, Cameron, Schwarz, and Worp 1987, 1–25.

3. Symmachus here refers to the special consular *sella* as part of the consular procession; it is depicted, for example, in the *Codex Calendar of 354*; see Salzman 1990, fig. 13. The taking of the auspices as the consul began the year is an ancient rite, but its religious significance at this time depended on the eye of the beholder, although some, like Callu (1972, 145 n. 1), have doubted

this. For multiple responses to religious rituals, even games, see Salzman 1990, 237–39; the same point on circus processions is made by Curran 2000, 236–59.

Letter 1.102: Symmachus to Syagrius
Date: 380–382[1]

This letter indicates that Syagrius was at the imperial court in Milan, and if consul designate, his rumored fame would be what Symmachus alluded to in this letter.

Text

Mediolani te agere ante litteras tuas fama pertulerat, quae nihil ignorari de conspicuis viris patitur. Sed quid iuvat desiderantes, quod pervectus in proxima nobis negaris? Aequius ferebam longinquam tui separationem; spes enim praesentiae tuae magno intervallo negata cessabat. Nunc expectationem nostram viciniae facilitate sollicitas. Nec te excusare collegis interventus Alpium potest eo quod iustior nobis ad querellam facta est via, qua tibi ad veniam causa deterior. Sed dolori meo faciendus est modus. Saltem posthac epistulae tuae Romam frequentent †Hyblae aut Hymetti favis iucundiores, quarum me in maximo fenore perceptio iuvat, solutio defetigat. Vale.

Translation

Rumor, which allows nothing to be unknown about famous men, brought me the news that you were at Milan even before I received your letter. But what does it avail us who long to see you that, though you come very near, you are denied to us? I was enduring quite patiently my distant separation from you, for hope for your presence, denied by the great distance, was subsiding. Now you arouse my expectation by the convenience of your proximity, nor can you offer the interposition of the Alps as an excuse to your colleagues,[2] insofar as we have the juster recourse for complaint as your case for pardon has become weaker. But I must put a limit to my distress. At least hereafter let your letters, sweeter than the honey of Hybla or Hymettus,[3] come frequently to Rome. Their reception, even at a very great debt, gives me pleasure; their repayment wears me out. Farewell.

Notes

1. The dating depends on Symmachus's description of Syagrius as "a famous man" (*conspicuus*), which fits the year 381, when he was consul, or it could be 380 when he was consul designate.

2. Symmachus's reference to Syagrius as a "colleague" is vague, but it builds a notion of shared fellowship and indicates that he, like Syagrius, is engaged in public office.

3. These mountains in Sicily and Attica were famous for their honey; see, for example, Martial 7.88.8: "Pascat et Hybla meas, pascat Hymettus apes" ("Should Hybla or Hymettus feed my bees").

Letter 1.103: Symmachus to Syagrius
Date: 381[1]

This letter is a thank-you note to Syagrius for the consular gift that he sent to Symmachus. Often these were expensive diptychs of ivory, silver, or gold, some of which have survived.[2] The sending of such gifts was an honor and obligation (*munus*) for the incoming consul, who was expected to send them in a timely fashion; indeed, Symmachus chastised two barbarian generals when the consular gifts they had sent to him arrived later than was considered proper (*Letters* 3.59; 4.15).[3]

Text

Quidquid in praesentes muneris contulisti, officio eorum videtur esse delatum; nos, qui consulatui tuo varia occupatione defuimus, amicitiae honore adfecti sumus, non mercede praesentiae. Ago igitur tibi <pro> oblatione consulari gratias uberes, sed pro bona mente maiores et, nisi verecundia tua verbis meis poneret modum, latius evagarer; atque ideo erit de hoc sermo interim parcus, memoria vero prolixior. Vale.

Translation

Whatever gifts you conferred upon those present seem to have been offered because of their dutifulness; I, who was absent from your consular inauguration because of various preoccupations, have been graced by the honor of our friendship, not as a reward for my presence. Therefore, I offer you abundant thanks for your consular gift but still greater for your good intentions, and I would go on at even greater length, if your modesty did not put a limit on my words. For that reason my letter will be brief for the moment, but my memory will be more protracted. Farewell.

Notes

1. The dating is based on Syagrius's consulship of 381. Consular gifts generally were sent soon after taking up the title.

2. For extant examples of ivory consular diptychs, see Delbrück 1929.

3. For more on consular gifts and on their obligatory nature, see Pellizzari 1998, 197–98. For Symmachus's attitude toward this breach of etiquette, see Salzman 2006b, 352–67.

Letter 1.104: Symmachus to Syagrius
Date: 379[1]

This is another letter of recommendation for Romanus; for more on this man, see the introduction to *Letter* 1.60, pp. 124–26, and *Letter* 1.73.

Text

Tuae equidem virtutis est omnes, qui palatinis stipendiis enitescunt, iuvare praesidio; sed specialis a me viro optimo Romano cura debetur amicitiae gratia, quae inter nos longa adolevit aetate. Quare si quid testimonio meo tribuis, nolo dubites dignum esse quem diligas et quem maximis officiis munereris. Certe si examen de eo habere digneris, pronuntiabis meis litteris defuisse, quae in illius meritis invenies redundare. Vale.

Translation

It is certainly in your power to aid with your protection all who distinguish themselves in palatine service, but I owe a special debt of care to the excellent man Romanus, because of the friendship that has developed between us over many years. So, if you consider my recommendation of any value, I do not want you to doubt that he is worthy of your affection and of the very greatest favors at your disposal. Certainly, if you think it proper to hold an examination of him, you will declare that the qualities you find in abundance in his merits were absent from my letter. Farewell.

Notes

1. Reference to Syagrius's palatine service suggests the year 379, when he was the *magister officiorum*. For Syagrius's career, see 169–70.

Letter 1.105: Symmachus to Syagrius
Date: after 376[1]

Symmachus is proud of his work, which he has sent to Syagrius. The reference to a "little book" (*libellus*) is probably to his *Oration on Behalf of Tryge-*

tius, noted earlier in this book.[2] However, in *Letter* 1.96 he referred to that speech simply as an oration (*oratio*). This change in terminology probably indicates a lengthened version of that speech, although it is also possibly a reference to another speech, *Oration* 4 (*On Behalf of His Father*), delivered later in 376 in gratitude for his father's consulate.[3]

Text

Ne me otiosum penitus arbitreris, committo eruditioni tuae vigiliarum mearum testem libellum, quo nuper in senatu sustuli civium secunda suffragia. Vides quo praeiudicio antevertam gravissimi examinis tui severitatem. Non stili mei praetendo meritum, sed ordinis iudicatum. Communis mihi et auditoribus meis causa est. Scient omnes aut consensum tuae de nobis sententiae aut contumeliam suae. Vale.

Translation

Lest you think I am completely lazy, I entrust to your learning as evidence of my wakeful nights a little book for which I have recently won in the Senate the favorable opinions of our fellow-citizens. You see with what preliminary judgment I am forestalling the severity of your most serious criticism.[4] I do not appeal to the merit of my pen but the judgment of the senatorial order. The situation is the same for me and for my audience. They will all know either of your agreement with their opinion about me or of the insult to their opinion.[5] Farewell.

Notes

1. Whether this refers to *Oration* 5 or 4, the date of this letter, so soon after both orations, is likely 376. For these orations, see 96–97 and 97 n. 2.

2. See 96–97 and 97 n. 2.

3. Ibid.

4. The notion of a preliminary judgment before a legal decision is familiar to Symmachus's contemporaries. See, for other instances, *Letter* 1.41 to Ausonius, p. 87.

5. The letter ends with a challenge to Syagrius's judgment that sounds rather more aggressive than usual for Symmachus. He has elsewhere, however, shown his high regard for the opinion of his peers, especially in regard to his own writing; see his praise of the Senate as "the better part of the human race" in *Letter* 1.52.

Letter 1.106: Symmachus to Syagrius
Date: before 382[1]

Symmachus writes openly about the workings of friendship networks. Here he is hoping to help a certain Theophilus, a senator (*clarissimus*) whose ties to the senator Priscus Attalus place him in Antiochan as well as Roman elite circles.[2] What is at stake for Symmachus here is his ability to help his friends.

Text

Posse me aliquid de vestris amicitiis aestimant. Hinc spes oritur amicorum meorum, quae Theophilo clarissimo viro tuam opem de meo sermone promittit. Quid igitur eius commodo velimus, in aperto est. Effice, oro te, ut eum fiducia mei non videatur esse frustrata. Vale.

Translation

Some think that I have some power over your friendships. For this reason a hope has arisen among my friends that holds out the promise that from my words your aid will come to the *clarissimus* Theophilus. In this way what we want for him is out in the open. Ensure, I pray, that the trust placed in me not seem to have failed him. Farewell.

Notes

1. See 176 n. 1.

2. Theophilus is identified with Theophilus 5, *PLRE* 1:908. Callu (1995, 174 n. 2) identifies him with the *vicarius* of Asia in 398, based on *C. Th.* 7.16.1. Theophilus was a friend of the Antiochene Attalus, identified as the son of Ampelius 3, *PLRE* 1:56–57, and see also Symmachus, *Letters* 2.83 and 7.15–25. If this identification is accepted, this Attalus would then go on to become a usurping emperor under the Gothic king Alaric; see Cecconi 2002a, 410–12.

Letter 1.107: Symmachus to Syagrius
Date: before 382[1]

Symmachus's last letter is a recommendation for one Alexander.[2] This letter is a short but open expression of the ways in which the aristocracy built ties both to provincial elites and to the imperial bureaucracy. Alexander was a provincial governor (*praeses*) in the fourth-century imperial bureaucracy.[3] Clearly, however, patronage was critical to his further promotion. Symmachus is, as this last letter reinforces, well-positioned to aid such a man through his ties to both provincial and imperial social networks. Thus, this letter provides a fitting conclusion to this epistolary book in which Symmachus strove, above all, to represent himself as politically and socially influential both in elite circles in Rome and in the provinces.

Text

Alexander vir ornatissimus sortitus provinciam praesidalem putat honori suo incrementa praestari, si tuo amore potiatur. Quare desiderii sui me adscivit interpretem, sciens apud te tantum loci esse litteris meis, ut haec commendatio maximi testimonii instar habeatur. Vale.

Translation

Alexander, a most distinguished man, having gained the office of provincial governor, thinks to gain an increase to his honor by winning your affection. For that reason he has enlisted me as an interpreter of his wishes, knowing that my letters have such status with you that this recommendation is considered as the strongest endorsement. Farewell.

Notes

1. See 176 n. 1.

2. Alexander is mentioned only here; see Alexander 10, *PLRE* 1:42.

3. The traditional provincial governorships included *praesides*, *correctores*, and *consulares*. As Cecconi (1994, 49–82) has shown, the titles of the governors in each province (*praeses*, *corrector*, etc.) do not, as many have claimed, offer a reliable guide to the status of each position except for the proconsuls; proconsulship was the only fourth-century position that indicated higher status for provincial governors.

Bibliography

Amidon, Philip R., trans. 1997. *Rufinus: Church History*. New York, Oxford: Oxford University Press.

Anderson, W. B., trans. 1936. *Sidonius Apollinaris: Poems, Letters 1–2*. 2 vols. LCL. Cambridge: Harvard University Press.

Arnheim, Michael T. W. 1972. *The Senatorial Aristocracy in the Later Roman Empire*. Oxford: Clarendon.

Astbury, Raymond, ed. 1985. *M. Terentii Varronis Saturarum Menippearum fragmenta*. Leipzig: Teubner.

Badel, Cristophe. 2005. *La noblesse de l'Empire romain: Les masques et la vertu*. Seyssel: Champ Vallon.

Bagnall, Roger S., A. Cameron, S. R. Schwarz, and K. A. Worp. 1987. *Consuls of the Later Roman Empire*. Philological Monographs 36. Atlanta: Scholars Press.

Barnes, Timothy D. 1976. The Historical Setting of Prudentius' *Contra Symmachum*. *American Journal of Philology* 97:373–86.

———. 1992. Augustine, Symmachus and Ambrose. Pages 7–13 in *Augustine: From Rhetor to Theologian*. Edited by Joanne McWilliam. Waterloo, Ont.: Wilfrid Laurier University Press.

Barrow, R. H., ed. 1973. *Prefect and Emperor: The 'Relationes' of Symmachus A.D. 384*. Translation and notes by R. H. Barrow. Oxford: Clarendon.

Beard, Mary, Simon Price, and John North. 1998–1999. *Religions of Rome*. 2 vols. Cambridge: Cambridge University Press.

Berti, G., and G. A. Cecconi. 1997. Vettio Agorio Pretestato in un'epigrafe inedita dal Valdarno? *Ostraka* 6:11–12.

Bloch, Herbert. 1963. The Pagan Revival in the West at the End of the Fourth Century A.D. Pages 193–218 in *The Conflict between Paganism and Christianity in the Fourth Century*. Edited by Arnaldo Momigliano. Oxford: Clarendon.

Boin, Douglas R. 2010. A Hall for Hercules at Ostia and a Farewell to the Late Antique "Pagan Revival." *American Journal of Archaeology* 114:253–66.

Bonner, S. F. 1965. The Edict of Gratian on the Remuneration of Teachers. *American Journal of Philology* 86.2: 113–37.

Bowersock, Glen. 1986. Symmachus and Ausonius. Pages 1–12 in Paschoud 1986.

Bowes, Kimberly. 2008. *Private Worship, Public Values, and Religious Change in Late Antiquity*. Cambridge: Cambridge University Press.

Bradbury, Scott, ed. 2004. *Selected Letters of Libanius from the Age of Constantius and Julian*. Translated by Scott Bradbury. Liverpool: Liverpool University Press.

Braun, René, ed. 1964. *Quodvultdeus: Livre des promesses et des predictions de dieu*. 2 vols. Sources Chrétiennes 101–102. Paris: Cerf.

Brennan, T. Corey. 2000. *The Praetorship in the Roman Republic*. 2 vols. Oxford: Oxford University Press.

Brown, Peter. 1992. *Power and Persuasion in Late Antiquity: Towards a Christian Empire*. Madison: University of Wisconsin Press.

Bruggisser, Pierre. 1993. *Symmaque ou le rituel épistolaire de l'amitié littéraire: Recherches sur le premier livre de la correspondance*. Fribourg: Éditions universitaires Fribourg Suisse.

Cain, Andrew. 2006. *Vox clamantis in deserto*: Rhetoric, Reproach, and the Forging of Ascetic Authority in Jerome's *Letters* from the Syrian Desert. *Journal of Theological Studies* 57:500–525.

———. 2009. *The Letters of Jerome: Asceticism, Biblical Exegesis and the Construction of Christian Identity in Late Antiquity*. Oxford: Oxford University Press

Callu, Jean-Pierre, ed. 1972. *Lettres [de] Symmaque: Livres I–II*. Paris: Belles Lettres.

———. 1976. En marge des vieux livres: Les manuscripts perdus de Symmaque. *Revue d'histoire des texts* 6:197–217.

———, ed. 1982. *Lettres [de] Symmaque: Livres III–V.* Paris: Belles Lettres.

———, ed. 1995. *Lettres [de] Symmaque: Livres VI–VIII*. Paris: Belles Lettres.

———, ed. 2002. *Lettres [de] Symmaque: Livres IX–X*. Paris: Belles Lettres.

———. 2005. Deux interpolations au Livre Ier des *Lettres* de Symmaque. Pages 181–96 in *Antiquité tardive et humanisme de Tertullien à Beatus Rhenanus*. Edited by Yves Lehmann, Gérard Freybeurger, and James Hirstein. Turnhout: Brepols.

———. 2009a. La lettre de Symmaque à L'Empereur Gratien (*Ep*. X.2; Printemps 376). Pages 183–98 in *Correspondances: Documents pour l'histoire de l'antiquité tardive*. Edited by Robert Delmaire, Janine Desmulliez, and Pierre-Louis Gatier. Lyon: Maison de l'Orient et de la Méditerranée.

———, ed. 2009b. *Symmaque: Discours – rapports*. Paris: Belles Lettres.

Cameron, Alan. 1965. The Fate of Pliny's Letters in the Late Empire. *Classical Quarterly* 15:289–98.

———. 1968. Gratian's Repudiation of the Pontifical Robe. *Journal of Roman Studies* 58:96–99.

———. 1970. *Claudian: Poetry and Propaganda at the Court of Honorius*. Oxford: Oxford University Press.

———. 1977. Paganism and Literature in Late Fourth Century Rome. Pages 1–31 in *Christianisme et formes littéraires de l'antiquité tardive en Occident*. Edited by M. Fuhrmann. Entretiens sur l'antiquité classique 23. Geneva: Fondation Hardt.

———. 1996. Orfitus and Constantius: A Note on Roman Gold-Glasses. *Journal of Roman Archaeology* 9:295–30.

———. 1999a. The Antiquity of the Symmachi. *Historia* 48:477–505.

———. 1999b. The Last Pagans of Rome. Pages 109–22 in *The Transformations of 'Urbs Roma' in Late Antiquity*. Edited by William V. Harris. Journal of Roman Archaeology Supplementary Series 33. Portsmouth, R.I. : Journal of Roman Archaeology.

———. 2002. Petronius Probus, Aemilus Probus and the Transmission of Nepos: A Note on Late Roman Calligraphers. Pages 121–30 in *'Humana sapit': Études d'antiquité tardive offertes à Lellia Cracco Ruggini*. Edited by Jean-Michel Carrié and Rita Lizzi Testa. Turnhout: Brepols.

———. 2007. The Imperial Pontifex. *Harvard Studies in Classical Philology* 103:341–84.

———. 2011. *The Last Pagans of Rome*. Oxford: Oxford University Press.

Carignani, A. 1993. La topografia antica della sommità del Celio: Gli scavi nell'Ospedale Militare (1982–1992). *Mitteilungen des Deutschen Archaeologischen Instituts, Römische Abteilung* 100:443–505.

———. 2000. La *domus* "dei Simmaci." Pages 149–52 in *Aurea Roma dalla città pagana alla città cristiana*. Edited by Serena Ensoli and Eugenio La Rocca. Rome: L'Erma di Bretschneider.

Cavallo, G. 2001. Scuola, libri, pratiche intellettuali a Roma tra il V e il IX secolo. Pages 92–103 in *Roma dall'Antichità al Medioevo: Archeologia e storia nel Museo nazionale romana Crypta Balbi*. Edited by Maria Stella Arena, P. Delogu, Lidia Paroli, M. Ricci, L. Saguì, and L. Vendittelli. Milan: Electa.

Cecconi, Giovanni Alberto. 1994. *Governo imperiale e élites dirigenti nell'Italia Tardoantica: Problemi di storia politico-amministrativa (270– 476 d.C.)*. Como: Edizioni New Press.

———. 2002a. *Commento storico al libro II dell'Epistolario di Q. Aurelio Simmaco*. Pisa: Giardini.

———. 2002b. L'Ipocondria di Simmaco: Critica a un piccolo mito storiografico. Pages 466–76 in *Prose et linguistique, médecine*. Vol. 2 of *Hommages à Carl Deroux*. Edited by Pol Defosse. Brussels: Latomus.

Champlin, Edward. 2001. Pliny's Other Country. Pages 121–28 in *Aspects of Friendship in the Graeco-Roman World: Proceedings of a Conference Held at the Seminar für Alte Geschichte, Heidelberg on 10–11 June 2001*. Edited by Michael Peachin. Journal of Roman Archaeology Supplementary Series 43. Portsmouth, R.I.: Journal of Roman Archaeology.

Chastagnol, André. 1960. *La préfecture urbaine à Rome sous le Bas-Empire*. Paris: Presses universitaires de France.

———. 1962. *Les fastes de la préfecture de Rome au Bas-Empire*. Paris: Presses universitaires de France.

———. 1987. Les *Quinquennalia* de Valentinien et Valens. Pages 255–68 in *Mélanges de numismatique: Offerts à Pierre Bastien à l'occasion de son 75e anniversaire*. Edited by Pierre Bastien, H. Huvelin, Michel Christol, and Georges Gautier. Wetteren, Belgium: Editions NR.

Chenault, R. 2008. Rome without Emperors: The Revival of a Senatorial City in the Fourth Century CE. Ph.D. diss. University of Michigan.

Chronopoulos, Tina. 2010. Brief Lives of Sidonius, Symmachus, and Fulgentius Written in Early Twelfth-Century England? *Journal of Medieval Latin* 20:232–61.

Clark, Gillian. 1993. *Women in Late Antiquity: Pagan and Christian Lifestyles*. Oxford: Clarendon.

Clauss, Manfred. 1981. *Der magister officiorum in der Spätantike (4–6 Jahrhundert):*

Das Amt und sein Einfluss auf die Kaiserliche Politick. Vestigia, Beiträge zur Alten Geschichte 32. Munich: Beck.

Conte, Gian Biagio. 1994. *Latin Literature: A History*. Translated by Joseph B. Solodow. Baltimore: Johns Hopkins University Press.

Conybeare, Catherine. 2000. *Paulinus Noster: Self and Symbols in the Letters of Paulinus of Nola*. Oxford: Oxford University Press.

Cooper, Kate. 2007. Approaching the Holy Household. *Journal of Early Christian Studies* 15:131–42.

Coşkun, Altay. 2002a. *Die gens Ausoniana an der Macht: Untersuchungen zu Decimius Magnus Ausonius und seiner Familie*. Prosopographica et Genealogica 8. Oxford: Unit for Prosopographical Research, Linacre College, University of Oxford.

———. 2002b. Symmachus, Ausonius und der Senex Olim Garumnae Alumnus auf der Suche nach Adressaten von Symm. *Epist.* 9, 88. *Rheinisches Museum für Philologie* 145:120–28.

———. 2003. Q. Aurelius Symmachus und die Stadtpraefecten unter Kaiser Valentinian II. (a. 383–87). *Prosopon* 13:8–17. http://users.ox.ac.uk/~prosop/prosopon/issue13-2.pdf.

Croke, Brian, and Jill Harries. 1982. *Religious Conflict in Fourth Century Rome*. Sydney: Sydney University Press.

Cugisi, Paolo. 1983. *Evoluzione e forme dell'epistolografia Latina nella tarda repubblica e nei primi due secoli dell'impero: Con cenni sull'epistolografia preciceroniana*. Rome: Herder.

Curran, John R. 2000. *Pagan City and Christian Capital: Rome in the Fourth Century*. Oxford: Oxford University Press.

Curtius, Ernst Robert. 1953. *European Literature and the Latin Middle Ages*. Translated by W. R. Trask. Princeton, N.J.: Princeton University Press.

D'Arms, J. H. 1970. *Romans on the Bay of Naples: A Social and Cultural Study on the Villas and Their Owners from 150 B.C. to A.D. 400*. Cambridge: Harvard University Press.

Degrassi, Attilio. 1963. *Fasti et elogia*. Inscriptiones Italiae 13.2. Rome: Libreria dello Stato.

Del Chicca, Fanny. 1984. *Q. Aurelii Symmachi V. C. Laudatio in Valentinianum Seniorem Augustum Prior*. Rome: Herder.

Délage, Marie-José, ed. 1971. *Césaire d'Arles: Sermons au peuple*. Paris: Cerf.

Delbrück, Richard. 1929. *Die Consulardiptychen und verwandte Denkmäler*. Berlin: de Gruyter.

Disselkamp, Gabrielle. 1997. *"Christiani senatus lumina": Zum Anteil römischer Frauen der Obersicht im 4. und 5. Jahrhundert an der Christianisierung der römischen Senatsaristokratie*. Bodenheim: Philo.

Ebbeler, Jennifer V., and Cristiana Sogno. 2007. Religious Identity and the Politics of Patronage: Symmachus and Augustine. *Historia* 56:230–42.

Ensslin, Wilhelm. 1894–1980. "Ponticianus 2." Col. 26 in vol. 22.1 of *Paulys Real-Encyklopädie der classischen Altertumswissenschaft*. New edition by Georg Wissowa and Wilhelm Kroll. 50 vols. in 84 parts. Stuttgart: Metzler and Druckenmüller.

Evans Grubbs, Judith. 2002. *Women and the Law in the Roman Empire: A Sourcebook on Marriage, Divorce, and Widowhood*. London: Routledge.

Evelyn-White, Hugh G., trans. 1919. *Ausonius, Works: In Two Volumes*. LCL. 2 vols. London: Heinemann.

Evenepoel, William. 1998. Ambrose v. Symmachus: Christians and Pagans in AD 384. *Ancient Society* 29:283–306.

Faller, Otto, ed. 1968–1996. *Sancti Ambrosii Opera*. 4 vols. Corpus scriptorum ecclesiasticorum latinorum 82. Vienna: Hoelder-Pinchler-Temsky.

Flower, Harriet. 1996. *Ancestor Masks and Aristocratic Power in Roman Culture*. Oxford: Clarendon.

Foerster, Richard, ed. *Libanius Opera*. 12 vols. Leipzig: Teubner, 1903–1927. Repr., Hildesheim: Olms, 1963.

Frakes, Robert M. 2001. *Contra potentium iniurias: The Defensor Civitatis and Late Roman Justice*. Münchener Beiträge zur Papyrusforschung und antiken Rechtsgeschiche 90. Munich: Beck.

Frasca, Rosella. 1996. *Educazione e formazione a Roma: Storia, testi, immagines*. Bari: Dedalo.

Frei-Stolba, R. 2003. Coelia Concordia, la dernière grande vierge Vestale, et la participation des femmes au discours politique du IVe s. apr. J-C. Pages 281–315 in *Les femmes antiques entre sphère privée et sphère publique*. Edited by Regula Frei-Stolba, Anne Beilman, and Olivier Bianchi. Bern: Lang.

Gallego, José Antonio Valdés, ed. 2000. *Símaco, Cartas: Libros I–V.* Madrid: Gredos.

———, ed. 2003a. *Símaco, Cartas: Libros VI–IX*. Madrid: Gredos.

———, ed. 2003b. *Símaco, Informes: Discursos*. Madrid: Gredos.

Giardina, Andrea. 1983. Lettura epigrafica e carriere aristocratiche: Il caso di Petronio Probo. *Rivista di filologia e di istruzione classica* 111:170–82.

Gibbon, Edward. 1901. *The History of the Decline and Fall of the Roman Empire*. Edited by J. B. Bury. 7 vols. London: Methuen.

Gillett, Andrew. 2003. *Envoys and Political Communication in the Late Antique West, 411–533*. Cambridge: Cambridge University Press.

Giomini, Remo, and Maria Silvana Celentano, eds. 1980. *C. Julii Victoris Ars rhetorica*. Leipzig: Teubner.

Gorce, Denys. 1925. *Les voyages: L'hospitalité, et le port des lettres dans le monde chrétien des IV. et V. siècles*. Paris: Picard.

Green, R. P. H. 1980. The Correspondence of Ausonius. *L'Antiquité classique* 49:191–211.

———, ed. 1991. *The Works of Ausonius*. Oxford: Clarendon.

Guenther, Otto. 1895. *Epistulae imperatorum pontificum aliorum inde ab a. CCCLXVII usque ad a. DLIII datae Avellana quae dicitur collectio, Pars 1: Prolegomena. Epistulae I–CIV*. Corpus scriptorum ecclesiasticorum latinorum 35.1. Vienna: Tempsky.

Hall, Ralph G. 1977. Two Panegyrics in Honor of Valentinian I by Q. Aurelius Symmachus: A Translation and Commentary. Ph.D. diss. University of North Carolina at Chapel Hill.

Harries, Jill. 1988. The Roman Imperial Quaestor from Constantine to Theodosius II. *Journal of Roman Studies* 78:148–72.

———. 2003. *Favor populi*: Pagans, Christians and Public Entertainment in Late Antique Italy. Pages 125–41 in *Bread and Circuses: Evergetism and Municipal Patronage in Roman Italy*. Edited by Kathryn Lomas and Tim J. Cornell. London: Routledge.

Haverling, Gerd. 1988. *Studies on Symmachus's Language and Style*. Studia Graeca et Latina Gothoburgensia 49. Göteberg, Sweden: Acta Universitatis Gothoburgensis.

Heather, Peter. 1998. Senators and Senates. Pages 184–210 in *The Late Empire, A.D. 337–425*. Volume 13 of the *Cambridge Ancient History*. Edited by Averil Cameron and Peter Garnsey. Cambridge: Cambridge University Press.

———. 2006. *The Fall of the Roman Empire: A New History of Rome and the Barbarians*. Oxford: Oxford University Press.

Hedrick, Charles, W. 2000. *History and Silence: Purge and Rehabilitation of Memory in Late Antiquity*. Austin: University of Texas Press.

Hillner, Julia. 2003. *Domus*, Family and Inheritance: The Senatorial Family House in Late Antique Rome. *Journal of Roman Studies* 43:129–45.

Hout, M. P. J. van den, ed. 1954. *M. Cornelii Frontonis epistulae*. Leiden: Brill.

Jones, A. H. M. 1986. *The Later Roman Empire 284–602: A Social, Economic and Administrative Survey*. 2 vols. Repr., Baltimore: John Hopkins University Press.

Kahlos, Maijastina. 2002. *Vettius Agorius Praetextatus: A Senatorial Life in Between*. Acta Instituti Romani Finlandiae 26. Rome: Institutum Romanum Finlandiae.

Kaster, Robert A. 1988. *Guardians of Language: The Grammarian and Society in Late Antiquity*. Berkeley: University of California Press.

Keil, Heinrich. 1880. *Scriptores de orthographia*. Leipzig: Teubner.

Kelly, Chris. 1998. Emperors, Government and Bureaucracy. Pages 162–75 in *The Late Empire, A.D. 337–425*. Volume 13 of the *Cambridge Ancient History*. Edited by Averil Cameron and Peter Garnsey. Cambridge: Cambridge University Press.

Klein, Richard. 1970. Die Kaiserbriefe des Ambrosius: zur Problematik ihrer Veröffentlichung. *Atheneum* 48:335–71.

Kohns, Hans Peter. 1961. *Versorgungskrisen und Hungerrevolten im spätantiken Rom*. Antiquitas 1, Abhandlungen zur alten Geschichte 6. Bonn: Habelt.

Krautheimer, Richard. 1982. *Three Christian Capitals: Topography and Politics*. Berkeley: University of California Press.

Kroll, Wilhelm. 1891. *De Q. Aurelii Symmachi studiis graecis et latinis scripsit*. Breslauer philologische Abhandlungen 6.2. Breslau: Köbner.

Kübler, Bernhard, ed. 1888. *Iuli Valeri Alexandri Polemi Res gestae Alexandri Macedonis translatae ex Aesopo Graeco*. Leipzig: Teubner.

Lançon, Bernard. 1988. Maladie et médecine dans la correspondence de Jérôme. Pages 355–66 in *Jérôme entre l'Occident et l'Orient: XVIe centenaire du départ de saint Jérôme de Rome et de son installation à Betheléem: Actes du Colloque de Chantilly (Septembre 1986)*. Edited by Yves-Marie Duval. Paris: Études augustiniennes.

Leach, Eleanor W. 1999. Ciceronian "Bi-Marcus": Correspondence with M. Terentius Varro and L. Papirius Paetus in 46 B.C.E. *Transactions of the American Philological Association* 129:139–79.

Lepelley, Claude. 1981. *Les cités de l'Afrique romaine au Bas-Empire*. 2 vols. Paris: Études augustiniennes.

———. 2003. Un témoinage sur la procedure par libelle et rescrit dans une lettre de Symmaque à son frère Celsinus Titianus. Pages 285–97 in *Consuetudinis amor: Fragments d'histoire romaine (IIe–VIe siècles) offerts à Jean-Pierre Callu*. Edited by François Chausson and Étienne Wolff. Rome: L'Erma di Bretschneider.

Liebeschuetz, J. H. W. G. 1999. The Significance of the Speech of Praetextatus. Pages 185–205 in *Pagan Monotheism in Late Antiquity*. Edited by Polymnia Athanassiadi and Michael Frede. Oxford: Clarendon.

———. 2004. The Collected Letters of Ambrose of Milan: Correspondence with Contemporaries and with the Future. Pages 95–107 in *Travel, Communication and Geography in Late Antiquity: Sacred and Profane*. Edited by Linda Ellis and Frank L. Kidner. Aldershot, U.K: Ashgate.

———, ed. 2005. *Ambrose of Milan: Political Letters and Speeches*. Translated with an introduction and notes by J. H. W. G. Liebeschuetz, with the assistance of Carole Hill. Liverpool: Liverpool University Press.

Lindsay, Wallace M. 1913. *Festus Grammaticus: Sexti Pompei Festi De verborum significatu quae supersunt cum Pauli Epitome*. Leipzig: Teubner.

Lizzi Testa, Rita. 2002. Policromia di cultura e raffinatezza editoriale: Gli esperimenti letterati dell'aristocrazia romana nel Tardo Impero. Pages 199–206 in *Humana sapit: Études d'antiquité tardive offertes á Lellia Cracco Ruggini*. Edited by Jean-Michel Carrié and Rita Lizzi Testa. Bibliothèque de l'Antiquité tardive 3. Turnhout: Brepols.

———. 2004. *Senatori, Popolo, Papi: Il governo di Roma al tempo dei Valentiniani*. Bari: Edipuglia.

———. 2007. Christian Emperors, Vestal Virgins and Priestly Colleges: Reconsidering the End of Roman Paganism. *Antiquité tardive* 15:251–62.

Lomanto, Valeria. 1983. *Concordantiae in Q. Aurelii Symmachi opera: A Concordance to Symmachus*. Hildesheim: Olms.

Lorenz, Stefan. 1997. *Imperii fines erunt intacti: Rom und die Alamannen 350–378*. Frankfurt: Lang.

Machado, Carlos. 2006. Urban Space and Power in Late Antique Rome (284–535). D.Phil. diss. Oxford University.

Mango, Cyril A. 1986. *The Art of the Byzantine Empire 312–1453: Sources and Documents*. Medieval Academy Reprints for Teaching 16. Toronto: University of Toronto Press in association with the Medieval Academy of America.

Marcone, Arnaldo. 1983. *Commento storico al libro VI dell'epistolario di Q. Aurelio Simmaco*. Pisa: Giardini.

———. 1987. *Commento storico al libro IV dell'epistolario di Q. Aurelio Simmaco*. Pisa: Giardini.

Markus, Robert A. 2006. *Christianity and the Secular*. Notre Dame, Ind.: University of Notre Dame Press.

Martin, René, ed. 1976. *Palladius: Traité d'Agriculture*. Paris: Belles Lettres.

Martindale, J. R. 1967. Note on the Consuls of 381 and 382. *Historia* 16:254–56.

Matthews, John. 1971. Symmachus and the *Magister Militum* Theodosius. *Historia* 20:122–28.

———. 1974. The Letters of Symmachus. Pages 58–99 in *Latin Literature of the Fourth Century*. Edited by James W. Binns. London: Routledge & K. Paul.

———. 1975. *Western Aristocracies and Imperial Court A.D. 364–375*. Oxford: Clarendon.

———. 1986. Symmachus and His Enemies. Pages 163–175 in Paschoud 1986.

———. 2000. *Laying Down the Law: A Study of the Theodosian Code*. New Haven: Yale University Press.

McGeachy, John Alexander. 1942. Quintus Aurelius Symmachus and the Senatorial Aristocracy. Ph.D. diss. University of Chicago.

McLynn, Neil. 1994. *Ambrose of Milan: Church and Court in a Christian Capital*. Berkeley: University of California Press.

Mommsen, Theodor. 1892–1898. *Chronica minora saec. IV. V. VI. VII*. 3 vols. Berlin: Weidmann.

Morello, Ruth, and A. D. Morrison, eds. 2007. *Ancient Letters: Classical and Late Antique Epistolography*. Oxford: Oxford University Press.

Mullett, Margaret. 1997. *Theophylact of Ochrid: Reading the Letters of a Byzantine Archbishop*. Birmingham Byzantine and Ottoman Monographs 2. Aldershot, U.K.: Variorum.

Nauroy, Gérard. 2009. La crise Milanaise de 386 et les lettres d'Ambroise: Difficultés d'interprétation et limites d'un témoinage épistolaire. Pages 227–58 in *Correspondances: Documents pour l'histoire de l'antiquité tardive*. Edited by Robert Delmaire, Janine Desmulliez, and Pierre-Louis Gatier. Lyon: Maison de l'Orient et de la Méditerranée.

Nieddu, Giuseppe. 1986. Il portico degli Dei Consenti. *Bolletino d'Arte* 71:37–52.

Niquet, Heike. 2000. *Monumenta virtutum titulique: Senatorische Selbstdarstellung im spätantike Rom im Spiegel der epigraphischen Denkmäler*. Heidelberger althistorische Beiträge und Epigraphische Studien 34. Stuttgart: Steiner.

Nixon, C. Edward V., and Barbara S. Rodgers. 1994. *In Praise of Later Emperors: The Panegyrici Latini*. Berkeley: University of California Press.

Norman, A. F., ed. 1992. *Libanius, Autobiography and Selected Letters*. 2 vols. Cambridge: Harvard University Press.

North, J. A. 2007. Religions in the Roman Empire. Pages 318–63 in *A Handbook of Ancient Religion*. Edited by John R. Hinnells. Cambridge: Cambridge University Press.

O'Daly, G. 2004. "Sunt etiam Musis sua ludicra": Vergil in Ausonius. Pages 141–54 in *Romane memento: Vergil in the Fourth Century*. Edited by Roger Rees. London: Duckworth.

O'Donnell, James. 1978. The Career of Virius Nicomachus Flavianus. *Phoenix* 32:129–43.

———. 1979. The Demise of Paganism. *Traditio* 35:43–77.

Osgood, Josiah. 2006. *Caesar's Legacy: Civil War and the Emergence of the Roman Empire*. Cambridge: Cambridge University Press.

Otto, August. 1890. *Die Sprichwörter und sprichwörtlichen Redensarten der Römer: Gesammelt und erklärt von Dr. A. Otto*. Leipzig: Teubner.

Pabst, Angela, ed. 1989. *Quintus Aurelius Symmachus Reden*. Texte zur Forschung 53. Darmstadt: Wissenschaftliche Buchgesellschaft.

Palanque, Jean-Rémy. 1931. Famines à Rome à la fin du IVe siècle. *Revue des études anciennes* 33:346–56.

Paschoud, François. 1965. Réflexions sur l'idéal religieux de Symmaque. *Historia* 14:215–35.

———. 1967. *Roma Aeterna: Études sur le patriotisme romain dans l'Occident latin à l'époque des grandes invasions*. Bibliotheca Helvetica Romana 7. Rome: Institut suisse.

———, ed. 1986. Colloque genevois sur Symmaque: À l'occasion du mille six centième anniversaire du conflit de l'autel de la Victoire. Paris: Belles Lettres.

Peiper, Rudolf, ed. 1886. *Decimi Magni Ausonii Burdigalensis opuscula*. Leipzig: Teubner. Repr., Stuttgart: Teubner, 1976.

Pellizzari, Andrea. 1998. *Commento storico al libro III dell'Epistolario di Q. Aurelio Simmaco: Introduzione, commento storico, testo, traduzione, indici*. Biblioteca di studi antichi 81. Pisa: Instituti editoriali e poligrafici internazionali.

Peter, Hermann Wilhelm Gottlob. 1965. *Der Brief in der römischen Literatur*. Repr., Hildesheim: Olms.

Pohlsander, H. A. 1969. Victory: The Story of a Statue. *Historia* 18:588–97.

Polara, Giovanni. 1967. Le iscrizioni sul cippo tombale di Vettio Agorio Pretestato. *Vichiana* 4:40–65.

———. 1972. La fortuna di Simmaco dalla tarda antichità al secolo XVII. *Vichiana* 1:250–63.

———. 2000. Epitafi e propaganda: Ancora sulle iscrizioni del cippo tombale di Pretestato. Pages 107–26 in *Letteratura e propaganda nell'Occidente latino da Augusto ai regni romano-barbarici: Atti del Convegno internazionale, Arcavata di Rende, 25–26 Maggio 1998*. Edited by Franca Ela Consolino. Saggi di storia antica 15. Rome: L'Erma di Bretschneider.

Radice, Betty, ed. and trans. 1969. *Pliny: Letters, Volume 1*. LCL 55. New York: Heinemann.

Rees, Roger. 2007. Letters of Recommendation and the Rhetoric of Praise. Pages 149–68 in Morello and Morrison 2007.

Reynolds, Joyce Maire, and J. B. Ward-Perkins. 1952. *The Inscriptions of Roman Tripolitania*. Rome: British School at Rome.

Ribbeck, Otto. 1897. *Tragicorum romanorum fragmenta*. Vol. 1 of *Scaenicae Romanorum poesis fragmenta tertiis curis*. Bibliotheca scriptorum Graecorum et Romanorum Teubneriana. Leipzig: Teubner.

Richardson, Lawrence, Jr. 1992. *A New Topographical Dictionary of Ancient Rome*. Baltimore: Johns Hopkins University Press.

Ridley, Ronald T. 1982. *Zosimus: New History*. Canberra: Australian Association for Byzantine Studies.

Rivolta Tiberga, Paola. 1992. *Commento storico al Libro V dell'epistolario di Q. Aurelio Simmaco*. Pisa: Giardini.

Roda, Sergio. 1981a. *Commento storico al libro IX dell'epistolario di Q. Aurelio Simmaco.* Pisa: Giardini.

——. 1981b. Una nuova lettera di Simmaco ad Ausonio. *Revue des études anciennes* 83:273–80.

——. 1986. Polifunzionalità della Lettera Commendaticia: Teoria e Prassi nell'epistolario Simmachiano. Pages 177– 207 in Paschoud 1986.

Rolfe, John C., trans. 1935–1939. *Ammianus Marcellinus.* 3 vols. LCL 300, 315, 331. Cambridge: Harvard University Press.

Rougé, J. 1961. Une émeute à Rome au IVe siècle: Ammien Marcellin XXVII 3.3–4: Essai d'interprétation. *Revue des études anciennes* 63:59–77.

Ruggini, Lellia Cracco. 1979. *Il paganesimo romano tra religione e politica (384–394 d.C.): Per una reinterpretazione del "Carmen contra paganos."* Atti della Accademia nazionale dei Lincei. Memoriae/Classe di Scienze morali, storiche e filologiche 8.23.1. Rome: Accademia nazionale dei Lincei.

——. 1984. Simmaco e la poesia. Pages 477–521 in *La poesia tardoantica: Tra retorica, teologia e politica*. Messina: Centro di studi umanistici.

——. 1989a. La donna e il sacro tra paganesimo e cristianesimo. Pages 243–375 in *La Donna nel mondo antico.* Edited by Renato Uglione. Atti dei Convegni della Delegazione torinese dell'Associazione italiana di cultura classica. Turin: Regione Piemonte, Assessorato alla cultura.

——. 1989b. Simmaco, Ausonio e l'enigma del numero tre. Pages 167–76 in *Polyanthema: Studi di letteratura cristiana antica offerti a Salvatore Costanza.* Studi Tardoantichi 7. Messina: Ed. Siciana.

——. 1995. *Economia e società nell'Italia annonaria: Rapporti fra agricoltura e commercio dal IV al VI secolo d.C.* 2nd ed. Bari: Edipuglia.

Rüpke, Jörg, 2007. *Religion of the Romans.* Translated by Richard Gordon. Cambridge: Polity.

Salzman, Michele Renee. 1990. *On Roman Time: The Codex-Calendar of 354 and the Rhythms of Urban Life in Late Antiquity.* Berkeley: University of California Press.

——. 2002. *The Making of a Christian Aristocracy: Social and Religious Change in the Western Roman Empire.* Cambridge: Harvard University Press.

——. 2004. Travel and Communication in the *Letters* of Symmachus. Pages 81–94 in *Travel, Communication, and Geography in Late Antiquity: Sacred and Profane.* Edited by Linda Ellis and Frank Kidner. Aldershot, U.K.: Ashgate.

——. 2006a. Symmachus and His Father: Patriarchy and Patrimony in the Late Roman Senatorial Elite. Pages 357–75 in *Le trasformazioni delle elites in età tardoantica.* Edited by Rita Lizzi Testa. Saggi di storia antica 28. Rome: L'Erma di Bretschneider.

——. 2006b. Symmachus and the "Barbarian" Generals. *Historia* 55:352–67.

——. 2010. Ambrose and the Usurpation of Arbogastes and Eugenius: Reflections on Pagan-Christian Conflict Narratives. *Journal of Early Christian Studies* 18:191–224.

——. 2011. The End of Public Sacrifice in Post-Constantinian Rome and Italy. Pages 167–83 in *Sacrifice in the Ancient Mediterranean.* Edited by Jennifer W. Knust and Zsuzsa Várhelyi. Oxford: Oxford University Press.

Savon, Hervé. 1995. Saint Ambroise a-t-il imité le recueil de lettres de Pline le Jeune? *Revue des études augustiniennes* 41:3–17.

Scafoglio, Giampiero. 2003. Ausonio poeta della pace: Un interpretazione della "Mosella." *Revue des études anciennes* 105:521–39.

Schanz, Martin, and Carl Hosius. 1909. *Geschichte der römischen Litteratur bis zum Gesetzgebungswerk des Kaisers Justinian.* Handbuch der Klassischen Altertums-Wissenschaft 8.1.2. Munich: Beck.

Scheid, John, and Janet Lloyd. 2003. *An Introduction to Roman Religion.* Bloomington: Indiana University Press.

Schlinkert, Dirk. 1996. *Ordo senatorius und nobilitas: Die Konstitution des Senatsadels in der Spätantike: Mit einem Appendix über den praepositus sacri cubicula, den "allmächtigen" Eunuchen am kaiserlichen Hof.* Hermes Einzelschriften 72. Stuttgart: Steiner.

Schmidt, Manfred G. 1999. Ambrosii carmen de obitu Probi. Ein Gedicht des Mailänder Bischofs in epigraphischer Überlieferung. *Hermes* 27:99–116.

Seeck, Otto. 1883. *Q. Aur. Symmachi opera quae supersunt.* Monumenta Germaniae historica: Inde ab anno Christi quingentesimo usque ad annum millesimum et quingentesimum. Auctores antiquissimi 6.1. Berlin: Weidmann.

Seyfarth, Wolfgang. 1970. Petronius Probus: Legende und Wirklichkeit. *Klio* 51:411–25.

Shackleton Bailey, D. R. 1965. *Cicero's Letters to Atticus.* Vol. 1. Cambridge: Cambridge University Press.

Shanzer, Danuta. 1989. The Date and Composition of Prudentius's *Contra Orationem Symmachi Libri. Rivista di Filologia e Istruzione Classica* 117:442–62.

———. 1997. The Date and Literary Context of Ausonius' *Mosella*: Ausonius, Symmachus, and the *Mosella*, Pages 284–305 in *The Discipline of the Art: Studies of Style and Tradition in Latin Literature in Honor of Wendell Clausen.* Edited by P. Knox and C. Foss. Stuttgart: Teubner.

Sherwin-White, Adrian N. 1966. *The Letters of Pliny: A Historical and Social Commentary.* Oxford: Clarendon

Sivan, Hagith. 1992. The Dedicatory Presentation in Late Antiquity: The Example of Ausonius. *Illinois Classical Studies* 17:83–101.

———. 1993. *Ausonius of Bordeaux: The Genesis of a Gallic Aristocracy.* New York: Routledge.

Sogno, Cristiana. 2005. Aegidius Beneventanus and the *Epistulae* of Q. Aurelius Symmachus. *Mittellateinisches Jahrbuch* 40:407–16.

———. 2006. *Q. Aurelius Symmachus: A Political Biography.* Ann Arbor: University of Michigan Press.

———. 2007. Age and Style in Late Antique Epistolography: The Polemics against the Rhetoric of the Old. Pages 85–102 in *Old Age in the Middle Ages and the Renaissance.* Edited by Albrecht Classen. Berlin: de Gruyter.

Souter, Alexander. 1997. *A Glossary of Later Latin to 600 A.D.* 1949. Repr., Oxford: Oxford University Press.

Starr, R. J. 1987. The Circulation of Literary Texts in the Roman World. *Classical Quarterly* 37:213–23.

Stewart, Peter. 2003. *Statues in Roman Society: Representation and Response*. Oxford: Oxford University Press.

Stirling, Lea Margaret. 2005. *The Learned Collector: Mythological Statuettes and Classical Tastes in Late Antique Gaul.* Ann Arbor: University of Michigan Press.

Teitler, Hans C. 1985. *Notarii and Exceptores: An Inquiry into the Role and Significance of Shorthand Writers in the Imperial and Ecclesiastical Bureaucracy of the Roman Empire: From the Early Principate to c. 450 A.D.* Dutch Monographs on Ancient History and Archaeology 1. Amsterdam: Gieben.

Thomson, H. J., ed. and trans. 1949. *Prudentius, Volume 1*. LCL 387. Cambridge: Harvard University Press.

Trapp, Michael B. 2003. *Greek and Latin Letters: An Anthology with Translation*. Cambridge: Cambridge University Press.

Van Haeperen, Françoise. 2002. *Le collège pontifical (3e s. a.C.–4e s. p.C.): Contribution à l'étude de la religion publique romaine.* Études de philologie d'archéologie et d'histoire anciennes 39. Rome: Institut historique belge de Rome.

Vera, Domenico. 1977. Sulle edizioni antiche delle *Relationes* di Simmaco. *Latomus* 36:1003–36.

———. 1981. *Commento storico alle "Relationes" di Q. Aurelius Symmachus*. Biblioteca di studi antichi 29. Pisa: Giardini.

———. 1983. Lotta politica e antagonismi religiosi nella Roma tardoantica: La vittoria sarmatica di Valentiniano II. *Koinonia* 7:133–55.

———. 1986. Simmaco e le sue proprietà: Struttura e funzionamento di un patrimonio aristocratico del quarto secolo d.C. Pages 231–76 in Pascoud 1986.

Vessey, Mark. 1993. Jerome's Origen: The Making of a Christian Literary Persona. *Studia Patristica* 28:135–45.

Weisweiler, John. 2010. Inscribing Imperial Power: Letters from Emperors in Late Antique Rome. In *Historische Erinnerung im städtischen Raum: Rom in der Spätantike.* Edited by Christian Witschel and Ralf Behrwald. Heidelberg: Steiner.

———. 2011. The Price of Integration: State and Élite in Symmachus's Correspondence. Pages 346–75 in *Staatlichkeit und Staatswerdung in Spätantike und Früher Neuzeit.* Edited by Peter Eich, Sebastian Schmidt-Hofner, and Christian Wieland. Heidelberg: Universitätsverlag Winter.

West, M. L., ed. 1971–1972. *Iambi et elegi Graeci ante Alexandrum cantati*. 2 vols. Oxford: Clarendon.

Whittaker, C. R., and Peter Garnsey. 1998. Rural Life in the Later Roman Empire. Pages 277–311 in *The Late Empire, A.D. 337–425.* Vol. 13 of *The Cambridge Ancient History.* Edited by Averil Cameron and Peter Garnsey. Cambridge: Cambridge University Press.

Wickham, Christopher. 2005. *Framing of the Early Middle Ages: Europe and the Mediterranean,* Oxford: Oxford University Press.

Wistrand, Erik Karl Hilding. 1950. *Textkritisches und Interpretatorisches zu Symmachus. Göteborgs Högskolas årsskrift* 56:87–105. Repr. in idem, *Opera selecta*. Lund: Åström, 1972.

Wright, Wilmer Cave, trans. 1913–1923. *The Works of the Emperor Julian*. 3 vols. Cambridge: Harvard University Press.

Zangemeister, Karl, ed. 1967. *Paulus Orosius: Historiarum adversum paganos libri VII.* Hildesheim: Olms.

Zelzer, Michaela. 1989. Plinius Christianus: Ambrosius als Epistolograph. *Studia Patristica* 23:203–8.

Zetzel, James E. G. 1981. *Latin Textual Criticism in Antiquity.* New York: Arno.

Subject Index

www.ingramcontent.com/pod-product-compliance
Lightning Source LLC
Chambersburg PA
CBHW031226120726
47905CB00002B/482

* 9 7 8 1 5 8 9 8 3 5 9 7 9 *